NEW DEVELOPMENTS IN DISTRIBUTED APPLICATIONS AND INTEROPERABLE SYSTEMS

IFIP - The International Federation for Information Processing

IFIP was founded in 1960 under the auspices of UNESCO, following the First World Computer Congress held in Paris the previous year. An umbrella organization for societies working in information processing, IFIP's aim is two-fold: to support information processing within its member countries and to encourage technology transfer to developing nations. As its mission statement clearly states,

IFIP's mission is to be the leading, truly international, apolitical organization which encourages and assists in the development, exploitation and application of information technology for the benefit of all people.

IFIP is a non-profitmaking organization, run almost solely by 2500 volunteers. It operates through a number of technical committees, which organize events and publications. IFIP's events range from an international congress to local seminars, but the most important are:

- The IFIP World Computer Congress, held every second year;
- open conferences;
- working conferences.

The flagship event is the IFIP World Computer Congress, at which both invited and contributed papers are presented. Contributed papers are rigorously refereed and the rejection rate is high.

As with the Congress, participation in the open conferences is open to all and papers may be invited or submitted. Again, submitted papers are stringently refereed.

The working conferences are structured differently. They are usually run by a working group and attendance is small and by invitation only. Their purpose is to create an atmosphere conducive to innovation and development. Refereeing is less rigorous and papers are subjected to extensive group discussion.

Publications arising from IFIP events vary. The papers presented at the IFIP World Computer Congress and at open conferences are published as conference proceedings, while the results of the working conferences are often published as collections of selected and edited papers.

Any national society whose primary activity is in information may apply to become a full member of IFIP, although full membership is restricted to one society per country. Full members are entitled to vote at the annual General Assembly, National societies preferring a less committed involvement may apply for associate or corresponding membership. Associate members enjoy the same benefits as full members, but without voting rights. Corresponding members are not represented in IFIP bodies. Affiliated membership is open to non-national societies, and individual and honorary membership schemes are also offered.

NEW DEVELOPMENTS IN DISTRIBUTED APPLICATIONS AND INTEROPERABLE SYSTEMS

IFIP TC6 / WG6.1 Third International Working Conference on Distributed Applications and Interoperable Systems September 17–19, 2001, Kraków, Poland

Edited by

Krzysztof Zieliński
University of Mining and Metallurgy
Kraków, Poland

Kurt Geihs
University of Frankfurt
Germany

Aleksander Laurentowski
University of Mining and Metallurgy
Kraków, Poland

SPRINGER SCIENCE+BUSINESS MEDIA, LLC

DOI 10.1007/978-0-306-47005-9

Electronic Services <http://www.wkap.nl>

Library of Congress Cataloging-in-Publication Data

A C.I.P. Catalogue record for this book is available from the Library of Congress.

Printed on acid-free paper.
www.springer.com/mycopy

Contents

Preface

The conference program of the Third IFIP WG 6.1 International Working Conference on Distributed Applications and Interoperable Systems (DAIS'2001) held in Kraków, Poland, on September 17th through 19th, 2001, presents the state of the art in research concerning distributed and interoperable systems. This is a topical research area where much activity is currently in progress. Interesting new aspects and innovative contributions are still arising regularly. The DAIS series of conferences is one of the main international forums where these important findings are reported.

The papers presented in this volume cover distributed context aware applications, integration and interoperability of distributed systems, software architectures and services for open distributed systems, management, security and quality of service issues in distributed systems, software agents, mobility, Internet and other related problem areas.

These proceedings contain 16 regular and 10 short papers, which have been selected in a careful reviewing procedure with at least three reviews for each paper plus two ballot phases. In addition, the extended abstracts of two invited talks by Liba Svobodova and Adam Wolisz are included. There were 60 submissions to the conference.

DAIS'2001 was sponsored by IFIP (International Federation of Information Processing) and it is the third conference in DAIS series of events organized by IFIP Working Group 6.1 of the IFIP Technical Committee TC6 (Communication Systems). The first conference in this series, DAIS'97, took place in 1997 in Cottbus, Germany and the second one in 1999 in Helsinki, Finland.

DAIS'2001 was organized by the Department of Computer Science and Academic Computer Centre at the University of Mining and Metallurgy in Kraków. Formally, the local host organization was also supported by the Committee of Computer Science of Polish Academy of Science and Polish Information Processing Society. The conference was financially sponsored by the Polish State Committee for Scientific Research, Motorola Software Center Kraków, Sun Microsystems, Solidex S.A., Comarch S.A., Microsoft Research and other IT companies.

Finally, I would like to take this opportunity to thank the numerous people whose work made this conference possible. The reviewing was a major effort and it was completed by experts from all around the world. The reviewers are listed in this proceedings. The local organizing committee, listed also in this book, was responsible for preparing and running the conference.

I believe that the stay in Kraków, the Capital of European Culture for the year 2000, will be one more thing to remember DAIS'2001 for.

KRZYSZTOF ZIELIŃSKI
(CONFERENCE CHAIR)

Conference Committees

Conference Chairmen

Krzysztof Zieliński, UMM Kraków, Poland
Conference Chair, PC Committee Member

Kurt Geihs, University of Frankfurt, Germany
Conference Co-chair, PC Committee Member

Aleksander Laurentowski, UMM Kraków, Poland
Organizing Committee Chair

Program Committee

Y. Berbers, Katholieke Universiteit Leuven, Belgium
J. Brzeziński, Technical University of Poznań, Poland
W. Cellary, Poznań University of Economics, Poland
S. Chanson, University of Science And Technology, Hong Kong
P. Dembiński, Polish Academy of Sciences, Poland
N. Dulay, Imperial College, UK
F. Eliassen, University in Oslo, Norway
J. Filipiak, ComArch SA, Poland
K. Geihs, University of Frankfurt, Germany
A. Hopper, AT&T Research Cambridge, UK
J. Indulska, University of Queensland, Australia
H. König, BTU Cottbus, Germany
H. Krumm, University of Dortmund, Germany
L. Kutvonen, University of Helsinki, Finland
W. Lamersdorf, University of Hamburg, Germany
P. Linington, University of Kent, UK
C. Linnhoff-Popien, RWTH Aachen, Germany
L. Logrippo, University of Ottawa, Canada
Q. Mahmoud, Carleton University, Canada
E. Najm, ENST Paris, France
M. Noga, ACC Cyfronet UMM, Kraków, Poland

T. Plagemann, University in Oslo, Norway
K. Raymond, DSTC, Australia
P. Robinson, University of Cambridge, UK
J. Rolia, Carleton University, Canada
A. Ruiz, Universidad de Sevilla, Spain
A. Schill, TU Dresden, Germany
A. Schiper, EPFL, Switzerland
M. Tienari, University of Helsinki, Finland
A. Wolisz, TU Berlin, Germany
A. Wolski, Solid, Finland
K. Zieliński, UMM Kraków, Poland

Additional Reviewers

Peter Urban
Paweł Wojciechowski
David Holmes
Rafael Corchuelo Gil
Octavio Martin Díaz
Joaquin Peña Siles
Kay Roemer
Peter Herrmann
Christian Zirpins
Glenford Mapp
Andrzej M. Borzyszkowski

Organisation Committee

Aleksander Laurentowski (Chair), UMM Kraków, Poland
Elzbieta Alda, UMM Kraków, Poland
Jacek Kosiński, UMM Kraków, Poland
Zofia Mosurska, ACC Cyfronet UMM, Kraków, Poland
Radosław Ruchała, WSB-NLU Nowy-Sącz, Poland
Milena Zając, ACC Cyfronet UMM, Kraków, Poland

I

INVITED LECTURE

THE INTELLIGENT INFRASTRUCTURE FOR E-BUSINESS

(an extended Abstract)

Liba Svobodova
IBM Research
Zurich Research Laboratory
CH-8803 Rüschlikon
Switzerland
svo@zurich.ibm.com

As e-business continues to gain momentum, it also develops into more complex and more dynamic forms, both in the B2C (Business to Consumer) sector, and even more so in the B2B (Business to Business) arena. These trends need to be enabled by increased intelligence and capabilities in the network infrastructure and services, which will evolve into an intelligent infrastructure for e-business.

Dynamic e-business will enable very rapid establishment of business partnerships and contracts over the global network, without any prior business relation developed in the traditional way. Online business directories, e-markets, and other kinds of e-intermediaries will be deployed to locate suitable partners who can provide desired products, parts, consulting on a specific issue, or financial investment. Trusted e-intermediaries will also offer services to verify the trustworthiness of potential partners and facilitate the negotiation and closure of a contract. All of this will happen at electronic speed, as these processes will be conducted over the network in a highly automated way. Such dynamic processes will be particularly useful in the creation and provisioning of application-level, fully electronic services, or e-services. The providers need to introduce such services to the market quickly and test their market value and acceptance without heavy investments in their own equipment; this need will be addressed by e-utilities, which will become an inseparable part of the intelligent infrastructure. E-utilities will manage thousands of modular servers and storage units that can be allocated on demand to a specific customer, service, or business process, as well as securely released and reallocated as the demand changes.

E-utilities themselves will require a very flexible infrastructure that will be able to support an almost instantaneous reallocation of resources. This needs to be supported by sophisticated monitoring of the utilization across these huge server and storage farms and scheduling and optimization based on the immediate application requirements and their specific service level agreements (SLA) as well as on the total demand, resource status, and overall policies. Dynamic pricing of computing and network resources usage will be deployed to control the demand. The *Project Oceano* [1] is addressing these multifaceted issues of e-utilities.

On the end-user side, e-services have to become much more interactive and personalizable. The proliferation of mobile devices having data communication and processing capabilities is one of the main drivers of new kinds of services. A well-known example of a highly personalized service is monitoring performance of selected stocks - the user should be able to specify in simple terms what information he/she wants and how it should be delivered. The service, supported by the intelligent infrastructure, needs to determine whether and how to notify the subscriber, and based on the device the subscriber is using at the time, choose the appropriate retrieval mode (push or pull), the presentation mode (text, voice), and the format. The research platform *Whale* [2] is a middleware supporting multichannel applications with these features. As the number of users who wish to receive real-time information in a highly personalized way grows to tens or even hundreds of thousands, an intelligent form of personalized distribution will be needed. *Gryphon* [3] is a highly scalable and personalizable publish/subscribe middleware aimed at distributing large volumes of data in real time over a global network.

The Internet has already evolved significantly from no more than pipes that deliver data in packets to an infrastructure that provides a multiplicity of services, such as multicast, secure connections, directories, caching, and transcoding. To grow the intelligence in the network requires powerful computing resources - these will be provided at the edge of the core networks by edge servers. The transport network will become increasingly less visible to the end users of e-services and applications. E-business processes will run on top of dynamically established virtual private networks [4]. As the bottom line, this infrastructure has to be extremely dependable. Not only does it have to be able to automatically heal from component failures, it has to withstand targeted attacks from hackers, as well as deal effectively with very sudden shifts in resource availability and demand. Continuous intrusion detection [5] will become a standard function in the integrated system and network management. The intelligent infrastructure for e-business will be in fact a very large and complex distributed system environment, where interoperability requirements will go far beyond the functional aspects.

The IBM Research Division has many projects addressing the different aspects of the Intelligent Infrastructure. The cited projects [1]–[5] are illustrative examples.

References

[1] e-utilities - Project Oceano: http://www.research.ibm.com/oceanoproject/

[2] Mobile Computing Platform (Whale): http://www.zurich.ibm.com/csc/mobile/index.html

[3] Gryphon: http://www.research.ibm.com/gryphon/home.html

[4] Dynamic Service Provisioning: http://www.zurich.ibm.com/csc/distribsys/icorp.html

[5] Intrusion Detection: http://www.zurich.ibm.com/csc/infosec/gsal.html

II

CONTEXT AWARE APPLICATIONS

MIDDLEWARE SUPPORT FOR CONTEXT-AWARE MULTIMEDIA APPLICATIONS

Hani Naguib, George Coulouris and Scott Mitchell
Laboratory for Communications Engineering, Cambridge University
http://www-lce.eng.cam.ac.uk/qosdream/
{han21,gfc22}@cam.ac.uk, Scott.Mitchell@mail.com

Abstract We describe QoSDREAM, a middleware framework for the construction and management of context-aware multimedia applications. The contributions of QoSDREAM include (1) a novel approach to the handling of location data derived from sensors in the physical world which integrates sensor data from a variety of sources into streams of application-relevant events and (2) a component-based architecture for the construction of real-time multimedia and other context-aware applications. The component architecture supports the construction of application models that are used for quality of service analysis and management purposes. Working distributed applications are derived from the models.

1. INTRODUCTION

Many of the components found in conventional analogue audio and video systems (for example, VCRs, switches, mixers and editing desks) can now be found as software components running on high-performance desktop and mobile computers and using high-speed networks with QoS guarantees instead of point-to-point analogue cables. Other components (cameras, microphones, displays, loudspeakers) are computer peripherals whose operation is managed by software. Digitally stored audio and video streams are already widely exploited in the production and use of programme material.

Another important development is the emergence of *sentient computing* [17] as a valuable adjunct to mobile computing devices and wireless network technologies, enabling applications to behave in a context-aware manner that is, their behaviour takes into account sensor data such as the locations of people and things in order to better support users' tasks. The locations of people and equipment can be tracked using a variety of *location technologies*. These technologies employ infrared, radio, sonic or optical sensing techniques. They provide information about the *proximity* of a locator object to a sensor or they give *coordinates* of the locator object to some degree of precision. Some also provide information about the orientation of the locator object. Active Badge [15], Active Bat [16], and tag technologies [25] are representative examples of location technologies that depend upon the detection of small dedicated tags or badges. GPS and mobile phone technologies and handheld computers plus beacons can be exploited as location technologies when the handset is able to communicate with the relevant systems.

As these developments proceed, there is an increasing need for flexible application development and management environments, enabling context-aware software for the manipulation and management of multimedia streams to be developed and deployed quickly and cheaply. There is a profusion of potential application domains for such systems. They include factory and plant management, security surveillance, support for clinical workers, airport and seaport control and major incident coordination. Applications are likely to emerge wherever there is a need for multi-party communication employing video or audio links between users, many of whom are engaged in multiple tasks and migrate according to the needs of their work, within a workplace or more widely.

In Section 2 we define and discuss the goals of the QoSDREAM framework. Section 3 reviews some related work. Section 4 describes the architecture of the framework, emphasising the features for the management of location data and those that support extensibility, configurability and scalability. Section 5 reports briefly on our initial experience in using the framework to build a context-aware application. Section 6 concludes the paper.

2. DESIGN APPROACH

We have defined the following goals for the QoSDREAM framework:

1. It should be simple for applications to construct multimedia flows in terms of a uniform set of high-level components (sources, sinks, transforming elements and communication channels). The framework should mask differences in terminal equipment and communication links and enable applications to add and delete multimedia streams and modify their configurations in response to changes in resource availability, application needs and users' contexts.
2. The framework should maintain application-defined constraints on the integrity and quality of service properties of multimedia flows during configuration changes.
3. Location information should be made available to applications with reference to single spatial model of the physical world, regardless of the sensor system that was used to generate it.

4 The multitude of raw real-time events that are reported by context sensors should be filtered as required and presented to application components in a uniform format.

5 A set of persistent data describing the current set of running applications and a synopsis of the real-world model should be available, so that applications or components can be added or brought up to date in a manner that is consistent with the existing state.

Space does not allow us to describe fully our approach to all of these goals. Therefore in this paper we focus on goals 3, 4 and 5. Please refer to [20, 21],for details regarding our approach to goals 1 and 2.

3. RELATED WORK

We are not aware of any integrated middleware platform that aims to achieve all of the goals described above. In this section we review several projects that address major portions of the requirements space we have identified.

The SPIRIT project [16] at AT & T Labs, Cambridge, has built a substantial Corba-based application framework to manage and exploit location data from the Bat high-resolution location technology. The SPIRIT system holds real-world descriptions in an Oracle database to provide persistence and queryability, with a cache of Corba objects holding more up-to-date data about currently-active real-world entities. High-precision geometric modelling is used to support queries and invocations that request the locations of objects, whereas QoS-DREAM aims to limit the computational load on application hosts by building a spatial model in terms of a (potentially large) set of possibly-overlapping 2.5-D regions and to support a wider variety of location technologies.

The Glagow Context Server [18] is designed as a low-cost context-aware architecture for mobile applications. It exploits PDAs connected by a wireless network and receiving data from static infrared beacons that emit identity, location or other information. The bandwidth of the handheld devices and the network technology cannot support multimedia streams, but like QoS DREAM, it aims to support clinical applications to provide information on the locations of patients, staff and equipment and to enhance communication between clinical staff. Such an architecture can substantially reduce the cost and time required to deploy context-aware applications.

The Cooltown project [5, 19] is an architecture for the support of applications that span the physical and virtual worlds. It exploits the world wide web to hold the data modelling real-world objects. It does not provide any special support for multimedia streams and it is not clear to us how Cooltown addresses the problems of system loads in large-scale applications.

Other component-base multimedia middleware systems include Sumo-ORB [8] and CINEMA [2]. CINEMA also uses a model-based approach to reconfiguration; however QoS DREAM is novel in its use of an active runtime model encapsulating QoS and event management, as well as reconfiguration. In addition, the atomic action mechanism encourages the construction of reliable, yet highly dynamic, applications. Researchers at Lancaster University have been investigating mobile multimedia support for emergency services [10], such as equipping ambulances with videoconferencing systems.

4. ARCHITECTURE

Figure 1 shows the major constituents of the QoSDREAM architecture. It consists of four major parts. At the lowest level we have the **Location Service** It is in charge of gathering location information from specific location-technologies and presenting it to the rest of the system in a location-technology independent fashion. The Location Service's functionalities also include managing and filtering the potentially large amount of location information that can be generated. This information is made available to the rest of the system and applications through an **Event Messaging System**. The Event Messaging System distributes events to interested parties and provides a number of filtering services.

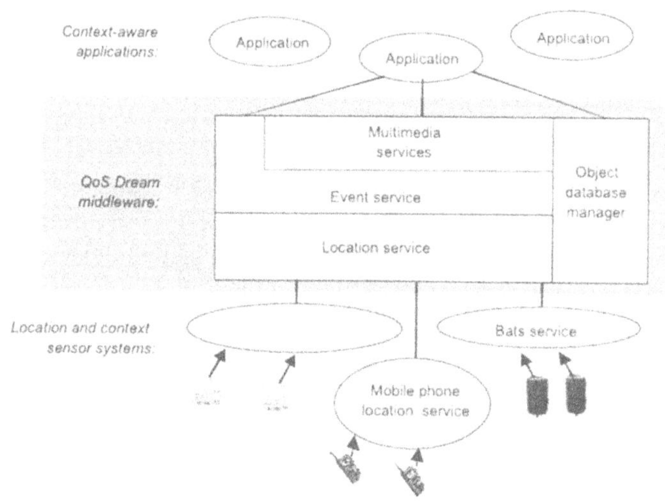

Figure 1. Overview of QoSDREAM's Architecture

Applications are exposed to three major APIs:

- The **Event Messaging Service**, which allows applications to subscribe to receive specific events (including those generated by the location service) and also to send their own application specific events.

- A **Distributed Multimedia Service**, which allows the application to construct and manage, distributed multimedia components. Multimedia applications are built as a collection of interconnected components, such as cameras and displays.

- A **Distributed Object Database Management Service,** which provides a means of sharing system wide properties such as information about known physical objects. The information held by the database is largely 'static' (i.e. it is not modified very often), although some location-specific data may also be stored with it.

4.1. Location Information

A wide range of location sensing technologies already exist and more are under development [25]. Some, such as the Active Badge system [15], provide information about the presence of a user in a region or a room. Other location technologies, such as the Active Bat system [16] are much more precise, providing information that is accurate to a few centimetres. All location technologies generate sensor events in response to changes in the locations of locatable objects. The rate at which they are generated is high, especially for high precision location technologies. Only a fraction of the sensor events are of interest to any specific application.

Our Location Service provides location-dependent information. The Location Service is a collection of objects that retrieve location information from existing location sensors and make this information available to QoSDREAM applications. The type of location information available is highly dependent on the location-technologies being used. QoSDREAM's Location Service interprets this information and presents it in a location-technology independent format. This is achieved by representing location information in terms of regions and the interactions between regions.

4.1.1 Modelling Location Information. Within QoSDREAM, applications are presented with a simplified model of the real physical world. This model contains the following abstractions:

- **Locators**, which represent objects whose location can be determined by a given location-technology. Active badges and Bats are examples of Locators.

- **Locatables**, these represent objects whose locations need to be tracked. Examples include people and equipment. Locatables must have at least one associated locator, so that their location can be inferred from its locator.

- **Locatable Regions**, Each locatable will in general have one or more regions. These regions define various location specific characteristics of Locatables. For instance in the case of a person, they may include in addition to the person's location, their visual and audible fields.

The main reason for using regions as a way of presenting location information is the varying degree of precision of location technologies. Active Badges will only place a badge within a room, Active Bats provide more fine grained information. Expressing location information as regions allows the incorporation of a wide range of location technologies. Furthermore the use of regions also aids in the management of location information particularly with regards to filtering this information in order to reduce location-related traffic. This is discussed in the following subsection.

Location related information is presented to applications as interactions between the various regions in the model. In particular the change in overlap status between regions (For example a person walks into a room, his 'location region' overlaps with the room's region).

4.1.2 Management of Location Information. Our Location Service performs management of location information. Figure 2 depicts the various abstractions that form this service.

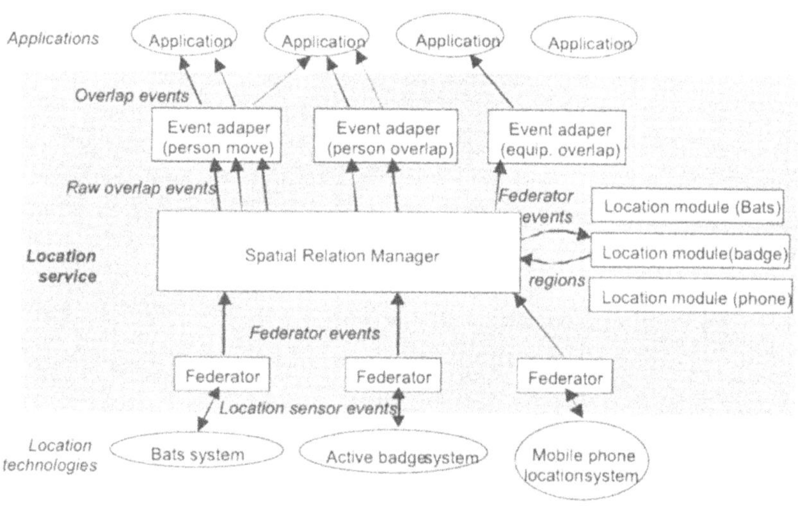

Figure 2. Location Service Architecture

At the lowest level we have **Federator** objects, these interface with specific location technologies and can detect location information. In our lab we have an 'Active Badge Federator' which is capable of interpreting the data being generated by the Active Badge System. The information gathered by Federators is exported through light-weight events called **Federator Events**. These contain generic information such as the type and id of the federator as well as federator-specific data.

These events can be monitored by applications that require very detailed location information. In general applications are only interested in specific location-related information and so can use other types of events (described below) to receive only events that it is interested in. Federator events are also sent to our **Spatial Relations Manager** (SRM). The SRM's task is to convert information gathered by Federators into overlapping events between the regions in our world model. Before the SRM can reason about the regions and their interactions, **Location Modules** translate Federator events into regions. For example a Location Module for an Active Badge System, would generate a location region for the given locator in the Badge Federator Event. The shape of this region would be the same as that of the room where the locator was detected. This can be derived from the sensorID field in the Federator Event.

Location Modules are Federator-type-specific, and can be loaded from the database by the SRM. The SRM uses the federatorType field of Federator Events to determine the required Location Module.

Once the SRM has obtained updated regions from Location Modules it analyses them looking for changes in overlaps between regions. If those are found then the SRM produces what we call **Raw Overlap Events**. These contain the type of overlap between two regions as well as their previous relationship.

Applications can register to receive these events, but again these events are too general for most applications and cannot be filtered. Instead application register to receive specialised overlap events produced by **EventAdaptors**. These types of events can be filtered and relate to higher level abstractions, such as people and equipment.

EventAdaptors are objects that receive Raw Overlap Events generated by the SRM and can filter and transform these into events that are of interest to applications. The events generated by EventAdaptors are called **OverlapEvents**, and are transmitted by QoSDREAM's Message Service. New EventAdaptors can be easily created and dynamically incorporated into QoSDREAM. By default we provide three types of EventAdaptors:

- **PersonMovement Adaptor**: This generates overlap events when a person's location region overlaps with a geographical location. This event contains a personID and a LocationID fields.

- **PersonOverlap Adapter**: This generates overlap events when a person's location region overlaps with that of another. This event contains a person1ID and person2ID fields.

- **EquipementOverlap Adapter**: This generates overlap events when a person's location region overlaps with that of an equipment. This event contains a personID as well as a equipmentID fields.

Applications are free to choose what events they wish to receive. They can further filter OverlapEvents on the value of the fields in the event. For example, an application interested in the arrival at work of person George can register to receive PersonMovement events whose personID field equals George's id.

To aid with the scalability the representation of the physical world is divided into zones. These zones can be used by the SRM to cut down on the number of regions it must analyse when looking for overlap events. Zoning also allows for a federation of SRMs to be set-up, each of which is responsible for specific zones (as long as those don't overlap). For instance floors in a building might each be handled by a separate SRM.

4.2. Event Messaging Service

The multiplicity of raw events occurring in context-aware systems determines the need for an event management system. Even after the processing of location information in the manner described above, the potential network and processing loads are substantial. A mechanism is required that will enable applications to see those events that are relevant to its responsibilities while filtering out those that are not. The event mechanism should be distributed to avoid the problem of hot-spots at network nodes where event traffic is concentrated.

The QoSDREAM framework provides an event abstraction that enables applications to register for events by event type. Further selection is performed by event filters which the application can instantiate. Options for event queuing, communication, fault tolerance, event persistence, reliability and security will be offered in a future version of the DREAM framework. The event handling abstraction outlined here is compatible with most general-purpose event handling systems including Corba Events [11], Elvin [1, 13] and Herald [3, 24].

QoSDREAM uses events primarily for delivery of contextual information to applications. The messaging service allows application objects to send and receive events and is also used by the Location Service to deliver events generated by EventAdaptors.

The Messaging Service facilitates the management of location information in a number of ways. It allows clients to request the delivery of events without having to know anything about the sources of these events. Similarly event sources do not require any knowledge about their clients. The messaging service also allows applications to specify filters on the events that are sent to it. This coupled with the location service greatly reduces location-related traffic. Without the location service and messaging service, applications would need to monitor all location information generated by the various underlying location technologies.

The Messaging Service is itself independent of the event delivery system used to transfer events from event sources to event clients. It provides the following abstractions:

- **Event Sources**: Are objects that produce events.

- **Event Clients**: Are objects that register an interest in receiving events.

- **EventDescriptors**: These are descriptions of the events generated by event sources. This includes information about the fields of an event as well as the event type name.

- **Message**: These are instances of events, and contain values for the fields in an event.

EventDescriptors are stored in the database by event sources and remain there while the source is registered to produce such events. Having EventDescriptors stored in the database in this fashion allows clients to easily discover the types of events currently available in the system. The database in this situation acts as an event broker.

Clients obtain a reference to an EventDescriptor from the database and through it can register their interest in receiving these types of events. EventDescriptors also allow clients to further filter the events they receive through a set of methods that specify specific value for fields in the event.

Our current implementation of the Messaging Service uses an implementation of the Cambridge Event Architeture called Herald [24] as the event delivery system. Herald contains similar abstractions to those listed above. Other event delivery systems can be easily added to our Messaging Service by the implementation of a single interface. Event sources can specify which underlying event delivery system is to be used if they so require.

4.3. Database Management System

While an application is running, its components in the physical world (cameras, screens, people, rooms) and the virtual world (conferences, phone connections, patient records) are modelled as objects in a distributed program and their attributes are manipulable by the application program. But the attributes of these components are also needed at application start time and whenever a new component is added to an application. For example, a 'locate a specialist' application might be invoked to find a cardiology specialist when a heart patient arrives in the emergency department of a hospital. The persistent data includes a synopsis (which is not necessarily up-to-the-second) of the locations of all of the doctors, nurses and patients in the hospital. It also includes details of doctors' specialisms. The persistent data should be queryable in order to resolve requests such as the example just mentioned.

The Database Management System (DMS) plays a central role within the QoSDREAM architecture. It is used to store static information about the system such as geographical information and information related to people and equipment. It is also used as an event broker, storing information that allows event sources and clients to interact, and contains a synopsis of the location-related information.

QoSDREAM exposes the DMS through an interface called the **QueryManager**. This interface allows for the objects stored within the DMS to be manipulated. Apart from providing a means to access the database the QueryManager also decouples the platform from the underlying database technology used (With the restrictions that it must support objects and be capable of handling OQL queries).

Our current implementation uses Castor from Exolab [9]. Castor is being used as an object-to-relational database mapping tool, and supports any relational database that is JDBC compliant and has full transactional support. (We currently use MySQL[14]).

The QueryManager interface still needs further refinement, for example it lacks direct support for transactions (which currently is only possible by obtaining a reference to the underlying castor Database object). Furthermore the database is a single point of failure and may become a bottleneck. We are currently investigating these issues.

5. EXPERIENCES

This section describes some of our preliminary experiences in building applications using the QoSDREAM architecture. The application described in this section is called **ActiveLab**, and is about to be deployed at our laboratory as a basis for our evaluation. Members of the laboratory will use it as a communications aid, allowing them to locate one another, establish and participate in audio/visual conferences. It exploits location information provided by the Active Badge System (through the QoSDREAM architecture), that is installed in our laboratory. Features of ActiveLab include:

- The ability to locate/track people, rooms and equipment.
- Reroute conferences and desktops as users move around the laboratory.
- Set alarms providing warnings for when given people enter or exit specific regions of the laboratory. (Useful to PhD students)
- Allow users to define default actions depending on the context in which they find themselves. For example to disable incoming phone or video calls when in a meeting.

The following sub-sections describe some of the experiences we have found while developing specific areas of the ActiveLab application.

5.1. Application Modelling

The ActiveLab application's model of the physical world contains a number of abstractions. These include people, computers, devices, rooms and regions as well as representations for the Active Badge System (badges and sensors). Creating representational objects for these abstractions was very simple, although our use of Castor requires that a mapping file be produced in XML. This file specifies the classes that are to be made persistent-capable and the names and types of fields that need to be kept persistent.

Additionally once the database objects have been designed, the database needs to be populated. We found this to be a slightly tedious task since measurements of our laboratory's rooms were required. Furthermore badge ids and people and equipment information were also gathered, although in this case we were able to import much of this information from pre-existing software.

We found that the use of OQL queries to interface with the database greatly simplified the retrieval of database objects.

5.2. Multimedia Modelling

Our approach to modelling the conferencing tools within the ActiveLab application was to build a composite component which we named **Conference**. A single instance of Conference is created for each of the ongoing conferences. This composite component contains a set of **Participant** components as well as an interface for adding/removing and connecting conference participants. A Participant is also a composite component in charge of controlling the multimedia components needed by a single conference participant. These include a camera, microphone, speaker and displays.

We have found a number of benefits from using our multimedia framework. Its component-based approach to application construction promotes reuse (In fact the Conference component can be used by any application which requires a conferencing ability with no modifications). Most of the atomic components used in the model were taken from pre-existing applications. This also meant that any preoccupations we might have had from platform-specific coding for multimedia devices were removed.

Unfortunately it is still too early to perform a thorough performance evaluation of QoSDREAM. Table 1 gives an indication of the typical location-specific traffic found in our lab. This traffic was measured over a five minute interval and at the time there were six members of the lab wearing badges.

The ActiveLab application registers interest only in PersonMovement events (in order to update its display). Thus in this application, the QoSDREAM

Table 1. Typical location related traffic

Event type	Count
Badge Events (Federator Events)	671
These are the events generated by the ActiveBadge Federator. They are generated whenever a badge is picked up by a sensor. Many of the rooms in the lab have more than one sensor and therefore a badge may be picked up by more than one sensor. Most of these events are as a result of a person's badge being detected, since equipment badges emit their signal less often, than badges worn by people.	
Raw Overlap Events	204
These are the events generated by the SRM.	
PersonMovement Events	12
These events are generated by the PersonMovement Adaptor in response to people moving in and out of rooms.	
PersonOverlap Events	40
These are generated by the PersonOverlap Adaptor. In this example those were caused by people moving into rooms where other people were present.	
EquipmentOverlap Events	48
These are generated by the EquipmentOverlap Adaptor. Those were caused by people moving into different rooms and their region overlapping with those of the equipment in the new room.	

location architecture reduces the event traffic that the application process is required to handle by a factor of approximately 17.

6. CONCLUSION

We have described those parts of the architecture and design of QoSDREAM that are concerned with location information management, a general-purpose framework to support the construction of context-aware multimedia applications. The contributions of the work include:

- a novel approach to the handling of location data derived from a variety of location-sensing technologies, integrating and representing them in terms of overlap events that are constructed by geometric analysis, thus reducing the incoming event traffic to proportions that are manageable by applications by its aggregation into relevant relations.

- an implemented framework that integrates an application-level service to handle a variety of types of location data with a service to configure and manage real-time multimedia streams.

The architecture encourages the use of pluggable components. Thus the components of the framework that support event-based communication and persistence are hidden behind generic interfaces that provide the abstractions required for the class of applications that the framework aims to support.. This makes the platform largely independent of the specific protocols and mechanisms used in providing its services.

Work is planned on the extension of the framework to support large-scale application domains, including the intelligent hospital. This will call for the incorporation of fault tolerance and security mechanisms and for refinements to the platform following an evaluation of its performance under large-scale application loads. The extension of the federator/relation approach to other types of data source (e.g. biometric data) – is seen as a promising direction for further research.

Work currently in hand is expected to result in the early availability of a public release of the QoSDREAM framework.

Acknowledgments

The following people have contributed to the development of the QoS DREAM framework: John Bates, Mark Spiteri, Martin Harper, Sarah Gunn, Eli Katsiri, Kasim Rehman. We thank the following for valuable advice and support: Andy Hopper, Mark Wharton, Pete Steggles, Tim Kindberg. Last but not least, we are grateful to Dr Tim Coats and the staff at the A& E Department of the Royal London Hospital for giving their time to our study of their requirements. This research is funded by EPSRC, the UK Engineering and Physical Sciences Research Council.

References

[1] David Arnold, Bill Segall, Julian Boot, Andy Bond, Melfyn Lloyd, Simon Kaplan, "Discourse with Disposable Computers: How and why you will talk to your tomatoes", Usenix Workshop on Embedded Systems (ES99), Cambrdige Mass, March 1999. http://www.usenix.org/publications/library/proceedings/es99/full_papers/arnold/arnold_html/

[2] I. Barth, "Configuring Distributed Multimedia Applications Using CINEMA", Proc. IEEE MMSD'96, Berlin, Germany, Mar 1996

[3] J. Bates, J. Bacon, K. Moody and M.D. Spiteri, "Using Events for the Scalable Federation of Heterogeneous Components", Proc. ACM SIGOPS EW'98, Sintra, Portugal, Sep 1998

[4] F. Bennett, D. Clarke, J. B. Evans, A. Hopper, A. Jones and D. Leask, "Piconet - Embedded Mobile Networking", IEEE Personal Communications 4:5, Oct 1997

[5] John Barton and Tim Kindberg , The challenges and opportunities of integrating the physical world and networked systems, paper submitted to Mobicom 2001, http://www.champignon.net/TimKindberg/

[6] Bluetooth Special Interest Group, "Bluetooth Specification v1.0B", Dec 1999. http://www.bluetooth.com/developer/specification/

[7] J. Bacon, K. Moody, J. Bates, C. Ma, A. McNeil, O. Seidel and M.D. Spiteri, "Generic Support for Asynchronous, Secure Distributed Applications", IEEE Computing, Mar 2000

[8] Gordon Blair and Jean-Bernard Stefani, Open Distributed Processing and Multimedia, Addison-Wesley, Harlow, England, 1998.

[9] The Castor Project. 2000. http://castor.exolab.org/

[10] G. Cugola, E. DiNitto, and A. Fugetta, "Exploiting an event-based infrastructure to develop complex distributed systems", Proc. ICSE'98, pages 261-270, 1998.

[11] G. Coulouris, J. Dollimore and T. Kinberg, Distributed Systems: Concepts and Design, Edition 3, Addison-Wesley 2001.

[12] E. Coiera, Clinical Communication & shy; A New Informatics Paradigm, Technical Report HPL-96-64, Hewlett-Packard 1996.

[13] G. Fitzpatrick, T. Mansfield, S. Kaplan, D. Arnold, T. Phelps, and B. Segall, "Instrumenting and augmenting the workaday world with a generic notification service called Elvin", Proc. ECSCW'99, Copenhagen, Denmark, Sep 1999

[14] P. Gulutzan, T. Pelzer, "SQL-99 Complete". CMP Books, April 1999

[15] A. Harter and A. Hopper, A Distributed Location System for the Active Office. IEEE Network, Vol. 8, No. 1, January 1994.

[16] A. Harter, A. Hopper, P. Steggles, A. Ward and P.Webster, The Anatomy of a Context-Aware Application. In Proceedings of the 5th Annual ACM/IEEE International Conference on Mobile Computing and Networking (Mobicom '99), Seattle, Washington, USA, August 15 - 20 1999 1999. ftp://ftp.uk.research.att.com/pub/docs/att/tr.1999.7.pdf

[17] Andy Hopper, Sentient Computing, The Royal Society Clifford Paterson Lecture, 1999, http://www.uk.research.att.com/abstracts.html# 108

[18] Chris Johnson and Kevin Cheng, The Glasgow Context Server: a Wireless System for Location Awareness in Mobile Computing. Submitted to IHM/HCI 2001, http://www.dcs.gla.ac.uk/~johnson/papers/context_aware/

[19] T. Kindberg, J. Barton, J. Morgan, G. Becker, D. Caswell, P. Debaty, G. Gopal, M. Frid, V. Krishnan, H. Morris, J. Schettino, B. Serra, and M. Spasojevic. "People, Places, Things: Web Presence for the Real World". Proc. 3 rd Annual Wireless and Mobile Computer Systems and Applications, Monterey CA, USA, Dec. 2000. p 19.

[20] R.S. Mitchell, Dynamic Configuration of Distributed Multimedia Components. Ph.D. Thesis, University of London, August 2000. http://www-lce.eng.cam.ac.uk/qosdream/publications/

[21] Scott Mitchell, Hani Naguib, George Coulouris and Tim Kindberg, A QoS Support Framework for Dynamically Reconfigurable Multimedia Applications. In Lea Kutvonen, Hartmut König and Martti Tienari (eds), Distributed Applications and Interoperable Systems II, pp 17-30. Kluwer Academic Publishers, Boston, 1999. Also in Proc. DAIS 99. http://www-lce.eng.cam.ac.uk/QoSDREAM/publications/

[22] Scott Mitchell, Mark D. Spiteri, John Bates and George Coulouris, "Context-Aware Multimedia Computing in the Intelligent Hospital", In Proc. SIGOPS EW2000, the Ninth ACM SIGOPS European Workshop, Kolding, Denmark, September 2000. http://www-lce.eng.cam.ac.uk/QoSDREAM/publications/

[23] QoS DREAM Project, "QoS DREAM Hospital User Study", November 2000. http://www-lce.eng.cam.ac.uk/QoSDREAM/applications/hospitalstudy.php

[24] M.D. Spiteri, An Architecture for the Notification, Storage and Retrieval of Events, Ph.D. Thesis, University of Cambridge, Jan 2000. http://www-lce.eng.cam.ac.uk/QoSDREAM/publications/

[25] R. Want, D. M. Russell. "Ubiquitous Electronic Tagging". Distributed Systems Online, IEEE 2000. http://www.computer.org/dsonline/articles/ds2wan.htm.

CAPEUS: AN ARCHITECTURE FOR CONTEXT-AWARE SELECTION AND EXECUTION OF SERVICES

Michael Samulowitz, Florian Michahelles, Claudia Linnhoff-Popien
University of Munich, Dept. of CS, Oettingenstr. 67, D-80538 Munich, Germany

Abstract This paper introduces a comprehensive framework that allows mobile users to access a variety of services provided by their current environment (e.g. print services). Novel to our approach is that selection and execution of services takes into account the user's current context. Instead of being harassed by useless activities as service browsing or configuration issues, environmental services get seamlessly aligned to the user's present task. Thus, the challenge is to develop a new service framework that fulfils these demands.

The paper proposes a document-based approach; so called Context-Aware Packets (CAPs) contain context constraints and data for describing an entire service request. The core framework, Context-Aware Packets Enabling Ubiquitous Services (CAPEUS), reverts to CAPs for realising context-aware selection and execution of services.

Keywords: Mobile Computing, Context-Awareness, Context Representation, Task-Driven

1. INTRODUCTION

Future environments will host a vast number of mobile and wireless devices, besides to general-purpose computers. These smart spaces [1] offer a variety of services to their visitors, which may include intelligent home or office services. Multi-service environments involve a number of research challenges for mobile computing scenarios. One challenge is how to discover services when a user moves into a new environment. This problem may be tackled by service discovery protocols, like JINI [2], IETF SLP [3], or SDP [4]; the user may access a local service access point, which returns available service interfaces. Another challenge is how to describe service interfaces; because a new discovered service interface can only be selected and used if it can be understood. This leads to abstract interfaces [5], first work on this issue can be found in [6]. A third challenge, considering multi-service environments, is *context-aware* service provision. In particular, the system selects and executes services in regards to the user's task in mind.

It is the third feature that has been least addressed by previous research projects. If for example a user's present task requires printing a document, then it should simply be printed. Of course this action should take into account her current context, here primarily the location. The printer should reside in her near neighbourhood, preferably in the same room, not in another building. Or, she is on the move, the system predicts her route and when passing the whereabout of her printout she gets the directions via a head-mounted display.

The paper presents a novel architecture for context-aware service provision in *ubiquitous computing* environments. We propose that just offering services to a user is not enough. Services should be aligned to a user's task; the user shouldn't be harassed with selecting the right service for the task at hand. Anymore, execution details should not be visible to the user.

The following issues were crucial to our architecture:

- service invocation mechanisms that regard arbitrary contextual constraints, e.g. location or time,
- a sophisticated representation scheme for representing contextual information, in particular constraints,
- reduce user's required interaction

In developing the architecture, we implemented and deployed some context-aware applications. Thereby we were able to proof our concept in practical use. Apart from satisfying the main design goals our architecture revealed three distinguishing features. Firstly, it is applicable to many context-aware scenarios, which outlines its general-purpose character. Secondly, it detaches context handling from service matters. By this separation of concerns services can be added without affecting context processing. Respectively, context handling may be manipulated without affecting underlying services. Thus, our design contributes to a simplified management. Finally, our work contributed to a new understanding of context. We do not only consider context information for deducing the current situation of an entity [8], but also *context constraints*. Here, context constraints are utilised to govern service selection and execution processes. Anyway, the concept of context constraints may be applied to many other problem areas.

2. DESIGNING A CONTEXT-AWARE SERVICE ARCHITECTURE

A user's device should act as a *portal* to its surrounding computing environment; it is an access point to the service and data space [5]. In our approach we refine this idea: The device acts as a *mediator* for expressing service needs to the environment; service needs result from the user's current context (or task). Our work mainly focuses on representing and interpreting the user's service needs.

As a solution for communicating service needs we endeavoured a uniform document format: *Context-Aware Packets* (CAPs). CAPs allow expressing service needs on a high abstraction level without knowing specifics about services available in the environment. CAPs are created by the user's device and put in the network; inside the network the CAP gets evaluated. The evaluation a CAP results in selection and execution of services fitting to the specified service needs. Service needs are expressed by *context constraints*, which describe the situation and circumstances under which the user intends to use a service.

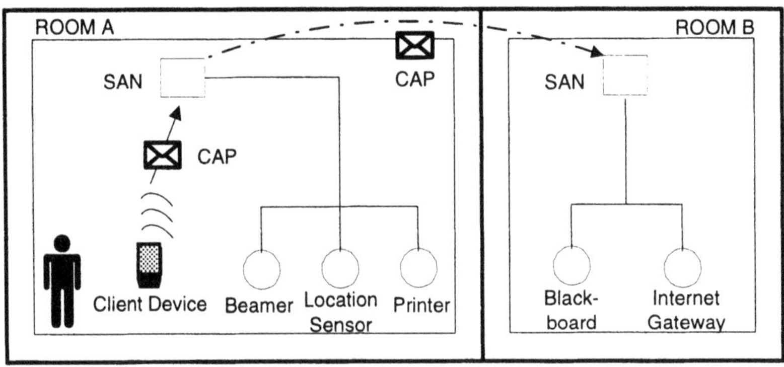

Figure 1. Testbed setup: Service Access Nodes control the services and sensors for a room. The user's device emits a CAP document via wireless link to the SAN in the room she stays. Then, system looks for a proper service and executes it.

Figure 1 depicts CAP evaluation from a networking perspective: A user injects a CAP to a local service access node (SAN). A SAN acts as a service proxy controlling the services available in its domain. For our testbed a domain always corresponds to a room and its hosted services (e.g. digital blackboard). The SAN evaluates the CAP; evaluation considers two phases: *selection* and *execution*. In the selection phase, the SAN checks whether the CAP is related to a service in its domain (room), or not. If not, the CAP is routed to a SAN meeting the needs; routing choices are governed by the CAP's embedded context constraints. In the second phase, a selected service is to be executed. Here, context constraints control the execution of a selected service.

In order to govern choices based on context constraints it is mandatory to determine the actual context, e.g. where is a user, or what services are available in the current environment. To find out, the SNA may read out sensor signals (e.g. location sensor) or check a service repository for available service interfaces.

Comprising, the architecture – using CAPs – controls the selection and execution of services based on context constraints, which reflect the user's service needs. The selection process initiated by CAP chooses a fitting service and its location (in which room); the execution process may bind services to context triggers, which control temporal issues.

2.1. The Concept of Context-Aware Packets (CAPs)

Technically, a CAP constitutes a kind of *remote procedure call* (RPC) [11] based on a document-based approach as XML-RPC [12]. CAPs feature some differences from the classical RPC concept: the receiver of the call is determined after it is issued. Specialised network nodes, SANs, route the CAP to its receiver based on its embedded context constraints. Another difference relates to the execution, calls in respect of CAP may be deferred, or even be autonomously repeated. Further on, CAP processing may require user interaction. *Interactive* CAPs (see section 2.4) ask the user to confirm the execution of a pre-selected service. Or in the case of problems the user may be notified. And finally, CAPs may be nested, see 2.3 for details. Provision of these non-RPC features requires a novel representation scheme, which is described in the following.

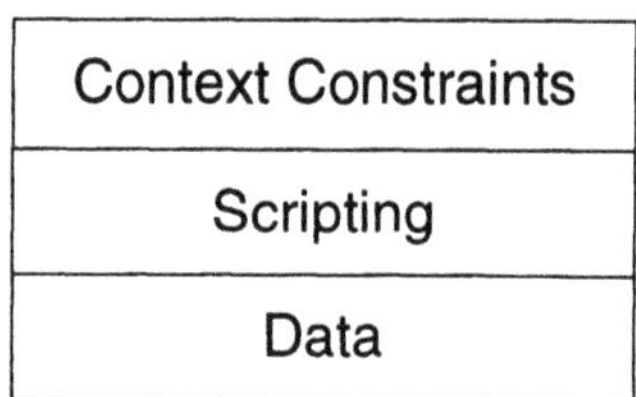

Figure 2. Context-Aware Packet (CAP)

As Figure 2 depicts a CAP document is organised into three parts: *context constraints*, *scripting*, and *data*. **Context constraints** play a major role inside CAP; as already mentioned they are used to mediate a user's service needs. The context constraints' semantics and representation will be explained in the subsequent section.

The **data** section provides data to be processed by the selected service. The data format is not restricted to one specific format, it relates to the service in mind. Hence, a beamer service might expect PowerPoint formatted data, and an Internet photo album might expect JPG. Data may be directly embedded in the document or referenced, e.g. by HTTP link. Referenced data allows implying dynamic data when executing a service, e.g. always display a user's day schedule when she enters the office.

The **scripting** section allows representing simple scripts executed on a selected service in order to embrace more complex semantics, which cannot be captured by context constraints or data section. In our current prototype implementation we did not make any use of the scripting feature. Scripting was added for completeness, so future applications of CAPs will not require any modification to the CAP format.

2.2. Context Constraints

This section outlines the semantics and representation of context constraints. Inspired by control theory [13], context constraints can be interpreted as a *set point.* The *actual value* is referred as a *context configuration.* A context configuration reflects the actual context of a set of entities; the value of a context configuration results from sensor measurements. In order to control service selection and execution processes, the system compares the context constraints to the context configuration. If the actual context configuration meets the context constraints, the CAP's data is applied on a specific service. In this moment the actual situation (deferred by the context configuration) exactly matches the requirements expressed by the context constraints.

If the context configuration does not meet the context constraints, the system may wait for the required situation to occur. Or it detects that the exposed context constraints cannot be fulfilled at all, e.g. the CAP relates to a service in another environment (room), hence the CAP has to be re-routed.

Context constraints are phrased using the following primtives: *abstract entities*, *relations*, and *events*. The primitives are described in the following paragraphs.

Abstract Entities

Abstract entities are categorised into three types: *Actors*, *Abstract devices*, *Items.*

Any user interacting with the system is an actor. Abstract devices represent devices, which offer services to their environment. These can be all kinds of devices from an abstract perspective, which means not related to concrete devices (e.g. printer luther in room D2). Finally, items denote passive elements. In contrast to abstract devices they do not offer services but are equipped with sensors, such that the item's state can be retrieved and used for denoting context triggers.

Printer
Attributes *Colour = "yes"* *Paper-size = "A4"* *Duplex = "yes"* *Technology = "laser"*
Interface

Figure 3. Printer Entity.

Entities are described by attributes. During the evaluation of context constraints, these attributes are used for mapping abstract entities to concrete units, which serve the requirements expressed by the entities' associated attributes. For example, specifying a colour laser-printer as an abstract device and "applying" it to an office returns an address to a suiting printer, if there is one. Chapter 3 shows how this functionality was implemented by inter-operating with a service discovery protocol. Figure 3 shows a sample entity, which uses common technical attributes. The concept of CAP does not restrict attributes to any types, but it has to be considered that the attributes are still applicable. Each CAP may relate to multiple entities.

Relations

Generally, a **relation** describes the dependencies of entities from each other in a spatial or temporary manner; a relation exists of a set of entities. One sample relation, *inRoom*, describes spatial information, such that the members of this relation have to be in the same room. Thus, starting with entities as atomic units, relations allow gluing those together for modelling dependencies. Relations constrain the selection of a desired service. Referring to the laser-printer example of the previous paragraph, an *inRoom* relation containing the printer entity and a user entity constraints printer selection to the same room as the user stays.

Events

Generally, events indicate actions or occurrences detected by a program. Usually, events can be user actions, such as clicking the mouse, or pressing a key. A system can subscribe to certain events and can respond to their occurrence.

An **event**, in the context of CAP, describes a trigger, which either activates (positive trigger) or aborts (negative trigger) the execution of a CAP initiated service call. Events report actions and occurrences detected by sensors, which are modelled by *item entities*.

Event conditions are represented by logical condition-expressions, which can be either ground or combined by logical operators (AND, OR). Figure 4 shows a condition in the CAP's XML format. Our representation scheme adopts to the trigger concept for policy-based management described in [15].

```
<AND>
   <condition subject = "day" object = "monday" type = "="/>
   <condition subject = "user\_location" object = "at_work" type = " ="/>
</AND>
```

Figure 4. "Triggering a reminder if the user gets to work on Monday"

Regarding semantics, the event concept steps out the service selection, it rather allows to condition execution of a selected service.

2.3. Composing Services

The latter sections outlined the structure of a single CAP; this section explains how multiple CAPs may be composed by *nesting*. In particular, this is useful for re-transferring CAPs in case of error, or for tunnelling through converters.

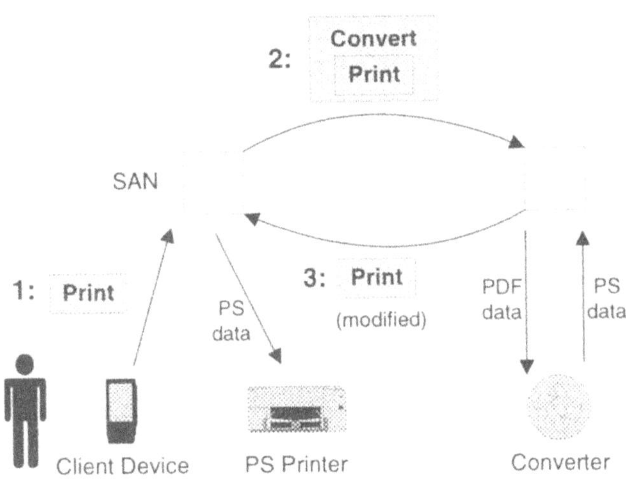

Figure 5. Tunneling a Print-Job

CAPs are nested, by putting one CAP into the data part of another one. Multiple nesting is also feasible. This recursive structure allows expressing cascaded use of multiple services. For example, a user wants to print a document in PDF format, but the printer in the current environment only accepts Postscript format. Instead of signalling the user that the demanded service request cannot be fulfilled, the system autonomously sends the document to a conversion service. There it is converted to the wanted format (Postscript) and is send back to the printer where the job is finally done.

For implementing this scenario (see Figure 5), the receiving service access node (SAN) wraps the incoming CAP, the outer CAP is directed to a conversion service. The SAN in the domain of the conversion service processes the nested CAP considering the context constraints of the outer CAP and data of the inner CAP. Hence, the data gets converted. Finally, the SAN removes the outer CAP and updates the data of the original CAP; the resulting CAP gets evaluated as usual.

2.4. Example: A CAP for local Printing

This section briefly discusses an example and explains vital CAP elements not covered by the previous sections. Figure 6 depicts a sample CAP document for printing a document locally (in the same room as the user stays). The begin of the document indicates the sender, the receiver and names the wanted action:

```
<CAP name="printing_locally" from="Florian"
put_to="Printer"
duration="one-shot" interactive="no">
```

Due to the fact that a CAP document may include a number of abstract entity descriptions the "put_to"-directive is used for labelling the *service entity*. The CAP's embedded data is applied to this service entity, here it is the printer entity. *Duration* signals if the CAP is only executed once or multiple times; *one-shot* denotes single execution, applying *multi-shot* a CAP is activated repeatedly.

```
...

<CAP name="printing_locally" from="Florian"
put_to="Printer" duration="one-shot">

<ContextC>

  <Entity type="abstractDevice" name="Printer">
        <attrib lextype="colors">greyscale</attrib>
        <attrib lextype="papersize">a4</attrib>
        ...
        <interface>
         <put name="lpr">
          <param lextype="lpr_filter">no</param>
          <param lextype="MIMEtype">
                stream/postscript
          </param>
          ...
         </put>
      </interface>

</Entity>

<Entity type="Person" name="Florian">
      <attrib lextype="date">02.02.2001 13:45</attrib>
      <attrib lextype="role">guest</attrib>
      ...
</Entity>

<Relation name="inRoom">
      <arg>Florian</arg>
      <arg>Printer</arg>
</Relation>

</ContextC>

<Data type="application/postscript">
  <![CDATA[ %!PS-Adobe-2.0
  ... ]]>
</Data>

<Scripting>future use</Scripting>

</CAP>
```

Figure 6. Example CAP

The *interactive* directive is a toggle for the CAP interaction facility. If the CAP is interactive, service execution has to be confirmed by the user. As can be seen in Figure 6 entities are optionally attributed by an *interface* section, which firstly describes if the entity is a data sink or source, and secondly it denotes the entities supported data types for exchange.

A data sink is indicated by a *put interface*, a data source is indicated by a *get interface*. As outlined in the previous section, a single service entity may provide both interface types, put and get. In case of the conversion service data is first written and consequently converted data is read back.

The *relation* element embraces entities belonging to a specific relation, here *inRoom*.

The complete XML DTD can be seen in [16].

2.5. CAP Life-Cycle

As outlined in Section 2.2 processing of CAPs and their associated services is controlled by context constraints. For managing and tracking the control process of multiple CAPs floating the system, each CAP always adopts to a discrete state. Figure 7 shows a CAP's main processing states and possible transitions. During its lifetime a CAP may traverse five different states: *Find*, *Wait*, *Ready*, *Talk To* and *Terminated.*

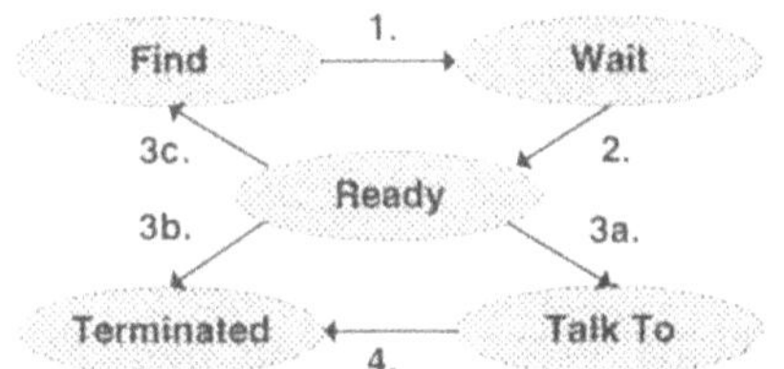

Find the location of the wanted service.

Wait for a matching context configuration.

Ready for processing.

Talk To the selected service

Terminated

Figure 7. CAP Life-Cycle

Find is the initial state the CAP is to be routed. When the CAP reached its final destination it adopts to *wait*, the system waits for a situation that matches the CAP's embedded context constraints. If there are no outstanding obstacles regarding service execution the CAP switches to *Ready*. *Talk To* relates to actual service execution. And ultimately, CAP processing is *terminated*, after execution or abortion has been performed.

3. IMPLEMENTATION

This chapter details the architecture of CAPEUS and its constituting components. Further on it describes technical features of our implementation.

3.1. CAPEUS Architecture

The overall architecture, CAPEUS (Context-Aware Packets Enabling Ubiquitous Services), is depicted by Figure 8. The left side of the picture relates to components running on the user's device. In brief, the CAP Organiser produces

CAPs on demand of user applications; the user model [17] provides personal preferences for service use.

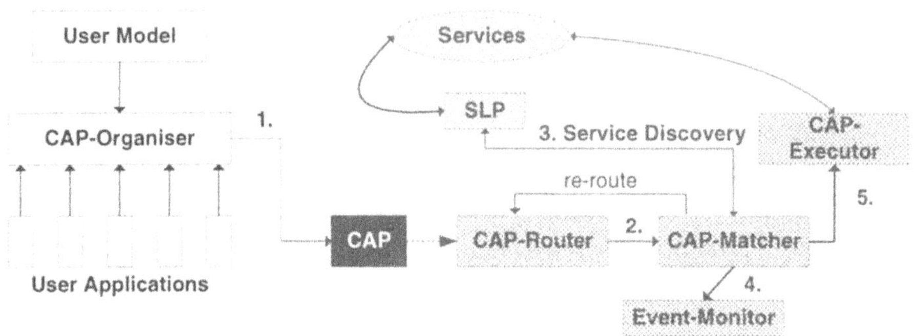

Figure 8. CAPEUS Architecture Design

The right side relates to components running on the service access node (SAN), which was the focus of our work: CAP Router, CAP Matcher, CAP Execution, Event Monitor, and SLP. The function of the SAN's components is described in the following sub-sections.

3.1.1 CAP Router. If a SAN receives a CAP via its network interface it is directed to the CAP router. The router component has mainly two tasks:

1 managing logical connections,

2 forwarding CAPs to other SANs based on symbolic attributes;

3 passing the CAP to the CAP Matcher.

We assume that network connections do only exist a short period of time, as featured by emerging networking standards, which offer ad-hoc peer-to-peer connectivity, e.g. Bluetooth [18]. Typically, a user's device establishes a wireless connection to its local SAN; then the CAP is transferred, and subsequently the network connection is closed.
But in some cases CAP execution may require interaction with the user, for signalling error, or successful service execution. Or in the case of *interactive* CAPs the user is asked if he really wants a service to be executed (when all context-constraints are evaluated valid). Hence, the router manages address data of the CAP sender, so it is possible to connect to her later. If a CAP is completely processed the user's associated data is deleted.

The second task relates to forwarding CAPs based on symbolic attributes, e.g. "Room D2, Building 10", "where the user is", or "to a proximate room". For implementing this functionality we endeavoured a hierarchy of routers as depicted in Figure 9.

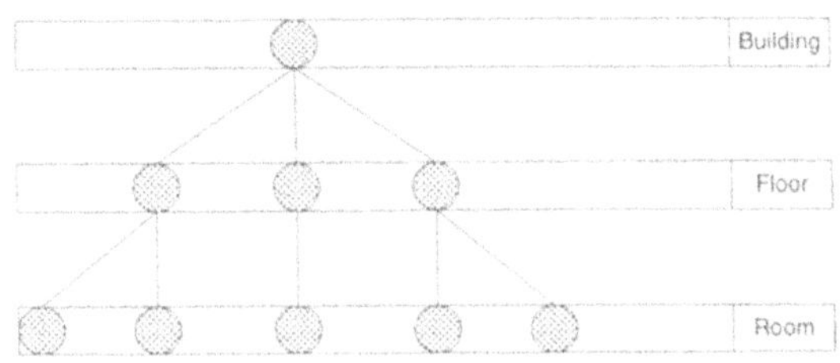

Figure 9. Hierarchy of CAP Routers

For routing a CAP to its destined environment (here room), the CAP is first routed to a floor level router. If context constrains do not allow processing the CAP in a room in this floor, the CAP is routed to the next higher level (building). Hence, the search domain is widened to the complete building. Obviously, this approach does not scale well, but it was sufficient for demonstrating the concept. Particularly, it was easy to express vicinity, e.g. room in the same floor.

Besides, a more sophisticated solution for routing messages based on attributes can be found in [19]; or a hierarchical lookup system for locating mobile objects is described in [20].

Finally, the router passes the CAP to the *CAP Matcher*. From the router's perspective, the matcher checks if the service is related to the current environment, and if it can be executed there. Otherwise, the CAP is send back to the router with additional addressing attributes.

3.1.2 CAP Matcher. Briefly, the *CAP matcher* compares the context constraints with the actual measured context configuration. If the context configuration matches the context constraints then the CAP's data is passed to the *CAP Executor,* which finally executes the service. Otherwise, the matcher calculates the *divergence*; in our context the divergence denotes *what* the matcher prevents from selecting or executing a specific service. For instance, if the matcher compares the CAP's context constraints to the actual context configuration and finds out that the CAP is related to another service domain, then the resulting divergence refers to location. Hence, the matcher may induce re-routing of the CAP. Altogether, the divergence is used to control the actions of the matcher in accordance to context constraints.

The resulting divergence may relate to *location*, *user interaction*, *wrong interface*, *trigger*, *equal*, or *general error*. Table 1 lists possible differences and associated actions. Location is sub-divided into two categories: *vicinity* and *other location. Vicinity* instructs the router to send the CAP to proximate domains for possible execution. *Other location* the CAP is related to another domain and has to be routed there.

Table 1.

Divergence		**Component/Action**
Location	Vicinity	Router: try proximate domains
	Other location	Router: route to specified address
User Interaction		Router: indicate state, user confirmation (interactive CAPs)
Trigger		Event Monitor: wait for matching situation
Wrong Interface		Matcher: convert data, nested CAP (see Section 2.3)
Equal		Executor: apply data on selected service
General Error		Router: Error message to user; Matcher: abort processing

In the following it is outlined how the matcher parses CAP documents: firstly the matcher evaluates the *relations* for selecting a suiting service. The matcher applies the CAP's embedded triggers for governing the execution of the previously selected service.

Evaluating Relations

The matcher represents nested relations as tree, nodes represents relations and leaves represent abstract entities. Figure 10 shows a simple example, it is used to select the cheapest printer in the same room as the user. As already, mentioned the *inRoom* relation requires entities to reside in the same room. The *min(X)* relation selects among multiple entities the one with minimum value for attribute X.

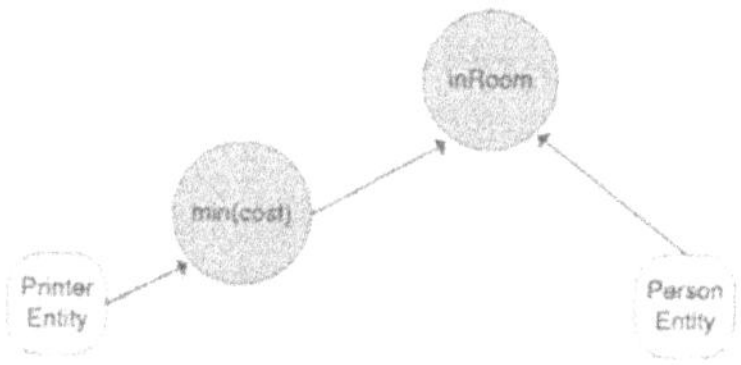

Figure 10. The cheapest printer in the same room as the user stays.

The relation tree is evaluated bottom-up; hence the matcher first evaluates the *min* relation and thereafter the *inRoom* relation. Figure 11 depicts the matching algorithm for relations. When applying the algorithm the set of possible candidates (service entities) gets stepwise reduced. Lastly, a set of suitable service entities remains; one of them is selected randomly.

For service discovery the system compiles a request based on the attributes of the abstract entity; in turn the service discovery returns all service entities which match the attributes. Sometimes it may be necessary to convert the attributes to a format compatible to the chosen service discovery protocol. Hence, we implemented a transducer component, which converts an attribute schema to a schema in question.

1 Enter next relation (bottom-up).
2 Execute service discovery for all abstract entities of the relation.
3 Evaluate relevant entity attributes by applying the relation.
4 Discard service discovery results, which do not fulfil the relation.
5 Continue with 1 until complete tree is processed.

Figure 11. Matching Algorithm for Relations

We deployed service location protocol SLP [3] for service discovery, for supporting other service discovery systems, like UPnP [22], JINI [2], or Salutation [23], we applied the strategy pattern [24]. Hence, the transducer component can be exchanged without affecting other components.

Evaluating Events

After evaluating the relations, the desired service is selected. In contrast, *Events* control the execution of this service.

For each event defined in the CAP the *matcher* spawns an individual *Event monitor*. An Event Monitor senses the environment for the event in question. If the event occurs the matcher is notified. As described in Chapter 2, events may be combined by logical operators. Special care has to be taken for evaluating conjunctive operators ("AND"), because the system has to decide whether two events are considered to be coeval or not. Hence, two events are considered coeval if they occur in a time period shorter than a defined threshold. For most applications a threshold less than a second seemed to be reasonable.

If all events evaluated true the event monitors get killed. Consequently, the matcher hands the CAP's data and the address of the selected service to the *CAP Executor*, which ultimately executes the selected service.

3.1.3 CAP Executor. The *CAP Executor* embodies the interface from CAPEUS to extern services. It is supplied with one single service location, which was determined by the *Matcher*. Further on, it accesses the CAP's embedded data. Services that do not comply to the executors expected streaming interface may be wrapped; as in CyberDesk [25] we could apply observable APIs [26]. In future projects, the executor will also process the scripting part, for facilitating more complex semantics.

3.2. Prototype

The CAPEUS prototype was implemented in JAVA [27] and is based on the principles discussed in the latter chapter. The objective is that the prototype will be suitable to implement and also validates the main concepts described above. In addition, to the features discussed and implemented within this project CAPEUS is meant to be used and refined in various future projects. CAPEUS was implemented and tested in conjunction with the DWARF project [28] on augmented reality [29]. The DWARF prototype provided several features, which could be used for demonstrating CAPEUS in practical use. On the other hand CAPEUS supplemented DWARF by adding spontaneous use of environmental services, whereby selection and execution of services is governed by pre-defined context constraints. In the current implementation DWARF offers besides of WaveLan [30] and Bluetooth [18] connectivity also location sensing. Up to now the system provides GPS for outdoor environments. It is planned to use RF tags for indoor environments.

We implemented a few context-aware applications for demonstrating our architecture in practice, two of them are briefly described in the subsequent paragraphs.

Context-Aware Notes

In analogy to the stick-e framework [31] this application mimics the post-it metaphor. If the user takes a note, it is tagged by the current available context information, particularly the location. If the user comes back to this place in future, her handheld[1] will display the note. The application also allows creating public notes, visible for anybody.

We implemented this application just by creating a repository of *multi-shot* CAPs. Each reflecting a user's note, the CAP's context constraints reflect the note's related context information. For personal notes the service access node (SAN) runs on the handheld. Anytime a note's related context occurs the associated CAP triggers a display service on the handheld.

For public notes the CAP is transferred to the location's responsible SAN. In this case the note is displayed to any user entering the location.

Task Aligned Local Service Use

We implemented an application for local service use, considering the user's task, here document viewing. In particular it is a document viewer running on a laptop computer. To any document, the viewer offers service options related to the currently displayed document type. For instance, viewing a text document the system offers the following service options: *print, blackboard, and note.* Each service option is related to a specific CAP: *print* issues a local

[1]For the prototype we used laptops with WaveLan connectivity.

print job as described see Section 2.4. *Blackboard* is similar to *print* it displays the document on a local digital blackboard. And finally *note* reverts to the context-aware note service described in the previous section.

In case of the print and blackboard service the viewer creates associated CAPs just by filling up the data part; the context constraints reflect pre-defined preferences of the user. The *note* is handled as described in the previous paragraph.

Due to the fact that the system pre-selects service options related to a specific document type, and transparently handles all interaction regarding remote service use (context-aware selection and execution), the system significantly reduces required attention by the user. Additionally, this technique allows saving *display estate* by simplifying the menu structure, what is crucial to handheld computing.

4. RELATED WORK & FUTURE DIRECTIONS

Work on service provision for mobile users as [34] or [35] are mainly based on the idea of service adapters. Using service adapters remote services appear local to applications running on the mobile device; service adapters mainly handle intermitted network connections and pass method calls to a remote service. Additionally, the mobile device can detect the service peers in its proximity, as featured by Bluetooth [18].

These approaches are similar to our architecture in the way that they enable the use of environmental services to a mobile user. But in contrast to CAPEUS, service use is restricted to services in coverage of the wireless network. Thereby, the spatial structure of environments is not reflected. Further on, CAPEUS enhances plain service use by supporting selection and execution processes taking in account arbitrary context information, not only location. Service invocations are modelled by documents, so it is not required to implement an individual service adapter for a specific service.

Our work profited from the Stick-e framework [33], which introduced the concept of virtual post-it notes; the implied context trigger mechanism influenced our design. The representation of service interfaces was inspired by the work of Hodes and Katz, see [5].

And finally, our work was fostered by work done on context-awareness [7,21,10,31].

Future work will focus on the following issues: Firstly, we will continue research on automatic creation of CAPs considering a user model, which reflects the user's preferences. Secondly, we will add support for other interface types. For the moment CAPEUS only handles streaming interfaces. Thirdly, scripting is to be supported in future versions of CAPEUS. Finally, we will consider security in order to protect the user's privacy.

References

[1] G. Abowd, J.P.G. Strebenz. Final Report on the Inter-Agency Workshop on Research Issues for Smart Environments. IEEE Personal Communications, October 2000.

[2] Jini(TM), 1998. http://java.sun.com/products/jini.

[3] C. Perkins. Service Location Protocol White Paper, May 1997.

[4] S. Czerwinski, B. Zhao, T. Hodes, A. Joseph, and R. Katz. An Architecture for a Secure Service Discovery Service. In Proceedings of MobiCom '99, Seattle, WA, August 1999.

[5] G. Banavar, J. Beck, E. Gluzberg, J. Munson, J. Sussmann, D. Zukowski. Challenges: An Application Model for Pervasive Computing. In Proceedings of MobiCom 2000, Boston August 2000

[6] T. Hodes and R. Katz. A Document-based Framework for Internet Application Control. In 2nd USENIX Symposium on Internet Technologies and Systems, October, 1999.

[7] G. Nelson. Context-Aware and Location Systems. PhD thesis, University of Cambridge, Computer Laboratory, Cambridge, UK, January 1998.

[8] Anind Dey and G.D. Abowd. Towards a Better Understanding of Context and Contex-Awareness. Technical report, GeorgiaTech, 1998.

[9] Daniel Salber, Anind K. Dey, and Gregory D. Abowd. The Context Toolkit: Aiding the Development of Context-Enabled Applications. In CHI'99, Pittsburgh, PA, US, 1999.

[10] Christos Efstratiou. Developing a Context-aware Electronic Tourist Guide: Some Issues and Experiences. Technical report, Department of Computing, Lancaster University, Lancaster, LA14YR, U.K., 2000.

[11] Sun Microsystems, Inc. RPC: Remote Procedure Call Protocol Specification Version 2, June 1988. RFC 1057.

[12] UserLand Software, Inc. XML-RPC. http://www.xmlrpc.com/

[13] Brogan, W.L., Modern Control Theory, (Prentice Hall, NJ, 1991).

P. Pin-Shan Chen. The Entity-Relationship Model-Toward a Unified View of Data. ACM Transactions on Database Systems, 1(1):9,1976.

[14] Morris Sloman and Emil Lupu. Policy Specications for Programmable Networks. In First International Working conference on Active Networks (IWAN'99), Berlin, June 1999.

[15] F. Michahelles. Designing an Architecture for Context-Aware Service Selection and Execution. Diploma Thesis. University of Munich, 2001.

[16] Michael Samulowitz. Designing a Hierarchy of User Models for Context-Aware Applications. Workshop on Situated Interaction in Ubiquitous Computing. CHI 2000, The Hague, April 2000.

[17] The Bluetooth SIG. WWW. http://www.bluetooth.com/v2/document.

[18] William Adjie-Winoto, Elliot Schwartz, Hari Balakrishnan, and Jeremy Lilley. The Design and Implementation of an Intentional Naming System. In Proceedings of the ACM Symposium on Operating Systems Principles, Charleston, SC, 1999.

[19] James Weatherall and Andy Hopper. Predator: A Distributed Location Service and Example Applications, 1999. In proceedings of Cooperative Buildings 1999, Springer-Verlag Lecture Notes in Computer Science.

[20] S. Fels, S. Sumi, T. Etani, N. Simonet, K. Kobayashi, and K. Mase K. Progress of C-MAP: A context-aware mobile assistant. In Proceeding of AAAI 1998 Spring Symposium on Intelligent Environments, March 1998.

[21] Universal Plug and Play Device Architecture. www.upnp.org

[22] Salutation, 2001. http://www.salutation.org.

[23] Erich Gamma, Richard Helm, Ralph Johnson, and John Vlissides. Design Patterns: Elements of Reusable Object-Oriented Software. Addison-Wesley, Reading, MA, 1995.

[24] A. Dey, G. Abowd, M. Pinkerton, and A. Wood. CyberDesk: A Framework for Providing Self-Integrating Ubiquitous Software Services. Proc. ACM UIST'97, 1997

[25] A. Wood. CAMEO: Supporting Observable APIs. Position Paper for the WWW5 Programming the Web Workshop, April 1996.

[26] J. Gosling, B. Joy, G. Steele, and G. Bracha. The Java Language Specification. Addison-Wesley, Reading, Mass., 2 edition, June 2000.

[27] P. J. Brown. The Stick-e Document: a Framework for Creating Context-aware Applications. In Proceedings of EP'96, Palo Alto, published in EP, January 1996.

[28] Martin Bauer, Asa MacWilliams, Florian Michahelles, Christian Sandor, Stefan Riß , Martin Wagner, Bernhard Zaun, Christoph Vilsmeier, Thomas Reicher, Bernd Brügge, and Gudrun Klinker. DWARF: System Design Document. Internal Report. Technical University Munich.

[29] Ronald T. Azuma. A Survey of Augmented Reality. August 1997.

[30] Airport Wireless Technology. http://www.apple.com/airport/.

[31] P. J. Brown. The Stick-e Document: a Framework for Creating Context-aware Applications. In Proceedings of EP'96, Palo Alto, published in EP, January 1996.

SENTIENT COMPUTING FOR EVERYONE

Diego López de Ipiña (1) and Sai-Lai Lo (2)
(1) Laboratory for Communications Engineering, Department of Engineering, University of Cambridge, Cambridge, UK
(2) AT& T Laboratories Cambridge, 24a Trumpington Street, Cambridge, UK

Abstract Sentient Computing gives perception to computing systems so that they can detect, interpret and respond to changing aspects of user contexts. The location attribute of a user's context is of special interest because it makes human-computer interactions more natural. In the last few years, several sophisticated indoor location technologies, which can track user whereabouts, have been developed. However, they are yet to be widely adopted because of their high cost and complexities in deployment, configuration and maintenance. This paper describes a novel vision-based software location system, known as TRIP, whose low-cost, off-the-shelf hardware requirements and easy deployment features overcome other systems' limitations. Nevertheless, in order to foster the deployment of "sentient spaces" that bring services to users wherever they are or about to move to, a location system must also be accompanied by the middleware to facilitate user-bound software service activation, migration and deactivation. LocALE addresses this issue by providing a CORBA-based solution that deals with heterogeneous object lifecycle and location control. Some distributed applications combining TRIP's and LocALE's capabilities are presented to demonstrate that Sentient Computing can be made readily available for everyone and everywhere.

Keywords: Context-Aware Computing, Location-Aware Computing, CORBA, Mobility

1. INTRODUCTION

Ubiquitous Computing [16] envisions physical spaces, such as offices, meeting rooms or homes, to be augmented with fully integrated computing devices. It aims to make services provided by these devices as commonly available as electricity. With Ubiquitous Computing, personal computers are no longer the focus of attention. Instead, the devices in the physical space provide their services unobtrusively and may not require the direct commands from the user.

Sentient Computing [5] is our approach to make Ubiquitous Computing a reality. It stems from the basic idea that to make computerised services pervasive in our life, the devices providing such services must be given *perception*, i.e. the capability to *see* or *hear* what entities are around them; what these entities are doing; where they are and when something is happening. Only then it is possible for the underlying computing system to undertake suitable actions to match the end user expectations. For example, when a user enters his office, depending on the time and day of the week, the sentient environment could automatically initiate the playback of a specific kind of music. If a colleague later on comes into the room to discuss some project ideas, the music volume could be automatically adjusted to facilitate communication. In order to do so, Sentient Computing must collect data from a variety of sensors in the environment and act upon these stimuli according to previously specified user preferences.

Location-Aware Computing [9], whose behaviour is determined by the position of objects in the environment, represents an interesting subset of the Sentient Computing paradigm since location is often an essential attribute of the context. This has motivated the development of several indoor location systems featuring different location granularity, ranging from room-scale resolution such as the infrared-based Active Badge [15], to the more accurate 3D resolution offered by systems such as the ultrasound-based Active Bat [4] or the radio-based 3D-iD [17]. These systems require people or objects to wear an electronic tag that transmits a unique identifier via infrared, ultrasound or radio to a network of sensors on the walls or ceilings. A *Location Server* then polls and analyses the data from the sensors and makes the information available to applications. These systems share several drawbacks. The tags they use need battery power and are expensive. The infrastructure required, a network of sensors, is complex and expensive to install and maintain. These factors may limit their practical use outside research laboratories. We have devised an alternative sensor technology, called TRIP, that provides a better trade-off between the price and flexibility of the technology and the accuracy of the location data provided. TRIP is a vision-based sensor technology that recognises and locates printed 2D circular barcode tags using inexpensive low-resolution CCD cameras.

In order to promote the use of the Sentient Computing paradigm in our living spaces, it is not sufficient to make computing systems aware of the user's presence, movement or precise location, it is important that these systems are provided with the capability to automatically activate services on behalf of the user when the appropriate contextual conditions are met. Furthermore, it is desirable to enable user-bound services to follow the user as he moves through the physical space, and to deactivate such services when the user leaves the space. In other words, what is needed is a middleware infrastructure that gives sentient applications the control over a computing object's lifecycle and location in a network. The LocALE framework is our middleware solution to this need. Sections 2 and 3 explore the TRIP technology and the distributed system infrastructure built on top of it. LocALE is introduced in section 4. Section 5 describes some applications combining TRIP and LocALE. Section 6 summarizes some related research. This is followed by the conclusions in section 7.

2. TRIP: A DOWNLOADABLE LOCATION SENSOR

TRIP (Target Recognition using Image Processing) [8] is a novel vision-based sensor system that uses a combination of visual markers (2-D *ringcodes*) and conventional video cameras to identify tagged objects in the field of view. Relatively low CPU demanding image processing and computer vision algorithms are applied to video frames to obtain the identifier (*TRIPcode*) and pose (3D location and orientation) of the targets relative to the viewing camera.

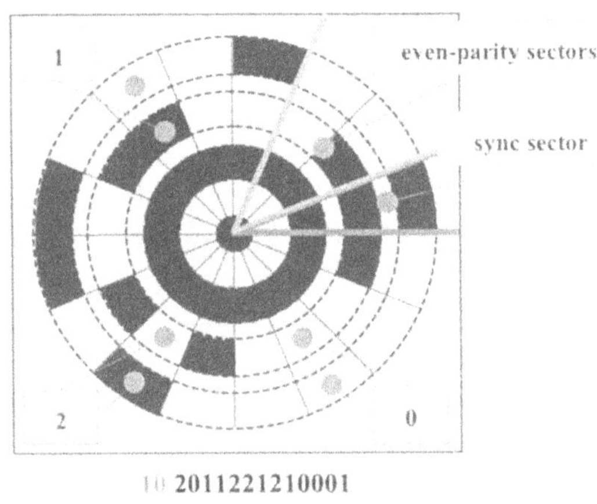

Figure 1. TRIPcode representing number 1,160,407

TRIP constitutes a very cheap and versatile sensor technology. Its 2-D ringcodes are printable, and can therefore be attached even to low-cost items, such as books or office stationeries (e.g. stapler). A TRIPcode (see Figure 1), read in counter-clockwise fashion from its synchronisation sector, represents a ternary number in the range $1\text{-}3^{13}(1{,}594{,}323)$. Only off-the-shelf hardware is required, i.e. low-resolution CCD cameras and CPU processing power.

The TRIP software will be made publicly downloadable in due course. Users with a web-cam attached to their PCs can easily install and run this software sensor and hence provide visual awareness to their computers.

When the Target Recognition Algorithm is applied to the images, a set of image processing stages is executed in order to determine the identities and positions (x-y coordinates in the image) where TRIPcodes are spotted. [8] fully describes the mathematics involved. In addition, a Pose Extraction Algorithm is employed. Given a single view of a target, this method determines the translation vector (t_x, t_y, t_z) and rotation angles (α, β, γ) that define the rigid body transformation between the camera coordinate system and the target-centred coordinate system. The method applied is based on the POSE_FROM_CIRCLE method given in [3].

The C++ implementation of the Target Recognition Algorithm processes 15 640x480 pixels frames per second on an 800 MHz Pentium III. When the target recognition and pose estimation are simultaneously undertaken, the performance achieved is about 12Hz. TRIPcodes are recognised as long as the target's plane orientation angles are less than 70° and its image occupies at least 20x20 pixels. The 3D location of the centre of a target relative to the viewing camera is obtained with less than 5% error. An even error parity check (see Figure 1) is used to prevent the identification of false positives.

3. TRIP: A DISTRIBUTED SENSOR SYSTEM

An event-based distributed architecture has been devised around TRIP in order to manipulate and distribute the sensor data provided by this technology. The functionality of the TRIP system, i.e. its target recognition and pose extraction, has been encapsulated by a CORBA [11] component, named *TRIParser*. This component offers a UNIX `pipe`-like interface that enables applications to connect distributed *Frame Grabber* components, which supply images from cameras, to TRIParsers. A TRIParser may consume images supplied by one or more *Frame Grabbers*. TRIP processing results are, by default, asynchronously communicated in an event-form to a CORBA Notification Channel [10], which is associated with each TRIParser. The Notification Channel serves as a de-coupler between the frame analysers and the components interested in the results.

A TRIParser pushes *TRIPevents* (see Figure 2) to its associated Notification Channel. The parties interested in a given TRIParser's location data subscribe to its associated channel and convey a set of constraints that specify the events they are interested in receiving. The Notification Channel undertakes consumer registration, event filtering and communication on behalf of its representing TRIParser. The filter constraint language supported is the constraint language defined by the OMG Trading Service. Hierarchical interconnections of these Notification Channels can be created in order to ensure the efficient and scalable dissemination of the TRIParser output. The TRIParser also provides a synchronous invocation interface (`processFrame`) that analyses a submitted frame and returns the location data inferred from it. Hence, applications can interact with a TRIParser either synchronously or asynchronously. However, for efficiency purposes, an application should establish direct communication between a *Frame Grabber* and a TRIParser, and register as an event consumer to the parser's Notification Channel.

```
Struct TRIPevent {
  string TRIPcode; // code ternary representation
  string cameraID; // capturing camera identifier
  paramsEllipse params; // bull's-eye's outer ellipse parameters (x,y,a,b, Θ)
  targetPosition pose;  // translation vector from camera origin to target centre
  targetOrientation angels; // (α, β, γ)
};
```

Figure 2. TRIPevent contents

3.1. The TRIP Directory Server

A TRIP Directory Server (TDS) has been created with the purpose of regulating the TRIPcode granting process and establishing mappings between real-world objects and TRIPcodes. This component ensures the efficient utilisation of the TRIPcode address space and its classification into categories. The TDS offers CORBA interfaces for the creation, modification, deletion and retrieval of both TRIPcodes and their categories.

3.2. The Sentient Information Framework

The Sentient Information Framework (SIF) defines an application construction model to streamline sentient application development. SIF isolates context capture and abstraction from application semantics. At the same time, it provides efficient mechanisms for context communication. Its main function is to transform context information into the formats demanded by the applications. SIF is not constrained to TRIP since it is sensor-technology independent. In this framework, components are categorised into 3 types (see Figure 3): (1) *Context Generators* (CGs), (2) *Context Channels* (CCs) and (3) *Context Abstractors* (CAs). *Context Generators* encapsulate sensors, such as TRIP, and the software that extracts information from them. They are sources of sensorial events. *Context Channels*, in our case implemented as CORBA Notification Channels, receive events and, after consumer specified filtering, pass the events to the consumers. *Context Abstractors* achieve the separation of concerns between context sensing and application semantics. They consume the raw sentient data provided by CGs (e.g. TRIPcode 1234 spotted), interpret its contents (e.g. user Diego spotted) and augment it (e.g. Diego's login is dipina) to produce enhanced contextual events that can be directly used by applications. They can also *correlate* other CAs' or CGs' outcomes to generate the required sentient data. For a more detailed description of SIF refer to [6].

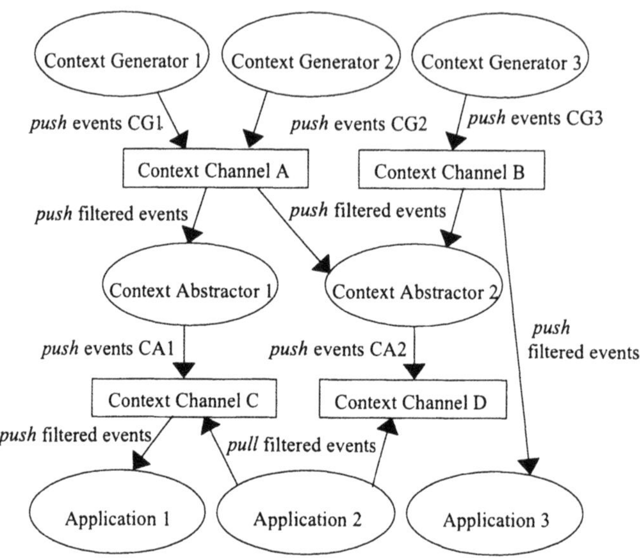

Figure 3. The SIF Architecture

4. LocALE: MIDDLEWARE FOR OBJECT LIFECYCLE AND LOCATION CONTROL

In order to make sentient computing available for everyone and everywhere, we have, so far, described a new cost-effective and easily deployable location sensor technology, TRIP, and a sentient application construction model, SIF, for the efficient manipulation and dissemination of sensorial data. However, one question still has to be answered, i.e. once a sentient system receives a high level event (e.g. Diego enters his office), how can the system effectively trigger the required action, i.e. activates, deactivates or migrates a user-bound software service?

Our experience with sentient application development has pointed us to the need for an infrastructure to streamline the lifecycle control of user-associated services. Otherwise, every time a new sentient application is developed, the distributed components involved in its operation have to be manually started. This makes sentient application deployment very cumbersome. Moreover, user-related services are often bound to user locations, e.g. the activation of an MP3 player must take place in one of the PCs in a room where a user presence is detected. Therefore, it is desirable to control both the lifecycle and location of user-bound services by a middleware designed for this purpose.

The LocALE (Location-Aware Lifecycle Environment) framework [7] defines a simple mechanism for managing the lifecycle and location of distributed CORBA objects residing on a network. In addition, it provides load-balancing and fault-tolerance features to the objects whose lifecycle it manages. The emphasis of its design is placed on providing a suitable interface for third party *object-location controllers*. These controllers can intelligently direct when and where components are activated or moved based on the inputs on user whereabouts and the location, load and capabilities of computing resources. LocALE offers an object-lifecycle infrastructure, simplifying sentient application deployment and enabling CPU intensive systems, such as TRIP, to reuse the spare resources available in a network.

4.1. LocALE Architecture

The LocALE middleware has a $3^1/_2$-tier architecture (Figure 4). It consists of client applications and the following 3 types of components:

- The *Lifecycle Manager* (LCManager) provides object-type independent lifecycle control interfaces and mediates the lifecycle operations over any CORBA object residing in a location domain. A location domain is a group of machines on a LAN that are physically located in the same place, such as a building, a floor or a room. Every object creation, movement or deletion request is routed through this component. This permits the LCManager to cache the current location of every object in a domain and thus act as a forwarding agent that redirects client requests after object references held by clients are broken due to either object movement or failure. In the latter case, the LCManager tries to recover the failed object, and, in case of success, returns the new object reference.
- *Lifecycle Server(s)* (LCServer) are containers of LocALE-enabled objects that are subjected to lifecycle control. Lifecycle operations invoked on an LCManager are delegated to suitable LCServers. They subsume standard strongly typed factory functionalities by providing a type specific creation method with hard-coded types. Furthermore, they also assist their local objects on their migration to other LCServers. They can be started either manually or by the local LCManager after a creation or migration request arrives at a location where the required LCServer type does not exist. In either case, they register with the manager by passing on their physical location (host), their CORBA object reference (or IOR) and data specific to the type of objects they handle.
- *Type-specific Proxy Factories* are placed in between clients and LCManagers. They save client applications from dealing with the generic object creation interface offered by an LCManager. Using type-specific interfaces makes client code far shorter and simpler to understand. With the generic version, if a mismatch in the type of a constructor argument occurs, the client would only receive an error at run-time rather than at compile time. *Type-specific Proxy Factories* offer type specific object-

creation methods with the same argument types and semantics as the LC-Servers they represent. They map type specific requests to the generic format demanded by LCManagers. They are on demand activated by the local LCManager.

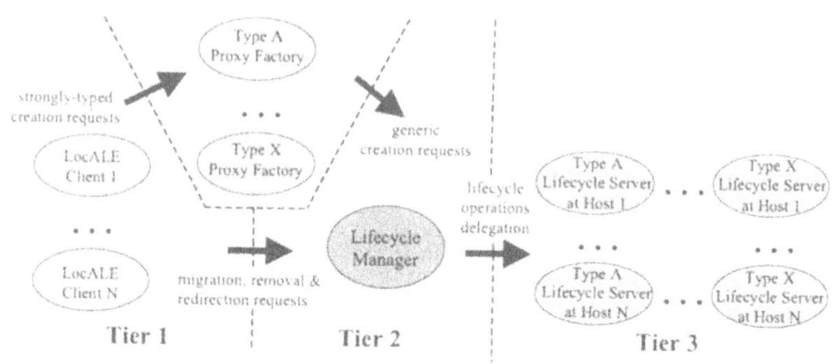

Figure 4. LocALE $3^1/_2$-tier architecture

The LocALE architecture guarantees compile-time type safety of clients with respect to the lifecycle control of their services. Clients find, through the LCManager, object references to type-specific proxy factories and issue through them object creation requests. Object migration and deletion requests are directly invoked on the LCManager because they are object type independent. The LCManager then delegates incoming lifecycle operations to the appropriate LCServers.

4.2. Location-constrained Lifecycle Control

One of the main advantages of CORBA [11] is that it offers location transparency to applications, i.e. it makes method invocations as simple on remote objects as on local objects. LocALE leverages on CORBA's location transparency but it is able to control *where* services are located. It can also set the constraints under which these services can later be re-located. We think these functions may bring important benefits. For example, load-balancing systems may wish to initiate new service instances on the hosts of the same LAN with the lowest processing load. Follow-me sentient applications may want to move objects tied to a user's physical location to the nearest host with the required capabilities. LocALE allows applications to control the location of CORBA objects. It extends conventional object factories with additional distributed object construction semantics. The following two attributes are appended to the object creation interfaces offered by the proxy factories:

- *Location* attribute (`LocSpec`): specifies *"where"* a service should be instantiated (or moved to). The formats available for location specification are:

  (1) `hostDN(hostName)`,

  (2) `roomID(room)` and

  (3) `hostGroup(listHostName)`.

  `hostDN` and `roomID` are used when the application wants to create an object on a specific host or in a specific room. By setting `hostName` or `room` attribute to `"ANY"` in either of these `LocSpecs`, the programmer can instantiate location-independent services. The `hostGroup` format is useful to specify an arbitrary set of hosts where an object may be created, e.g. hosts in a room with audio capabilities.
- *LifeCycle contraints* (`LCconstraints`) attribute: determines whether the object created should be considered as `RECOVERABLE` and/or `MOVABLE` within the location scope in which it is created, i.e. on a host, in a room or a host group. A recoverable object is either a stateless or a persistent object whose state can be restored after failure.

With respect to the ability to create objects based on the location constraints supplied, the LCManager provides a similar function as a conventional Trader. The LCManager matches client object creation specifications against the registered object Lifecycle Server types and locations, and delegates the operation to a suitable LCServer.

4.3. LocALE Implementation

The LCManager has been implemented in C++ using the CORBA 2.3 C++ ORB omniORB [1]. Its implementation makes extensive use of some advanced features provided by the CORBA 2.3's Portable Object Adapter (POA). Among these, it relies on the POA defined standard mechanism to generate LOCATION_FORWARD reply messages. These messages are sent by LCManagers to client ORBs to indicate the new location of an object where previously issued requests have to be redirected. A detailed description on the implementation of the LocALE middleware is available in [7].

5. TRIP-ENABLED SENTIENT APPLICATIONS

This section describes three sentient applications[1] that combine TRIP sensing with LocALE's object lifecycle and location management. They demonstrate

[1]The first two applications are available at: http://www-lce.eng.cam.ac.uk/~dl231/#Demos.

how our work streamlines the deployment of sentient systems and make it a cost-effective process.

5.1. The LCE Sentient Library

This system augments a conventional library catalogue system with sentient features. Apart from the typical functionalities expected in a book cataloguing system, the LCE Sentient Library offers contextual information about the books in our lab. Details on the last seen book location and its proximity to other fixed items in the environment are offered. This application is an illustration of TRIP's versatility for tracking any tag-able entities in the environment.

Figure 5. LCE Sentient Library snapshot

Every location where a book may be located in our lab has been tagged with a *location-category* TRIPcode. Similarly, *book-category* TRIPcodes have been attached to book spines. Periodically, the LCE librarian wanders around our lab with a video camera recording TRIP tagged locations and books. The system automatically updates the book database by the off-line processing of the book-sighting video. This process involves the co-operation of a Video Frame Grabber, which provides access to the video frames, a TRIParser, which analyses those frames, and the TRIP Directory Server, where book details and contextual data are recorded. The Video Frame Grabber and TRIParser components are automatically activated by LocALE.

A web interface allows LCE members to (1) browse all the book categories, (2) list books in a category, (3) obtain book details and (4) perform keyword-based search of books. Figure 5 shows the result of a book search with this web interface.

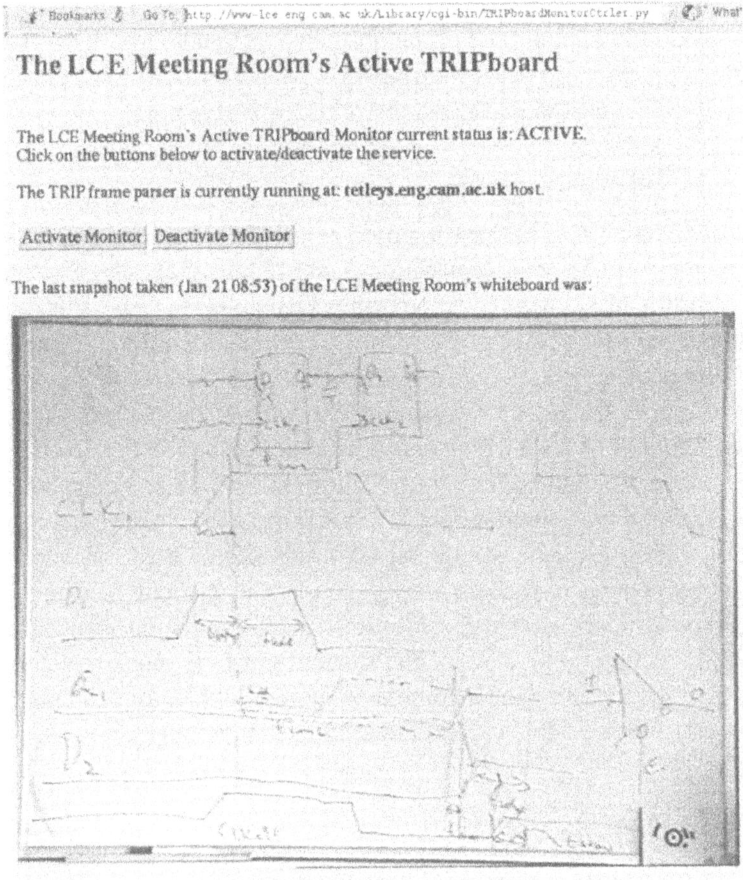

Figure 6. Active TRIPboard snapshot

5.2. Active TRIPboard

This application augments a conventional whiteboard with interactive commands issued by placing TRIPcodes in the field of view of a camera pointing at the whiteboard. Some example actions that can be triggered are: (1) capture whiteboard snapshot and email its web link to people currently present in the room, (2) printout a copy of the whiteboard snapshot for each person in the room. The application components: a Frame Grabber and a TRIParser are activated via LocALE either when a person appears in the meeting room or through a web interface (see Figure 6). The Active Badge indoor location system deployed in our lab is used to determine person presence. In future, the meeting room will be populated with sufficient cameras to cover all the field of views of the room, and so permit people wearing TRIPcode tags to be detected. Through LocALE, the TRIParser is activated in a load-balancing way by randomly picking one of the hosts in a candidate list. If the TRIParser fails, the application recovers transparently because LocALE's fault-tolerance support will recreate the parser on one of the available host.

5.3. Follow-me Audio

This application provides mobile users with music from the nearest speakers wherever they are. The source of music is an MP3 jukebox server whose operation is controlled by showing jukebox-type TRIPcodes to web-cams attached to some of our lab's PCs. A personal software agent, associated with each lab person, listens for that person's movement events generated by a *Person Location Monitor Context Abstractor*. This component obtains people sightings from the *Context Channels* of the TRIParsers corresponding to the PC web-cams spread throughout the laboratory. From raw TRIP sighting events, it generates personnel presence and movement events. The personal agent, acting as a component migration controller, requests LocALE to migrate the audio player and MP3 decoder components to the host nearest to the user that can deliver the music. As the user wanders around the location-aware computing environment, the music follows him. The state of the system and time index into the current song persists as the components migrate. This application makes use of TRIP's tracking capabilities, SIF's context modelling features and LocALE's migration support.

6. RELATED WORK

SONY's CyberCode [12] is a visual tagging system based on a 2D square barcode that can be used to determine the 3D position and identifier of tagged objects. Several augmented reality applications have been produced based on this system, e.g. the visitor view of CyberCode tagged items in a museum is augmented with synthesised information. The geometric features of CyberCodes require higher image resolution for their accurate recognition and location than TRIP. BBC's free-d [14] location system measures the precise position and orientation of studio cameras, by using an auxiliary camera mounted on the back of a conventional moving camera pointing to circular markers, similar to TRIPcodes, placed on the ceiling of a TV recording studio. A hardware implementation of its algorithms was necessary to achieve real time processing. The system is used for virtual reality TV production. It is expensive and cumbersome to deploy.

GeorgiaTech's Context Architecture project [2] attempts to make sentient application development as simple as GUI development. For that it introduces Context Widgets that separate context sensing from context-use. It has some similarities to SIF but doesn't tackle efficient context information dissemination. Microsoft's EasyLiving [13] project tries to create reactive context-aware living spaces without the user having to wear any location tag or computing device. Their approach tracks people based on colour histograms without requiring the user to wear any marker. This has a much heavier computational demand and produces less reliable results than TRIP. AT& T's Sentient Computing project [5] aims to replace human- computer direct interaction (through mouse or keyboard) by enabling users to instead interact with their surrounding space based on the precise location and orientation provided by the Active Bat Location System [4]. This concept has been explored with several sophisticated sentient applications.

7. CONCLUSION

TRIP, a novel cost-effective and easily deployable location sensor technology, has been introduced. This sensor requires only inexpensive and off-the-shelf hardware, which makes the creation of location-aware reactive environments, even in the home, an affordable proposition. All that is required to augment a standard PC with visual awareness is a web-cam and TRIP's downloadable software.

SIF, an application construction model to ease the development of distributed sensor-driven systems has also been described.

LocALE, an object lifecycle and location control middleware that streamlines user-bound service activation, migration and deactivation and, at the same time, permits application developers to reuse the spare networked computing resources in a LAN, has been presented. LocALE complements TRIP's minimal cost and deployment complexity. It is a very useful tool for sentient applications that have to trigger user-related services in response to captured sensor data.

To validate our contributions, several TRIP-enabled applications, following the SIF model and leveraging on the LocALE infrastructure have been developed and described in this paper. The initial results are encouraging.

Acknowledgments

Diego López de Ipiña is very grateful to the Basque Government's Department of Education for the sponsorship of his PhD studies. Thanks are also due to AT& T Laboratories Cambridge for sponsoring the TRIP project.

References

[1] AT& T Laboratories Cambridge, "omniORB C++ CORBA ORB", http://www.uk.research.att.com/omniORB/omniORB.html

[2] Dey A.K., Salber D., Futakawa M. and Abowd G. "An architecture to support context-aware applications", 12th ACM's UIST, 1999

[3] Forsyth D., Mundy J.L., Zisserman A., Coelho C., Heller A. and Rothwell C. "Invariant Descriptors for 3-D Object Recognition and Pose", IEEE Transactions on Pattern Analysis and Machine Intelligence, Vol. 13, No. 10, pp. 971-991, October 1991

[4] Harter A., Hopper A., Steggles P., Ward A. and Webster P. "The Anatomy of a Context-Aware Application", Proceedings of MOBICOM'99, August 1999

[5] Hopper. A. "Sentient Computing", The Royal Society Clifford Paterson Lecture, AT& T Laboratories Cambridge, Technical Report 1999.12, 1999

[6] López de Ipiña, D. "Building Components for a Distributed Sentient Framework with Python and CORBA ", Proceedings of the 8th International Python Conference, January 24 - 27, 2000

[7] López de Ipiña, D. and Lo S. "LocALE: a Location-Aware Lifecycle Environment for Ubiquitous Computing", Proceedings of ICOIN-15, February 2001

[8] López de Ipiña D., "TRIP: A Distributed vision-based Sensor System", Technical Report, Laboratory for Communication Engineering, Cambridge, September 1999

[9] Nelson G. "Context-Aware and Location Systems". PhD Thesis. Cambridge University Computer Lab, UK, January 1998

[10] Object Management Group. "Notification Service Specification", June 2000

[11] Object Management Group. "The Common Object Request Broker Architecture: Architecture and Specification", October 1999

[12] Rekimoto J. and Ayatsuka Y. "CyberCode: Designing Augmented Reality Environments with Visual Tags", Designing Augmented Reality Environments (DARE 2000), 2000

[13] Shafer S, et al. "The new EasyLiving Project at Microsoft Research, Microsoft, 1999

[14] Thomas G. A., Jin J., Niblett T., Urquhart C. "A versatile camera position measurement system for virtual reality in TV production", Proceedings of IBC'97, September 1997

[15] Want R., Hopper A., Falcão A. and Gibbons J. "The Active Badge Location System", ACM Transactions on Information Systems, Vol. 10, No. 1. 91-102, January 1992

[16] Weiser M. "The Computer for the 21st Century". Scientific American, September 1992

[17] Werb J. and Lanzl C. "Designing a positioning system for finding things and people indoors", IEEE Spectrum, pp.71-78,
September 1998

THE ACTIVE GUIDEBOOK

Information retrieval by keyword and location

Trevor Boyd & Peter Robinson
University of Cambridge, Computer Laboratory

Abstract The active guide book is a context-aware information management system that uses a combination of spatial and keyword indexing to retrieve data. The system has three principal components:

- A new document description language extends HTML to include facilities for tagging with spatial locations.
- Retrieval uses two separate indexes – a segment tree is used for spatial indexing and an inverted file is used for keyword indexing.
- A user interface allows queries involving keywords and location data to be expressed, and presents their results.

The system has been evaluated with the implementation of an interactive guidebook. The test data was drawn from existing Web pages describing the City of Cambridge in England, which were augmented with spatial information. A GPS system is used to provide the default location information for retrieval, but can be overridden with explicit coordinates.

Keywords: Context-aware applications, mobility, location.

1. INTRODUCTION

Improvements in communications bring the benefits of distributed computing to mobile users. Moreover, cellular wireless systems can identify the user's location with considerable precision. This paper considers the use of position as part of an information retrieval system. An experimental system has been built to investigate the combined use of spatial and keyword indexing to retrieve data.

Traditional guidebooks present text and pictures with an alphabetical index of keywords and using maps as the sole source of spatial information. It would be better to allow more flexible indexing of material that included audio and video content.

The *active guidebook* presents tourists with a system that guides them around a new city and provides useful information on local landmarks and places of interest. This guidebook uses a positioning system to enable it to display the user's current location and tailor information accordingly. For example, relevant information can be automatically displayed as the user walks past an historic building.

The system runs on a portable unit, equipped with a Global Positioning System (GPS) or equivalent module that identifies the location of the user. This allows the information presented to be keyed to the location of the user. Content can be taken from any suitable source, such as a conventional tourist guide or continuous media from CD-ROM or the Internet. This is indexed and annotated with positional information and presented to the user.

The information to be stored and presented will contain both spatial and context information and it must be possible to retrieve information in a variety of ways. Most importantly, it is necessary to enable the efficient retrieval of information by its spatial reference to exploit the system's knowledge of the user's current position.

Spatial data differs in important ways from normal keyword data. This project demonstrates how the two can be combined in a retrieval system providing a uniform interface to the data.

Others have considered the problem of content and presentation for electronic tourist guides [1, 5]. We focus on the problems of indexing and retrieval.

2. DESIGN

The system draws on the work of Professor Peter Brown and others at the University of Kent on context-sensitive information retrieval [2, 3, 7]. His *Stick-e notes* associate a context with pieces of information and retrieval is triggered when the user's current context matches that associated with the information. The data files in this system are also referred to as *notes*.

The focus of this work is on retrieval rather than content generation, so notes are stored simply as Hypertext Markup Language (HTML). This allows the inclusion of different media types in the notes, and also allows them to be displayed easily using a conventional web browser. It also allows existing publications to be reused for content and to write new notes without any specialist skills. Guidebooks consist of a collection of HTML notes and several extra index files, which can be generated quickly within the system.

Each note's context consists of two separate components: spatial location and keywords. Following Brown's suggestion [2], two separate structures are used to index the data.

Different data structures were needed to allow efficient searching and retrieval of notes in these two indices. The spatial index uses a *segment tree* for fast and efficient retrieval of notes covering a given point. The keyword index uses an inverted file structure. These are described in more detail in below.

A tree of filters is used to sift the notes, with each filter implementing either a restriction on keyword or location, or combining two streams through a Boolean operation.

2.1. Document Structure

The HTML notes are augmented with meta tags to store keywords and values, along with a type field for the value. The work from the University of Kent proposes using Standard Generalised Mark-up Language (SGML) to represent the context associated with a given document, but this was considered unnecessarily complex for this application and HTML is sufficient.

Brown also proposes designing an object-oriented model for the values and information stored in the documents [3]. While this is a very elegant system, it is also unnecessarily complicated for this application.

The context information is stored as `meta` tags in the head section of the HTML. These take the form:

```
<meta name = "..." value = "..." type = "...">
```

We refer to the contents of the `name` field as the *keyword* and those of the `value` field as the *value*. Together, these make up a (keyword, value) pair.

A variety of data types are provided for information in the notes. These are integers, strings, point locations and lines. The `meta` tags include an explicit `type` field for each keyword. This was designed to allow easy reading of the files by the system, as types do not need to be inferred.

By convention, spatial information uses the keyword `location` as this presents a consistent naming convention for the whole system.

The process of creating notes is simplified by the provision of a special editor to facilitate the addition of the `meta` tags to existing HTML documents.

2.2. Spatial Index – Segment Tree

Each location has an associated *area of interest*, an arbitrarily shaped zone surrounding the object. A similar, circular zone surrounds the user's current position. The retrieval system must identify any objects whose areas of interest overlap that of the user.

Areas of interest are stored as sets of disjoint rectangles. Each rectangle is stored in a pair of data structures, one recording horizontal extents and one vertical. *Segment trees* are used to store the intervals corresponding to these extents.

A segment tree [8, 10] is a binary tree used to store sets of intervals. Each leaf node represents an interval. For example, consider the following set of intervals:

```
A. 1 - 8
B. 3 - 12
C. 6 - 8
D. 6 - 9
E. 1 - 9
```

The segment tree corresponding to this set would be as follows:

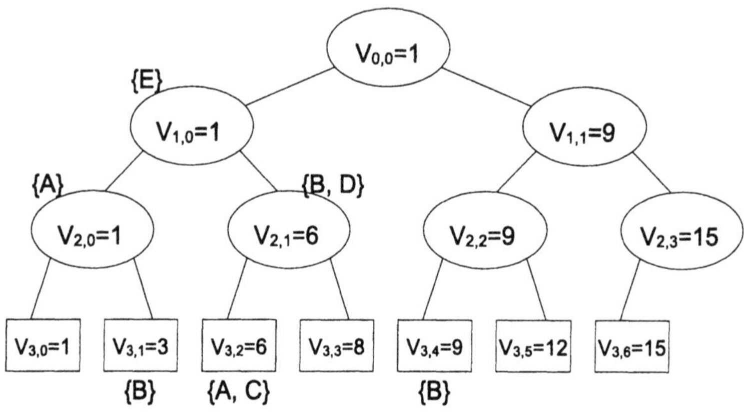

In this structure, node $n_{l,\,x}$ is at level l (where level 0 is the top of the tree and level *leaf* is the leaf node level) and horizontal position x (where x runs from 0 to $2l-1$). The two children (if they exist) of node $n_{l,\,x}$ are the nodes $n_{l+1,\,2x}$ and $n_{l+1,\,2x+1}$. $v_{l,\,x}$ is the value stored in node $n_{l,\,x}$. Each leaf node $n_{leaf,\,x}$ is marked with an integer and the node is deemed to span the interval $[v_{leaf,x}, v_{leaf,x+1})$, where $[a, b)$ is the half-open interval $\{\, z \mid a \leq z < b \,\}$. In the diagram above, *leaf* = 3 and node $n_{3,2}$ spans the interval [6, 8).

Note that the tree need not be perfectly balanced in the sense that the leaf node level need not be complete if there are insufficient values. Some nodes are simply missing from the right hand side.

Nodes higher in the tree are deemed to span the intervals spanned by their children. Node $n_{l,x}$ where $l \neq$ *leaf* spans the interval $[v_{l+1,2x}, V_{l+1,2x})$. Thus, we can mark higher nodes with the same value as their left child and the same rule applies to nodes at the same level in the tree.

This data structure allows us to store sets of rectangles easily. We simply have two segment trees, one each for the latitude and longitude information. To build the latitude tree, we create a sorted list of all the unique latitude values at which edges of rectangles occur. These values are then used to mark the leaf nodes in the tree. The values are then propagated up the tree in the way discussed above. A similar process creates the longitude tree.

Each node can then be marked with a set of rectangles that cover the interval denoted by the node. The intervals should mark nodes as high in the tree as possible. The sets of intervals are shown next to the nodes in the tree above. A given interval can mark several nodes at different levels in the tree, but never two adjacent nodes at the same level.

Extracting the list of rectangles that cover a given point in such a structure is clearly easy and can be accomplished with a simple scan down the tree.

Starting with $l = 0$ and $x = 0$, and searching for the rectangles covering point p we perform the following function recursively:

Compare p with $v_{l,x}$

- If $p < v_{l,x}$ then point p is not covered by any rectangles in the tree and we exit.

- If $v_{l,x} \leq p < v_{l+1,2x+1}$ set $l = l + 1$ and $x = 2x$ and continue.

- If $p \geq v_{l+1,2x+1}$, set $l = l + 1$ and $x = 2x + 1$ and continue.

At each stage we add any rectangles in the current node's list to our result list and then return this as the result when we reach $l =$ *leaf*.

2.3. Keyword Index – Inverted File

The (keyword, value) pairs stored in the HTML files are used to build an inverted file structure to allow retrieval of the notes based on keyword searches.

An inverted file is a structure that allows the retrieval of documents by reference to the keywords contained in them. This is clearly the inverse of simply retrieving all the keywords in a given document. The design of the file structure and means of reading it is based on the system designed by Mike Burrows for the index in the AltaVista internet search engine [4].

The retrieval of notes from the index is based on a data-driven model. Information from retrieved notes 'flows' from readers through a tree of filters and is made available to the application. These readers and filters could be implemented as separate threads using buffers with synchronized methods to pass values between them, but explicit transfer of the information proved more efficient.

3. IMPLEMENTATION

The system is implemented in Java and has the following overall structure:

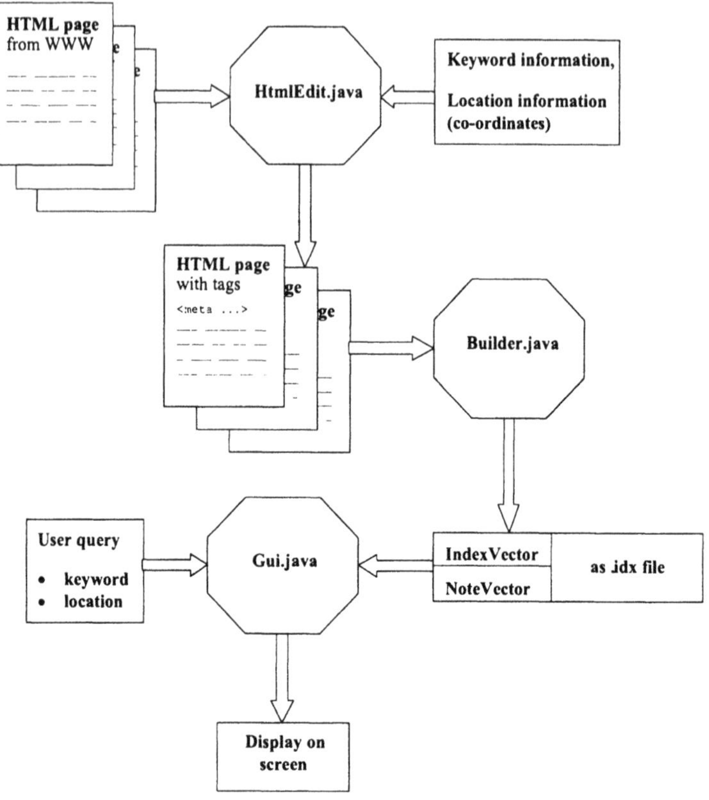

HtmlEdit is a simple utility that allows the quick and easy addition of meta tags of the correct form to HTML documents. Its GUI contains text fields to allow the entry of the keyword and value fields of the tag and a drop-down menu to allow selection of a type for the value. These are then combined into a suitable `meta` tag in the format described above and this is inserted into the `<head>` section of the HTML.

Builder is responsible for generating the inverted file structure used in the indexing and retrieval of notes by context in the main GUI of the system. The program takes a list of HTML files and directories and scans each file in turn, recursing down through directories, extracting tags. For each file containing at least one such tag, a `Note` object is generated. This contains a list of all the keywords and their values in the HTML. The `Note` object also contains a pointer to the HTML file from which it was generated to allow the file to be retrieved later for display.

Gui provides the map display, GPS controls and the query interface.

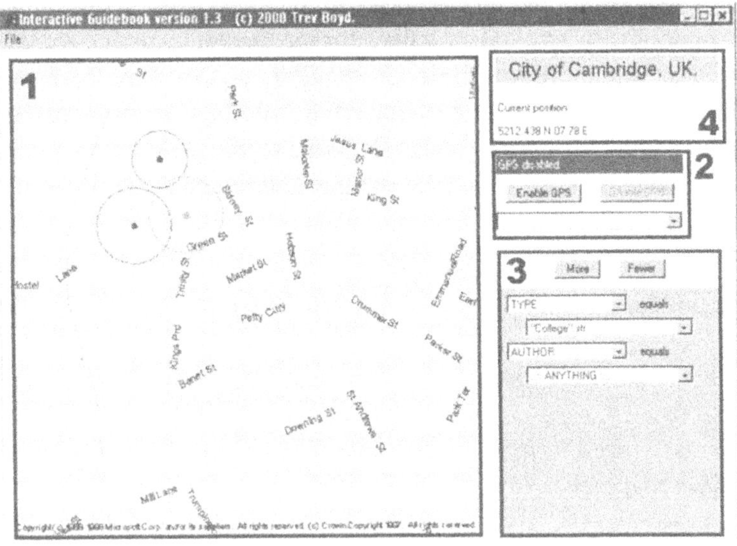

The user's current position is displayed on the map (Area 1 in the screen shot above) as a green dot surrounded by a circle. This circle represents the user's area of interest and only notes overlapping this circle will be displayed. As notes are retrieved by the search system, their locations are shown on the map as red dots and circles to show the locations and (spatial) sizes of the notes. The figure below shows the display after a query has returned two notes of interest.

The user's location can be updated as either the result of a mouse click in the map window, or on receipt of an NMEA location message from the GPS unit if serial communication has been enabled using the controls in Area 2.

Queries are constructed in Area 3. Terms are added to the query through two pull-down menus, one for a keyword and the other for its value. The value can be set to 'Anything', which allows the retrieval of all notes with the given keyword specified, independently of its value. The terms are then ANDed together with the position information to retrieve all notes of interest.

Finally, Area 4 gives some general information, including the name of the current guidebook and the user's current position.

A separate window displays the list of notes recovered by the query. Clicking on a note's name opens the relevant document in a Web browser.

3.1. Segment Tree

The system's performance depends on fast spatial indexing using the segment tree. Two trees are used (one each for the latitude and longitude values), so two lists are returned, which must be intersected to find the list of rectangles covered by the given point. This is achieved by sorting the two lists into two arrays, which can then be scanned in parallel.

Rectangles are inserted into the tree using the following algorithm. Suppose x_1 and x_2 are the two boundary values for the rectangle, with $x_1 < x_2$. Nodes are named $n_{l,x}$ as before with the index marking a node being $v_{l,x}$ The rectangles marking a node are represented by $R_{l,x}$. We write $R^*_{l,x}$ to represent the new list created by adding the current rectangle to the rectangle list $R_{l,x}$.

At each node $n_{l,x}$, there are four options to consider.

1 The current node is a leaf node ($l = leaf$).
In this case, we simply mark it with the rectangle ($R_{l,x} = R^*_{l,x}$ and return.

2 Both boundary values are less than the index of the right child ($x_1 < x_2 \leq v_{l+1,2x+1}$).
We only need to mark nodes in the left sub-tree, so we simply proceed down that branch ($l = l + 1$; $x = 2x$).

3 Both boundary values are greater than the index of the right child ($v_{l+1,2x+1} \geq x_1 > x_2$).
The rectangle only covers intervals in the right sub-tree, so we can proceed down that branch only ($l = l + 1$; $x = 2x + 1$).

4 The index of the right child lies between the two boundary values ($x_1 < v_{l+1,2x+1} < x_2$).
In this case, the rectangle covers intervals in both sub-trees. We proceed down both branches and then check on our return to see if both children are marked. If so, we unmark both of them and mark the current node instead.

An ordering is imposed on the rectangles to allow the easy intersection of two lists to be calculated. This ordering is the numerical order of the notes from which the rectangles were generated. If two rectangles are from the same note, the co-ordinates of their corners distinguish them. This allows the production of an ordered output compatible with the remainder of the search system.

3.2. Query Processing

All classes in the retrieval subsystem are derived from an abstract class, `Streamer`. This provides the basis for a class that will produce a *stream*, or lazily evaluated list, of notes matching given criteria. These criteria might be containing a given (keyword, value) pair, matching a given location or a logical combination of two inputs.

These derived classes can be combined to form tree structures for retrieving notes matching complex search criteria:

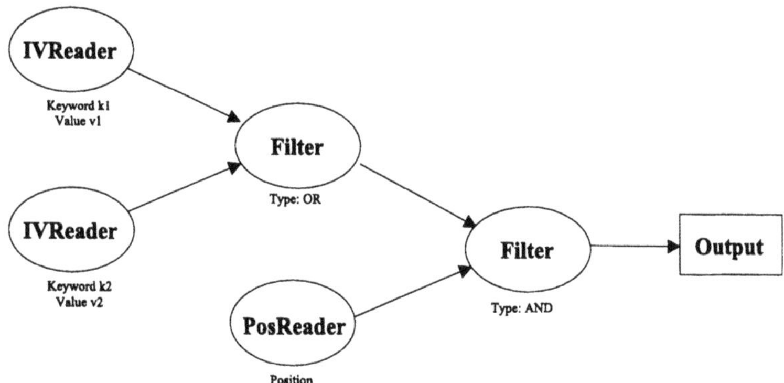

Each class has a selection of inputs (either one or two, although more could easily be supported) and a single output, which is then connected to the input of another class. Notes are presented on the inputs and only those matching the criteria set in that object will be passed to the output. Thus, by constructing a tree of such objects, we can build a complex query with many inputs and a single output at the top of the tree.

Three concrete instantiations of `Streamer` are used:

- An `IVReader` yields a sequence of notes containing a given (keyword, value) pair.
- A `PosReader` yields a sequence of notes that include an area of interest intersecting the user's area of interest.
- A `Filter` combines two streams using AND or OR.

Each note carries a unique identifier and data in each stream is sorted by this identifier. `Streamers` are initialised with their output as `Integer.MIN_VALUE`. When a `Streamer` has reached the end of its input, it returns a result of `Integer.MAX_VALUE` to signal the end of the data stream.

If either of the inputs are `Integer.MIN_VALUE` (i.e. this child has not yet been asked for a result), we call `getFile()` on the child to start it searching. Obviously, this may result in the child making calls to its children if it is not a leaf node in the search tree.

Once the inputs are both valid, we compare them and the subsequent behaviour depends on the type of `Filter`.

If it is an AND node:

- If either input is `Integer.MAX_VALUE`, the node has finished and can set its output to `Integer.MAX_VALUE`.
- Otherwise, if the two inputs are equal, one input is copied to the output and both input streams are advanced.

- If they are not equal, the output is not changed and the input with the lowest value is advanced. The lower valued input continues to advance until either the two inputs are equal or one of them finishes.

If the current node is an OR node:

- If both inputs are `Integer.MAX_VALUE`, the node has finished and can set its output to `Integer.MAX_VALUE`.
- Otherwise, if the two inputs are equal, one input is copied to the output and both the input streams are advanced.
- If they are different, the smaller input is copied to the output and its input stream is advanced.

4. RESULTS

This section shows the system in use in its intended environment, i.e. in the hands of a tourist visiting Cambridge and looking for directions to nearby points of interest. Performance figures for the segment tree are also presented.

4.1. Using the Guidebook

The guidebook in use in the example is that compiled during development. It contains notes attached to most of the major landmarks, including colleges, churches and museums.

The following screen shots show the changing display as the user moves, refines the search criteria and finally opens a note:

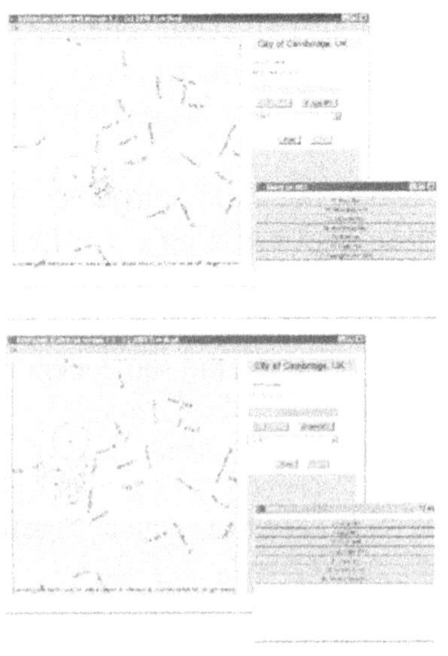

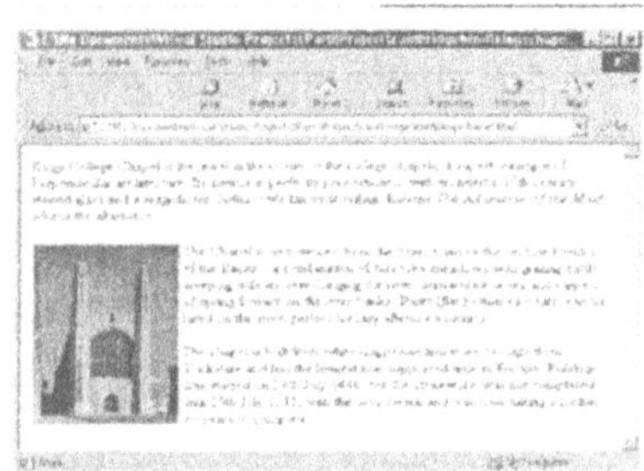

4.2. Segment Tree Performance

Rapid spatial indexing is vital to the system's performance, and the segment tree achieves this. Tests with randomly generated data yield the following results on a modest (133MHz Pentium) lap-top computer.

Two main tests were conducted:

- time taken to construct a segment tree as a function of the number of rectangles,
- time taken to retrieve a list of rectangles covering a fixed point as a function of both segment tree size and the length of the retrieved list.

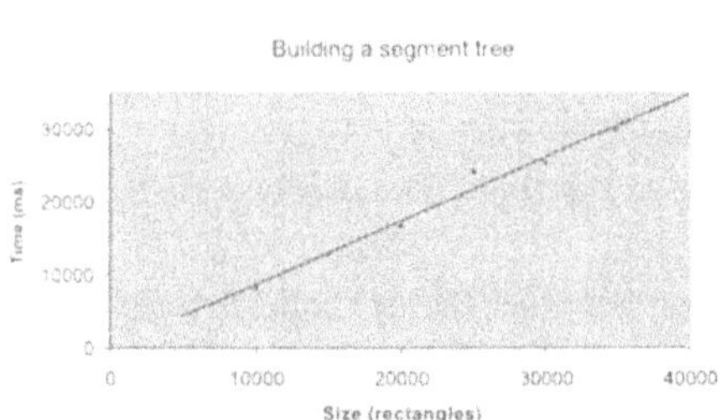

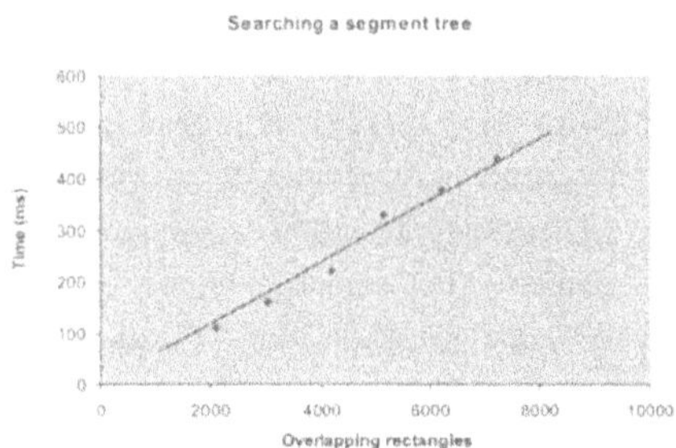

These test results show a clear linear (order O(n)) relationship between the number of rectangles in a tree and the time taken to build it. The search time also shows a linear relationship to the number of rectangles in the result list. The number of enclosing rectangles is also related by a linear relationship to the tree size. Thus, the search time is also O(n) with tree size. This is extremely good and shows that the system is very efficient in the spatial retrieval of information. We can run many searches a second, even on very large trees, providing us with a low-latency retrieval system.

These tests are using large search trees, several orders of magnitude larger than any expected to be used in the system in practice.

5. CONCLUSIONS

The main aim of this project was to investigate techniques for spatial indexing and the possibility of combining it with keyword indexing of information. The resulting system shows that the combination is not only possible but can be implemented efficiently by a search system based on segment trees and `Streamers`. The two indices complement each other well and combine to provide considerable power and flexibility.

One possible extension of the system is to make use of the position information available from GSM mobile phones, as provided by *Cambridge Positioning*

Systems' Cursor system [6]. This provides an accuracy of around 50 metres from a standard GSM digital phone, which would be much more convenient and cheaper than the use of a dedicated GPS receiver. It has the added advantage over GPS of working indoors.

The recently announced Cambridge Open Mobile System [9] will be used to develop this system in further experiments with information retrieval based on location.

References

[1] ABOWD, G.D. et al. Cyberguide: A Mobile Context-Aware Tour Guide. *Wireless Networks, 3(5), pg 421-433,* October 1997.

[2] BROWN, P.J. (1998). Triggering Information by Context. *Personal Technologies, 2(1),* pg. 1-9, September 1998.

[3] BROWN, P.J. (1996). The Stick-e Document: a framework for creating context-aware applications. *Proceedings of EP '96,* Palo Alto, pg. 259-272.

[4] BURROWS, M. (1999). A Library for Indexing and Querying Text. *Computer Laboratory seminar,* Michaelmas 1999.

[5] DAVIES, N. et al. (1998). Developing a Context Sensitive Tourist Guide. Proceedings of the *First Workshop on Human Computer Interaction for Mobile Devices,* University of Glasgow, pg 64-68, May 1998.

[6] DUFFET-SMITH, P. (1996). High precision CURSOR and digital CURSOR: the real alternatives to GPS. *Proceedings of EURONAV 96 Conference on Vehicle Navigation and Control.*

[7] PASCOE, J. (1997). The Stick-e Note Architecture: Extending the Interface beyond the User. Proceedings of the *1997 International Conference on Intelligent User Interfaces,* pg. 261-264.

[8] SAMET, H. (1990). *The Design and Analysis of Spatial Data Structures.* Addison – Wesley Publishing Company, Inc., USA.

[9] UNIVERSITY OF CAMBRIDGE (2000). *Vodafone and University Announce Experimental Network in Cambridge.* Press release, 11 October 2000. `http://www.admin.cam.ac.uk/news/pr/2000101103.html`.

[10] VAN LEEUWEN, J. (ed) (1990). *Handbook of Theoretical Computer Science Volume A: Algorithms and Complexity.* Elesevier Science Pulishers B.V., Amsterdam.

III

INTEGRATION & INTEROPERABILITY

SOFTWARE CONNECTORS AND THEIR ROLE IN COMPONENT DEPLOYMENT*

Dušan Bálek[1], František Plášil[1,2]
[1] *Charles University,*
Faculty of Mathematics and Physics, Department of Software Engineering,
Malostranské námìstí 25, 118 00 Prague 1, Czech Republic,
http://nenya.ms.mff.cuni.cz
[2] *Academy of Sciences of the Czech Republic, Institute of Computer Science,*
Pod vodárenskou vìží 2, 180 00 Prague 8, Czech Republic,
http://www.cs.cas.cz

Abstract To support rapid software evolution, it is desirable to construct software systems from reusable components. In this approach, the architecture of a system is described as a collection of components along with the interactions among these components. Whereas the main system functional blocks are components, the properties of the system also strongly depend on the character of the component interactions. This fact gave birth to the "connector" concept which is an abstraction capturing the nature of these interactions. The problem tackled in this paper is that even though the notion of connectors originates in the earliest papers on software architectures [20, 15], connectors are currently far from being a typical first class entity in the contemporary component-based systems.By articulating the "deployment anomaly", the paper identifies the role connectors should play when the distribution and deployment of a component-based application is considered. Further, we introduce a connector model reflected at all the key stages of an application's development: ADL specification, deployment, and implementation.

Keywords: Software component, deployment, connector

1. INTRODUCTION

A few years ago, the trend to construct software systems as a collection of cooperating reusable components emerged and has become widely accepted

*This work is partially supported by the Grant Agency of the Academy of Sciences of the Czech Republic (project number A2030902), the Grant Agency of the Czech Republic (project number 201/99/0244)

since. Influenced by the academic research projects focused on components [8, 19, 21, 7, 1, 14, 5], several industrial systems on the market [22, 23, 12, 13, 24] advertise support of component technology. As for *components*, there is a broad agreement on grasping them as reusable black/grey-box entities with well-defined interfaces and specified behavior. Usually, a component can have multiple interfaces; some of them to provide services to the component's clients, other to require services from the surrounding environment. Components can be nested to form hierarchies; a higher-level component can be composed of several mutually interconnected, cooperating subcomponents. Serving as tools for specifying component interfaces and architecture, a number *architecture description languages (ADLs)* [8, 21, 1, 14, 17] have been designed. To describe component interactions, an ADL may encompass the connector concept: Typically, a *connector* is a first class architectural element that reflects the specific features of interactions among components in a system [21, 1, 14, 10, 3]. Even though the notion of a connector originates in the earliest papers on software architectures [20, 15], no widespread consensus on how to incorporate it into the existing application development systems and languages has been reached until present.

1.1. Connectors: overview and related work

Studying the related work [8, 21, 1, 3, 14], the following basic approaches to specifying component interactions can be identified: (1) using *implicit connections*, (2) via *connectors*, which can be either *built-in* or *user-defined.*

The Darwin language [8] is a typical representative of ADLs that use implicit connections. The connections among components are specified via direct bindings of their *requires* and *provides* interfaces. The semantics of a connection is defined by the underlying environment (programming language, operating system, etc.), and the communicating components should be aware of it (to communicate, Darwin components directly use ports of the underlying Regis environment).

In addition to making system maintenance easier, letting components communicate via connectors has also other significant benefits: increased reusability (the same component can be used in a variety of environments, each of them providing specific communication primitives) direct support for distribution, location transparency and mobility of components in a system, support for dynamic changes in the system's connectivity, etc.

The UniCon language [21] is a representative of ADLs with (only) built-in connectors. A developer is provided with a selection of several predefined built-in connector types that correspond to the common communication primitives supported by the underlying language or operating system (such as RPC, pipe, etc.). However, the most significant drawback of a UniCon-like ADL is that there is no way to capture any interaction among components that does not correspond to a predefined connector type.

User-defined connectors, the most flexible approach to specifying component interactions, are employed, e.g., in the Wright language [1]. The interactions among components are fully specified by the user (system developer). Complex interactions can be expressed by nested connector types. However, the main drawback of the Wright language is the absence of any guidelines as to how to realize connectors in an implementation. (In Wright, connectors exist at the specification level only, which results in the problem of how to correctly reflect the specification of a connector in its implementation.)

Based on a thorough study of existing ADLs, Medvidovic et al. [10] presented a classification framework and taxonomy of software connectors. This taxonomy is an important attempt to improve the current level of understanding of what software connectors and their building blocks are. Not addressing all the issues of designing connector types, it is focused mainly on classification (thus better comprehension) of connector types. In addition, the selection of basic connector types in [10] may be questionable, as not all of them seem to be at the same abstraction level (e.g., adaptor, arbitrator and distributor vs. procedure call, event, stream).

1.2. Challenges and the goals of the paper

Component-based systems and ADLs have become fields of study in their own right, however their practical application is still to be demonstrated. Reuse of components is an attractive idea, but the real life has proved many times that to combine the business components provided by third parties into a running application can be very demanding. The main problem of the current ADLs is that they either do not capture component interactions at all, or they focus on application design stages only. However, the component interactions have to be reflected throughout the whole application lifecycle, otherwise they may become a serious obstacle in component reusability. In particular, the deployment phase has turned out to be critical in this respect.

The first goal of the paper is to bring an additional argument for considering connectors as first class ADL entities by analyzing their role in component deployment (deployment anomaly is articulated). The second goal of the paper is to propose a connector model that allows to describe a variety of (possibly complex) component interactions, helps system developers target the deployment anomaly, and at the same time allows to generate the corresponding interaction code (since none of the existing connector models/ADL systems provides a sufficient support for that).

The paper has the following outline. Reviewing the basic ADL concepts for illustration purpose, Section 2 briefly introduces a simple component model and introduces the deployment anomaly. The set of basic connector tasks and requirements is identified and studied in Section 3. A new connector model is proposed in Section 4. As a proof of the concept, it is integrated into the SOFA/DCUP component model in Section 5. Finally, the main achievements and future intentions are summarized in the concluding Section 6.

2. COMPONENTS AND THEIR LIFECYCLE

2.1. A component model

For the purpose of this paper we adopt the following component model (event though based on [16,17] in some details, it very much follows the basic spirit of most ADL languages): An application is viewed as a hierarchy of software components. A *software component* is an instance of a *component template* (*template* for short). A template is defined by a pair <component frame, component architecture>. In principle, the *component frame* determines a component type as the set of interfaces *provided* and *required* by every instance of T (reflecting a blackbox view on T's instances). Similarly, the *component architecture* reflects a gray-box view of each of T's instances by describing its internal structure in the terms of its direct subcomponents and their interactions (interface ties, "wiring"). A component architecture can be specified as *primitive* which means that there are no subcomponents and the component frame is directly implemented in the underlying implementation language, for example as a set of Java classes, a shared library, or even a binary executable file. If a component C is an instance of a template with a primitive architecture, we say that C is a *primitive component*, otherwise C is a *composed component.*

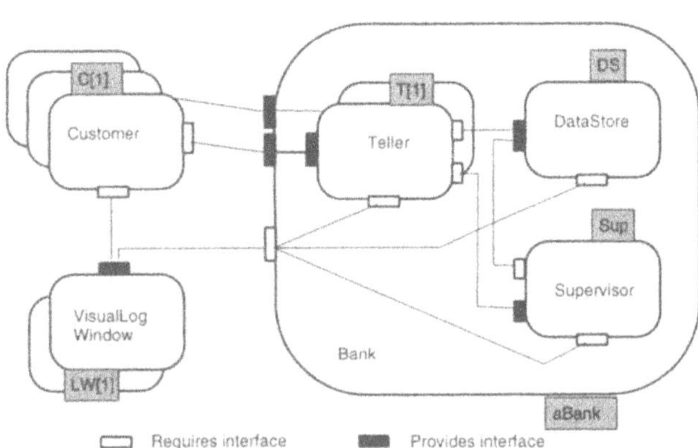

Figure 1. BankingDemo Architecture

For illustration, consider a bank where tellers serve a number of customers. Each customer requests a teller to perform a desired financial transaction(s) on an account(s). Certain transactions, such as an overdraft, require the teller to ask the supervisor for an approval. Each of these entities can be modeled as a component (Figure 1). The core of the application is the instance aBank of the Bank template (Bank component for short). The Bank component internally contains an array of Teller subcomponents (T[1], T[2], ... , T[N]), the Supervisor subcomponent, and the DataStore subcomponent. The Bank component features a number of provide interfaces, each of them being tied to a Customer component's requires interface, and internally tied (delegated) to the provides interface of a Teller subcomponent. The remaining part of the application is formed by the Customer and VisualLogWindow components, the latter serving for system administration purposes. The communication of the Customer components with the Bank component is based on procedure calls, while all the interaction with the VisualLogWindow components relies on event delivery.

2.2. Component lifecycle

The lifecycle of a component is characterized by a sequence of design time, deployment time, and run time phases (potentially repeated). In a more detailed view, a design time phase is composed of the following design stages: development and provision, assembly, and distribution.

Development and provision. The component is specified at the level of its template, i.e. component frame and component architecture is specified in an ADL; if the architecture is primitive, its implementation in an underlying programming language/environment has to be also supplied. As a frame F can be implemented by potentially several component architectures, each of such templates can be viewed as a design version of components of the type F.

Assembly. An application is assembled by choosing one particular component architecture for each frame involved recursively in the topmost frame of the application. Consequently, an executable form of the application is based on all the primitive architectures involved recursively in the component architecture associated with the topmost frame.

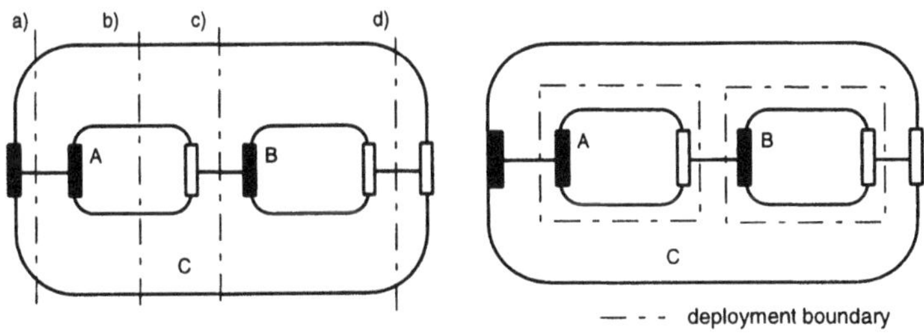

Figure 2. Deployment boundaries crossing interface ties

Distribution. To reflect its future distribution, the assembled application is divided into deployment units. Here, two approaches are to be considered: (1) Deployment unit boundaries can cross the component interface ties, but not the component/frame boundaries (Figure 2, right part). Advantageously, the deployment description of composed/nested components can be done on a top-down basis, following the hierarchy of components. (2) Deployment boundaries are orthogonal to component/frame boundaries. Thus, deployment boundaries can cross a component/frame boundary. Assuming that a primitive component cannot be distributed (see **Deployment** below), deployment boundaries can cross a component/frame boundary of compound components only (the alternatives a), c) d) in the left part of Figure 2 are permitted, b) is not). Thus there is no difference in comparison with (1) when deploying primitive components. As to composed components, the following two problems are not easy to overcome: (i) the deployment description cannot parallel the hierarchy of component nesting, and (ii) the deployment of a composed component into more deployments docks (see below) may be a complex process.

Deployment time. The goal is to achieve *deployment* of the application, i.e. to associate each of its deployment units with a deployment dock and let these deployment docks start the application. In principle, a *deployment dock* serves as a component factory and a container which controls the lifecycle of running components. A deployment dock may be an instance of Java Virtual Machine, capable to load, instantiate, and run components written in Java, a processes capable to load dynamically linked native libraries and instantiate components into its address space, a daemon that instantiates components by starting new processes from binary executables, etc. In such settings, it is natural to require a primitive component not to be distributed.

2.3. Deployment anomaly

If a deployment unit boundary crosses the interface tie of two components A and B, the actual deployment of A and B in general substantially influences the communication of A and B. For example, in Figure 3a), the method calls on the r and q interfaces have to be modified in order to use an appropriate middleware technique of remote procedure calls (RPC), e.g. RMI stub and skeleton is to be employed. These modifications include changes to the internal architectures of A and B. Analogously with the inheritance anomaly concept [9, 18], we refer to this kind of a post-design modification of a component enforced by its deployment as *deployment anomaly*.

As a quick fix, one can imagine employing an ordinary component DC mediating the communication of A and B (Figure 3b)). In principle, however, this leads to the deployment anomaly again: (1) If a component DC was added to handle change in communication enforced by the deployment, the parent component of A and B would be modified by this adjustment of its architecture; (2) As it is unrealistic to imagine a primitive component spanning more deployment docks, DC has to be a composed component; this leads to the issue of adjusting the internals of some inner components of DC.

To illustrate the deployment anomaly on the BankingDemo example, consider the DataStore component is to be deployed in a separate deployment dock, compared to the rest of the application. Thus, inside the Bank component, all the interactions with DataStore have to be modified to be based on RPC. This post-design modification affects the Teller, Supervisor, and DataStore components.

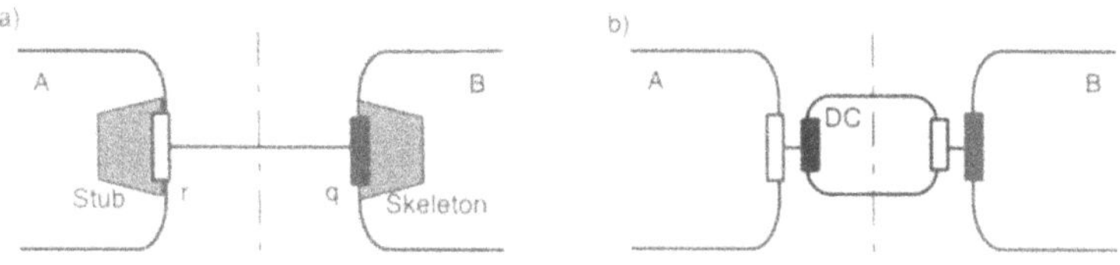

Figure 3. Deployment anomaly

2.4. Targeting the deployment anomaly: connectors

Basically, the deployment anomaly could be addressed by introducing a first class abstraction being: (a) inherently distributed, and (b) flexible enough to accommodate changes to the component communication enforced by a particular deployment. The connector abstraction can meet this requirement if defined accordingly: (1) It should be a part of the system architecture from the very beginning (being a first class entity at the same abstraction level as a component). (2) To absorb the changes in communication induced by the deployment modification, a flexible parametrization system of the connector internals has to be provided. (3) To reflect inherent distribution, the deployment of a connector should not be specified explicitly, but inferred from the deployment description of the components involved in the communication the connector conveys. As a consequence, the lifecycle of a connector inherently differs from the lifecycle of a component as its underlaying code has to be supplied (e.g. semiautomatically generated) as late as its deployment is known (Section 4.3).

3. BASIC CONNECTOR TASKS

To understand the connector concept properly, it is useful to identify and analyze the basic tasks a connector should perform; here, the taxonomy of software connectors presented in [10] can be used for guidance. From the main service categories and the basic connector types of this taxonomy, we have selected the connector tasks listed below that we generally consider the key ones. In Section 5, we will show that most of the basic connector tasks can be provided through a simple hierarchical composition of a few primitive connector elements.

Control and data transfer. A connector specifies the mechanisms on which possible control and/or data transfer is based (like procedure call, event handling, and data stream). Each of these mechanisms has specific characteristics and properties, e.g., a procedure call can be local or remote. As to RPC, various kinds of middleware can be used to implement it. Similarly, event handling can be based on an event channel, a centralized event queue, etc.

Interface adaptation and data conversion. When facing the need to tie two (or more) components that have not been originally designed to interoperate, a straightforward idea is to include an *adaptor* into the connector abstraction. As mentioned in [16], there is the option (and challenge) to devise a mechanism for automatic or semi-automatic generation of adaptors and/or data convertors.

Access coordination and synchronization. In principle, the ordering of method calls on a component's interface is important (the protocol concept in [11]). The permitted orderings are usually determined by a behavioral specification of the component (e.g., interface, frame and architecture protocols in SOFA [17], CSP-based glue and computation in Wright). Thus another connector task is access coordination and synchronization - enforcing compliance with the protocol of an interface (set of interfaces). As an example, consider a server component, implemented for a singe-threaded environment, to be deployed into an environment with multiple client threads. The necessary serialization of threads can be achieved by a connector mediating the clients' access to the component.

Communication intercepting. Since connectors mediate all interactions among components in a system, they provide a natural framework for intercepting component communication (without the participating components being aware of it) which might help implement various filters (with applications in cryptography, data compression, load monitoring, debugging, etc.).

4. CONNECTOR MODEL

To reflect the variety of interactions among components in a hierarchically structured system, a connector model supporting the creation of a connector by a hierarchical composition of its internal elements is a natural choice. This complies with the observation that the complexity of interactions among components depends on the granularity of the system's architecture description. A finer granularity implies a larger number of components with simpler interactions, while a coarser granularity implies a smaller number of components with more complex interactions.

In this section, we propose a connector model designed as follows: Every interaction among components in an application is represented by a *connector* which is an instance of a *connector template.* Being generic in principle, a connector template is a pair <*connector frame*, *connector architecture*> that can be parameterized by *interface type* and *property* parameters. Given a connector template T, the *connector frame* specifies the black-box view of a T's instance (thus it can be referred to as connector type), while the *connector architecture* specifies the structure of a T's instance in terms of its *internal elements* (primitive elements, component instances, and instances of other connector templates) and their interactions (thus it can be referred to as connector implementation).

4.1. Connector frame

A connector frame is represented by a set of role instances. In principle, a *role* is a generic interface of the connector intended to be tied to a component interface. In a frame, a role is specified either as a *provides* role or *requires* role. A *provides* role serves as an entry point to the component interaction represented by the connector template instance and is intended to be tied to a (single) requires interface of a component (or to a requires role of another connector). Similarly, a *requires* role servers as an outlet point of the component interaction represented by the connector template instance and is intended to be tied to a (single) provides interface of a component (or to a provides role of another connector). In general, a role is an entity of a generic interface type; the actual interface type of a role R of a template T is implicitly determined by the specific interface (of a component or another connector) tied to R at the instantiation time of T.

4.2. Connector architecture

Depending on the internal elements employed, a connector architecture can be *simple* or *compound.* The internal elements of a simple connector architecture are instances of *primitive elements* only (Figure 4a); some of them can be specified as optional. Primitive elements are typed (usually generic types are employed - both the interface type and property parameters are allowed). For every primitive element type, in addition to functional specification in plain English, a precise specification of its semantics is given by mappings to underlying environments. For example: "Stub and skeleton elements provide the standard marshaling and unmarshaling functionality of RPC". Each of these elements is parameterized by its remote interface type and by the underlying implementation platform (specified as a property parameter). The mappings of the stub and skeleton element types exist for each of the implementation platforms supported (CORBA, Java RMI, etc.).

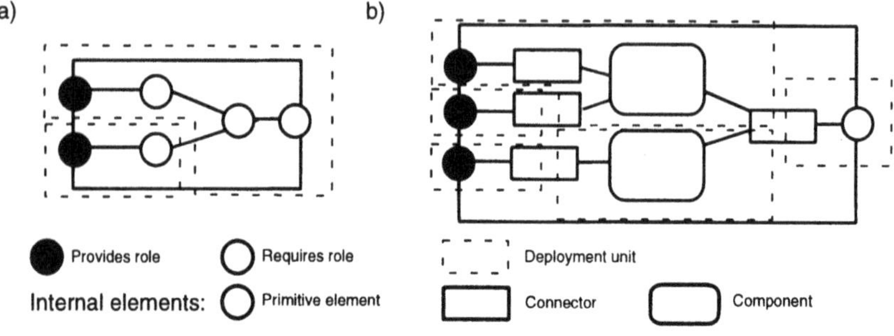

Figure 4. Connector model: a) simple architecture, b) compound architecture

The internal elements of a compound connector architecture are instances of other connector types and/or components (Figure 4b). This concept allows for creating complex connectors with hierarchically structured architectures reflecting the hierarchical nature of component interactions. For examples, we refer the reader to Sections 5.1 and 5.2.

4.3. Connector lifecycle

The connector lifecycle substantially differs form the component lifecycle. It can be viewed as a sequence of the design time, instantiation time, deployment and generation time, and runtime phases.

Connector design. The connector is specified as a template in ADL. For each of its primitive element types, a functional specification and definition of corresponding mappings (at least one) are to be provided. Since connectors are inherently distributed entities, the connector architecture is divided into a number of disjoint *deployment units.* A deployment unit is formed by the role instances and internal elements designed to share the same deployment dock.

Connector instantiation. The connector is instantiated within an application. Since the actual interface types of the entities tied by the connector instance become known at this point, the interface type parameters of the connector's roles can be resolved. Also the actual need for some of those primitive elements specified as optional at the design time (e.g. interface adaptors) reveals. A part of the connector instance remains generic – due to the unresolved property parameters related to a future deployment of the connector.

Connector deployment and generation. Connectors are deployed at the same time as the components the interactions of which they convey. To each of the connector's deployment units, a specific deployment dock is assigned. For a connector of simple architecture, the actual deployment docks of the connector's deployment units can be inferred from the locations of the components interconnected by the connector. The deployment of potential internal components of a connector is specified in the same way as the deployment of "ordinary" components in the application.

Once the deployment of a connector is known, the connector's implementation code is (semi-automatically) generated to use the communication primitives offered by the deployment docks's underlying environments. Note that the generated code of the primitive elements either follows their mapping to the underlying programming environment, or it can be null (e.g., no need for an adaptor). Note that the connectors with primitive architectures are considered for code generation while the connectors of compound architectures are created by composition of their internal elements.

A typical scenario of the code generation of a connector is as follows: (1) Using a deployment tool, the deployment of components (the interaction of which the connector conveys) is specified. (2) Each of the selected deployment docks is then asked to automatically generate the implementation code of those internal elements of the connector that are intended to be deployed in it. (3) The deployment dock replies the list of technologies offered by its underlying environment on which the generated implementation could be based (the returned list can be empty). (4) All returned lists are examined by the deployment tool in order to find a match in the offered technologies. (5a) If a matching technology exists, the deployment docks are asked to generate the connector's implementation code for the technology. (5b) If no matching technology exists, the user is given the options to either change the application's deployment, or to provide the connector's implementation manually.

5. CASE STUDY: SOFA/DCUP CONNECTORS

As a proof of the concept, the connector model described in Section 4 have been integrated into the SOFA/DCUP component mode [16,17]. This section describes this integration by introducing the *SOFA/DCUP connector model.*

5.1. Predefined connector templates

To avoid specifying the frequently used connector templates repeatedly, SOFA/DCUP provides a set of predefined connector templates – *CSProcCall*, *EventDelivery*, and *DataStream*. For brevity, only the CSProcCall connector template (Figure 5a) will be described here (for details see [2]).

CSProcCall is the predefined connector template representing the (possibly remote) procedure call interaction semantics. The interaction is based on the existence of multiple *caller* entities (client components) invoking operations on a *definer* entity (server component).

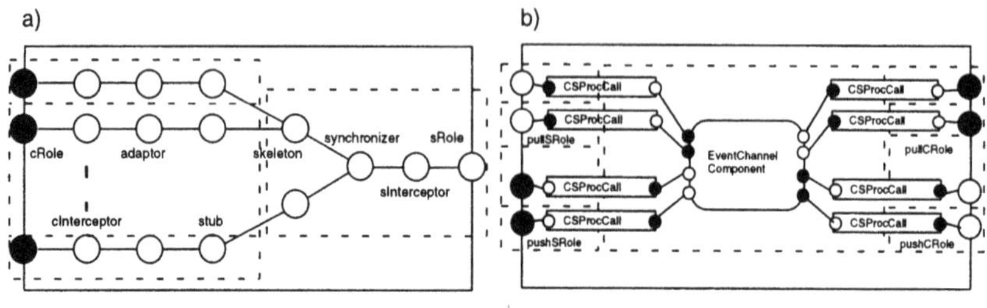

Figure 5. a) CSProcCall connector template, b) EventChannelDelivery connector template

The CSProcCall frame consists of a requires role to connect a server component (`sRole`), and of any number of provides roles to connect client components (`cRole`). All of the roles are generic entities with interface type parameters.

The CSProcCall architecture is simple. It consists of several primitive elements interconnected in the way illustrated in Figure 5a). The `cInterceptor` and `sInterceptor` instances of `TInterceptor` provide a framework for plugging in an additional connector functionality to support logging, debugging, etc. An interface `adaptor` is (optionally) included in a connector instance if a particular client's interface does not match the server interface. A (`TStub`, `TSkeleton`) instance pair is used if a remote invocation is needed. These primitive elements provide the standard RPC marhalling and unmarshalling. A `synchronizer` is (optionally) included if the server component requires client invocations to be synchronized when accessing its interface.

There is an exactly one *server deployment unit* (composed of `sRole`, `sInterceptor`, `synchronizer`, and `skeleton`) and any number of *client deployment units* (each of them composed of `cRole`, `cInterceptor`, `adaptor`, and a `stub`). There is one client deployment unit per connected client component.

The following fragment of source text illustrates the main parts of the CSProcCall specification using the modified SOFA CDL notation.

```
connector frame CSProcCall<CT, ST> (Properties properties){
     provides: optional multiple Role<CT> Crole;
     requires:  Role<ST> Srole;
};
connector architecture CSProcCall {
     inst optional multiple TInterceptor<CT> cInterceptor;
     inst optional multiple TAdaptor<CT, ST> adaptor;
     inst optional multiple TStub<ST> stub;
     inst optional multiple TSkeleton<ST> skeleton;
     inst optional TSynchronizer<ST> synchronizer;
     inst optional TInterceptor<ST> sInterceptor;
     delegate cRole to cInterceptor;
     bind cInterceptor to adaptor;
     bind adaptor to stub;
```

```
    bind stub to skeleton;
    bind skeleton to synchronizer;
    bind synchronizer to sInterceptor;
    subsume sInteceptor to sRole;
};
```

5.2. User-defined connector templates

The process of creating a new connector template can be illustrated on the example of *EventChannelDelivery*, a connector template reflecting event-based communication via an event channel. Similarly to the CORBA Event Service, this connector template allows multiple suppliers to send data asynchronously to multiple consumers in both the push and pull modes.

The EventChannelDelivery frame consists of a number of roles to connect supplier components in the push and pull modes (`pushSRole` and `pullSRole`), and of a number of roles to connect consumer components in the push and pull modes (`pushCRole` and `pullCRole`). All of the roles are generic entities with interface type parameters.

The EventChannelDelivery architecture is compound. As depicted in Figure 5b), the core element of the EventChannelDelivery architecture is an instance of the `EventChannel` component. The other internal elements of EventChannelDelivery are instances of the CSProcCall connector template to tie EventChannelDelivery's roles to the EventChannel's interfaces.

The division into deployment units is illustrated in Figure 5b). It should be emphasized that while the deployment of the internal CSProcCall connectors is partially determined by the EventChannelDelivery's roles, the deployment of the EventChannel component (and related parts of CSPracCall connectors) has to be stated explicitly as with "ordinary" components.

5.3. Using SOFA/DCUP connectors

To demonstrate how the SOFA/DCUP connectors can be used, consider the DataStore and Supervisor components from the banking application introduced in Section 2.1. The following fragment of CDL specification illustrates their interconnection using the CSProcCall connector instance.

```
inst DataStore DS;
inst Supervisor Sup;
bind Sup.dsi to DS.dsi using CSProcCall;
```

Since the actual interfaces of the DataStore and Supervisor components are known at this point, the interface type parameters of the conveying connector are resolved. Assuming that the actual interfaces match, the interface adaptor (as an optional element of the CSProcCall architecture) will be omitted. However, the rest of the connector architecture still remains generic due to the unresolved property parameters related to future deployments of the application.

Consider a deployment scenario which assumes that the DataStore and Supervisor components are to be deployed into separate deployment docks. Since both components do not share an address space, a cross-address space communication is needed. The stub and skeleton internal elements are therefore generated and included in the resulting connector.

6. EVALUATION AND CONCLUSION

As the first goal of the paper, we articulated the deployment anomaly as the necessity for a post-design modification of components caused by their particular deployment. This is a serious obstacle in using component-based real-life applications. In a practical setting, the deployment of a component-based application can be efficiently done by system staff members, experts in the underlying system environment (typically in the brands of middleware to be employed). To realize the necessary deployment modifications, these people would have to study the business logic details of the components subject to the deployment. This is inherently inefficient, if not even impossible, since some of the components may be of a third-party origin. A symmetrical inefficiency would be to ask the business logic designers to deal with the local networking/middleware details. For these reasons it is very desirable to separate the business and communication part of the component-based application. This issue can be addressed by the connector concept presented in the paper .

None of the current ADL languages/systems, such as [14, 19, 7, 21, 1], targets the deployment issue directly nor combines it with connectors). The second goal of the paper was therefore to propose a novel connector model allowing not only to express and represent a variety of possible interactions among components in an application at all key stages of the application lifecycle, but in particular to reflect component distribution.

In summary, in the presented component model, the **key difference between a component and connector** is in (1) distribution (a primitive connector can be distributed, while primitive component cannot) and (2) in the lifecycle (parts of the connector can be generated only after all component deployment has been determined). In addressing the deployment anomaly, a **connector helps** in (3) separation of concerns (by separating the business and communication part of a component-based application), and in (4) reusability – if the primitive elements are designed properly, they can be reused in many of the typical component communication patterns. The important trick supporting the reusability is that the primitive elements are very generic (work almost for “any interface”); the modification of the communication pattern for the actual interfaces is done in an automatized way, i.e. it can be generated.

Having finished a pilot implementation of our connector model, we currently focus on finding techniques for at least semi-automatic generation of primitive elements, including interface adaptors, stubs and skeletons for remote communication, etc. We believe this can be done by defining a mapping of every primitive element type to the underlying programming environment. Another future intention is to apply behavioral protocols [17] in connector specification to express the interplay of its internal elements.

References

[1] Allen, R. J.: A Formal Approach to Software Architecture. Ph.D. Thesis, School of Computer Science, Carnegie Mellon University, Pittsburgh, 1997.

[2] Balek, D., Plasil, F.: A Hierarchical Model of Software Connectors, Tech. Report No. 2000/2, Department of SW Engineering, Charles University, Prague, 2000.

[3] Bishop, J., Faria, R.: Connectors in Configuration Programming Languages: are They Necessary? Proceedings of the 3rd International Conference on Configurable Distributed Systems, 1996.

[4] Ducasse, S., Richner, T.: Executable Connectors: Towards Reusable Design Elements. In Proceedings of ESEC/FSE'97, Lecture Notes in Computer Science no. 1301, Springer-Verlag, 1997.

[5] Issarny, V., Bidan, C., Saridakis, T.: Achieving Middleware Customization in a Configuration-Based Development Environment: Experience with the Aster Prototype. In Proceedings of ICCDS '98, 1998, http://www.irisa.fr/solidor/work/aster.html.

[6] Leavens, G.T., Sitaraman,M.(eds.): Fundations of Component-Based Systems, Cambridge University Press 2000.

[7] Luckham,D. C., Kenney, J. J., Augustin, L. M., Vera, J., Bryan, D., Mann, W.: Specification and Analysis of System Architecture Using Rapide. IEEE Transactions on Software Engineering}, 21(4), 1995.

[8] Magee, J., Dulay, N., Kramer, J.: Regis: A Constructive Development Environment for Distributed Programs. In Distributed Systems Engineering Journal, 1(5), 1994.

[9] Matsuoka, S., Yonezawa, A.: Analysis of Inheritance Anomaly in Object-Oriented Concurent Programming Languages. Research Directions in Concurrent Object-Oriented Programming, MIT Press, 1993.

[10] Mehta N. R., Medvidovic, N.,Phadke S.: Towards a Taxonomy of Software Connectors. In Proceedings of the 22th International Conference on Software Engineering (ICSE 2000), Limerick, Ireland, 2000.

[11] Nierstrasz, O.: Regular Types for Active Objects, In Proceedings of the OOPSLA '93, ACM Press, 1993, pp. 1–15.

[12] OMG orbos/99-04-16, CORBA Component Model. Volume 1, 1999.

[13] OMG orbos/99-04-17, CORBA Component Model, Volume 2, 1999.

[14] Oreizy, P., Rosenblum, D. S., Taylor, R. N.: On the Role of Connectors in Modeling and Implementing Software Architectures, Technical Report UCI-ICS-98-04, University of California, Irvine, 1998.

[15] Perry, D.E., Wolf, A. L.: Foundations for the Study of Software Architecture. ACM Software Engineering Notes, vol. 17, no. 4, 1992.

[16] Plasil, F., Balek, D., Janecek, R.: SOFA/DCUP Architecture for Component Trading and Dynamic Updating. In Proceedings of ICCDS '98, Annapolis, IEEE CS, 1998, pp. 43–52.

[17] Plasil, F., Besta, M., Visnovsky, S.: Bounding Component Behavior via Protocols. In Proceedings of TOOLS USA '99, Santa Barbara, USA, 1999.

[18] Plasil, F., Mikusik, D.: Inheriting Synchronization Protocols via Sound Enrichment Rules. In Proceedings of JMPLC, Springer LNCS 1204, March 1997.

[19] Purtilo, J. M.: The Polylith Software Bus. ACM Transactions on Programming Languages and Systems, 16(1), 1994.

[20] Shaw, M.: Procedure Calls Are the Assembly Language of Software Interconnection: Connectors Deserve First-Class Status. In D.A. Lamb (ed) Studies of Software Design, Proceedings of a 1993 Workshop, Lecture Notes in Computer Science no. 1078, Springer-Verlag 1996.

[21] Shaw, M., DeLine, R., Klein, D. V., Ross, T. L., Young, D. M., Zalesnik, G.: Abstractions for Software Architecture and Tools to Support Them. IEEE Transactions on Software Engineering, Vol. 21, No. 4, April 1995, pp. 314–335.

[22] Sun Microsystems: JavaBeans 1.0 Specification. http://java.sun.com/beans/docs/spec.html.

[23] Sun Microsystems: Enterprise JavaBeans 1.1 Specification. http://java.sun.com/products/ejb/docs.html.

[24] Rogerson, D.: Inside COM. Microsoft Press 1997.

[25] Yellin, D. M., Strom, R. E.: Interfaces, Protocols, and the Semi-Automatic Construction Of Software Adaptors. In Proceedings of the OOPSLA '94, ACM Press, 1994, pp. 176–190.

AN EXTENSION TO A CORBA TRADER TO SUPPORT XML SERVICE DESCRIPTIONS

Twittie Senivongse and Wuttichai Nanekrangsan
Department of Computer Engineering, Chulalongkorn University, Bangkok, Thailand

Abstract Search functionality of a CORBA trader is restricted to search for service offers and assumes clients' knowledge of service types of those offers. It would be more flexible if the clients can also import other information, i.e. service types and interfaces, before trading for service offers, or conduct keyword search. With this requirement, making service descriptions into XML format can be helpful. This paper focuses on the trader extension that can transform service types and service offers within a CORBA trader into XML service descriptions, and vice versa. The transformation is based on our Document Type Definitions for service types and service offers. This transformer module can be used to create XML service descriptions that will enable flexible XML-based service discovery. The transformer also facilitates clients in viewing details of CORBA services from Web browsers and helps with exporting service descriptions to the trader.

Keywords: service discovery, XML, trader, CORBA

1. INTRODUCTION

CORBA Trader [1] (Trading Object Service) is one of the common services in CORBA [2] that serves as a directory, allowing service exporters (servers) to advertise their service type and service offer descriptions, and allowing service importers (clients) to discover service offers they desire. The trader is designed for trading for service offers, and thus its clients are assumed to know details about types and interfaces of those offers. We aim to provide a flexible service discovery service that can discover service information, i.e. service types, interface definitions, and service offers, with no assumption on clients' exact knowledge of the services and the clients can trade for information in a similar way they do with search engines [3]. With this objective, we use Extensible Markup Language (XML) [4] to represent service descriptions because its self-describing characteristic can contribute to more flexible search, and its accepted status as a data interchange medium will open a way for future integration of service information from several directory services. Our experimental service discovery service obtains XML service descriptions from CORBA traders; these traders are extended with a module that can transform CORBA service descriptions into XML documents. This paper focuses on the architecture of this transformation module although the overview of the service discovery service will also be discussed in Section 5.1.

The transformation module can transform trader's service type descriptions, with interface definitions from the Interface Repository (IR) embedded, as well as service offer descriptions into XML documents, and vice versa. The transformation is based on our Document Type Definitions (DTDs) for service types and service offers. Since we are focusing more on flexible features for discovery of services than on the interchange of service descriptions among several directory services, we describe CORBA service descriptions by using our own simple DTDs rather than the standard XML Metadata Interchange (XMI) [5] in our experimental prototype. It is foreseen that service descriptions can be represented as XMI documents and used by the transformation module to overcome this limitation. Apart from being used in our service discovery service, the transformation module provides a convenient way to access CORBA service descriptions from other architecture like World Wide Web.

There are several efforts to describe component and service descriptions in XML. WebTrader [6] provides an infrastructure to handle Web-based service market where users can export and import services in XML. A DTD is defined for users to describe their services but it does not provide for all characteristics of CORBA service descriptions. Other works include Open Software Description (OSD) [7] that describes general software descriptions, and Deployable Software Description (DSD) [8] that uses XML to describe components for deployment management purpose; nevertheless, they are too general for describing CORBA services.

Section 2 of this paper gives the explanation of service descriptions that can be found in the trader and IR followed by our proposed DTDs that will be used to describe them. Section 3 discusses the extension to the trader to facilitate CORBA/XML transformation. Our prototype implementation is explained in Section 4 and Section 5 discusses possible use of the transformation module. Section 6 summarises the paper with future work.

2. SERVICE DESCRIPTIONS IN CORBA

Service descriptions within a CORBA trader can be divided into two categories – service type and service offer. A service type is an abstract definition of a service and it is, therefore, a template for advertising service offers. A service offer is the information describing a particular instance of a service that conforms to a service type. We define two straightforward DTDs for XML service descriptions, i.e. service type DTD and service offer DTD.

2.1. Service type and service type DTD

A service type description within a trader comprises service type name, service interface, base service types from which the service type inherits, and a set of service properties. This information is trader-owned and stored in the Service Type Repository module of the trader. It is described by the following BNF:

```
Service <ServiceTypeName> [:<BaseServiceTypeName>
[,<BaseServiceTypeName>]*]{
  interface <InterfaceTypeName>;
  [[mandatory][readonly] property <IDLType> <PropertyName>;]*
}
```

InterfaceTypeName above is the link to the interface definition expressed in OMG IDL and stored in the IR. With this interface definition, the service type description is augmented with information such as the interface name, the set of attributes, and the set of operations that this service can respond to. Hence, our service type DTD that constrains XML service type descriptions is composed of two main parts: the DTD for the interface definition from the IR and the DTD for the service type information from the trader.

Table 1 shows our service type DTD. The design principle is to capture as many CORBA service type characteristics as possible. The *Interface* element in the service type DTD describes the computational signature of the interface definition from the IR, while the *TraderServiceType* element shows the service type description from the trader. The *Interface* element consists of the interface identifier, base interfaces represented as structured graph (adapted from [9]), list of constants, list of attributes, and list of operations. The *TraderServiceType* element comprises the interface id that corresponds to an interface definition in the IR, base service types, and a list of property templates. Note that the DTD does not yet support a full description of any user-defined type; only type name is supported.

2.2. Service offer and service offer DTD

Service offers are stored within the Offer List of the trader, each describing the service type name, name-value pairs of service properties, and the object reference (IOR) used to locate the service instance. The service offer DTD is simple, as shown in Table 2, capturing the service type name, zero or more property values and the reference to the offer instance. The *DynamicPropEval* elements describe exported dynamic properties.

Table 1. Service type DTD

```
 1 <!ELEMENT ServiceTypeDescription (Interface?, TraderServiceType)>
 2 <!ELEMENT Interface (BaseInterfaces?, Constant*, Attribute*, Operation*)>
 3 <!ATTLIST Interface Id CDATA #REQUIRED Name CDATA #REQUIRED
 4                     Version CDATA #REQUIRED>
 5 <!ELEMENT BaseInterfaces (BaseInterface*, Link*)>
 6 <!ELEMENT BaseInterface EMPTY>
 7 <!ATTLIST BaseInterface Id CDATA #REQUIRED Name CDATA #REQUIRED>
 8 <!ELEMENT Link EMPTY>
 9 <!ATTLIST Link Source CDATA #REQUIRED Dest CDATA #REQUIRED>
10 <!ELEMENT Constant EMPTY>
11 <!ATTLIST Constant Id CDATA #REQUIRED Name CDATA #REQUIRED
12                     Version CDATA #REQUIRED Type CDATA #REQUIRED
13                     Value CDATA #REQUIRED Derived (YES | NO) "NO">
14 <!ELEMENT Attribute EMPTY>
15 <!ATTLIST Attribute Id CDATA #REQUIRED Name CDATA #REQUIRED
16                     Version CDATA #REQUIRED Type CDATA #REQUIRED
17                     Mode (NORMAL | READONLY) "NORMAL"
18                     Derived (YES | NO) "NO">
19 <!ELEMENT Operation (Parameter*, Exception*, Context*)>
20 <!ATTLIST Operation Id CDATA #REQUIRED Name CDATA #REQUIRED
21                     Version CDATA #REQUIRED Type CDATA #REQUIRED
22                     Mode (NORMAL | ONEWAY) "NORMAL"
23                     Derived (YES | NO) "NO">
24 <!ELEMENT Parameter EMPTY>
25 <!ATTLIST Parameter Name CDATA #REQUIRED Type CDATA #REQUIRED
26                     Mode (IN | OUT | INOUT) "IN">
27 <!ELEMENT Exception (Member)*>
28 <!ATTLIST Exception Id CDATA #REQUIRED Name CDATA #REQUIRED
29                     Version CDATA #REQUIRED Derived (YES | NO) "NO">
30 <!ELEMENT Member EMPTY>
31 <!ATTLIST Member Name CDATA #REQUIRED Type CDATA #REQUIRED>
32 <!ELEMENT Context (#PCDATA)>
33 <!ELEMENT TraderServiceType (BaseServiceTypes?, Property*)>
34 <!ATTLIST TraderServiceType Id CDATA #REQUIRED Name CDATA #REQUIRED
35                          Masked (YES | NO) "NO">
36 <!ELEMENT BaseServiceTypes (BaseServiceType*, Link*)>
37 <!ELEMENT BaseServiceType EMPTY>
38 <!ATTLIST BaseServiceType Name CDATA #REQUIRED>
39 <!ELEMENT Property EMPTY>
40 <!ATTLIST Property Name CDATA #REQUIRED Type CDATA #REQUIRED
41                     Mode (NORMAL|READONLY|MANDATORY|
42                          MANDATORY_READONLY) "NORMAL"
43                     Derived (YES | NO) "NO">
```

Table 2. Service offer DTD

```
 1 <!ELEMENT ServiceOfferDescription (OfferType, Property*, ObjectReference)>
 2 <!ELEMENT OfferType EMPTY>
 3 <!ATTLIST OfferType Name CDATA #REQUIRED>
 4 <!ELEMENT Property (DynamicPropEval, ExtraInfo)?>
 5 <!ATTLIST Property Name CDATA #REQUIRED Value CDATA #IMPLIED>
 6 <!ELEMENT DynamicPropEval (#PCDATA)>
 7 <!ATTLIST DynamicPropEval ReturnType CDATA #REQUIRED>
 8 <!ELEMENT ExtraInfo EMPTY>
 9 <!ATTLIST ExtraInfo Type CDATA #REQUIRED Value CDATA #REQUIRED>
10 <!ELEMENT ObjectReference (#PCDATA)>
```

3. AN EXTENSION TO A CORBA TRADER

An extension to a trader, called the CORBA/XML Transformer (CXT), is responsible for transformation of service descriptions between the CORBA description format and XML (Figure 1). The CXT is designed as a separate module, in addition to existing components of the trader, so that it does not affect the normal operation of the trader. At present, resultant XML documents from the transformation are kept in the underlying file system.

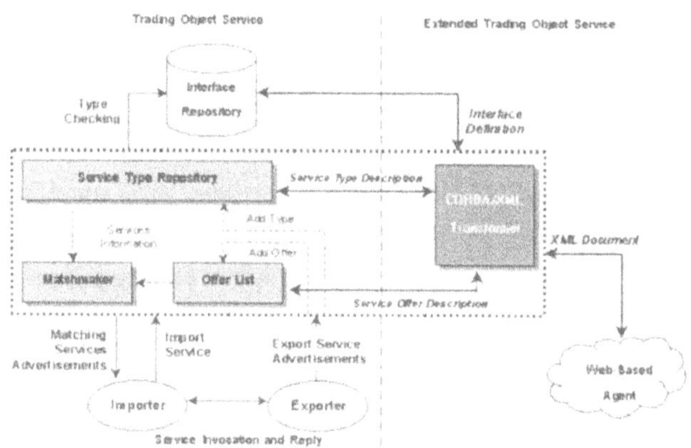

Figure 1. Trader with CORBA/XML transformer

We extend a CORBA trader by adding to CosTrading.idl the following interface definition of the CXT.

```
interface CorbaXmlTransformer {
    typedef Istring Identifier;
    exception InvalidXmlFileLocation { string location; };
```

```
    exception InvalidXmlDocument{};
    exception UnknownInterface { Identifier if_name;};
    exception ServiceTypeExists { ServiceTypeName name;};
    long transform_all_type();
    boolean transform_type(in ServiceTypeName type)
        raises(UnknownServiceType, IllegalServiceType);
    long transform _all_offer(out OfferIdSeq ids);
    long transform _offer(in ServiceTypeName type, out OfferIdSeq ids)
        raises(UnknownServiceType, IllegalServiceType);
    boolean transform_offer_id(in OfferId id)
        raises(UnknownOfferId, IllegalOfferId);
    OfferId transform_xml(in string file)
        raises(InvalidXmlFileLocation, InvalidXmlDocument,
            UnknownInterface, UnknownServiceType,
            ServiceTypeExists);
};
```

The behaviour of the CXT can be described as follows:

transform_all_type() : This operation is used to transform all service type descriptions within the trader. Its return type is *long* indicating the number of service types that have been transformed.
transform_type() : This operation is used to transform the description of the specified service type. Its return type is *boolean* indicating success or failure of the transformation. Two exceptions may be raised during the operation:

- *CORBA::CosTrading::UnknownServiceType* : The specified service type does not exist in the Service Type Repository of this trader.
- *CORBA::CosTrading::IllegalServiceType* : The specified service type is malformed.

transform_all_offer() : This operation is used to transform all service offers within the trader. The number of offers successfully transformed is returned in a *long* value and their offer ids are returned in the *OfferIdSeq* output parameter.
transform_offer() : This operation is used to transform all service offers of the specified service type. This also includes offers of subtypes of the specified type. The number of offers that are successfully transformed and their offer ids are returned. Two exceptions may be raised during the operation:

- *CORBA::CosTrading::UnknownServiceType* : The specified service type does not exist in the Service Type Repository of this trader.
- *CORBA::CosTrading::IllegalServiceType* : The specified service type is malformed.

transform_offer_id() : This operation transforms an offer with the specified offer id. It returns *boolean* to indicate success or failure of the transformation. Two exceptions may be raised during the operation:

- *CORBA::CosTrading::UnknownOfferId* : There is no offer with the specified offer id within this trader.
- *CORBA::CosTrading::IllegalOfferId* : The specified offer id does not comply with the rules for object identifiers defined in [1].

transform_xml() : This operation transforms an XML service description into the CORBA description format according to the root of the document which specifies the type of the information. That is, a service type document will be transformed to a service type description and a service offer document to a service offer description. Several exceptions may be raised during the operation:

- *CORBA :: CosTrading :: CorbaXmlTransformer :: InvalidXmlFileLocation*: The XML document location specified as a URL is malformed, or the specified file location does not exist.
- *CORBA :: CosTrading :: CorbaXmlTransformer :: InvalidXmlDocument*: The XML document is not valid according to the service type DTD and service offer DTD.
- *CORBA::CosTrading::CorbaXmlTransformer::UnknownInterface*: This exception may occur when tranforming from a service type document. If the IR does not store the definition of base interfaces of the service type (i.e. interfaces of the base service types), the transformation fails with no descriptions added to the Service Type Repository and IR.
- *CORBA::CosTrading::UnknownServiceType*: This exception may occur in two cases. One is when transforming from a service type document. If base service types of the service type do not exist in the Service Type Repository of the trader, the transformation fails with no descriptions added to the Service Type Repository and IR. The other is when transforming from a service offer document. If the service type of the offer does not exist in the Service Type Repository, the transformation fails with no descriptions added to the Offer List.
- *CORBA::CosTrading::CorbaXmlTransformer::ServiceTypeExists*: This exception may occur when transforming from a service type document. If the service type already exists in the Service Type Repository of the trader, the transformation fails with no description added to the Service Type Repository and IR. This is to prevent the existing service type from being replaced by a different description with the same name. Note that if the interface definition for this service type already exists in the IR, it may be the case that there is another service type, which exhibits that

interface, stored within the trader. The transformation will be allowed because more than one service type may support the same interface.

4. IMPLEMENTATION OF CORBA/XML TRANSFORMER

The CXT (Figure 2) is implemented to retrieve service descriptions from the Service Type Repository, Offer List, and IR when a client program requests for transformation of a service type or service offer. It then creates an instance of the Document Object Model (DOM) [10] to represent those descriptions before generating an XML document. On the other hand, the CXT can also construct a DOM instance by parsing an XML service description before writing the information as CORBA descriptions into the trader and IR.

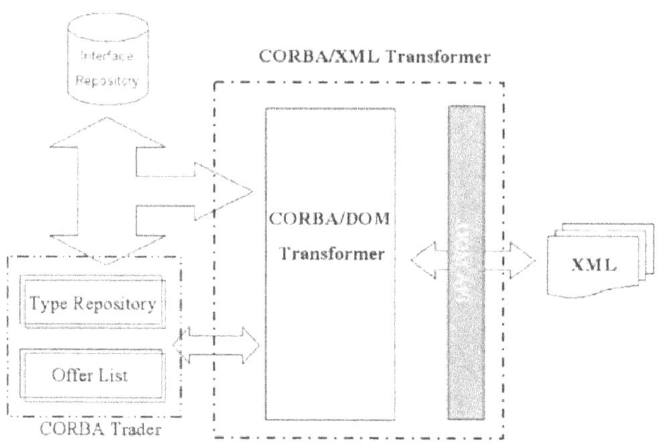

Figure 2. CORBA/XML transformer components

We have developed a prototype of the CXT using Java. This prototype uses the implementation of DOM called Java API for XML Parsing (JAXP) from Sun Microsystems [11]. An extension is added to a JacORB trader [12] that works with the IR from ORBacus [13]. The CXT is implemented in such a way that it uses only the operations specified in the standard IDL interfaces of the trader and IR so that it can be easily integrated with various implementations of the trader and IR. XML service descriptions generated by our CXT are stored as files in a location that is also accessible by HTTP.

The class model of our implementation is presented in Figure 3. The implementation is composed of three main classes that can be added to any Java implementations of CORBA-compliant traders: *ServiceTypeExporter* for transformation of CORBA service types to XML, *ServiceOfferExporter* for transformation of CORBA service offers to XML, and *ServiceImporter* for trans-

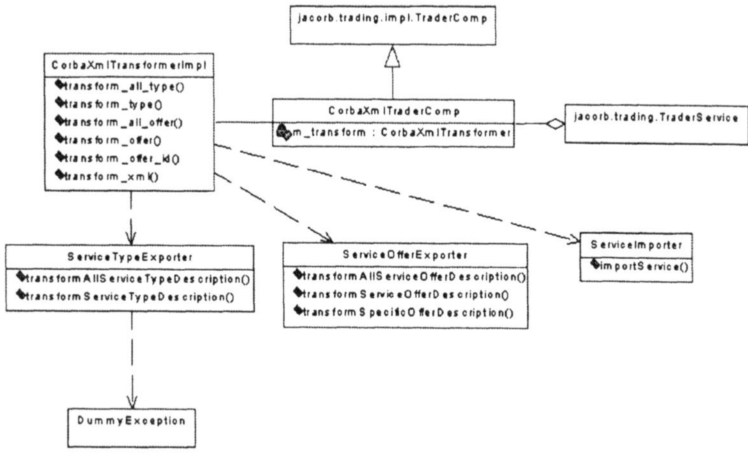

Figure 3. CORBA/XML transformer class model

formation of XML service descriptions to CORBA description format. Other classes are used for integrating with the JacORB trader.

5. USE OF CORBA/XML TRANSFORMER

In this section, we discuss some possible use of the CXT.

5.1. Service discovery service

As mentioned earlier, the CXT has been used to provide our Service Discovery Service (SDS) prototype with service descriptions in XML format [3]. Figure 4 shows the overview of the SDS.

The SDS obtains service descriptions from multiple traders and can also federate with other SDSes to extend search space. A Trader Agent will intercept new service advertisements or updates that are sent to its associated trader and requests the CXT to transform the service descriptions into XML documents before passing onto the Service Provision Centre of the SDS for storage. Search on these XML service descriptions can be conducted via the Search Interface that supports multiple XML query languages and keyword search and is accessible to both CORBA clients and Web users. SDS users can discover service types, service offers, and service interfaces information without having to know exact details of the required services. Details and the comparison between a trader and the SDS can also be found in [14].

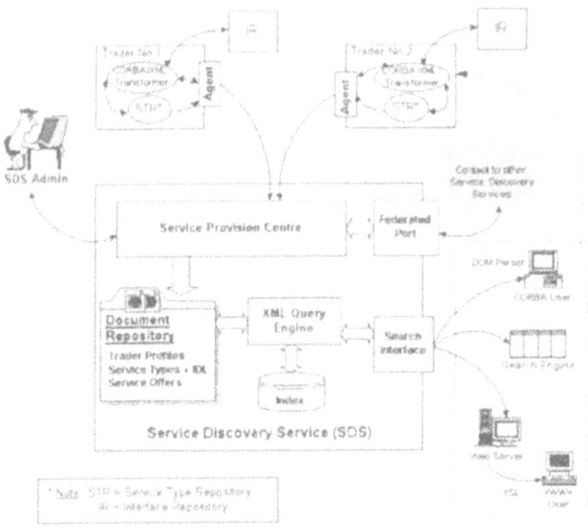

Figure 4. Service discovery service components

5.2. Convenient access to trader

Another advantage of having the trader extended with the CXT is that access to service descriptions within the trader from other environment like World Wide Web is more convenient by using HTTP directly. Normally, a Web user can access the trader's service descriptions (as CORBA objects) using IIOP via a browser with ORB plug-in, but this requires a user-side effort (e.g. by an applet) to represent those CORBA service descriptions in a form that is understandable to the user. Associating the CXT with the trader allows server-side manipulation that makes service descriptions Web-ready as XML documents, and hence the access can be by HTTP. The user does not require a browser with ORB plug-in and if the browser is XML-enabled, service descriptions can be displayed directly; otherwise simple use of the Extensible Stylesheet Language Transformations (XSLT) [15] is required.

We have tried with our Web-based client system in Figure 5. A user can invoke operations on the CXT from the Web environment using Java Servlet and JavaServer Page (JSP). The Servlet mediates between the browser and a Java ORB service, while JSP renders dynamic HTML to be displayed on the browser. Within this architecture, there exist JavaBeans that accept requests from the browser and invoke operations on the extended trader. The results are sent to their associated JSPs and then back to the browser. The functions of the JavaBeans are:

- View service types and service offers within the trader.
- Display a specified service type description.

- Display a specified service offer description.
- Request the CXT to transform a specified service type into XML.
- Request the CXT to transform a specified service offer into XML.
- Request the CXT to transform a specified XML service description for the trader.
- Call XSLT to render an HTML document from a specified XML file.

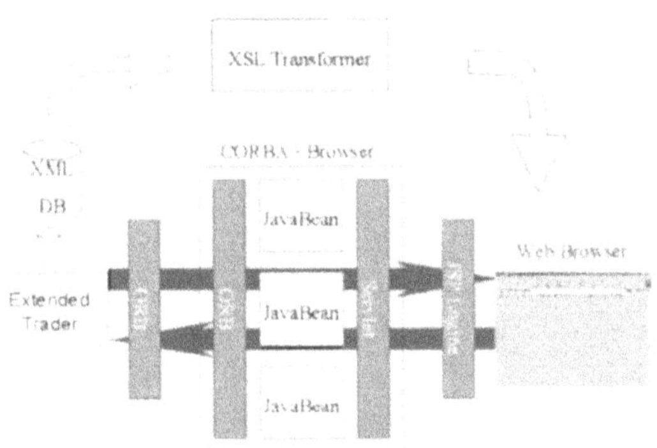

Figure 5. Web-based client prototype

Our model has been tested on Linux 2.2.13 using Apache 1.3.6 as a Web server, Tomcat 3.1 as a Servlet/JSP engine, and JDK version 1.2.2. Test data comprise 7 service types and 12 service offers added to the trader and the CXT is called by the Web-based client system. We have also successfully tested on Windows 98 using Sun's JavaServer Web Development Kit (JSWDK) 1.0 as a Servlet/JSP engine and JDK version 1.1.7b. Figure 6(a) and 6(b) show sample results of the transformation of a service type called PlainConnection and its offer, respectively as a raw XML document and as an HTML document rendered from XML.

Other means of cross-platform communication via HTTP is also possible by an XML protocol such as the Simple Object Access Protocol (SOAP) [16] that allows a message in XML format to be enclosed with some binding protocols including HTTP. Our Web-based client system may use SOAP for the communication between the browser or JSP and the Servlet for request/reply of transformation. However, this is not of our concern since it is only another access protocol; both sides of the communication still have to understand and process the XML message enclosed with the request and reply.

Since the CXT also allows transformation of XML service descriptions into CORBA format, service providers may use this feature for Web-based export

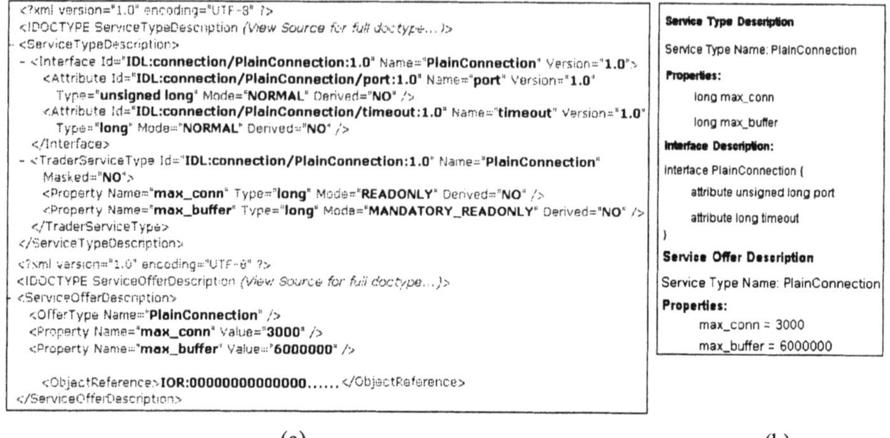

Figure 6. Example of results of transformation in XML and HTML

of service types and service offers without having to write CORBA programs to do so. The CXT can conveniently help with the exchange or import of trader contents, e.g. when exchanging service descriptions between traders or when constructing a replica of a particular trader.

6. CONCLUDING REMARKS

The CXT extension to a CORBA trader provides a way to describe and generate XML version of CORBA service descriptions and also to transform XML descriptions back to the CORBA format. The transformation is straightforward based on our simple service type and service offer DTDs and this extension is now used within our prototype of the service discovery service. We have also integrated it with our service change notification system [17] that notifies subscribing clients about change of advertised services with details of change in XML documents. Another benefit is that the CXT makes trader's descriptions Web-ready for HTTP access by Web users. We hope that the CXT can be applied further to other applications.

As stated earlier, the transformation of service descriptions can be more standardised by adopting XMI to describe the trader's service description model. This will enable further exchange of service information between several kinds of traders or directory services. We may also used XML Schema [18] to constrain service descriptions instead of DTDs.

Acknowledgments

This work is supported by the Thailand-Japan Technology Transfer Project (TJTTP-OECF) and the Development Grants for New Faculty/Researchers of Chulalongkorn University.

References

[1] Object Management Group, "Trading Object Service Specification", Revised Ed., March 1997.

[2] Object Management Group, "The Common Object Request Broker: Architecture and Specification", Revision 2.2, February 1998.

[3] W. Suphasanthitikul and T.Senivongse, "An Architecture for a Service Discovery Service in CORBA", Proceedings of the National Computer Science and Engineering Conference (NCSEC 2000), Bangkok, Thailand, 16-17 November 2000, pp. 49-54.

[4] T. Bray, J. Paoli, C.M. Sperberg-McQueen, and E. Maler, "Extensible Markup Language (XML) 1.0 Specification (2nd Edition)", W3C Recommendation, 6 October 2000, http://www.w3c.org/xml.

[5] Object Management Group, "XML Metadata Interchange (XMI)", 16 July 1998.

[6] V. Vasudevan and T. Bannon, "WebTrader: Discovery and Programmed Access to Web-Based Services (Draft)", OBJS Techinical Report, 1999, http://www.objs.com/agility/tech-reports/9812-web-trader-paper/WebTraderPaper.html.

[7] A. van Hoff, H. Partovi, and T. Thai, "The Open Software Description Format (OSD)", Submitted to W3C, 13 August 1997, http://www.w3.org/TR/NOTE-OSD.html.

[8] R.S. Hall, D. Heimbigner and A.L. Wolf, "Specifying the Deployable Software Description Format in XML", SERL Technical Report CU-SERL-207-99, Software Engineering Research Laboratory, Department of Computer Science, University of Colorado, March 1999.

[9] O. Liechti, M.J. Sifer, T. Ichikawa, "Structured Graph Format: XML Metadata for Describing Web Site Structure", Computer Networks and ISDN Systems Vol. 30 No. 1-7, 1 April 1998, pp. 11-21.

[10] L. Wood et al., "Document Object Model (DOM) Level 1 Specification Version 1.0", W3C Recommendation", 1 October 1998, http://www.w3.org/TR/REC-DOM-Level-1.

[11] Java API for XML Parsing (JAXP), http://java.sun.com/xml.

[12] JacORB – a free Java ORB, http://jacorb.inf.fu-berlin.de.

[13] ORBacus, http://www.ooc.com/.

[14] T. Senivongse and W. Suphasantithikul, "An XML-Based Architecture for Service Discovery", Submitted to the 5th International Enterprise Distributed Object Computing Conference (EDOC'2001), Seattle, Washington, USA, 4-7 September 2001, http://www.cp.eng.chula.ac.th/faculty/tsv/research/publications/home.html.

[15] J. Clark, "XSL Transformations (XSLT) Version 1.0", W3C Recommendation, 16 November 1999, http://www.w3c.org/TR/xslt.

[16] D. Box et al., "Simple Object Access Protocol (SOAP) 1.1", W3C Note, 8 May 2000, http://www.w3c.org/TR/SOAP.

[17] P. Suriyentrakorn and T. Senivongse, "An Approach for Service Change Notification in Distributed Systems", Proceedings of the National Computer Science and Engineering Conference (NCSEC 2000), Bangkok, Thailand, 16-17 November 2000, pp. 43-48.

[18] D.C. Fallside, "XML Schema Part 0: Primer", W3C Recommendation, 2 May 2001, http://www.w3c.org/TR/xmlschema-0.

ON THE CONSTRUCTION OF DISTRIBUTED RM-ODP SPECIFICATIONS

Xavier Blanc(+)(*), Marie-Pierre Gervais(*) and Raymonde Le Delliou(+)
(*)Laboratoire d'Informatique de Paris 6 - 8 rue du Capitaine Scott F75015 PARIS
(+)EDF Research Division - 1, av du Gnl De Gaulle F92141 CLAMART Cedex

Abstract LIP6, is association with EDF R& D[1] , proposes a framework that deals with the construction of heterogeneous and distributed specifications. This paper focuses on the part of work devoted to the distribution aspects of a specification, especially the distributed specifications consistency and management. It describes our approach to deal with these two aspects. Regarding the distributed specifications consistency, we advocate that the modeling language must enable the partitioning of the specification into several pieces and provide means to express the dependencies between them. For this reason, we make use of RM-ODP language as it includes some concepts that fit these requirements. However, RM-ODP is not prescriptive enough to be really helpful when elaborating distributed specifications. Thus we propose distributed specifications construction rules in identifying the needed concepts and in defining their usage rules. Concerning the distributed specifications management, we provide a so-called Distributed Specifications Management System (DSMS), that is an RM-ODP specifications repository built in conformance with the MOF and CORBA standards. Such a repository provides facilities to distribute specifications, to link pieces of specifications and to handle them.

Keywords: Distributed Specifications, Modelling, RM-ODP, MOF.

1. INTRODUCTION

Thanks to the object-oriented technologies and to the growing evolution in the semi-conductors, there are more and more distributed applications. For example, Information Systems of companies are now distributed, e-commerce is everywhere and we can send e-mails with our mobile phones. If these distributed applications provide helpful services to the end users, however they are more and more complex.

[1]This work is supported by grant # I26/B32617/IMA375 from EDF R& D

Modeling languages and methods can be useful to face this complexity. They lead to the elaboration of specifications that help for building, documenting and maintaining applications. In this paper, we are particularly interested in using RM-ODP standard for elaborating specifications. RM-ODP is an ISO standard that defines concepts and structuring rules for building specifications of distributed systems [1][2][4].

Considering that applications are built by big teams composed of designers, architects or developers, consequently specifications are now themselves distributed. It should be noted that specifications can also be distributed because some entities of the applications have been already specified and developed. In this case, building a specification consists in integrating existing with new ones.

Let us consider a project such as the building of an e-shop. The goal of this e-shop is to sell some products to its customers. For this, the e-shop must receive some orders, manage stocks and deliver the products. To increase its customers, the e-shop must do advertising and marketing.

The project team developing the e-shop is distributed over the USA, Europe and Japan and must build the specification. As the team is distributed, then the specification will be distributed. For example, the USA part of the team will specify the e-shop marketing while the Europe part of the team will specify the delivery service and the Japan part will specify the stocks.

Elaborating distributed specifications give new problems that the current specification techniques do not deal with. LIP6, is association with EDF R& D, addresses this issue and proposes a framework that deals with the construction of heterogeneous and distributed specifications [5]. This framework makes use of various standards from the distributed object computing and meta-modeling communities, such as RM-ODP from ISO, CORBA, MOF and XMI from OMG and XML from W3C. Considering the RM-ODP language as a reference formalism, the framework provides translation mechanisms between various formalisms enabling to build a new specification by composing heterogeneous existing pieces of specifications with new ones. Moreover, it deals with the taking into account that the various pieces to be composed can be distributed and stored in various locations.

This paper focuses on the part of work devoted to the distribution aspects of a specification, especially the distributed specifications consistency and management. As a specification can be composed of several pieces depending on each other, building one piece impacts the others. Thus maintaining the consistency of the whole specification becomes very difficult but is needed. Moreover, understanding the whole specification, which is distributed, requires that some relations be established between the various pieces stored. As a calculation can be performed by several distributed pieces of code providing the same result as a single run-time, "linking" together pieces of specification stored in various locations must transparently provide the same view as a unique specification.

Current techniques do not provide mechanisms, which first enables the consistency maintenance and second the distributed specifications management. Actually, these problems respectively require an adapted modeling language and a Distributed Specifications Management System (DSMS). The modeling language must provide some mechanisms enabling the partitioning of the specification into several pieces and means to express the dependencies between them. The DSMS, also called repository, must provide facilities to distribute specifications, to link pieces of specifications and to handle them.

We present in this paper our approach to deal with these two aspects. Regarding the modeling language aspect, we make use of RM-ODP language because it includes concepts that fit the requirements presented above. However, RM-ODP is not prescriptive enough to be really helpful when elaborating distributed specifications. Thus we propose distributed specifications construction rules in identifying the needed concepts and defining their usage rules. Concerning the DSMS, we detail how we built an RM-ODP specifications repository enabling the management of these specifications. Our DSMS is developed in conformance with the MOF and CORBA standards [9][10].

The paper is structured as follows. We first introduce main concepts of the RM-ODP standard we use. For sake of simplicity, we only focus on the Enterprise viewpoint[2] and illustrate the Enterprise specification construction rules we prescribe with the e-shop example. We then present our Distributed Specifications Management System by describing its construction based on the MOF and CORBA standards.

2. CONSTRUCTION OF AN RM-ODP ENTERPRISE SPECIFICATION

2.1. The RM-ODP Enterprise Viewpoint

RM-ODP (Reference Model for Open Distributed Processing) is an ISO standard that defines concepts and structuring rules for specifying open distributed systems [1][2][4]. In particular, RM-ODP defines the concept of "viewpoint" that deals with the separation of concerns needed to specify different facets of a system. Five viewpoints are then defined. The set of RM-ODP concepts is composed of concepts common to all the viewpoints and those that are specific for some viewpoints.

[2]Although there is no sequence or hierarchy between the RM-ODP viewpoints, it is generally considered that building RM-ODP specifications often starts by building the Enterprise one.

The Enterprise viewpoint focuses on the purpose, scope, and the policies that apply to a system [3]. The basic concepts of RM-ODP Enterprise language are object, role, community, objective, behavior and action. An *object* is a model of an entity, either an entity of the system to be specified or an entity of the system environment. Objects can be grouped to form a *community*. In that case, they exhibit the *behavior* needed to realize the *objective* of the community. By doing this, they fulfill roles of the community since a *role* identifies a behavior. This is a set of *actions* with constraints on when they appear. Actions can be *interactions* between several objects or internal actions.

More sophisticated concepts are defined in the Enterprise viewpoint, namely the *C-object and Interface role* concepts. They are particularly useful when building distributed specifications. A *C-Object* is an object that represents a community [3]. It enables to specify interactions between communities. As it represents a community, it is composed of several objects. Thus, when it performs an action, in fact one of its components really performs the action. To express this, RM-ODP defines the concept of *interface role* as an identifier of a behavior exhibited by a C-Object [3]. Thus the system and its environment can be modeled in several interacting communities.

2.2. Steps of the construction of an Enterprise specification

RM-ODP is not prescriptive on how to build an Enterprise specification, that's why we propose the following steps [13]:

1 Defining the objective;

2 Enumerating all the roles enabling to perform this objective;

3 Among the roles of the community, identifying those that can correspond to a distinct community. Assign then to these communities the roles that must be attached to them;

For each community:

4 Identifying the Enterprise objects fulfilling the roles of the community. If some objects are C-objects, describing the corresponding interface roles;

5 Describing the behavior of the community;

6 Describing the policies.

2.3. RM-ODP Enterprise specification of the e-shop

Applying these steps on the e-shop example, we elaborate the Enterprise specification of the e-shop. It should be noted that the specification we present here is a very simplified one, but sufficient to highlight our proposal. In particular, some steps (namely step 6) will not be considered as they are not relevant in the context of this paper.

The objective of the e-shop is to sell products to the customer. To accomplish this objective, we have identified the role "Customer", the role "Delivery Service" (DS) , the role "Stock", the role "Marketing Service" (MS) and the role "Order Taker".

The role "Customer" defines the behavior of the customer. The Customer can **create a new profile**, which is needed to order some products. The Customer can **order some products**. The Customer can **trace its order**, to know where it is. The Customer can **receive its order**. And finally, the Customer can **pay its order**.

The role "Delivery Service" (DS) defines the behavior of the delivery service. The DS can **package an order**. It can **deliver the package**. And finally, it can **provide the trace of an order**.

The role "Stock" defines the behavior of the stock. It can **buy new products**. And finally, it can **prepare the products for an order**.

The role "Marketing Service" (MS) defines the behavior of the marketing service. The MS can **send some advertising**. It can **perform some survey**. And finally, it can **define some special prices**.

The role "Order Taker" (OT) defines the behavior of the order taker. It can **create a new profile** for a new customer. It can **accept or deny a new order**. It can **deliver the order**. And finally, it can **cash the order**.

Among the actions listed for each role, some of them are interactions. For example, when a Customer creates a new profile, it interacts with the OT in order that this creates a new customer profile.

The figure 1 represents the e-shop community, with the interactions between these roles.

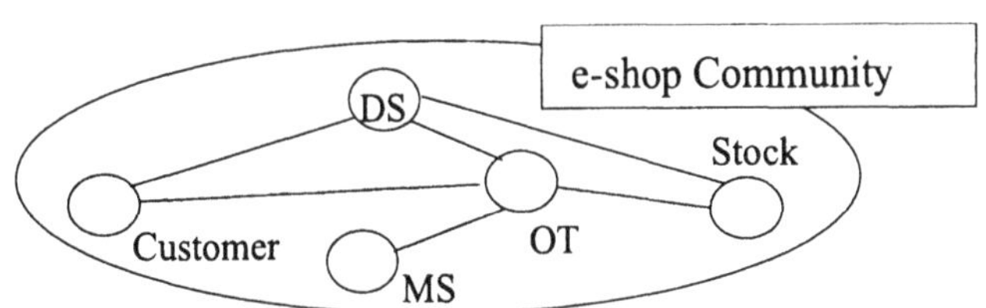

Figure 1. The e-shop community with its roles and their interactions

Applying the step 3 and according to our modeling choices, we consider that the DS role identifies a behavior that can be defined more precisely in a distinct community called the DS community. This defines the roles of the

"Trace Service" (TS), the "Stock Manager" (SM), the "Global Delivery Service" (GDS) and the "Local Delivery Service" (LDS).

The role "Trace Service" (TS) can receive information about an order to know where it is localized and **provide a trace of the order**.

The "Stock Manager" (SM) is responsible for finding the nearest stocks from the client that contain the products of an order.

The "Global Delivery Service" (GDS) **asks for some stocks to the SM** and **then delegates the delivery of the order** to a Local Delivery Service.

The "Local Delivery Service" (LDS) is responsible for **packaging the order** and **delivering the package** to the customer.

We can now, for each community, allocate roles to objects (step 4). Depending on modeling choices, various results can be obtained.

In the e-shop Community, for sake of simplicity, we choose to allocate one role to one object, except for the customer role where several objects can fulfill the role, one for each custom of the e-shop. Let us notice that the object fulfilling the DS role in this community is a C-object that represents the DS community.

In the DS Community, for the same reason of simplicity, we decide that each role is fulfilled by a distinct object.

The figure 2 shows the relationship between the e-shop community and the DS community.

As mentioned previously, the C-Object does not really perform actions. To define which component performs the action, we must describe its corresponding interface roles. In our example, the C-Object performs three actions that are **package an order, deliver the package and trace an order**

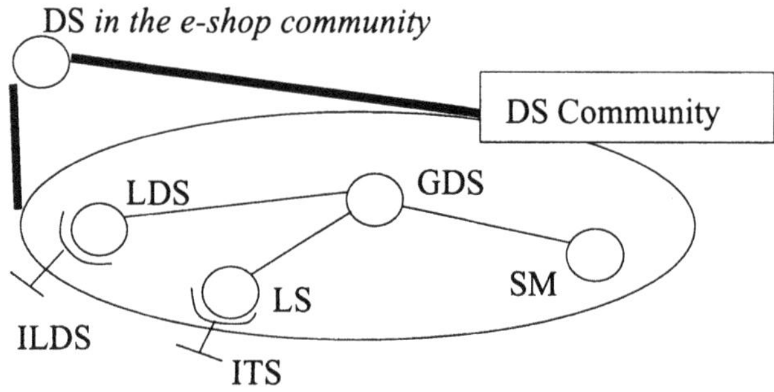

Figure 2. Relationships between a C-Object and its corresponding community

To define that the actions **package an order** and **deliver the package** are performed by the object fulfilling the role LDS, we define an interface role into the DS community that identifies these two actions. It should be noted that behavior identified by this role is only a part of the behavior already identified by the LDS roles of the community. This interface role we define is named ILDS for Interface of LDS. It expresses that the actions "package an order" and "deliver the package" specified in the behavior of the C-object fulfilling the DS role in the e-shop community is in fact achieved by an object fulfilling the LDS role in the DS community. To define that the action **trace an order** is performed by the object fulfilling the role TS, we define another interface role into the DS community that identifies this action. This interface role, named ITS, expresses that the action "trace an order" specified in the behavior of the C-Object fulfilling the DS role in the e-shop community is in fact achieved by an object fulfilling the TS role in the DS community. It should be noted that the DS role of the e-shop community is a composition of the interface roles of the DS community. By this way, dependencies between the two communities are well expressed.

2.4. Conclusion

RM-ODP standard proposes very useful concepts such as C-Object and interface roles for specifying the relationships between communities, that are themselves very useful to partition specifications. However, the standard does not mention any guideline for elaborating an Enterprise specification in using these concepts. By proposing our construction rules of an enterprise specification, we provide such a guideline helpful for building specifications that can be distributed between the designers, as demonstrated in our example. This illustrates the specification of the e-shop can be distributed in such a way that the DS Community building is under the responsibility of the Europe team while the Stock community building is achieved by the Japanese team and so on.

Using these concepts while applying the rules we defined enables the designers to maintain consistency of the whole specification. Each piece of the specification is clearly delimited (community concept) and can be independently defined once the interfaces between communities (c-object and interface role concepts) have been properly identified and expressed.

3. THE DISTRIBUTED SPECIFICATIONS MANAGEMENT SYSTEM (DSMS)

When developing a specification distributed in various locations, the concerned team in a location must be able to access to the other pieces of the specification developed by the other teams. Reciprocally, it must offer access to its own piece. Thus all pieces of the specification must be accessible for all the teams who handle them.

We then propose a Distributed Specifications Management System (DSMS) that is a repository enabling the management of specifications. A DSMS stores specifications and offers facilities to handle them. Since the project team working on the elaboration is distributed, then the DSMS is distributed too. More precisely, it is designed as a set of local repositories interconnected by a CORBA bus. A specification is then distributed among these repositories. Each local repository stores and manages the piece of specification of the local team. Each team can access the piece of another team, i.e., access a remote repository.

The figure 3 shows the specification of the e-shop distributed into three repositories.

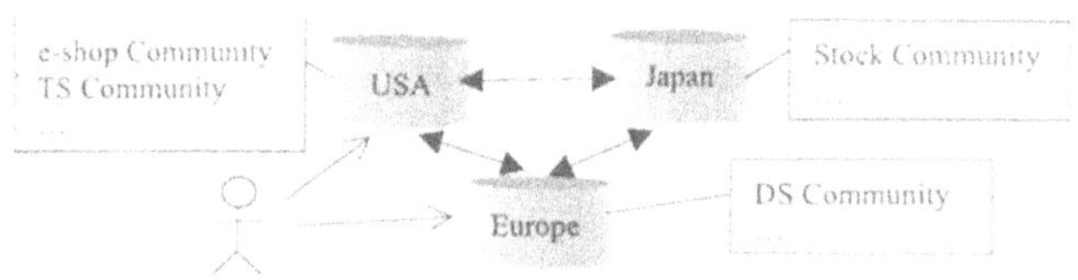

Figure 3. The e-shop specification in three repositories

Building a repository requires defining first how to encode the RM-ODP specifications and second how to provide the access to the repository. To address these two issues, our DSMS is built according to the MOF standard. We detail hereafter the use of the MOF standard we made in order to achieve the DSMS.

3.1. The MOF (Meta Object Facility)

The MOF is an OMG standard that defines mechanisms to handle meta-data [9]. Meta-data are data that describe other data. The MOF standard is mainly composed of two parts. The first part defines the so-called MOF model, that is a set of concepts needed to define the structure of meta-data. The main concepts defined in the MOF model are packages, classes, attributes and associations. This explains why the meta-model looks like UML class diagrams. The second part of the standard is a set of rules used to generate APIs for handling meta-data. These APIs are defined in IDL (Interface Description Language) [10]. They are generally used to build repositories.

3.2. Building an RM-ODP specifications repository

Our approach for the building of our RM-ODP specifications repository (i.e., the DSMS) in conformance with the MOF standard can be summarized as follows.

Advocating that specifications can be considered as meta-data, thus it is possible to define the structure of a specification in terms of a meta-model. As we deal with RM-ODP specifications, then we defined the structure of the RM-ODP specifications by building the so-called RM-ODP meta-model. Then we applied on it the rules to generate the repository APIs. Since APIs are described in IDL, we have implemented classes that realize the interfaces of the APIs.

To achieve these steps detailed hereafter, we have developed M3J, a tool dedicated to the construction of MOF compliant repositories.

3.2.1 The RM-ODP meta-model. The RM-ODP meta-model we built makes use of the MOF model concepts. The figure 4 illustrates a part of this meta-model. It is composed of five classes representing the RM-ODP concepts of Community, Role, Object, C-Object and Behavior. Relationships between these classes represent the relationships between the RM-ODP concepts as defined in the RM-ODP standard. For example, a relationship between Role and Behavior concepts expresses that a role identifies a behavior. For sake of simplicity, we do not represent here some elements of the meta-model, such as the multiplicity of the associations or the attributes of the classes.

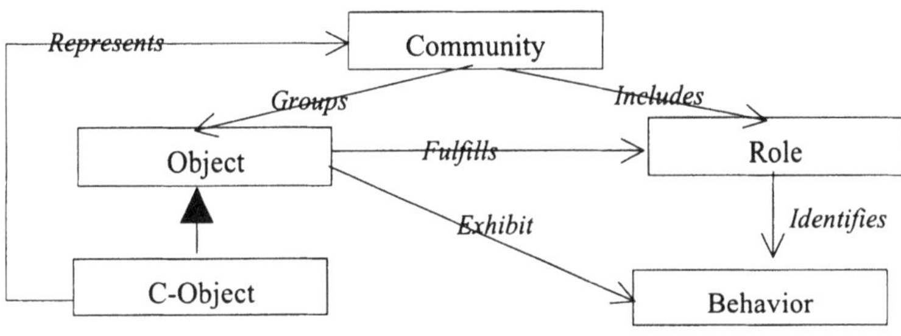

Figure 4. A part of the RM-ODP meta-model

The whole Enterprise RM-ODP is composed of 15 classes and defines the structure of the Enterprise RM-ODP specifications. It should be noted that this meta-model is a part of our contribution to the ISO working group elaborating the "RM-ODP Enterprise Language" standard, which is still in work.

3.2.2 The APIs and implementation classes generation. Rules defined in the MOF standard for generating the APIs generate two IDL interfaces for each class of the meta-model. One interface represents the instance of the concepts while the other represents a factory used to create instances.

For example, considering the Community concept, one interface named "Community" will represent the instance of a community. This interface will describe services to handle a community, such as the service "add_role" enabling the addition of a role in a community. The other interface named "Community-Class" will contain a service named "create_community" to create communities.

Moreover, an interface representing the repository itself is also generated. It describes services to obtain references to the factories. For example, the service "community_ref" enables to obtain the reference to the communities factory. The table1 presents a simplified version of the API of the repository.

Table 1. A simplified version of the API of the repository

interface Community {
add_role(in Role r);
add_object(in Object o);
...
};
	interface CommunityClass {
	Community create_community();
	...
	};

interface Object{
set_role(in Role r);
...
};
	interface ObjectClass {
	Object create_object();
	};

interface Repository{
CommunityClass community_ref();
Object object_ref();
...
};	

The APIs definition in IDL provides two advantages. First, the API is independent of any programming language, i.e., repositories can be compliant to the API while developed in any language such as Java or C. Secondly, repositories can be developed using CORBA and consequently can be distributed.

We make use of these benefits in developing our DSMS with CORBA and Java, thus a repository is composed of a set of CORBA objects. For example, let us consider an Enterprise RM-ODP specification composed of one community with three roles. Then, the repository storing this specification is composed of five CORBA objects, one representing the repository itself and four others representing the community and the three roles.

3.2.3 The M3J Tool. To implement the steps described above, we developed M3J, a tool dedicated to the construction of MOF compliant repositories [5][7]. M3J is a tool that proposes a graphic interface to elaborate MOF compliant meta-models. It provides IDL interface generation as specified by the rules defined in the MOF standard. It also provides generation of implementation classes. M3J has been developed in Java. The description of other tools with similar facilities can be found in [6][8].

3.3. Use of the an RM-ODP specifications repository

To illustrate how a set of repositories enables the management of distributed specifications, let us consider that in our example, we have three sites, respectively in the USA, in Europe and in Japan. Each of these sites implements a local repository as a CORBA object. Thus, there are three CORBA objects, each representing the Enterprise specifications repository of each location.

The USA team starts in building the e-shop community. For this, it uses the service "create_community" proposed by the "CommunityClass" interface (see table 1 the list of services of each interface corresponding to the concept). Then it creates the roles of the e-shop community using the "create_role" service of the "RoleClass" interface and adds the roles to the community using the "add_role" service of the "Community" interface. Then the USA teams creates the objects of the community using the "create_object" service of the "ObjectClass" interface and it links the objects to the roles using and the "set_role" service of the "Object" interface. For the C-Object, the "create_c_object" service of the "C_ObjectClass" interface is used.

The Europe team creates the DF community using the "create_community" service of its "CommunityClass" interface. As the DF community is represented by a CORBA object, the Europe team can export its reference towards the USA team. Getting this reference, the USA team can use the "set_community" service of the "C-Object" interface to set the link between the C-Object and its representing community, namely the DF community. The Europe team creates the interface roles, giving that the links between the C-Object and its interface roles are derived from the link between the C-Object and the represented community.

The figure 5 represents this part of the e-shop specification and the corresponding CORBA objects. The Enterprise specification is totally represented by CORBA objects and is distributed between the USA and Europe. The same mechanism can be applied to the complete specification and its distribution between the USA, Europe and Japan.

Figure 5. A part of the e-shop specification distributed over the USA and the Europe

4. CONCLUSION

Due to the fact that teams leading projects are more and more distributed and to the emergence of new paradigms such as the component paradigm, all specifications will be distributed in a few years. However, current technologies do not provide the mechanisms required in the elaboration of distributed specifications.

We identify that two aspects must be encompassed when dealing with distributed specifications. First, the modeling language must define some concepts to ensure the consistency of the distributed specification and secondly, some facilities must be available in order to manage and to handle the distributed specifications.

We then propose an approach to build Enterprise RM-ODP distributed specifications. It is based on the use of RM-ODP concepts and the definition of construction rules together with the provision of the M3J tool enabling the construction of an RM-ODP repository that is MOF compliant. Such a repository, also called DSMS, is based on CORBA. This enables interactions between remote repositories and thereby the provision of a distributed DSMS. Let us notice that M3J is more than an RM-ODP repository constructor. Actually, it enables the construction of any repository, which is MOF compliant. For example, this tool can be easily used to create a UML repository enabling the elaboration of UML distributed specifications.

This paper focused on the distribution aspects on the specification and illustrated how CORBA technology can be used to manage the distribution. However, other technologies are available and we have already investigated the building of repositories based on XML. For this, we use the XMI standard to generate the structure of the XML documents [5].

This work highlights the potential benefits of distributed specifications. It is particularly of interest to face the growing use of the component paradigm in the distributed software development. According to the approach presented in this paper, one can easily consider the storage of components specifications in repositories providing access facilities. Then, designers should be able to look at the description of a particular component. They could choose to get this specification in order to check if the component can be easily integrated or not.

References

[1] ISO/IEC, "ISO/IEC 10746-2 Information Technology Open Distributed Processing Reference Model: Foundations", 1996

[2] ISO/IEC, "ISO/IEC 10746-3 Information Technology Open Distributed Processing Reference Model: Architecture", 1996

[3] ISO/IEC "ISO/IEC 15414 Information Technology – Open Distributed Processing – Reference Model – Enterprise Language" Committee Draft Madrid 2000 Output 10 July 2000.

[4] P.F. Linington "An ODP approach to the development of large middleware systems" IFIP TC6 WG6.1 Second International Working Conference on Distributed Applications and Interoperable System (DAIS'99) June 28-July 1, 1999, Helsinki, Finland pp.61-74

[5] X. Blanc, M.P. Gervais and R. Le Delliou, *The Specifications Exchange Service of an RM-ODP Framework*, to appear in Proceedings of the 4th International Enterprise Distributing

Object Computing Conference (EDOC'00), IEEE Press (Ed), Makuharin, Japan, September 2000

[6] Unisys, Universal Repository (UREP), http://www.unisys.com

[7] X. Blanc "M3J Project Web Site", http://www.lip6.fr/meta/Projects/M3J

[8] DSTC, "dMOF 1.0 An OMG Meta Object Facility Implementation", http://www.dstc.edu.au/Products/CORBA/MOF/, 2000

[9] OMG "Meta Object Facility (MOF) Specification v1.3" TC. Document ad/99-09-05. OMG 1999. http://www.omg.org

[10] OMG "The Common Object Request Broker : Architecture and Specification v2.4" TC. Document ad/00-11-07 OMG 2000. http://www.omg.org

[11] OMG "XML Metadata Interchange (XMI) v1.1" TC. Document ad/99-10-02. OMG 1999. http://www.omg.org

[12] OMG "Unified Modeling Language Specification v1.3" TC. Document ad/00-03-01. OMG 2000. http://www.omg.org

[13] M.P. Gervais,"ODAC : une méthodologie de construction de systèmes à base d'agents fondée sur ODP", rapport LIP6 n°2000.028 (in French), novembre 2000, http://www.lip6.fr/reports/lip6.2000.028.html

IV

SHORT PAPERS I

ASPECTIX: A QUALITY-AWARE, OBJECT-BASED MIDDLEWARE ARCHITECTURE

Franz J. Hauck, Ulrich Becker, Martin Geier,
Erich Meier, Uwe Rastofer, Martin Steckermeier
Informatik 4, University of Erlangen-Nürnberg, Germany
http://www.aspectix.org/

Abstract: Quality of service is becoming more and more important in distributed systems. Current middleware systems lack quality-of-service support on the application and on the system level. *AspectIX* is a CORBA-compliant middleware platform that defines generic interfaces to control quality-of-service and an infrastructure for quality implementations. *AspectIX* is based on a fragmented object model that can provide transparent client-side quality implementations. Quality implementations can be weaved into functional fragments using a hierarchy of Weavelets which are modular code-transforming software components. A distributed policy decision engine allows administrators to influence object-internal decisions, e.g., decisions about how to implement the current quality-of-service requirements.

Keywords: Quality of Service, Middleware, Distributed Objects, Programming Models for Distributed Systems, CORBA, Policy-Enabled Application

1. INTRODUCTION

Quality of service (QoS) becomes more and more relevant for distributed applications. Not only do multimedia applications need a certain bandwidth and a well-defined delivery time, but also a broad variety of traditional applications asks for some quality in terms of accuracy, security, scalability, fault tolerance, and many more. Most middleware platforms today do not address quality of service: neither do they support applications in expressing their requirements on services or application components, nor do they provide mechanisms to integrate quality implementations into the system. Furthermore, distributed applications should adapt to domain-local policies that may prescribe certain quality levels and implementation mechanisms, e.g., a certain encryption algorithm for security reasons.

This paper introduces the ongoing research project *AspectIX* that is about the design and implementation of a quality-aware middleware platform on the basis of distributed objects.

2. THE ASPECTIX MIDDLEWARE

AspectIX is a CORBA-compliant middleware system [2]. Thus *AspectIX* supports distributed objects that can be transparently invoked in a distributed system. The interface of an object is described in CORBA IDL [6]. *AspectIX* integrates quality-of-service awareness on the basis of distributed objects. So, the clients of an object and the administrators of domains and applications may want to configure their requirements on an object's behavior. The object implementation in turn will consider those requirements and use various quality implementations to not only provide its functional behavior but also the requested quality.

2.1 Quality-of-Service Interface

The client interface of an *AspectIX* object has two additional methods that can be used to configure quality-of-service requirements. This QoS interface is generic, i.e., it is the same for every quality-aware object regardless which quality requirements and implementations are supported by the object.

For historical reasons, we name every category of quality an aspect of the functional object implementation. This relates to the term aspect of aspect-oriented programming [3]. On the basis of object references, a client can provide aspect-configuration objects that describe the quality-of-service requirements of the client with respect to certain aspects (e.g., one configuration object for configuring security, another one for fault tolerance). The client can investigate which aspect configurations are supported by the object. An object can immediately refuse to accept requirements if it cannot fulfill them.

If the object accepts the aspect-configuration objects of a client, it will implicitly promise to provide the corresponding quality of service. If an object implementation can no longer fulfill those requirements (e.g., because the network is currently congested) the client will be informed via a callback interface and an exception. In such a case, the client gets not only a list of the failing aspect configuration objects but also a set of alternative configurations. The latter can be influenced by the client by assigning priorities to the different aspect configuration objects. Configuration objects with higher priority will preferably not be changed compared to the current configuration whereas others with lower priority might be changed to compute an alternative configuration that the object implementation is able to fulfill.

Administrators can influence the QoS behavior of objects by providing so-called policy rules. Such rules contain small decision programs that provide a decision for a certain decision type, e.g., shall a communication link send encrypted messages and what encryption algorithms shall be used. As we will see later, the object will request those policy decisions and thus consider the administrators wishes, especially their demands on the QoS behavior of an object.

2.2 Application Programming Model

AspectIX adopts a partitioned or fragmented object model for programming applications. A distributed object is partitioned over multiple hosts. Every client that has bound to a distributed object gets a fragment of the object in its local address space. This fragment serves as a local access point to the object. The fragment will communicate with other fragments of the same object in order to locally implement the object's functionality. In case of modelling a standard CORBA object, most fragments have simply CORBA-stub behavior whereas there is one designated server fragment that is contacted by all the stub fragments.

When it comes to quality-of-service requirements by the client, a simple stub may be not enough, as it can only communicate with a single server using CORBA's remote invocation protocol. For several quality requirements there is a need for other protocols (e.g., real-time protocols) or for some communication with multiple other fragments (e.g., for implementing fault tolerance and scalability by replication).

The local fragment is dynamically loaded by the ORB when a client binds to an object the first time. This binding process is completely transparent to the client. A client just uses CORBA's standard binding techniques (`string_to_object` and reference passing via method calls). The local fragment implementation is also able to transparently replace itself by another implementation. Repositories and location services help in loading fragment implementations and in locating the other fragments of a particular object.

Client-side quality-of-service requirements can be expressed on a per-fragment basis. For the client, all object references to the same local fragment own the same set of aspect configuration objects. There may be multiple fragments of the same distributed object in a local address space, so that different requirements to the same object can be expressed by having an own fragment for each of them.

For all kinds of strategic decisions inside of the object's fragment implementations, a policy decision engine is consulted. Instead of hard-wiring decisions into the fragment code, they are strictly separated from the corresponding mechanisms and expressed as policy rules. For every necessary decision type, the fragment and object developers provide a dedicated policy rule that can decide eventually by considering system conditions and the result of queries to external services. The decision of those developer-provided rules can be delegated to policy rules from administrators. Thus, administrators are allowed to influence not only the quality-of-service but also the object's strategic behavior. We call this concept *policy-enabled application* [5].

2.3 Object-Based Quality Implementations

We assume that fragment implementations contain the quality implementations they need, e.g., consistency protocols for replication and encryption algorithms for security. By replacing the local fragment implementation, the distributed object may switch to alternative quality implementations according to current system conditions and client requirements.

However, interlocking the functional code with different quality implementations is intricate and requires deep knowledge of the quality implementation from the developer of a service. The *AspectIX* approach to that problem is to allow quality implementors to describe a code transformation process that converts quality-unaware functional code into a fragment implementation including the required quality implementations. The object developer just has to write the functional code which is then automatically converted to a fragment implementation. Of course, there is some need for additional parameters to be given by the object developer. Those can be used to control and influence the conversion process. Examples are the tagging of methods as read or write methods, the tagging of variables as transient or persistent, etc.

The code conversion is similar to the weaving process of aspect-oriented programming (AOP) [3]. With AOP, an aspect weaver generates code from both, a functional program and an aspect program. An aspect program contains the concise code for describing an aspect of the functional program which otherwise would need code scattered over the whole functional program. Thus, the aspect program compares to the additional parameters an object developer has to provide for generating fragment implementations. As weaving is a complex process, *AspectIX* supports the quality implementor in defining it. The weaving process is modularized in a hierarchical way. The units of composition are called Weavelets which are internally represented as objects. Elementary Weavelets are provided by the *AspectIX* code generator. They can add new code at the beginning or end of a method, add new variables, change parameters and exception declarations, etc. Complex Weavelets are built by using elementary and other composite Weavelets. A top-level Weavelet finally describes the complete process of integrating a certain quality implementation with functional code. Weavelets create not only code but also skeletons for the policy rules that are necessary to decide on the decision requests inserted into the quality implementations. The skeletons have to be filled with decision code by application developers. As an alternative, the decision code can be provided as additional information to the weaving process.

Still, the interlocking of the functional code with the quality implementations is an intricate process. However, instead of scattering quality implementations over the functional code, the application developers are asked to define the necessary weaving process. This process is expressed by Weavelets. Thus, the knowledge about the weaving process is collected, preserved, and can be reused for other applications. The definition of a weaving process will become the easier the more suitable Weavelet implementations already exist.

Inside of a fragment, the quality implementation has to provide means to monitor and react on changes of the current quality characteristics. This process is supported by *AspectIX* in form of so-called QoSlets. QoSlets are code sections that can be activated by internal events, e.g., on communication failures, incoming and outbound messages, time-triggered events, etc. A QoSlet manager takes care about the correct execution of QoSlets. An activated QoSlet implements certain reactions with respect to the required quality of service, e.g., re-establishing a communication link, metering and monitoring timing and usage behavior, etc. Thus, the code of many QoSlets can be reused in different environments and forms a building block for quality implementations. Special Weavelets can insert QoSlets and QoSlet managers into a fragment implementation and thus automate the integration process.

2.4 Middleware-Based Quality Implementations

Some quality-of-service implementations have to be put into the middleware or the operating system as they touch inherent system behavior like memory management, thread scheduling and communication protocols. So far, *AspectIX* only supports protocol modules that can be dynamically loaded into the ORB in order to adapt it to varying application demands.

To make protocol modules accessible from the application, AspectIX introduces the notion of communication end points (CEPs) that form a well-defined system-independent interface for communication via arbitrary protocols. So far three different kinds of CEPs are supported: message-based, connection-based and invocation-based CEPs.

The distributed policy decision service introduced in Section 2.2 provides the evaluation of policy rules on request of a fragment implementation or even of the system itself. The core of this service consists of a distributed rule base that distributes the necessary policy rules to every location on which a decision request may be necessary. The rule base maintains rules of administrators for all locations that belong to the administrators domain. Thus, domain-dependent decisions are supported.

3. CONCLUSION

We introduced *AspectIX*, a CORBA-compliant middleware system that supports quality-of-service on a per object basis. *AspectIX* compares to some related systems: *MAQS* [1] and *QuO* [7] also integrate quality-of-service implementations into CORBA, but do not have transparent object binding, if the object should immediately use quality implementations. *AspectIX* has transparent binding, as does the *Squirrel* system [4]. Unlike *Squirrel* and *QuO*, *AspectIX* has well-defined interfaces to negotiate quality-of-service requirements. Unlike any of the other systems, *AspectIX* especially supports automatic interlocking between functional and QoS implementation by a modular weaving process.

A complete prototype of *AspectIX* is still under construction. However, a first part, the *AspectIX* IDL compiler IDL*flex* will be released in May 2001. The prototype components have been developed entirely in Java. The current status of the project can be looked up at: `http://www.aspectix.org`.

REFERENCES

1. C. Becker, K. Geihs: Generic QoS specifications for CORBA. *Proc. of Kommunikation in Verteilten Systemen*—KiVS. Informatik aktuell. Springer, 1999.
2. F. J. Hauck, E. Meier, et.al.: A middleware architecture for scalable, QoS-aware and self-organizing global services. *Proc. of the USM Conf. 2000*. LNCS 1890, Springer, 2000.
3. G. Kiczales, J. Lamping, A. Mendhekar, C. Maeda, C. Lopes, J.-M. Loingtier, J. Irwin: Aspect-oriented programming. *Proc. of the ECOOP Conf.* LNCS 1241, Springer, 1997.
4. R. Koster, T. Kramp: Structuring QoS-supporting services with smart proxies. *Proc. of the Middleware 2000 Conf.*. LNCS 1795, Springer, 2000.
5. E. Meier, F. J. Hauck: *Policy-enabled applications*. Tech. Report TR-I4-99-05, IMMD IV, Univ. Erlangen-Nürnberg, July 1999.
6. Object Management Group, OMG: *The Common Object Request Broker: architecture and specification*. Rev. 2.4.2, OMG Doc. formal/01-02-33, Feb. 2001.
7. P. Pal, J. Loyall, R. Schantz, J. Zinky, R. Shapiro, J. Megquier: Using QDL to specify QoS-aware distributed (QuO) application configuration. *Proc. of the 3rd ISORC Symp.*, 2000.

PROVIDING MESSAGING INTEROPERABILITY IN FIPA COMMUNICATION ARCHITECTURE

Heikki Helin[1] and Stefano Campadello[2]
[1]*Sonera Corporation*
P.O.Box 970, FIN-00051 Sonera, Finland
Heikki.j.Helin@sonera.com
[2]*Nokia Research Center*
P.O.Box 407, FIN-00045 Nokia Group, Finland
Stefano.Campadello@nokia.com

Abstract We describe an on-going technical work done by FIPA standardization organization in the field of agent communication between heterogeneous FIPA agent platforms. The goal of this work is enabling flexible agent communication while providing sufficient interoperability. The flexibility is achieved by introducing several options for different layers of communication. Interoperability is assured by messaging gateways translating between incompatible options.

Keywords: Software Agent Technology, Agent Communication, Gateways, FIPA

1. INTRODUCTION

In a distributed system communications is an essential component. This is also true in the software agent systems where multiple agents are involved. In order to exchange the knowledge, agents should be able to communicate with each other. In the lower layers, the agent communication does not necessarily differ from the communication in traditional distributed systems. In fact, same transport protocols and messaging techniques as in modern distributed systems should be used. From the lower-layers point of view, agents are just sending data. What makes the software agent communication different from the communication in the traditional distributed systems is the usage of the agent communication languages (ACLs). Typically, the ACLs are based on a speech act theory: messages are actions—communicative acts—as they are intended to perform some action by virtue of being sent. In this paper we assume that agents do communicate with each other, using some ACL. Further, we assume that, at some level, the communication fails due to certain incompatibilities.

FIPA[1] is a non-profit standardization organization promoting development and specification of generic agent technologies. FIPA has specified several communication options in order to enable flexible communication in environments with different characteristics. For example, wireless environments are taken into account in FIPA communication model. Since wireless environments typically have significantly different characteristics than wireline environments, most of the communication layers have an option tailored for wireless environments.

Having various options obviously decreases the direct interoperability, as the message originator cannot assume that the destination understands the protocols and encoding the sender uses. In order to achieve reasonable interoperability between domains using different communication means, interoperability gateways can be used. These gateways translate between message transport protocols and encoding of message components where direct end-to-end interoperability is impossible, impractical or undesirable.

Mediators and gateways have been used in various architectures. In WAP architecture [13], the WAP-gateway translates between various layers in the WAP communication stack and Internet protocols. In the CORBA architecture, similar gateways are called "half-bridges" [12]. Additionally, application level proxies or gateways are used in many architectures where wireless and wireline environments are combined (see for example [10, 11]).

The rest of this paper is structured as follows. In Section 2 we give an overview of messaging in the FIPA communication architecture. Section 3 presents the concept of FIPA messaging interoperability gateway. Finally, Section 4 concludes the paper.

2. MESSAGING IN FIPA ARCHITECTURE

At the heart of the FIPA's model for the agent systems is agent communication, where agents can pass semantically meaningful messages to one another. Figure 1 depicts layered model of the FIPA agent communication. The transport protocol layer and Message Transport Protocol (MTP) layer provide together basic messaging between agents or agent platforms. These layers are not independent. In FIPA, there are three options for MTP: IIOP [7], HTTP [6], and WAP [8]. Each of the MTPs implicitly or explicitly also defines the transport protocol. The message envelope layer provides the communication stack with MTP independent message delivery information (e.g., how message should be routed, etc.). For the message envelope, three encoding options are specified: XML [4], bit-efficient [5], and one which concrete representation is defined in terms of an IDL interface [7]. The ACL layer defines both the semantics and

[1]Foundation for Intelligent Physical Agents; http://www.fipa.org

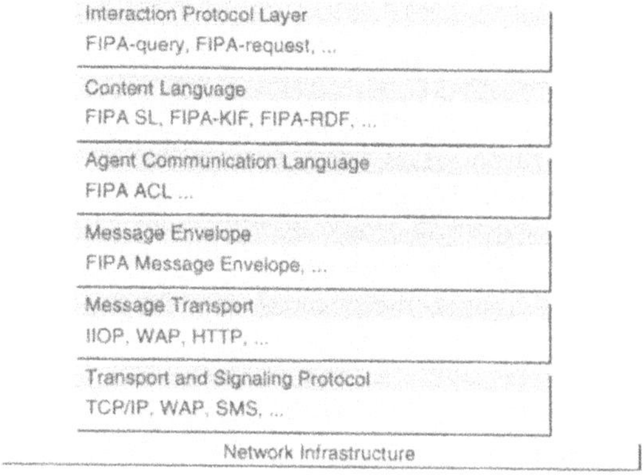

Interaction Protocol Layer
FIPA-query, FIPA-request, ...
Content Language
FIPA SL, FIPA-KIF, FIPA-RDF, ...
Agent Communication Language
FIPA ACL ...
Message Envelope
FIPA Message Envelope, ...
Message Transport
IIOP, WAP, HTTP, ...
Transport and Signaling Protocol
TCP/IP, WAP, SMS, ...
Network Infrastructure

Figure 1. Communication layers in FIPA architecture

the syntax for ACL messages. FIPA has defined three encoding options for its ACL [1, 2, 3]. FIPA-ACL defines only the outer language used in communication, but not the actual content of the message. For example, on the ACL level, the sender defines the type of the message, for example "request", but does say nothing about the action, which should be performed by the receiver. For this purpose, FIPA has specified several content languages (see [9] for details). Lastly, agent communication typically falls into common patterns (conversation layer). In the FIPA specifications, these are called interaction protocols. An interaction protocol defines a common pattern of conversations used to perform a task.

For successful direct end-to-end interoperability both the sender and the receiver should agree on the MTP and the encoding of various message components. Given that there are three options for MTP-, message envelope-, and ACL-layers, there are in total 27 combinations that can be used. The choices for the content language increase the number of combinations even more. In practice, however, the situation is better. For example, if HTTP is used as MTP, the message envelope and the ACL are typically encoded using XML.

3. MESSAGING INTEROPERABILITY GATEWAYS

In some cases direct end-to-end interoperability is impossible, impractical or undesirable. Obviously it is impossible when communicating platforms/agents do not support any common message transport protocol or encoding of FIPA-message component. Direct end-to-end interoperability might be impractical, for example, when communicating over a slow wireless link and the peer at the fixed network does not support message transport protocol suitable for wireless links.

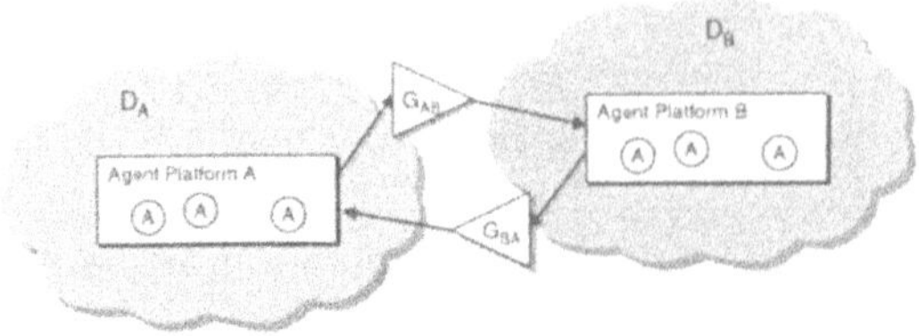

Figure 2. Gateways between incompatible domains D_A and D_B

Messaging interoperability gateways are needed in order to provide sufficient interoperability in different communication layers using different protocols or encodings. In this paper, we are interested in messaging gateways, but there might other type of gateways as well (e.g., gateways that translate between heterogeneous directory services).

Messaging interoperability gateways are logically situated between agent platforms belonging to different domains. Figure 2 depicts two agent platforms A and B belonging to domains D_A and D_B respectively. They employ the gateway G_{AB} in communication from A to B and the G_{BA} in communication from B to A.

Logical reference model of a gateway comprises four levels (Figure 3). A gateway on a given level is defined as a function that translates from a source protocol or encoding to a target protocol or encoding, respectively. At the lowest level of the reference model, translation between message transport protocols is performed. On the second level, the translation between concrete representation of the message envelope is performed. Similarly, third and fourth levels are for the ACL and the content language translations, respectively. Additionally, the gateway might perform translations between representations of the application data. This, however, is not a concern of FIPA. A gateway implementing the translation function from a to b is not required to implement the inverse function, although this might be the typical case.

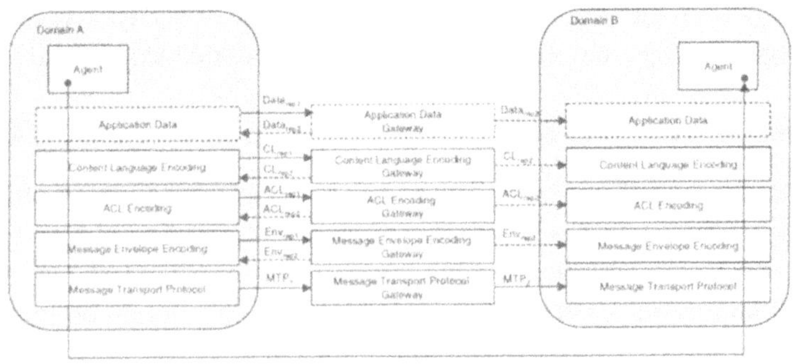

Figure 3. Reference model for messaging interoperability gateway

The communicating agents or agent platforms can request the messaging gateway service in two ways. Firstly, an agent that recognizes that it cannot directly communicate with its peer (which can be either the destination agent platform or some third party agent platform in between) asks the gateway to perform the necessary translations. The agent can both send the message to the gateway and implicitly ask the gateway to forward the message, or the agent can ask the gateway to perform the necessary translations and return the translated message back. Obviously, the latter method cannot be used in the case of the MTP translation. Secondly, an agent that knows that it can handle only specific encoding can request the gateway to perform necessary translations for each incoming message. For example, an agent that is situated in a mobile device, can request some gateway at the fixed network to translate all the incoming messages to a format which is suitable for the wireless link.

4. CONCLUSIONS

Flexible messaging is a desired feature in any communication architecture. We presented briefly the FIPA communication architecture and introduced the concept of a messaging interoperability gateway. FIPA has standardized flexible communication architecture, but in many cases direct end-to-end interoperability is impossible, impractical, or undesirable. Therefore, messaging interoperability gateways are needed.

A messaging interoperability gateway is able to translate between FIPA message transport protocols as well as between different concrete encoding of various FIPA message parts. At the time of writing, the standardization work in this area has just begun. The experimental standard is expected to be released in the beginning of the year 2002.

The security is an important issue that has to be addresses in the context of messaging interoperability gateways. This, however, is something that we have not yet considered thoroughly.

Acknowledgments

The authors express their thanks to the rest of the members of the FIPA Gateways Technical Committee, especially to Michael Berger, Kari Koivuniemi, Heimo Laamanen, Mikko Laukkanen, Jamie Lawrence, Milla Mäkeläinen, Satoshi Nishiyama, John Shepherdson, and Santtu Toivonen.

References

[1] Foundation for Intelligent Physical Agents. *FIPA ACL Message Representation in Bit-Efficient Specification.* Geneva, Switzerland, October 2000. Specification number XC00069.

[2] Foundation for Intelligent Physical Agents. *FIPA ACL Message Representation in String Specification.* Geneva, Switzerland, November 2000. Specification number XC00070.

[3] Foundation for Intelligent Physical Agents. *FIPA ACL Message Representation in XML Specification.* Geneva, Switzerland, October 2000. Specification number XC00071.

[4] Foundation for Intelligent Physical Agents. *FIPA Agent Message Transport Envelope Representation in XML Specification.* Geneva, Switzerland, November 2000. Specification number XC00085.

[5] Foundation for Intelligent Physical Agents. *FIPA Agent Message Transport Envelope Representation in Bit Efficient Specification.* Geneva, Switzerland, November 2000. Specification number PC00088.

[6] Foundation for Intelligent Physical Agents. *FIPA Agent Message Transport Protocol for HTTP Specification.* Geneva, Switzerland, October 2000. Specification number XC00084.

[7] Foundation for Intelligent Physical Agents. *FIPA Agent Message Transport Protocol for IIOP Specification.* Geneva, Switzerland, November 2000. Specification number XC00075.

[8] Foundation for Intelligent Physical Agents. *FIPA Agent Message Transport Protocol for WAP Specification.* Geneva, Switzerland, October 2000. Specification number XC00076.

[9] Foundation for Intelligent Physical Agents. *FIPA Content Languages Specification.* Geneva, Switzerland, October 2000. Specification number XC00007.

[10] S. Hadjiefthymiades and L. Merakos. A survey of web architectures for wireless communication environments. *Journal of Universal Computer Science*, 5(7):390–417, 1999.

[11] J. Jing, A. S. Helal, and A. Elmagarmid. Client-server computing in mobile environments. *ACM Computing Surveys*, 31(2):117–157, 1999.

[12] Object Management Group. *The Common Object Request Broker: Architecture and Specification*, 1999. formal/99-10-07. Version 2.3.1.

[13] WAP Forum. Wireless Application Environment Overview, Version 1.2, November 1999.

ARCHITECTURAL DESIGN AND PERFORMANCE ASPECTS OF DEVELOPING APPLICATIONS BASED ON MIDDLEWARE

Alexander Schill, Olaf Neumann, Christoph Pohl, Thomas Müller
TU Dresden, Fakultät Informatik, 01062 Dresden
{schill|neumann|pohl|muellet}@rn.inf.tu-dresden.de

Abstract For quite some time now, applications have been designed and developed in various projects of our research group by using middleware. In addition, various middleware products have been evaluated. An existing client/server system has been converted to EJB. The subject of this paper will be the results of these studies, along with the characteristics of the analyzed servers other concepts and related work.

Keywords: Enterprise JavaBeans, EJB, Performance

1. PERFORMANCE RESULTS

In the course of the performance analyses, the use of single servers and clustered application servers has been tested. Three commercial servers have been considered: Inprise Application Server [4], BEA WebLogic Server, and IBM Websphere.

As testing environment, the NT-Lab at the Chair of Computer Networks at the University of Science and Technology, Dresden, was used. This consists of several Dual-Pentium computers 766Mhz, 512MB that are interconnected via a switched 100Mbit LAN. The operating system used was Windows NT 4.0SP6a. On all application servers, an IBM Universal Database 7.0, powered by the jdbc.db2.net.Driver an XA-capable JDBC2.0 driver was used for efficient data access.

Special attention was given to providing as identical conditions as possible for testing the individual servers [1, 2, 3]. Therefore, the same test data and configurations were used.

Prior to a discussion of the performance comparison, some special aspects of the application servers shall be mentioned.

1.1. Deployment

All of the tested servers provided a graphical tool for creating deployment descriptors and supporting the actual deployment. In most cases, these tools are easy to use. However, they are not very efficient in the developing process of EJBs as the beans used in this process have to be re-deployed occasionally. In such cases it proved to be more helpful to perform script-controlled deployment, if that is supported by the server.

1.1.1 BEA Weblogic Server. To control the deployment, either a graphical tool or the command line can be used. The graphical tool should be used for the first configuration because it allows for an easy creation of the deployment descriptors. However, occasional crashs of this tool complicated routine work. Once the descriptors have been created, performing the deployment using the command-line can save a lot of time. To deploy the beans the next time the server is started, these have to be added to the file weblogic.properties. One could actually use the console for hot-deployment, or re-deploy already deployed beans at runtime, but these changes would only be valid while the server is running. Thus, it is always necessary to write the changes to the file weblogic.properties.

1.1.2 Inprise Application Server. Deployment is also performed with the help of the graphical console. The user can decide whether to comply more or less strongly with the J2EE standards. After deployment has been performed, it is possible to create a client-Jar containing the stubs needed. If a bean has been deployed, it exists even after the server has been restarted; it can only be removed if it is explicitly deleted from the server via the console.

1.1.3 IBM Websphere Application Server. Deployment in Websphere is rather slowly, both in regard to the steps necessary prior to deploying and the actual deployment process. The server allows deployment of several beans in one JAR simultaneously. In our tests, this simplification failed every time, so that each bean had to be deployed individually. After successful deployment, the beans are anchored in the server even after a restart. Websphere makes use of the serialized deployment-descriptors of EJB-version 1.0. As the descriptors have to be newly created, this interferes with one major objective of the J2EE standard: the reusability of the individual components. The internal deployment tool has been used to cope with this problem. This tool, however, is rather unstable and produces arbitrary errors. Moreover, changing the configuration requires a restart of the container, or the web-engine, which is rather time-consuming.

1.2. Clustering

All of the tested servers offer clustering to support fail-over and load-balancing. Even though these features have been differently realized on the respective servers, the basic concepts are very similar. Clustering can be performed on at least two levels. For one thing, it can be realized by distributing the requests of the servlets, i.e. on the web-level, for another, directly on the level of the EnterpriseBeans.

1.2.1 BEA Weblogic Server. Using replica-aware stubs, EJB's are automatically clustered on the Weblogic server. This can be easily configured. All one has to do is to start several servers so that they can be clustered. These servers must deploy the same beans under the same JNDI-names. It is important to remember that the ability to cluster is made possible by setting a property of the beans. For load-balancing, different procedures such as round-robin (standard), weight-based round robin, random, and parameter-based routing can be used. Parameter-based clustering requires the creation of a call-router that forwards the different calls to the corresponding server-instances.

1.2.2 Inprise Application Server. Clustering is realized via the JNDI-service. Only one instance of the name server is started in the cluster that is to be created. In order to achieve a fail-over of the name servers, these can also be started in a master-slave procedure. This distributes client requests among server instances according to the round-robin method. It is required that beans on the individual servers are addressable by identical JNDI-names and that the property vbroker.naming.propBindOn has been set to 1. Inprise supports clustering of Stateless Session Beans and claims to provide clustering of Statefull Session Beans via an additional Session State Service. However, the latter could not be verified in the current test, as no Stateful Session Beans were used.

1.2.3 IBM Websphere Application Server. The server supports clustering by means of an administrative database. All administration servers used in the cluster must use the same administrative database. Clones can be created based on a pre-configured application server. These clones can then be installed either on the same physical machine, or on other machines. In addition to the server clones, the EJBs must be WLM-enabled, i.e. so-called smart stubs for addressing the different servers must be installed on the client to allow load-balancing or fail-over, respectively. The methods round-robin and random can be used to distribute requests. These methods can be set to additionally include the option of preferring the local clone. Currently, IBM supports clustering of Stateless Session beans and servlets, or JSPs, while Statefull Session Beans are always assigned to a certain container.

1.3. Comparison

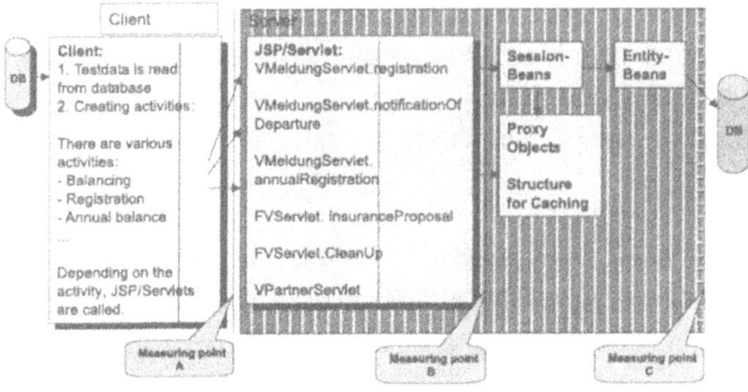

Figure 1. Measuring Points

For enabling a better evaluation of the various components' behavior, different measuring points have been implemented (see Figure 1).

Measuring point A determines the complete round trip time needed after an operation has been read from the database until the server has processed the request – including the time until to be displayed data has been received.

Measuring point B has been implemented in the servlets to determine processing times in the beans. This is actually not one single measuring point but rather several points where beans are called in the servlets.

Measuring point C determines the time needed for the internal processing in the database.

The figures of BEA and Inprise are about the same level. Inprise takes only slightly more time, and also shows leveling. Websphere consumes considerably more time. More precisely, IBM's round trip is longer especially for logic processing in the beans.

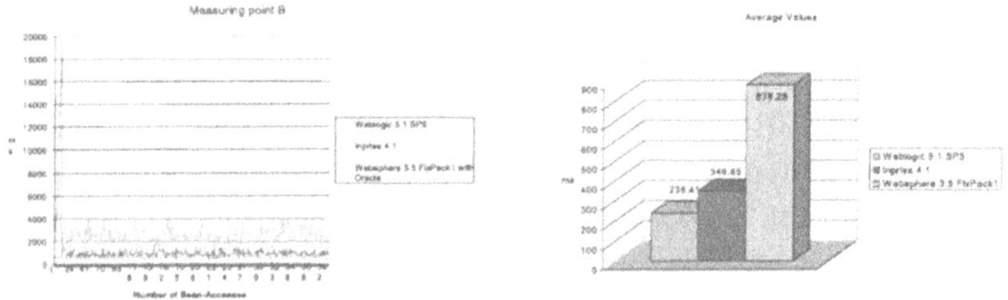

Figure 2. Results of Measure Point B. *Figure 3.* Average Values of Point C.

The diagram shown in Figure 3 summarizes the average measured results of the test in measuring point A. While Websphere needs about four times longer than BEA, Inprise's results are very similar to those of BEA. Even if the leveling behavior of Inprise is taken into account, it shows a slightly worse performance compared to BEA. In this example, measurings have been performed for 100 users. Unfortunately, even with such a small number server errors still occured. Inprise regularly stopped with an OutOfMemoryException that could not be corrected by increasing the memory assigned to the JVM, thus suggesting a server-internal memory problem. IBM could not complete some transactions because of internal, incomprehensible OSE problems. Both on IBM and BEA servers, tests have been run with 1,000 users. However, due to the errors results are not comparable.

2. RELATED WORK

This paper describes different aspects in the design process of applications with EJB. Furthermore, it gives details about the performance of a complex application. The comparison [11] and [12] as well as other benchmarks such as [10] give mostly an overview of server properties. Exact performance results can be found in [10]. Nevertheless, there are few publicly available facts about complex systems. A major problem about complex system evaluation is the mutual dependency of results, i.e. resources and components depend not only on equal component types. Although there are some good sources about patterns like [9], it is often not evident how to apply these concepts to real world applications based on EJB. A goal of this paper was to provide some contributions towards these aspects.

References

[1] Auswahl eines EJB-Applikations-Servers - Java-Spektrum 2/2000 S.12

[2] Special Interest Group - Enterprise JavaBeans - http://www.mgm-edv.de/ejbsig/

[3] Application Server Comparison Matrix - http://www.flashline.com/components/appservermatrix.jsp

[4] Inprise Applikation Server - Java Magazin 2/1999 S.71

[5] Read all about EJB 2.0 http://www.javaworld.com/javaworld/jw-06-2000/jw-0609-ejb.html

[6] Enterprise JavaBean Persistence 101 - http://www.sdmagazine.com/articles/2000/0004/0004b/0004b.htm

[7] Enterprise JavaBean Persistence 201 - http://www.sdmagazine.com/articles/2000/0004/0004c/0004c.htm

[8] Eberhard Wolff: EJB und das Java-Typsystem – Java Spektrum 6/2000 S. 62

[9] EJB DesignPatterns http://www.c2.com/cgi/wiki?EjbDesignPatterns

[10] http://nenya.ms.mff.cuni.cz/thegroup/EJBCOMP/ejb-public.pdf

[11] http://www.networkcomputing.com/1022/1022f2.html

[12] http://www.informationweek.com/759/java.htm

MANAGING EVOLUTION IN TELECOMMUNICATION SYSTEMS

G.Koutsoukos[1], J.Gouveia[1], L.Andrade[1,2], J.L.Fiadeiro[2,3]
[1] *Oblog Software S.A.*
Alameda António Sérgio 7, 2795 Linda-a-Velha, PORTUGAL
{gkoutsoukos,jgouveia,landrade}@oblog.pt
[2] *ATX Software S.A.*
Alameda António Sérgio 7, 2795 Linda-a-Velha, PORTUGAL
[3] *Department of Informatics*
Faculty of Sciences, University of Lisbon, Campo Grande, 1700 Lisboa, PORTUGAL
jose@fiadeiro.org

Abstract Recent advances in telecommunication technology, including wireless networks and the Internet, along with the competition of network operators for offering advanced and different services, are putting increasing pressure for building telecommunication software systems that are adaptive to new requirements and easily reconfigurable, even in run time. We propose a new modelling primitive – coordination contract – that we have developed and applied to other applications domains, as a means to provide an effective solution to this problem. We briefly describe coordination contracts and discuss how they can support the evolution of the specifications of the Wireless Application Protocol (WAP) Datagram layer.

Keywords: Component-based frameworks, Coordination, Evolution, Telecommunication Systems, Object-Oriented design, Reconfigurability, Scalability, Wireless Application Protocols

1. INTRODUCTION

Technology and system requirements in the telecommunications domain are changing very rapidly. Over the previous years, since the transition from analog to digital communications, and from wired to wireless networks, different standards and solutions have been adopted, implemented and modified, often to deal with new and different business requirements. Today, more and more, telecommunication network operators strive to provide new advanced services in an attractive and usable way. However, time-to-market is a business decision that can be severely conditioned by the capacity of systems to accommodate changes quickly and with minimum impact on the services already implemented. This challenge is often difficult to be met by hardware-based systems because hardware cannot be easily modified and integrated.

On the other hand, thanks to the explosive growth of the Internet and the emergence of wireless data technologies, we are witnessing a major shift from hardware to software-based systems in this sector. This is because more and more applications must process data and information, a task that is easier to be performed on software. Therefore, it is not surprising that, due to their popularity in more traditional software application domains, object-oriented development techniques are becoming a standard in the telecommunications software industry. However, for reasons we put forward in [1], it is now widely accepted that, although OO techniques such as inheritance and clientship make it easier to build systems, their support for evolution in general, and the ability of systems to exhibit the agility required by the volatility of business domains in particular, is quite limited. Yet, the ability to change is now much more important than the ability to create systems in the first place. Change has become a first-class design goal that requires functional and technical architectures whose components can be added, replaced and reconfigured dynamically.

In this paper, we argue that the modelling primitive – coordination contract – that we developed for superposing coordination mechanisms over existing components [1] can be applied to telecommunication systems in order to achieve increased flexibility and agility in reacting to change. By borrowing concepts and techniques from Reconfigurable Distributed Systems and Software Architectures, coordination contracts provide the ability for interactions between objects to be modelled as first-class entities and for changes that require a reconfiguration of such interactions to be performed without having to change the objects involved. Through an example related to the modelling of the Wireless Application Protocols, we discuss how coordination contracts can support such forms of evolution.

2. COORDINATION CONTRACTS

In general terms, a coordination contract is a connection that is established between a group of objects (participants), where rules and constraints are superposed on the behaviour of the participants, which determines a specific form of interaction. The way such an interaction is established between the partners is more powerful than what can be achieved within OO languages because it relies on the mechanism of *superposition* as developed for parallel and distributed system design [3]. When a call is made from a client object to a supplier object, the contract "intercepts" the call and *superposes* whatever forms of behaviour it prescribes. In order to provide the required levels of pluggability, neither the client, nor any other object in the system, needs to know what kind of coordination is being superposed. To enable that, a contract design pattern, presented in [2], allows coordination contracts to be superposed on given objects in a system to coordinate their behaviour without having to modify the way the objects are implemented (black box view). In general terms, a coordination contract is defined as follows:

```
contract class <name>
participants <list of partners>
constraints <the invariant the partners should satisfy>
attributes <private to the contract attributes>
operations <private to the contract operations>
coordination <interaction with partners>
end class
```

where each interaction under a coordination rule is of the form:

```
< name > when < trigger >
       with < condition >
       do < set of actions >
```

The condition under "when" establishes the trigger of the interaction. The trigger can be a condition on the state of the participants, a request for a particular service, or an event on one of the participants. The "do" clause identifies the reactions to be performed, usually in terms of actions of the partners and some of the contract's own actions. When the trigger corresponds to a request for an operation, three types of actions may be superposed on the execution of the operation: actions to be performed *before* the operation, a *replace* action which is performed instead of the operation (alternative) and actions that are performed *after* the operation. The "with" clause puts further constraints on the execution of the actions involved in the interaction. If any condition under the "with" clause is not satisfied none of these actions is executed. More details and references to other papers on the semantics and applications of coordination contracts can be found in [1,2].

3. THE WAP DATAGRAM PROTOCOL

The Wireless Application Protocol (WAP) is the latest attempt of the telecommunications industry to specify an application framework and network protocols for wireless devices with the main objective of bringing Internet content and advanced data services to digital cellular phones and other wireless terminals.A detailed description of the WAP architecture is presented in [4].

WAP layers are designed to operate over a variety of different bearer services supported by the various network types, i.e the data transport mechanisms used to carry data between two devices. For instance, WAP layers can operate over services such as GSM GPRS, CDMA CSD and so on. This functionality is accomplished in the layer referred to as the Wireless Datagram Protocol (WDP) [5]. WDP provides a common interface to the upper layers (Security, Session, and Application) of the protocol stack so that they are able to function independently of the underlying wireless network. This is achieved by adapting the transport layer to specific features of the underlying bearer. Therefore, the WAP layers architecture can, in fact, be considered as a 3 layered architecture of the upper layers, the underlying bearers and their interface (WDP).

In general terms, WDP has to perform 3 tasks: port addressing by assigning port numbers (identify the higher layer entity above WDP), segmentation of datagrams and re-assembly of packets and error reporting. Discussing the way WDP performs these tasks is out of the scope of this paper. The reader can consult [5] for more details. However, it is clear that the list of supported bearers will change over time with new bearer types and services being added as the wireless market evolves (projection made by WapForum in [4], pg 17). Moreover, specifications keep changing in order to improve the protocol, making relevant modifications to the implementation of the interface level (WDP) needed in order to continue offering transparent services to the upper layers of the WAP stack. Therefore, WDP must be flexible enough to accommodate the changes in the underlying level quickly and with minimum impact on the services already implemented.

4. COORDINATING WDP COMPONENTS

We will now discuss how the flexibility required on the WDP can be achieved using a contract based development methodology. As far as the evolution of bearers is concerned, a generic architecture of our proposal is shown below.

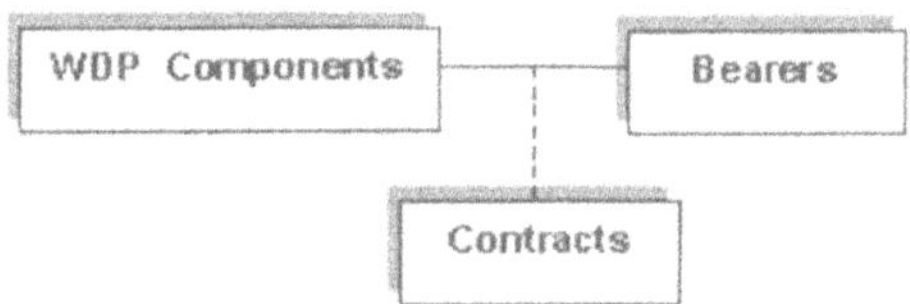

The WDP components correspond to the parts of the WDP layer that are identical for all bearer services supported by WDP. This means that they are computationally identical. However, their conditions for execution are different according to the underlying bearer. The WDP components can be implemented as "black boxes". It is the responsibility of the contracts to coordinate the behaviour of such components according to the specific requirements of a bearer service. When a new bearer (type or service) is to be added to the ones already supported by WAP, new contracts will be added to the system to support that bearer. As a result, the already implemented WDP components will remain unchanged, thus allowing support for the evolution of requirements and achieving software reuse.

Consider, for instance, the segmentation case. As already stated, WDP has to provide for segmentation and re-assembly of datagrams in a bearer dependent way. A datagram is a unit of information that consists of header fields and data fields. However, from the segmentation point of view, a datagram can be considered as a sequence of bits that is split into a number of packets being transmitted over the network. From the evolution point of view, the issue in segmentation is that the resulting packets must be of a size and format consistent with the underlying network service.

In a conventional design in which segmentation is implemented in different components in a bearer dependent way, the required evolution would be difficult to be achieved in a compositional way. However, contracts provide a very flexible solution to the problem. Consider a design in which a class Segmentation d9efines an operation Segment(Datagram) to perform the segmentation of a datagram into a number of packets. The Segmentation class and Segment are defined in such a way that they provide the necessary computational functionality that is common for all or some bearer types or services. All bearer specific features of segmentation, such as packet size, encoding of packets and so on are modelled in contracts. Each contract corresponds to a bearer service and is responsible for coordinating the segmentation operation according to the underlying bearer requirements. For instance, *GSM_Service_Segmentation* below could be the definition of a contract that is superposed on the Segmentation operation in order to support a GSM bearer service. The contract sets the maximum packet size for segmentation to be equal to the size required by the GSM Service. Moreover, it defines some operations for encoding the packet headers according to the particular GSM Service requirements. Additional operations or actions may be required based on more "low-level" design decisions.

```
contract class GSM_Service_Segmentation
constants gsm_N :Integer // number of bits per packet in the GSM service
participants x:  Segmentation;
operations GSM_Service_Ref_Encod(int);
coordination
   when * -- >> x.Segment(Datagram) AND NETWORK.bearer_type:="GSM_Service";
   with Datagram.data !=NULL;
   do  before   x.Size = gsm_N;
       after    for (int i=0, i<size (x.List_Packets), i++)
                x.List_Packets[i].ref_number=
                   GSM_Service_Ref_Encod(x.List_Packets[i].ref_number)
end contract
```

When a new service is added to the protocol, a new contract will be added to the system in a "plug and play" mode to support that service. This allows for the *Segmentation* component already defined and all client components using *Segmentation* to remain unchanged. It is also important to note that the condition specified by the keyword AND under the "when" clause checks whether the network service is the correct one. This is accomplished by using a *NETWORK* global component, defined only for illustrative purposes. If the condition is false, it may be possible for another contract, imposed on Segmentation and concerning another network type, to be executed. In that way, support for dynamic network reconfiguration may be achieved. This is an application of contracts that we intend to further investigate in the future. Finally, it should be mentioned that similar designs exist for the other operations of WDP as well as for telecommunications systems in general, but due to space limitations are not presented in this paper.

5. CONCLUDING REMARKS

The telecommunications sector is being governed by the expeditious growth of two networking technologies: the wireless data and the Internet. This growth has fuelled the creation of new and exciting information services and resulted in a major shift from hardware to software as far as the implementation of telecommunication systems is concerned. However, under this increasing pressure for new sophisticated services, and with the frequent adoption of new standards, software development in telecommunications cannot rely solely on traditional OO development techniques such as inheritance and clientship. We believe that the only hope for telecommunication organisations to be able to face the challenges of the fast market and technology evolution is to follow the emerging trend in software analysis and design based on predefined frameworks of skeletal applications, components, and design patterns that can be easily customized and integrated.

In this paper, we proposed the contract-based development methodology described in [1] as a discipline that can be applied when developing telecommunications systems in order to support the evolution of system requirements and achieve software reuse. We supported our view by briefly discussing how contracts can provide a compositional structuring mechanism with respect to changes occurring due to the evolution of specifications of the Wireless Application Protocol Datagram Layer. Based on our experience in applying the contract-based methodology in other domains, we believe that by adopting coordination contracts when building telecommunications systems increased levels of flexibility and reuse will be achieved.

Acknowledgments

Some of the ideas presented in this paper were developed as part of the first author's MSc thesis at King's College, University of London, September 2000, who would like to thank Prof. Tom Maibaum for his valuable guidance and comments.

References

[1] L.F.Andrade and J.L.Fiadeiro, "Coordination Technologies for Managing Information System Evolution", in *Proc. CAISE'01*, A.Geppert (ed), LNCS, Springer-Verlag 2001.

[2] J.Gouveia, G.Koutsoukos, L.Andrade and J.L.Fiadeiro, "Tool Support for Coordination-Based Software Evolution", in *Technology of Object-Oriented Languages and Systems – TOOLS 38*, W.Pree (ed), IEEE Computer Society Press 2001, 184-196.

[3] S.Katz, "A Superimposition Control Construct for Distributed Systems", in ACM TOPLAS 15(2), 1993, 337-356.

[4] The WapForum. "The WAP Architecture Specification", Version 30th April 1998 http://www.wapforum.org/what/technical.htm.

[5] The WapForum. "The WAP Wireless Datagram Protocol Specification", Version 19th Feb 2000, http://www.wapforum.org/what/technical.htm.

MOBILITY MANAGEMENT FOR PROVIDING QOS IN LOCAL AREA WIRELESS NETWORKS

J. Antonio García-Macías, Franck Rousseau, Gilles Berger-Sabbatel, Leyla Toumi, Andrzej Duda
LSR-IMAG Laboratory, Grenoble, France
{amacias, rousseau, gberger, toumi, duda}@imag.fr

1. INTRODUCTION

The purpose of this paper is to present our current work on mobility support integrated with QoS mechanisms in a wireless local area network. Such an environment becomes increasingly important with the emergence of ubiquitous mobile devices connected via wireless LANs and the development of future wireless telecommunication services such as UMTS. They contribute to the emergence of new real-time multimedia applications such as voice and video, networked games, or cooperative work that require better quality of service than current *Best Effort*. Integration of mobility with QoS support is a difficult challenge because of specific radio channel characteristics and complexity of mobility management.

Our approach is based on QoS mechanisms at the IP layer—*Differentiated Services (DiffServ)* [2]. We extend them to a wireless LAN environment so that we can provide consistent end-to-end quality of service to mobile hosts. If we want to support QoS for mobile hosts, we need to rethink our approach to mobility management. As the DiffServ QoS management is done at the IP level, we have to manage mobility also at the IP level, so that both issues can be addressed in an integrated way. However, the traditional approach to mobility at the IP level—Mobile IP [5, 6] does not take into account QoS requirements. Moreover, it is unsuitable for integration with QoS mechanisms because of its high overhead: triangular routing, address translation, and complex interaction between agents [3].

In our approach, we limit the scope of mobility management to a local subnetwork of wireless cells—we think that coupling QoS with mobility management makes sense only in such a case. We use a micro-mobility scheme implemented in the IPv6 layer with fast hand-offs between adjacent cells. It is the right level to deal with local mobility, because mobility is essentially a routing problem. Micro-mobility avoids address translation, traffic tunneling, and accelerates hand-offs. Coupled with the QoS management, it contributes to the overall end-to-end performance. A mobile station may decide to hand-off to an adjacent cell based on the current channel characteristics (signal to noise ratio), performance conditions, or access control policies.

The rest of the paper presents our mobility management scheme. Then we discuss briefly its integration with QoS management and compare with related work. We terminate with some conclusions and further developments.

2. MOBILITY MANAGEMENT FOR FAST HAND-OFFS

Each cell of a wireless LAN is managed by an *Access Router (AR)* that forwards packets between mobile hosts in a cell. Access Routers are interconnected via a wired network and linked to an *Edge Router (ER)*. There can be some intermediate routers between Access Routers and the Edge Router. For any pair of adjacent cells there is a cross-over router at the intersection of the routes going from Access Routers to the Edge Router. Figure 1 presents the main elements of the architecture.

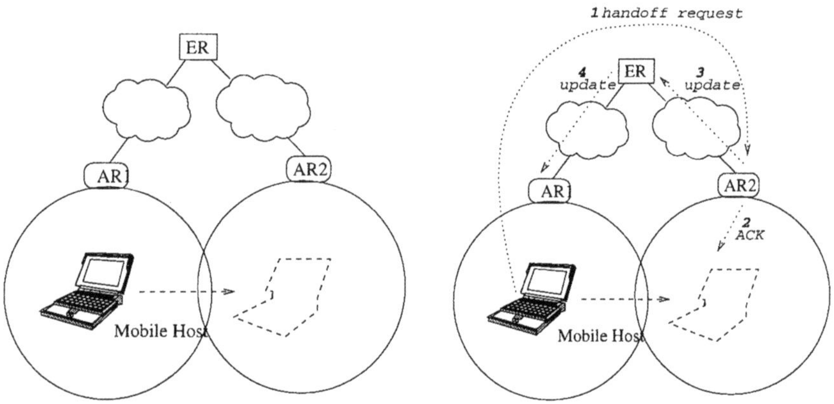

Figure 1. Architecture of mobility.

Figure 2. Mobility protocol.

As we have stated, one of the design requirements for our mobility management scheme was its integration with QoS support. Fast hand-offs can only be achieved when a mobile station keeps its IP address when moving to another cell, routes in the wired backbone being updated to reflect the new location of the station. Careful preparation of the new route in advance makes it possible to avoid lost packets and reduces the hand-off delay. We also assume that neighbour cells are overlapping so that the radio channels have sufficient quality during the hand-off.

We describe below the operation of our mobility management protocol during a hand-off (cf. Figure 2).

- *Hand-off initiation.* At some instant the mobile host decides to move to another cell. This decision can be based on some standard parameters such as the signal to noise ratio or it can take into account QoS parameters: the load or the number of stations in the current and in the adjacent cell (an increased number of stations means an increasing number of collisions at the MAC level). When the decision is taken, the mobile host sends a hand-off request to the target Access Router (AR2) via its current Access Router (AR1) to setup a new route (step 1). The request contains the address of the Access Router of the target cell and the current demand for bandwidth allocation.

- *Hand-off request propagation.* The current Access Router (AR1) propagates the hand-off request to the target Access Router (AR2) that checks whether the request can be satisfied or not. For example, if there are not enough resources, the hand-off may be denied. To avoid such a situation, which may severely affect QoS performance, Access Routers can pre-reserve resources in adjacent cells.

- *Hand-off granted.* If the hand-off request is accepted, the target router modifies its routing table by inserting a host route for the mobile host. The request is acknowledged to the mobile host via the wireless link of the target cell (step 2). The mobile host changes its routing table by specifying the target Access Router (AR2) as its default router. At this instant, the mobile host is able to communicate with mobiles in the target cell.

- *New route setup.* After sending the acknowledgment to the mobile host, the target Access Router (AR2) relays the hand-off request to all routers in the wired backbone up to the cross-over router (step 3). All routers update their routing tables by inserting a host route that goes via the target Access Router (AR2) to reflect the new location of the mobile host. At this instant, the traffic from hosts behind the Edge Router can be forwarded to the target cell using the new route.

- *Old route deletion.* The cross-over router forwards the hand-off request to all routers on the old route to the previous Access Router (step 4). The routers changes the old route in the routing tables. At this instant, the traffic from the previous cell can be forwarded to the target cell using the new route.

In our scheme, we initiate a hand-off by contacting the current Access Router before using any resource of the target cell. The mobile host changes its routes and start using the target cell after the target Access Router has granted permission. This means that there are enough resources to satisfy the QoS requirements of the mobile host. The order of route updates prevents transient routing loops or the creation of multiple traffic streams during hand-off. Moreover, the scheme is optimized so that the traffic can be delivered as soon as possible to the new location: after the first route setup at the target Access Router (AR2), some part of the traffic to the mobile host can be already delivered; after step 3 and 4, the rest of the traffic is rerouted to the new location. Note also that some part of the operation is performed in parallel: hand-off propagation in the wired network and the movement of the mobile towards the target cell.

3. QOS MANAGEMENT

Our QoS architecture aims at extending DiffServ to a wireless LAN so that mobile hosts can benefit from different performance classes in a similar way to wired networks. We assume that the wired backbone is an over-provisioned LAN such as for example a switched Ethernet, so that the only performance critical parts of the global network are wireless links. All mobile hosts and Access Routers are provided with the *DiffServ* mechanisms to control traffic sources in function of varying conditions of a cell: parameters of traffic shapers and bandwidth allocations for QoS classes can be adjusted to provide requested performance behavior.

A 802.11 WLAN environment has specific characteristics that make it difficult to provide adequate quality of service: the radio channel is shared between all stations and the access overhead increases with the number of stations. Our approach to providing quality of service in a 802.11 environment is based on the following constraints:

- we limit the area of a cell so that all stations use the same high bit rate of the radio channel,
- we constraint traffic sources by configuring traffic shapers in stations to obtain desired QoS effects,
- we limit the number of stations allowed to use a cell (a hand-off request can be denied if there is no enough available bandwidth in a cell).

An Access Router manages QoS allocations in a cell: a mobile host informs it about the required bandwidth and the Access Router configures the QoS mechanisms of the mobile host. More details on the QoS management are given elsewhere [4].

4. RELATED WORK

Our mobility management scheme is similar to those studied in the HAWAII project [7]. HAWAII proposes four schemes: MSF, SSF, UNF, and MNF. In MSF, hand-off is initiated via the old base station and results in transient loops, whereas SSF requires more descriptive routing tables. UNF and MNF rely on the capacity of the mobile host to communicate with both base stations: the old and the new one. When a mobile host hand-offs into a new cell, routing tables in routers involved in the movement are modified starting from the new base station. The HAWAII mobility schemes have been only validated by simulation and they do not provide any specific QoS support. At the beginning, we considered the UNF scheme, however it does not take into account the QoS management—before using a cell, the new Access Router has to check whether the QoS requirements of the mobile host can be satisfied or not. So, in our mobility scheme, the hand-off request is sent first to the old Access Router and relayed to the new one.

5. CONCLUSIONS AND FUTURE WORK

We have implemented the basic elements of our architecture: the micro-mobility scheme and the intra-cell QoS management based on DiffServ. We use FreeBSD PC boxes that act as Access Routers to provide all required functions to mobile hosts. They are connected using wireless 11 Mb/s 802.11b and 10 Mb/s wired Ethernet cards. Access Routers and mobile hosts use an IPv6 stack developed in a French Next Generation Internet project [1].

We have measured performance of differentiation between two traffic sources: an UDP source generating a priority EF traffic and a TCP source generating an elastic BE traffic. Configuring the DiffServ mechanisms in the mobile host allows to limit the BE traffic to a given value (2.4 Mb/s) so that the delay of the EF class is only slightly disturbed by the BE class. In the case when mobile host does not require configuration of QoS mechanisms, the hand-off has taken around 5 ms.

We are working on the integration of mobility management with QoS mechanisms: the in-band signaling protocol and the coupling of intra-cell QoS management with the management at the inter-cell level. This will allow dynamic changes in QoS allocations that adapt to varying conditions in the network. After the integration of the mechanisms, we will be able to provide more results on the performance of DiffServ classes during a hand-off.

Acknowledgments

This work has been supported by the French Ministry of Industry National Network of Telecommunication Research via the AIRS project: *"Integrated Architecture for Networks and Services"*.

References

[1] AIRS (2001). Integrated Architecture for Networks and Services. http://www-rp.lip6.fr/airs/.

[2] Blake et al., S. (1998). An Architecture for Differentiated Services. Internet RFC 2475.

[3] Chalmers et al., D. (1999). A Survey of Quality of Service in Mobile Computing Environments. *IEEE Online communication Surveys*, 2(2).

[4] García-Macías, J., Rousseau, F., Berger-Sabbatel, G., Leyla, T., and Duda, A. (2001). Quality of Service and Mobility for the Wireless Internet. In *submitted for publication*.

[5] Perkins, C. (1996). Mobile IP Specification. Internet RFC 2002.

[6] Perkins, C. and Johnson, D. (1996). Mobility Support in IPv6. In *Mobile Computing and Networking*, pages 27–37.

[7] Ramjee et al., R. (1999). HAWAII: A Domain-based Approach for Supporting Mobility in Wide-area Wireless Networks. In *IEEE Int'l. Conf. Network Protocols*.

V

INVITED LECTURE

INFORMATION ACCESS IS FINE, BUT WHO IS GOING TO PAY? *

(an extended Abstract)

Adam Wolisz

Technical University of Berlin, Telecommunication Networks Group

http://www-tkn.ee.tu-berlin.de

Abstract Modern telecommunication networks promise new perspective in information access at any time, from any place. On the other hand recent spectrum auctions made it clear, that the transmission capacity (at least for wireless access!) becomes really an economic issue. In this talk we advocate the thesis, that both flat rate and usage based charging of the end-users are structurally wrong, and discuss an alternative dual charging model.

Keywords: Internet, Mobile Computing, Wireless Access, Charging

Generally speaking, we are used to the fact that if we use something we have to pay for it. And we are fairly aware that there are different business models driving manufacturers and service providers, so that we can expect different charging principles. With the explosive growth of Internet – which seems to evolve to a universal platform for information access and dissemination, the basic question of how the charging model for internet should look like becomes an essential one.

In the evolution of Internet three phases can be defined as far as charging principles are concerned. In the early phase, due to governmental support for the new, evolving packet network technology, free usage has been natural. In the second phase, the principle of flat rate charging has been introduced: each user subscribing the access has is charged equally, independent from his/her real usage. The reasoning behind this model has been multifold. On one hand, it seemed natural that something which used to be covered in equal shares by all

* This is a modified version of an unpublished talk given during the Third Berlin Internet Economy Workshop, Mai 2001, Berlin, Germany.

taxpayers, will be in the second phase covered in equal shares by those who use it, and in the US, were the initial Internet deployment took place, there has been a long, good tradition of flat rate charging for information transfer (the local phone calls). On the other hand, the content reached by the internet used to be free, so it would make no sense to differentiate on the basis of the services used. Last, but not least, in the Internet infrastructure there has been no mechanisms which might have supported a different charging schema.

With the rapidly increasing volume of data, but also with the increasing spectrum of services offered via the internet, sincere doubts have been expressed concerning the soundness of flat-rate charging. The arguments for and against flat rate vs. the alternative volume-charging have been mostly of intuitive nature. Sure, nobody cares about economic use of something which is charged usage independent. Sure, if the total costs of the infrastructure increases (because of the strongly increased traffic volume) usage-based charging seems to be more fair. However, it is also possible that the costs of developing an infrastructure for supporting usage-based charging might be higher than the gains of more economical usage. Only recently some studies (eg. [8] – the Berkeley INDEX project) demonstrated the inefficiency of the flat-rate charging and provided founded arguments for the usage-based charging.

In parallel, recent trends for changing from the single best-effort service model towards some kind of QoS support (Integrated Services or Differentiated Services) will make it anyway necessary to diversify charges in different QoS classes (otherwise there would be no incentive at all for NOT using the highest service class!). So we approach a third period – the usage based charging era.

But – as mentioned before – at the moment there do not exist any efficient mechanisms for accounting and charging in the internet infrastructure. This gave a reason for quite a momentum in research – see eg. [6, 3, 4]. The importance of this topic has been recently recognized also by the IRTF were a special working group [1] has been commissioned. We believe strongly, that BEFORE real effort will be invested in development of accounting mechanisms, there is an essential need to discuss the basic philosophy of the future usage based charging model. This paper is intended as a contribution to such discussion. In the following we will first define a simplified view of the Internet used for our reasoning. Afterwards we will discuss a straightforward option in usage based charging: charging for transferred information volume. We will express our criticism towards this approach, and argue for charging per end-user relevant service as the proper model from the end-user perspective. Finally we will formulate and describe our suggested dual model.

Our view of the Internet

Further in this paper we will constrain ourselves to the following, simplified view of the internet, which we believe is a quite realistic one.

There are several **packet transfer providers** (PTPs), P_i, I = 1,2, . . . M each offering transfer of IP packets in different QoS (Quality of Service) classes. C_{ij} , j= 1,2,. . . N. Let us stress that the precise semantic of the quality delivered in each of the classes is irrelevant to our discussion, and that the semantic of the classes does NOT have to be identical in the case of different providers – i.e. semantic of the class C_{11} might be different from the semantic of C_{21}!.

We identify, as a special important role, **end users**. For the sake of this paper, we will associate an end-user temporarily with a single device (this association might be modified in time!). Let us also assume that this device has an Internet connectivity, which however does not necessarily imply that it has an own, permanent IP address. In fact, we cannot even assume, that the end-user's device will be sending/receiving IP packets, as usage of special proxies might be quite attractive (see for example [9], this issue will be elaborated in the talk in more detail).

The internet connectivity is assured via an ISP (this might be also an on-campus or company internal network). Information transmission form end-user to the ISP will be assured by the use of some access infrastructure. The owner of access infrastructure might be different from the ISP (although there is a strong tendency for the access infrastructure owners to offer the ISP functionality), thus the end user might have a choice of several ISP over the single access infrastructure. On the other hand, a single device might have a choice of several access infrastructure variants (e.g. telephone line, TV Cable, and wireless packet access). Each access infrastructure will be characterized usually by the mode of operation (permanent access, switched access) as well as the supported bit-rates, and possibly other quality of transfer parameters. On top of this ISPs might offer also different Quality of Service of Internet Access. In fact ISPs make available to the end-user devices the packet transfer services delivered by PTPs.

End users access Internet in order to use some services and utilities. In order to keep the generality, and avoid the multiple usage of the frequently misused word services, we will introduce the term: **servilities** to describe any kind of service which an end user might trigger via the Internet. For the sake of further discussion we will refer to a single servility, as to something which, from the point of view of the end-user is complete, and satisfies his specific need. A servility might be short or long, in fact we believe that servilities will include, for example such different items as: playing a movie, downloading (or playing!!) an MP3 song, a money transfer, booking a flight, phone call, waking in the morning, permanently observing the courtyard. . . and many, many others. . . Servilities are made available to the end-user by **serviders** (servility providers). We introduce this term as a more general than just content providers, or service providers. This should become clear after understanding the term servility.

WHAT DOES IT MEAN FLAT CHARGING? TIME BASED CHARGING?

After having introduced our vision of the internet, we can shortly elaborate on the notion of flat charging. In fact, in general we have to differentiate between charging for the use of access infrastructure and charging for the use of packet transfer service. Under the notion of flat charging both of this charges might be included (say charging for the CATV based Interent access or RICOCHET wireless packet access in the Bay Area). Alternatively, universities usually offer to the students free packet transfer, but charges for long distance modem transmission (the access infrastructure) have to be paid by the user, on a per minute basis. In Europe time dependent charging – namely a fixed charge per time unit for both: access infrastructure and unlimited packet transfer service – is widely deployed for the switched access type (phone or ISDN access) regardless of usage or non usage of any servilities in this time.

Although it has never been stated clearly, flat charging in the case of shared media is reasonable only in the case of servilities which are rather short in time, and elastic (meaning that the offered load is dependent on the feedback). Sure, a wireless packet network (like Ricochet) would break down under a traffic generated, for example by surveillance systems with permanently sending Web cameras.

So, what about charging by volume?

One, rather frequently mentioned alternative to the flat-rate charging is volume based charging ([2], [5]) meaning that the user will be charged depending on the amount of data being passed to/from end-user device. This approach can be in a very straightforward way extended for the case of different QoS classes (independent of their definition), by differently charging the volume of data passed in each of the priority classes. This is a direct analogy to charging for energy – by counting the amount of electricity taken in the different charging times (day, night). The advantage of this schema is an inherent possibility given to the end-user to verify the measurements (as the flow has to be generated in the end-system. And the ISP could – theoretically – compute the sum of the services obtained from the PTPs by adding the flows of individual end users.

We claim that such simple volume-based charging is not a proper one. Let us give some examples for this – even for the simplest case, when the end-system has a full protocol stack and IP packets are passed directly from the end-user device over the access network. In this case, the most natural approach would be counting the bytes as seen at the IP level.

Example A: Let our servility be the download of medical images. Let us assume that we attempt to download a rather huge image – say an X-Ray image. The volume of data would be dependent on the coding schema (Changing the coding may change the volume of data significantly, thus changing the charge proportionally). Why should the inefficient – or possibly just stupid! selection of a data format by the servider cause unavoidable costs for the user? (sure, your doctor, affiliated with the local hospital will not switch to another hospital only because they have a cleverer data processing guy... he will simply charge you more for your treatment.)

Example B: Electronic Payment. A user is not interested how many bits, bytes or gigabytes are transferred over the internet in order to support his payment. What he is interested in is security and timeliness of the transfer. In fact it would be highly annoying to the user, if – because of some technical reasons which might influence the amount of data used for individual transfers (like, say repeated authentication!) he would be asked to pay different amount of money for identical transactions. One could in fact imagine even a worse case: if due to errors a financial transaction cannot be completed at all, user would pay for data movement which did not have any value for him!

Example C: It is obvious, that for reliable transmission X Mbytes of USER data we will in fact transmit really some Y>X Mbytes. In fact, the INEFFICIENCY of the reliable transmission can be expressed as (Y–X)/Y. Let us note that charging by Y is the most unfair option: in fact providers with HIGH error/loss rate will have high INEFFICIENCY, thus requesting higher charges. And – frankly – which user does look at the real amount of data being transferred? Who compares the costs of individual transfers?

Combining the observations of the three examples given above, the user would never know what is the reason of the high prize, and furthermore, the prize will not be predictable! The situation becomes even worse if the end-user device is connected to the internet over a kind of proxy – say the WAP architecture. In this case data are converted at some intermediate server, in order to adjust at low-bit-rate access infrastructure. The amount of data downloaded to the end-system is by definition essentially smaller to the amount of data moved by the PTP. So a volume metering function, with measurements per end user! on the "backbone side" of the converters is needed. This does definitely scale much worse than the measurement at each end system. And in addition the result is unverifiable from the end system.

Let us have a look even one step further. If the end-user device is a mobile one, and uses temporary IP addresses, accounting can no longer be based solely on IP address of the end-device. Instead, additional complexity of the accounting system, and coupling of the accounting with authorization is unavoidable ([1]). This makes the simplicity questionable.

THE DUAL APPROACH TO INTERNET CHARGING[1]

Following these examples we advocate the position, that a new approach to internet services charging is needed. In fact, we argue that the end user is interested in the quality of application services – like the quality of the video which she is going to look at. Or obtaining an MP-3 Song. The end user might be ready to pay for a timely and high quality service, but not for the amount of data being shuffled in the backbone, which – by the way – is not transparent to them, and cannot be influenced by them. We also argue that the user is interested in having fixed, settled IN ADVANCE charges for successfully completed servilities – possibly offered under competitive conditions by several competing serviders. Or – frequently – offered free of charge for a specific class of users (customers, holders of a gold/platinum card, club members). On the other hand, the work done by the PTPs should be charged quite differently

Thus we recognize a duality in the intended charging approaches and suggest a novel approach based on two different charging schemata.:

- End users should be charged by serviders only on the basis of servilities used, independently of the volume of data, because only completing a servility has some value for the user. This is – by the way – consistent with the classical end-to-end argument. Charging schemata must be relevant to the APPLICATION SERVICE SEMANTICS (APS) and charged by actions - servilities – not volume of data, possibly unnecessary, or technology specific – generated at lower layers.
- PTPs (and possibly ISPs) should charge serviders for the amount of data (in each QoS class) transferred on their behalf, independently of the fact, for which servility, and for which customer, the transfer took place. In fact the PTPs are not interested who, and why generates the traffic they carry.

We will refer to this concept as to dual approach to charging. Let us explain this concept in more detail, and discuss the impact of such an approach on the design of serviders, as well as accounting and charging mechanisms.

Serviders – and only serviders! – can develop different, possibly quite complex charging policies for the end-users. One can imagine for this case the following approaches:

[1] Recently the author has discovered, that a similar idea has been independently developed by researchers at IBM Zürich [7]

- the game machine model – an end user is charged for a couple of minutes of using the game machine)

- the sushi-bar model – one is charged for the retrieving of objects (an MP3-song, a movie)

- the "all you can eat" approach: for entering a session – eg. chatting, ... until you deregister...

These models may be combined. We can imagine for example a "game model" charging of the search machine (which you might use to search for, say, recording of theater performances or movies including 10 second samples) combined with the "sushi-bar" charging for downloading the copies of the downloaded objects (the movies themselves). Which would be, by the way, similar to the pay TV in the hotels....

But charging by servilities makes also very straightforward more complex models, like: members of a society have free access to some subset of the journals and reports, but have to pay for another ones. Or: each servility has a fixed charge. Each member obtains some free allowance per month (year), without limits of the servilities used. After exceeding the allowance further servilities will be charged.

It is obvious that this way of charging per servilities can be in a natural way coupled with granting access right to use the servilities, thus the proper accounting mechanisms can (and should) be tightly coupled with the access and authentication mechanisms. Not necessarily contributing to an essential increase of their complexity. We expect that support for this kind of charging will be also increasingly provided in the WWW browsers, so that a prize of – say downloading an object, or starting an action might be presented in advance to the user.

Quite a different situation is to be considered for charging the packet transfer services by PTP (and possibly ISPs). As those services are to be covered by the serviders, there is no need to care for the high resolution of the carried flows, down to the identification of the end-user and counting IP packets or even bytes per end-user. Really meaningful is only the servider responsible for the traffic. An example for this might be the whole traffic of an ISP, or a whole traffic of some electronic commerce service provider. As this traffic is rather highly aggregated, there is no real need to go for a very high resolution of accounting: we will care rather for Megabits or Gigabits exchanged in a given service class. In fact totally different charging models apply. We expect typically the servider to make a contract with a PTP, assuring him the right to put on the PTP in some time frame, up to an agreed amount of traffic following a fixed traffic profile in each of the QoS classes suppoted. The charge might be computed from a component based on the negotiated upper limit as well as a component based on real usage. As for the real usage we conjecture that statistical sampling methods can effectively be applied, rather than precise counting of bytes or packets. We are quite convinced that only usage of statistical sampling methods will is a feasible way to determine the amount of data transferred by the PTPs. In fact development of such methods, which would provide an assesment with some predetermined accuracy, for individual traffic classes seems to be an interesting challenge, which we will investigate in detail separately.

As for the access technology charges, those might be alternatively carried by the servider on behalf of his customers, or covered by a flat rate by the end-user.

Last but not least: the dual charging approach delivers incentives for technological progress and competition both among the PTPS and the serviders. As for the PTPs the situation is clear: by creating competition on the charges for transport of just IP packets (possibly with different Quality of Service classes) without coupling to services, we create a situation similar to the market of long distance calls in US. Which proved to be very advantages for the customers, and has lead to very low tariffs in the US as compared, for example, to the situation in Europe.

As for the serviders the situation is even more convincing. Serviders have to compete only in the quality and charges for the offered servilities (sure, different composed blocks of servilities might be offered – like insurances are offered now). In order to remain competitive, in spite of equal access to the PTPs, serviders will have to optimize the cost of the infrastructure used for providing servilities.

In fact serviders will have to consider technical implication of mapping the user-defined operation into (a possibly complex) sequence of data transfers in different QoS classes, into possible caching, replicating etc. . And, based on how successful a given servider will be, he will be in the position to offer more or less attractive prizes to the end-user. In fact the end-user will most probably prefer obtaining an MP3 song for 50 cents from provider A rather than for one dollar from provider B. And we will not accept the 1 dollar offer with the explanation that this is justified by the higher volume of data used by provider B. . . .because of his less innovative technical solution.

Taking the example of search engines: looking for a keyword with different search engines might cause totally different traffic, depending on the location of the engines themselves (possibly replicated) , the location of the data bases, and – last but not least – their efficiency (if you get the best match as the first one. . .).

Conclusions

We have presented a concept of charging for Internet services, that distinguishes (A) charging of the end user based on the end-to-end service (denoted the servility offered by a servider), and (B) charging of serviders based on packet transfer volume per QoS class.

The main attraction of this concept of charging, which we call the dual approach, is giving incentives for optimization of the information infrastructure, like considering the tradeoff between information replication vs. transport of information, information compression vs. uncompressed tranport, etc. The dual charging approach opens, however, quite a couple of research issues. We will list here only a few of them:

How should the individual end-user services use the different possible data communication classes? How can the end-user oriented charges for these services be derived from the data communication charges? If the charges structure for data communication services changes, will this have a direct consequence to the end-user-oriented charges, or will there be a large freedom for the provider concerning which structure of charge to use? How to support on-line information about the prizes of individual operations (a user interface extension?) How to organize efficiently the accounting?

Acknowledgments

I would express my gratitude to Dr. Carle, Dr. Smirnov and Tanja Zseby for numerous discussion during the development of this concept.

References

[1] IRTF Authentication Authorisation Accounting ARCHitecture Research Group (AAAARCH), URL: http://www.irtf.org/charters/aaaarch.html

[2] Nevil Brownlee: New Zealand Experiences with Network Traffic Charging, ConneXions, Volume 8, No. 12, December 1994

[3] B. Briscoe, M. Rizzo , J. Tassel, K. Damianakis, N. Guba: Lightweight policing and charging for packet networks, BT Research, BT Labs, Martlesham Heath, 1999

[4] Georg Carle, Felix Hartanto, Michael Smirnow, Tanja Zseby: Charging and Accounting for QoS-enhanced IP Multicast, IFIP Sixth International Workshop on Protocols ForHigh-Speed Networks (PfHSN '99), August 25-27, 1999, Salem, MA, U.S.A.

[5] R. Edell, N. McKeown, P. Varaiya: Billing Users and Pricing for TCP, IEEE Journal on Selected Areas in Communications, Vol. 13, No. 7, September 1995, pp. 1162-1162.

[6] G. Fankhauser, B. Stiller, C. Vögtli, B. Plattner: Reservation-based Charging in an integrated services Network, 4th INFORMS Telecommunications Conference, Boca Raton, Florida, U.S.A., March 1998.

[7] B. Liver, G. Dermler: The E-Business of Content Delivery , Talk at Workshop on Internet Service Quality Economics, MIT, Dec. 2-3, 1999. http://www.marengoresearch.com/isqe/agenda_m.htm

[8] B. Rupp, R. Edell, H. Chand, P. Varaiya. INDEX: A Platform for Determining how People Value the Quality of their Internet Access. Proceedings of the Sixth IEEE/IFIP International Workshop on Quality of Service – IWQoS'98, Napa, CA, May 1998, pp. 85-90.

[9] A. Wolisz. Wireless Internet Architectures: Selected Issues. . . (invited paper) in: J.Wozniak, J. Konorski, editors "Personal Wireless Communications" Kluver Academic Publishers, Boston/Dordrecht/London 2000, pages 1-16

VI

ARCHITECTURES, SERVICES & APPLICATIONS

A FRAMEWORK FOR ASPECT–ORIENTED MULTIPARTY COORDINATION

José A. Pérez, Rafael Corchuelo, David Ruiz and Miguel Toro
Dep. de Lenguajes y Sistemas Informáticos
Universidad de Sevilla, Spain
{jperez, corchu, druiz,mtoro}@lsi.us.es

Abstract Separation of concerns has been presented as a promising tool to tackle the design of complex systems in which cross–cutting properties that do no fit into the scope of a class must be satisfied. In this paper, we show that interaction amongst a number of objects can also be described separately from functionality by means of the CAL language, and present a framework that provides the needed infrastructure. It is innovative because it supports open multiparty interactions.

Keywords: Multiparty interactions, coordination algorithms, aspect–oriented languages .

1. INTRODUCTION

Isolating coordination from computation has been paid much attention because it benefits from enhancing modularity, understandability or reusability, but also from being the best way to solve difficult problems such as the well-known inheritance anomaly. Unfortunately, aspect–oriented languages such as COOL, RIDL [Lopes, 1998], ASPECTJ [Lopes and Kiczales, 1998] or AML [Irwin et al., 1997] do not succeed in isolating computation from interaction with other objects in a system. COOL, for instance, allows us to define synchronisation policies, but interactions with other objects are embedded into the functional code. Therefore, objects are dependent on the interaction model used to coordinate them. This model relies on classical point–to–point communication primitives and, thus, emphasises a number of objects exchanging binary messages and requires a specific protocol for coordinating them that is usually scattered amongst functionality.

Besides point–to–point communication, many other interaction models have been proposed in the literature [Papadopoulos and Arbab, 1998], and many researchers have centred their effort on the novel multiparty interaction model, which has been introduced in many languages [Joung and Smolka, 1996]. It has also attracted the attention of the designers of the well–known Catalysis method

[D'Souza and Wills, 1999]. Catalysis has been used by Fortune 500 companies in fields including finance, telecommunication, insurance, manufacturing, embedded systems, process control, flight simulation, travel and transportation, or systems management, thus proving the adequacy of this novel interaction model in so different application domains.

Unfortunately, the languages that incorporate this powerful construct are usually intended to describe both functionality and coordination, thus producing components that are highly dependent on the environment in which they are intended to be integrated. We think that aspect–orientation is the key to describe coordinated behaviour separately from computation so that functional code can be kept clean.

In this paper, we present a framework for implementing multiparty coordination as an aspect. It has been used to implement the CAL language [Corchuelo et al., 2000], which is, to the best of our knowledge, the first multiparty coordination–aspect language to appear in the literature. The rest is organised as follows: section 2 sketches the interaction model on which CAL relies; section 3 presents the framework that provides the needed run–time infrastructure to implement it, and section 4 shows a brief description of the underlying algorithms; section 5 glances at other authors' work, and section 6 shows our conclusions and future work.

2. CAL INTERACTION MODEL

CAL [Corchuelo et al., 2000] is a language aimed at describing coordination patterns amongst a number of objects in a way that is independent from computation or other aspects. Coordination patterns are not dependent on the objects they coordinate, so that they can be easily reused.

To achieve this, CAL uses multiparty interactions as the sole mean to express coordination. In CAL, each interaction has a name, a number of roles and a number of slots associated to it.

The name of the interaction is a string which unambiguously identifies an interaction in the system. When an object is ready to coordinate with other objects, it offers to participate in one or more interactions by mean of their interaction names.

So, every object can offer participation in one or more interactions simultaneously. In every offer, a participant states which role it plays in the interaction, and may establish constraints on what objects should play the other roles. An interaction may be executed as long as a set of objects satisfying the following constraints is found: (i) there is an object per role willing to participate in that interaction and play that role; (ii) those objects agree in interacting with each other, i.e., the constraints they stablish are satisfied. A set of objects which can execute an interaction is what we call a *enablement*.

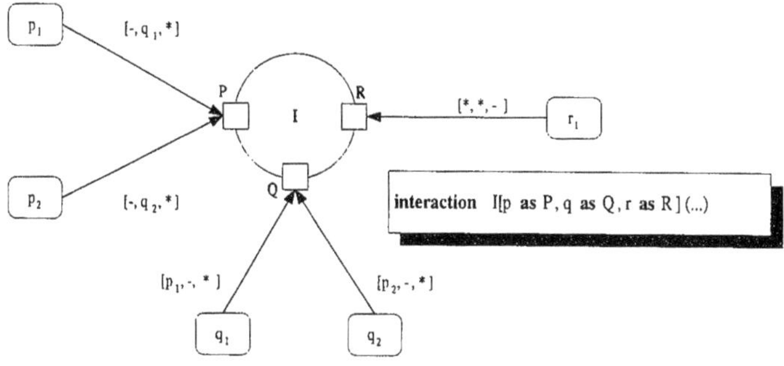

Figure 1. Offers made to the coordinator of an interaction I.

Figure 1 shows an example system with an interaction called I amongst three objects that must play roles P, Q and R. Objects p_1 and p_2 make offers to play role P, objects q_1 and q_2 make offers to play role Q, and object r_1 makes an offer to play role R. The objects p_1 and p_2 require that role Q must be played by q_1 and q_2 respectively, and vice versa. Neither p_1, q_1, p_2 nor q_2 establish constraints about what object should play role R. In the other hand, the object r_1 accepts that roles P and Q could be played by any object.

Since exclusion must be guaranteed, an object cannot commit to more than one interaction at a time. But, since an object can offer participation simultaneously in more than one interaction, it can be in more than one enablement. So, when two or more enablements share objects, they cannot be executed simultaneously. The set of enablements that cannot be executed are said to be *refused.*

When an enablement of an interaction is executed, the objects in it can communicate by means of the interaction slots. A slot is a shared variable among the objects in the enablement which is created when the enablement is executed. These slots make up a local state that simulates the temporary global combined state in IP [Francez and Forman, 1996], being the most important difference that an object does not need to have access to the local state of other objects in order to get the information it needs. Obviously, a multiparty interaction delays an object that tries to read a slot that has not been initialized yet by another object.

3. A FRAMEWORK FOR ASPECT-ORIENTED MULTIPARTY COORDINATION

We have carefully designed a framework that offers a number of high-level services for providing CAL run-time support. This framework is extensible so that new middlewares or coordination algorithms may be easily incorporated.

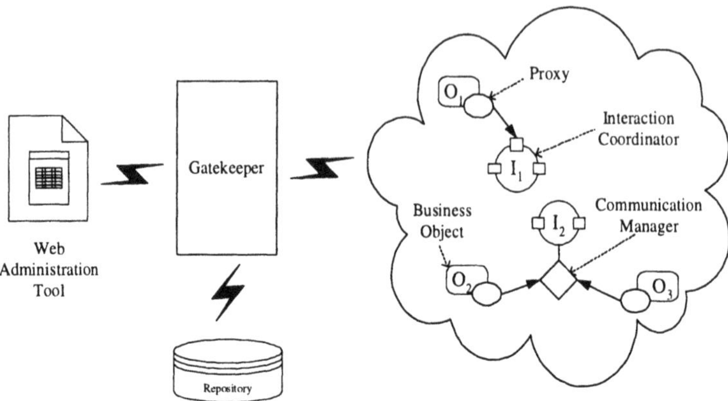

Figure 2. The architecture of our solution.

Figure 2 shows a snapshot of a running system that sketches the architecture of our implementation, which is composed of the following elements:

The gatekeeper: It is one of the most important components of our architecture because it is responsible for tasks such as security policies, billing, generating and managing UUIDs, locating interaction coordinators or interacting with the system administrator.

Interaction coordinators: They are responsible for detecting enabled interactions and umpiring amongst conflicting ones, i.e., interactions that cannot be executed simultaneously because they involve a common object. The algorithms we use are presented in section 4.

Proxies: In our framework, objects are considered to be external entities that use proxies to interact. This makes a clean separation between functionality and coordination details and simplifies the framework because it does only need to care about proxies, independently from the objects they represent.

Communication managers: They are responsible for managing communication amongst a number of objects that have committed to an interaction. They are also responsible for coping with faults during multiparty communication [Zorzo and Stroud, 1999].

At a first glance, it might seem that the gatekeeper is a bottleneck component of our framework, but it is not. The reason is that the functionality it offers is used only when new objects or interactions are added to the system, or when an object needs to fetch references to the coordinators responsible for the interactions in which it may be interested. It is also worth noting that nothing prevents us from creating several instances of the gatekeeper, thus reducing the impact of a crash. However we usually refer to this component as "the gatekeeper" because all of its instances are functionally equivalent.

It is also worth mentioning that having proxies does not amount to inefficiency because they reside in the same memory space as the objects they represent. Furthermore, separating coordination concerns from objects at run–time is worthwhile because this draws a clear line between the functionality they encapsulate and the way they interact with others.

4. IMPLEMENTING MULTIPARTY COORDINATION

In this section, we describe the algorithm we have devised to implement multiparty coordination. It is called α, and it is scattered amongst coordinators and proxies. It is responsible for the following tasks:

Enablement detection: The offers received from proxies are analysed sequentially to find sets of objects that agree in participating in an interaction, i.e, enablements.

Enablement selection: When one or more enablements have been detected, as many as possible should be executed simultaneously. Thus, an election under conflicting enablements needs to be held.

That is the reason why we have split α into two parts called *α–solver* and *α–core* that are further explained in the following subsections.

4.1. The *α–solver* Algorithm

α–solver is responsible for enablement detection, and the ideas behind it can be presented by means of the example in figure 1 at page 163.

α–solver processes offers as they arrive and form a consolidation graph that consists of tuples such as $[p_1, (q_1), ()]$. This tuple represents the offer made by p_1 and it means that it wants to play role P in interaction I, requires q_1 to play role Q, and does not care about which object should play role R. We say that role P is consolidated in this tuple, whereas role Q requires object q_1 and role R accepts any object.

Figure 3 shows the consolidation graph built by our algorithm as the offers made by the objects in our example arrive at the coordinator responsible for interaction I. Assume that the offer made by p_1 arrives first so that *α–solver* constructs a consolidation graph with only one node $[p_1, (q_1), ()]$. If the second offer is made by object p_2, a new node of the form $[p_2, (q_2), ()]$ is added to the graph, but no connecting node is constructed because the tuples so far processed cannot be consolidated, i.e., objects p_1 and p_2 cannot interact together. If the offer made by q_1 is then received, a node of the form $[(p_1), q_1, ()]$ is added. Since it consolidates with $[p_1, (q_1), ()]$, a connecting node of the form $[p_1, q_1, ()]$ is

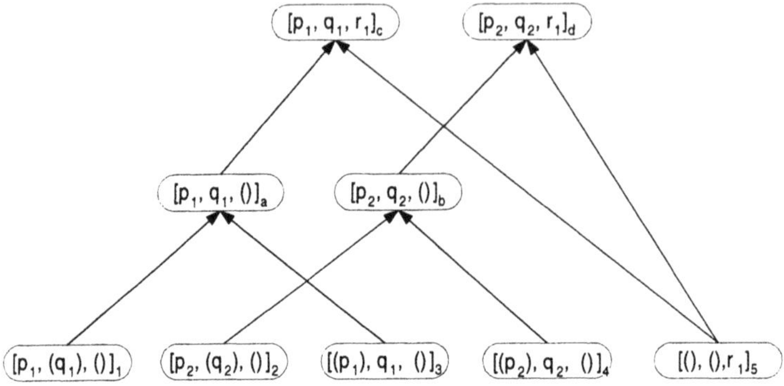

Figure 3. Consolidation graph for the system in figure 1.

added. It indicates that both p_1 and q_1 want to participate in interaction I and agree in committing to it together with any object playing role R. Notice that no enablement is found until object r_1 makes its offer. When this happens, two enablements are found simultaneously, but, unfortunately, they are conflicting because they share r_1.

In order to present *α–solver* code, we first need to define a consolidation operator that is defined on both the tuples of the consolidation graph and its elements. We refer to this operator as $\odot$ and it is defined on tuples as $[e_1, e_2, \ldots, e_n] \odot [e'_1, e'_2, \ldots, e'_n] = [e_1 \odot e'_1, e_2 \odot e'_2, \ldots, e_n \odot e'_n]$. It is defined on the elements of a tuple by means of the following axioms:

1 $p_1 \odot (p_2) = (p_2) \odot p_1 = p_1$, as long as $p_1 = p_2$

2 $(p_1) \odot (p_2) = (p_2) \odot (p_1) = (p_1)$, as long as $p_1 = p_2$

3 $p \odot () = () \odot p = p$

4 $(p) \odot () = () \odot (p) = (p)$

5 $() \odot () = ()$

The entry–point to *α–solver* is the routine called $ProcessOffer(T, G)$ presented in figure 4. (T is the offer being processed, and G is the current consolidation graph, which is built incrementally as new offers are received.) It simply iterates over the set of roots of graph G and calls routine $Search(T, R)$ presented in figure 5 on each one. (T represents the current offer, and R a root of graph G.) This routine first tries to consolidate tuples T and R, and if it is possible, the consolidated tuple is returned and inserted in the graph as a parent of both T and R. Otherwise, a recursive search is performed in the subgraph whose root is the left child of R. If a consolidation $left$ is found there, it then recursively tries to find a new consolidation of $left$ with a tuple in the subgraph

```
ProcessOffer (T: Tuple; G: Graph): Set of Tuple
 enablements: Set of Tuple
 roots: Set of Tuple
 C: Tuple
 enablements ← ∅
 roots ← the roots of G
 add T to G as an unconnected leaf
 for every root R in graph G do
  C ← Search (T, R)
  if C is not null and every role in C is consolidated then
   enablements ← enablements ∪ {C}
  end if
 end for
 return enablements
end ProcessOffer
```

Figure 4. *α–solver* entry–point.

```
Search (T: Tuple; R: Tuple): Tuple
 result: Tuple;
 left, right: Tuple;
 if T and R can consolidate then
  result ← T ⊙ R
  let result be the parent tuple of T and R
 else
  if T is not a leaf then
   left ← Search (T, left child of R)
   if left is not null then
    right ← Search (left, right child of R)
    result ← (right is not null ? right : left)
   else
    right ← Search (T, right child of R)
    result ← (right is not null ? right : null)
   end if
  else
   result ← null
  end if
 end if
 return result
end Search
```

Figure 5. *α–solver* recursive consolidation function.

whose root is the right child of R. If such a consolidation if found, then it is returned because it is the most consolidated tuple that has been found; else, $left$ is returned. If no consolidation is found while examining the left subgraph of R, then the right subgraph is also explored. If no consolidation is found, then $null$ is returned.

4.2. The *α–core* Algorithm

The *α–core* algorithm takes the enablements detected by *α–solver* and selects for execution as many as possible. If a enablement is rejected, that is because it conflicts with another that has already been selected. An enablement can be conflicting in two different ways:

- It may be *locally* conflicting with another enablement of the same interaction. This is the case of enablements c and d in the example in figure 3.
- It may be *remotely* conflicting with another enablement of another interaction.

For the sake of simplicity, in this section, we assume that each coordinator is responsible for only one enablement. We drop this restriction in the next section.

The idea behind *α–core* is quite simple. Shared objects are considered to be shared resources amongst the coordinators which coordinate the enablement where they appear. In order for an enablement to be selected, its coordinator must ensure exclusive access to every shared object participating in it. So, a coordinator must *lock* every shared object in its enablement before it can be selected for execution. For instance, consider the example in figure 6: there are two coordinators for two interactions I_1 and I_2 that are conflicting because p_2 is offering participation in both. Figure 7 shows a scenario for this system, and table 1 describes the messages *α–core* uses.

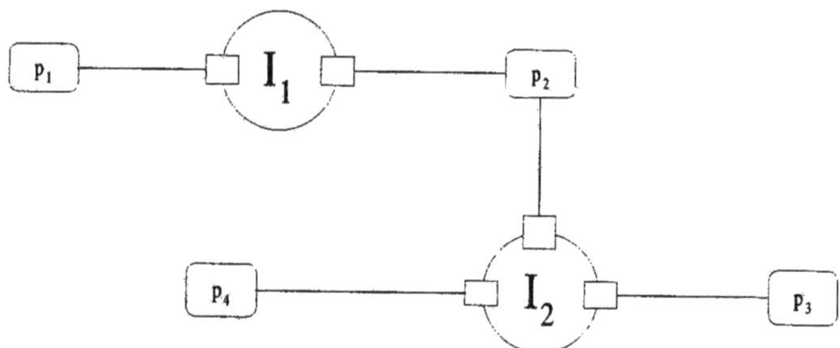

Figure 6. Two conflicting coordinators with one enablement each one.

In this scenario, p_1 is the first object ready to participate in I_1. Since it is only interested in this interaction, it notifies its offer to coordinator I_1 by means of a $PARTICIPATE$ message, and then waits for a $START$ message before beginning the execution of this interaction. Assume that p_2 gets then ready to participate in either I_1 or I_2. Since it offers participation to more than one coordinator, it sends two $OFFER$ messages by means of which the

Table 1. Messages used by *α–core*.

Message	*Description*
$ACKREF$	Message sent from a coordinator to acknowledge it has got a $REFUSE$ message from an object.
$LOCK$	Message sent from a coordinator to a shared object to request exclusive access.
$OFFER$	Message sent from an object to a number of coordinators to offer them participation in the interactions they manage.
OK	Message sent from an object to a coordinator to notify that it grants it exclusive access. This message is sent as a reply to a $LOCK$ message.
$PARTICIPATE$	Message sent from an object to only one coordinator to inform it that it is only interested in the interaction it manages.
$REFUSE$	Message sent from an object to a coordinator to cancel an offer.
$START$	Message sent from a coordinator to a locked object to notify it that the interaction it manages may start.
$UNLOCK$	Message sent from a coordinator to a shared object to release exclusive access.

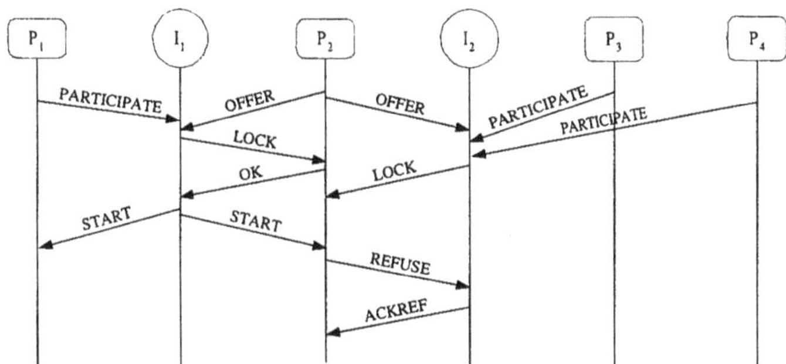

Figure 7. A possible scenario for the system in figure 6.

coordinators that receive them can infer that this object is shared with others, although they need not know each other directly.

When coordinator I_1 processes this offer, it detects enablement $[p_1, p_2]$. Since p_2 is a shared object it tries to lock p_2 by sending it a $LOCK$ message. There is no need to lock p_1 because this object is interested in only one interaction; thus it is not a shared object. Assume that p_3 and p_4 decide then to participate in I_2 and send a $PARTICIPATE$ message to its coordinator. It then detects enablement $[p_2, p_3, p_4]$ and tries to lock p_2, too. Unfortunately, the $LOCK$ message sent to p_2 by I_1 is received before the $LOCK$ from I_2 arrives. Thus, p_2 notifies I_1 that it accepts to be locked by means of an OK message, but it shall not acknowledge the lock message received later from coordinator I_2, but shall record it, just in case I_1 cannot be executed. Coordinator I_2 waits until it gets an answer from p_2 before going on, thus it cannot lock an object if another lock is still pending. When I_1 receives the OK message, it knows that it has exclusive access to its shared object, and thus sends a $START$ message to p_1 and p_2. When the shared object p_2 receives the $START$ message from I_1, it knows that it can execute that interaction and cancels the offer made to I_2 by sending it a $REFUSE$ message that is acknowledged by means of an $ACKREF$ message.

Therefore, the idea behind *α–core* consists of making the coordinators compete to lock their shared objects, allowing an enablement to be executed as long as its corresponding coordinator has acquired exclusive access to all of its shared objects. The problem is that locks need to be carried out carefully in order to avoid deadlocks. We use an idea proposed in [Coffman et al., 1971]: *α–core* assumes that coordinators may sort their objects according to a given immutable property, e.g., their net address or UUID, so that lock attempts are made in increasing order. This idea was proven not to produce deadlocks and it is quite effective.

4.3. Putting *α–solver* and *α–core* Together in an Efficient Way

In the previous section, we sketched the way *α–core* resolves conflicts amongst conflicting enablements, but we assumed an important restriction: every coordinator coordinated just one enablement. This is not realistic because, as we showed in the example in section 4.1, an offer may lead to several enablements.

The solution to this problem is straightforward because *α–core* can easily be generalised to coordinate an arbitrary number of enablements: if a coordinator finds more than one enablement, it just executes *α–core* for every enablement. For example, the coordinator of interaction I in figure 1 would execute *α–core* for the enablement $[p_1, q_1, r_1]$ and for the enablement $[p_2, q_2, r_1]$.

Notice that the coordinator of I should send two $LOCK$ messages to object r_1: one for the enablement $[p_1, q_1, r_1]$ and another one for the enablement $[p_2, q_2, r_1]$. Obviously, it does not make sense that a coordinator needs to send more than one $LOCK$ message to the same object because it compromises efficiency. The solution to this problem is that every coordinator associates a *lock count* to every shared object that is initialised to zero. When it needs to lock an object for the first time, it sends it a $LOCK$ message and set its lock count to one. When the coordinator needs to lock again an object with a lock count greater than zero, it just increases by one its counter, and no $LOCK$ message is sent again to it. Symmetrically, when an object needs to be unlocked, its lock count is decreased by one. If the resulting counter is greater than zero, no $UNLOCK$ message should be sent since the object is already locked. If the lock count reaches zero, then no enablement is locking the object, so an $UNLOCK$ message must be sent then.

5. RELATED WORK

Several solutions to implement multiparty interactions have been proposed in the literature. We have found a variety of centralised and distributed techniques for dealing with multiparty synchronisation and exclusion. For instance, synchronisation may be solved by means of polling, message–counts [Bagrodia, 1989], or auxiliary resources such as tokens [Chandy and Misra, 1988]; the exclusion problem may be solved by using time stamps, auxiliary resources [Bagrodia, 1989], probabilistic techniques [Joung, 2000], and so on. Our α algorithm solves synchronisation by means of its enablement detection algorithm (α*–solver*), and the exclusion problem by the selection algorithm (α*–core*), which locks objects in a given order. This idea was presented in [Coffman et al., 1971] in the context of operating systems. Although it did not work well in this field, because resources of an operating system are difficult to sort and usually cannot be requested in increasing order, it has been successfully applied in α*–core*.

The simplest algorithm can be found in [Francez and Forman, 1996], for instance, and it consists of using a central scheduler responsible for every interaction. In [Corchuelo et al., 1999], a slightly modified version of the basic algorithm was presented. In this solution, there is a manager per interaction responsible for detecting enablement, but also a central scheduler responsible for umpiring amongst conflicting managers. Although this solution is suitable for some problems in the traffic control arena, the central conflict resolutor is not adequate in the general case.

The first distributed algorithms for coordination were produced in the context of CSP, but they were restricted to two–party interactions. Later, the problem became of great interest, and Bagrodia devised the EM and MEM algorithms [Bagrodia, 1989], which are the most cited in this field. EM uses a number of interaction managers, each one responsible for managing a subset of interactions. When an object wants to participate in a number of interactions, it sends $READY$ messages to the corresponding managers, which use a message–count technique for detecting enablement; mutual exclusion is achieved by means of a circulating token that allows the manager having it to execute as many non–conflicting interactions as possible. Having a circulating token has several drawbacks because it amounts to additional network load, even if no interaction is enabled, which may be quite problematical in bus networks. The token also needs to circulate amongst managers in a given order, thus organising them in a unidirectional ring, which may lead to a situation in which a manager can never execute one of the interactions for which it is responsible, because it never gets to have the token at the right time.

For these problems, Bagrodia devised a modified version of EM that was called MEM. It combines the synchronisation technique used in EM with the idea of using auxiliary resources to arbitrate between conflicting interactions. The exclusion problem is solved by mapping the multiparty exclusion problem onto the well–known dining philosophers problem. Thus, conflicting managers are considered to be philosophers that need to acquire shared forks placed between them in mutual exclusion. MEM has an important drawback because the number of forks a manager has to acquire to guarantee mutual exclusion increases steadily as the number of potentially conflicting interactions increases. This implies that the probability of acquiring all the forks decreases accordingly, even if the managers are not conflicting at run–time.

6. CONCLUSIONS AND FUTURE WORK

In this paper, we have explored the aspect–oriented paradigm, the multiparty interaction model, and how programming distributed systems may benefit from both. The multiparty interaction model captures three main issues in the design of distributed systems: synchronisation, communication and exclusion, and we have presented a framework to implement it as an aspect.

A variety of solutions exist in the literature, and ours is innovative in the sense that we do not require the set of active objects in a system to be fixed and known in advance. In addition, coordinators need not know all of the processes in a system, and objects are not directly dependent on each other, which is an important drawback in other proposals. This way, our solution can be easily applied in open contexts such as the Internet where multiparty interactions can be used to coordinate an arbitrary number of objects.

References

[Bagrodia, 1989] Bagrodia, R. (1989). Process synchronization: Design and performance evaluation of distributed algorithms. *IEEE Transactions on Software Engineering*, 15(9):1053–1065.

[Chandy and Misra, 1988] Chandy, K. and Misra, J. (1988). *Parallel Program Design: A Foundation*. Addison–Wesley.

[Coffman et al., 1971] Coffman, E., Elphick, M. J., and Shoshani, A. (1971). System deadlocks. *Computing Surveys*, 3(2):67–78.

[Corchuelo et al., 2000] Corchuelo, R., Pérez, J., and Toro, M. (2000). A multiparty coordination aspect language. *ACM Sigplan*, 35(12):24–32.

[Corchuelo et al., 1999] Corchuelo, R., Ruiz, D., Toro, M., Prieto, J., and Arjona, J. (1999). A distributed solution to multiparty interaction. In *Recent Advances in Signal Processing and Communications*, pages 318–323. World Scientific Engineering Society.

[D'Souza and Wills, 1999] D'Souza, D. and Wills, A. (1999). *Objects, Components, and Frameworks with UML: The Catalysis Approach.* Addison–Wesley, Reading, Mass., 1 edition.

[Francez and Forman, 1996] Francez, N. and Forman, I. (1996). *Interacting processes: A multiparty approach to coordinated distributed programming.* Addison–Wesley.

[Irwin et al., 1997] Irwin, J., Loingtier, J.-M., Gilbert, J. R., and Kiczales, G. (1997). Aspect–oriented programming of sparse matrix code. In Springer-Verlag, editor, *Proceedings of the 1997 International Scientific Computing in Object–Oriented Parallel Environments*, volume 1343 of *Lecture Notes in Computer Science*, pages 249–256. Springer–Verlag.

[Joung, 2000] Joung, Y. (2000). Two decentralized algorithms for strong interaction fairness for systems with unbounded speed variability. *Theoretical Computer Science*, 243(1–2):307–338.

[Joung and Smolka, 1996] Joung, Y. and Smolka, S. (1996). A comprehensive study of the complexity of multiparty interaction. *Journal of the ACM*, 43(1):75–115.

[Lopes, 1998] Lopes, C. (1998). *D: A Language Framework for Distributed Programming.* PhD thesis, Xerox Palo Alto Research Center.

[Lopes and Kiczales, 1998] Lopes, C. and Kiczales, G. (1998). Recent developments in AspectJ. In Demeyer, S. and Bosch, J., editors, *Object-Oriented Technology: ECOOP'98 Workshop Reader*, volume 1543 of *Lecture Notes in Computer Science*, pages 398–401. Springer–Verlag.

[Papadopoulos and Arbab, 1998] Papadopoulos, G. and Arbab, F. (1998). Coordination models and languages. In *Advances in Computers*, volume 46. Academic Press.

[Zorzo and Stroud, 1999] Zorzo, A. F. and Stroud, R. J. (1999). A distributed object-oriented framework for dependable multiparty interactions. *ACM Sigplan*, 34 (10):435–446.

AN OPEN ARCHITECTURE FOR PERVASIVE SYSTEMS

J.Indulska[♯♮], S.W Loke[♯], A.Rakotonirainy[♯], V. Witana[♯], A. Zaslavsky [♯♭]
[♯] *CRC for Distributed Systems Technology*
Level 7, General Purpose,
The University of Queensland, QLD 4072, Australia
[♮] *School of Computer Science and Electrical Engineering*
The University of Queensland, QLD 4072, Australia
[♭] *School of Computer Science and Software Engineering*
Monash University, Caulfield VIC 3145, Australia
jaga@csee.uq.edu.au, swloke@dstc.monash.edu.au, andry@dstc.edu.au,
varuni@dstc.uts.edu.au, A.Zaslavsky@csse.monash.edu.au

Abstract Recent advances in mobile devices create a need for computing architectures and applications which are able to react to environmental changes in order to adapt to the changing context of computation. To date insufficient attention has been paid to the issues of defining an open component-based architecture which is able to describe complex computational context and handle different types of adaptation for a variety of new and existing pervasive enterprise applications. In this paper an architecture for pervasive enterprise systems is proposed. The architecture uses a component based modelling paradigm and an event-based mechanism which provides significant flexibility in dynamic system configuration and adaptation. The architecture includes context management which captures descriptions of complex user, device and application context including enterprise roles and role policies, and allows easy extension by new types of context. The architecture provides an open approach to adaptation which allows easy extension with adaptation mechanisms. In addition, the coordination language used to coordinate system events provides the flexibility needed in pervasive computing applications to support dynamic reconfiguration and a variety of communication paradigms[1].

[1]The work reported in this paper has been funded in part by the Co-operative Research Centre Program through the Department of Industry, Science and Tourism of the Commonwealth Government of Australia.

1. INTRODUCTION

Pervasive (ubiquitous) systems are built to support a large number of heterogeneous and ubiquitous devices which utilise heterogeneous networks and computing environments. The ubiquitous system is a system in which components, in spite of this heterogeneity, can react to environmental changes caused by mobility of users and/or devices by adapting their behaviour, and can be dynamically reconfigured (added or removed dynamically). Ubiquitous systems need to offer a variety of services to a diverse spectrum of entities in a dynamic system in which services can appear or disappear, run-time environments can change, failures may increase, and user roles and objectives may evolve (i.e. the context of user applications may change).

A major factor in pervasive systems is their ability to adapt to the context changes. Many adaptation problems (both application adaptation and environment adaptation, e.g. middleware adaptation) have been already addressed by existing research and industry approaches. There is, however, no architecture that is open, flexible and evolvable, and therefore allowing to use a variety of concepts in one architectural framework including (i) rich context description, (ii) generic approach to decisions about adaptability methods, (iii) dynamic definition of communication paradigms, (iv) dynamic reconfiguration of the architecture components, (v) incorporation of enterprise aspects like roles of participants and policies governing roles in the dynamic context management (the dynamic change of roles and policies needs to be recognised by the ubiquitous system in order to deliver appropriate services to the user. Most of the existing pervasive systems have been influenced by a specific type of adaptation or by the type of underlying technology, thereby resulting in a lack of generality (see Section 2).

In this paper we describe the m3 architecture and its Run-Time Environment (m3-RTE). The architecture supports adaptation and dynamic reconfiguration of the system. The proposed approach separates clearly the computation aspect from the component coordination aspect. These two aspects are often merged into a monolithic framework preventing flexibility and extensibility.

The structure of this paper is as follows. Section 2 characterises related work. Sections 3 describes the design requirements and modelling concepts used in the proposed architecture. Section 4 characterises the architecture and describes the functionality of its main components and their interfaces. Section 5 discusses several issues related to the architecture prototype including coordination of events, characterises the current status of the prototype and provides examples of applications adapted by the prototype architecture. Section 6 concludes the paper.

2. RELATED WORK

In Sumatra [1], adaptation refers to resource awareness, ability to react and privilege to use resources. Sumatra provides resource-aware mobile code that places computation and data in response to changes in the environment. Rover [14] combines architecture and language to ensure reliable operations and is similar to Sumatra in the sense that it allows loading of an object in the client to reduce traffic. It also offers non-blocking RPC for disconnected clients. Bayou [8] takes a different adaptability approach by exposing potentially stale data to the application when the network bandwidth is poor or down. Bayou is similar to Coda [21] in that respect. Coda is a distributed file system that supports disconnected operation for mobile computing.

Mobiware [3] and Odyssey [17] are more focused on adaptability measurement. Mobiware defines an adaptation technique for bandwidth changes based on a utility-fair curve. Odyssey's approach to adaptation is best characterised as application-aware adaptation. It is based on control system theory where output measurements are observed from the input reference waveform variation. The information about the change in availability of resources is delivered to the application which should adapt to the change.

PIMA, Aura, Limbo and Ensemble address issues about architecture as m3 does. Limbo [7] and Ensemble [19] are concerned with the mobile architecture and the programming model. Limbo offers an asynchronous programming model (tuple space) and defines an architecture for reporting and propagating QoS information that might be related to the system. Adaptability is achieved by filtering agents. Ensemble's architecture consists of a set of protocol stacks which are micro-protocol modules. Modules are stacked and re-stacked in a variety of ways to meet application demands. Adaptation is done transparently to the application. The lowest stack tries to adapt first. If it cannot, then it passes the notification to the next upper layer. This repeats until, eventually, the application itself has to reconfigure.

PIMA [2] is a framework that focuses on providing a device-independent model for pervasive applications that facilitates application design and deployment. It provides functionalities such as an application adaptation enabler, and dynamic application apportioning to services.

Aura [24] is a task-driven framework that helps the user to gather information about available services, selecting suitable services to carry out a tasks and binding them together. A Service Coordination Protocol controls adaptability mechanisms required when the environment changes.

Open-ORB [4] and dynamicTao [15] use reflection mechanisms to address dynamic configuration and adaptation of middleware. The two approaches make use of reflective CORBA ORB that gives program access to meta information that allow to inspect, evaluate and alter the current functionality and configuration of components.

As can be seen, most the above work addresses specific types of adaptability for networks, operating systems or middleware and hence caters for only specific kinds of contextual information. The cited works do not provide an open, evolvable architecture enabling the use of a broad range of concepts related to adaptation of enterprise applications. Furthermore, dynamic coordination of heterogeneous components, dynamic definition of communication paradigms and context awareness are not addressed in the existing solutions.

3. BASIC CONCEPTS

The design of the m3 architecture was driven by the following requirements: *(i)* **Reactivity**: the architecture should allow easy programming of reactions to context changes. The changing context of a component determines its interactions with other components and the service it can offer. *(ii)* **Open dynamic composition**: the system must support inter-operation with open components such as legacy applications or new components. New components may exhibit new types of interactions which go beyond the currently common but very static and asymmetric Remote Procedure Call (RPC). Dynamic composition (plug and play) configuration and customisation of services is essential in a pervasive environment as lack of resources to carry out a task may require a partial/complete reconfiguration of services. *(iii)* **Enterprise focus**: As enterprise applications are complex and their complexity increases if they operate in pervasive environments, we need abstractions that capture the purpose, scope and policies of the system in terms of behaviour expected of the system by other entities within the enterprise.

To meet the above requirements the m3 architecture utilises three modelling concepts: components, their roles and the events to which components can react.

Event is an atomic modelling concept from which interaction protocols such as message passing, RPC, streams and other communication paradigms can be expressed. We assume that interactions between all components are event based.

In object-oriented terminology, a component is a set of interacting objects (or even a single object). Components can be composed of other components. Components describe their relationship with other components by means of interfaces. The interface of a component has a unique ID, role permissions, pre/post conditions and event type. An interface is a subset of the event interactions of a component.

m3 focuses on enterprise specifications which define the purpose, scope and policies for a system in terms of roles played, activities undertaken, and policy statements about the system. An enterprise role is an identifier for a behaviour (e.g. Director). It focuses on the position and responsibilities of a component within an overall system to carry out a task. A role is a placeholder that can be fulfilled by one or more interfaces. Roles provide abstractions required for enterprise modelling and allow dynamic addition/removal of roles during the lifetime of a component.

4. M3 ARCHITECTURE

The m3 architecture is organised into three layers as shown in Figure 1 and characterised in the following subsections: *(i)* **Coordination layer**: a coordination manager that executes a coordination script written in MEADL (Mobile Enterprise Architecture Description Language). *(ii)* **Dedicated manager** layer consisting of three fundamental parts of pervasive computing environments. They are the Context, Adaptation and Policy managers. *(iii)* **Distributed Service layer**: existing services such as notification, security and network protocols.

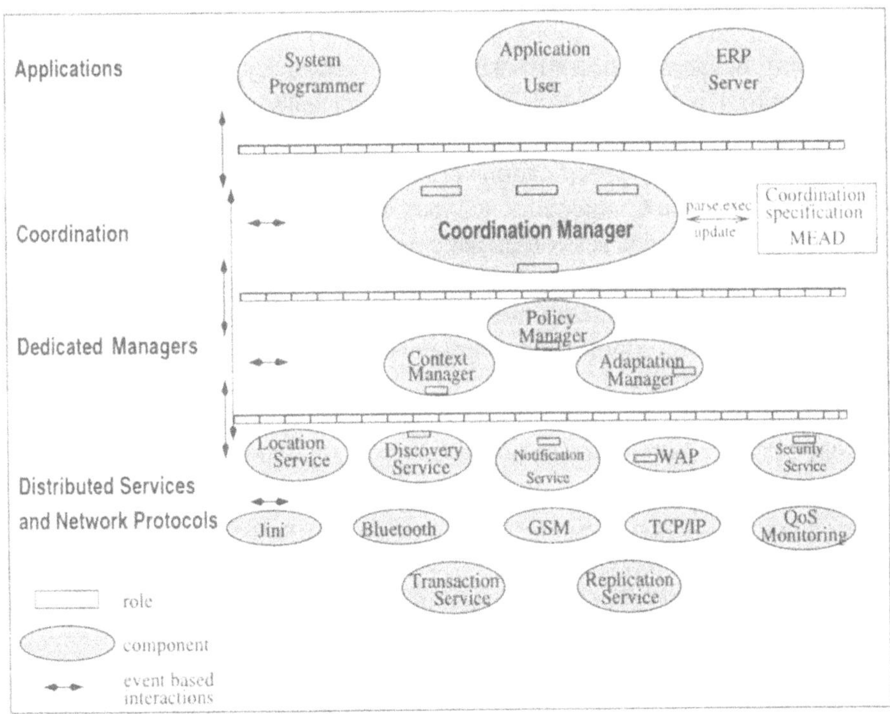

Figure 1. m3 Architecture

4.1. Coordination Layer

The need for increased programmer productivity, rapid development for dynamic changes within complex systems is the main motivation that led to the development of coordination languages and models. Coordination-based methods provide a clean separation between individual software components and their interaction within the overall software organisation. This separation makes large applications more tractable, more configurable, supports global analysis, and enhances reuse of software components.

There exist Architecture Description Languages (ADL) which are modelling notations to support architecture-based development [16].
Their scalability, in a large scale system and pervasive environments, are yet to be proven [20]. In addition, these languages do not cater for dynamic change of communication paradigms between components.

The coordination layer is the core of the m3 architecture. The coordination focuses on concepts necessary to manage the implications of mobility for enterprise-wide activities. The coordination consists of two parts (i) specifying with MEADL the interaction between enterprise roles and (ii) executing MEADL scripts by a coordination manager.

Coordination specification with MEADL. MEADL specifies the coordination of events. It is a rule-based coordination script that separates the behaviour's specification (functionalities) of components from the communication between components. MEADL specifications provide means to dynamically configure interactions between components, to change dynamically the communication paradigm and to provide session management. We take a pragmatic (not based on formal description techniques) approach to specify coordination. The script offers two main advantages: (i) interaction between components can be changed dynamically, and (ii) coordinated components can be added or removed dynamically.

Events belong to roles, and therefore, MEADL specifies the coordination of roles. Roles can be fulfilled by users, ERP(Enterprise Resource Planing) servers, network protocols or dedicated managers. A role's description is the interface of tasks that a component can provide. A role's duty is described in a set of input/output events.

The m3 architecture is a reactive architecture and this is reflected in the use of reaction rule syntax `on event` as first class construct of MEADL. `on event` $R_j : E_i$ waits for the occurrence of a set of events E_i from a defined set of roles R_j. The value of E_i parameters is checked with a `WHERE` clause. The relevant context is also checked with `in context` or `out context` clauses.

The MEADL syntax is summarised in Code 4.1. An example of a MEADL sentence is shown in Code 4.2. Code 4.2 specifies a rule that waits for the

Code 4.1 MEADL EBNF syntax

```
rule    : "on" pexpr [guard] "{" actions "}"
pexpr   : "event" role "("[ident(","ident)*] |"(" pexpr ")"
          | pexpr op pexpr
guard   : "not"* ( "in" | "out" ) "context" string
actions : [action(";"action)*]
role    : ident ":" ident
op      : "where" | "and" | "or" | "eq" | "neq"
action  : ("call" | "emit") ident "(" [expr (","expr)*] ")"
```

occurrence of event `http:get(balance, account)` from the role `Director`. If the current context is secure and the balance is more than 10,000 then it emits a new event featuring the new balance then calls a function `foo`.

Code 4.2 Example of MEADL specification

```
ON EVENT Director:http:get(balance, account)
        WHERE (balance > 10,000)
        IN CONTEXT ``secure_environment''
    {
      EMIT employee_chat_line(``DSTC has'',balance);
      CALL foo(account, 23);
    }
```

To allow rules to affect other rules (a form of reflection) and to allow dynamic change of the above reaction rule, the body of the reaction rule can use the following methods: (I) create a reaction rule, (ii) delete a reaction rule, (iii) map an event to a set of operations, (iv) inhibit a reaction rule, (v) reactivate an inhibited reaction rule.

Coordination manager. The coordination manager is an engine that executes a MEADL script. MEADL scripts are transformed into XML [23]. Then, the coordination manager coordinates the events based on the generated XML specification. The coordination manager coordinates components by sending/receiving events. Using XML is a provision for the future use of different coordination mechanism (e.g. workflow engine) and language independent coordination.

4.2. Dedicated managers layer

The middle layer of the architecture is composed of three dedicated managers which provide the three major functionalities. The three managers are context, adaptation and policy managers. The Context Manager (CM) provides awareness of the environment and feeds the Adaptation Manager(AM) with context information in order to enable selection of an appropriate adaptation method. The Policy Manager(PM) ensures that the overall goals of the roles involved are maintained despite adaptation and that a change of roles is followed by appropriate adaptation. The use of these managers is invisible for the applications running in m3-RTE. They are autonomous components with well defined interfaces that interact together to provide the appropriate level of services to applications. The coordination manager has an impact on the way the three dedicated managers interact.

Context Manager (CM). Context management in pervasive systems must contain at least three separate but complementary functionalities. They are: (i) context sensing (gathering contextual information) from variety of hardware and software sensors, (ii) interpretation of context information gathered from various sensors (may involve complex processing and resolution of conflicting context information), (iii) context description represented in a generic way.

Context sensing and interpretation depends on the type of context and is reasonably well understood for various types of context information. In our architecture we, therefore, concentrate on the final context description which is used to evaluate context changes in order to make adaptation decisions. The CM is responsible for gathering context descriptions and making it available to the other entities. The CM enables consistent addition, deletion and modification of the context (value, attribute and relationship between attributes) and the detection of context changes. The CM represents context using RDF (Resource Description Framework) graphs. RDF enables the definition of schemata which describe the gathered context as well as allowing the use of relationship operators between attributes. The use of RDF enables us to use the work of the W3C CC/PP [5] WG which is defining a vocabulary for describing device capabilities as well as protocols to transmit these device profiles from the client. We are extending the CC/PP vocabulary to include user and application context.

Adaptation Manager (AM). As the mobile environment is dynamic, devices may switch from one kind of network to another, users may move causing changes in terms of communication, security, device capabilities and reliability (context changes). The role of AM is to make decisions about adaptability if context changes and to install/invoke appropriate adaptability methods. The AM is able to incorporate various types of adaptation.

The AM concept is based on `Event Condition Action` (ECA) rules. `Event` is an event that might trigger the `Action`. `Conditions` are related to the event and `Action` is a reference to an adaptation action. Such rules support multimedia (continuous) and operational (discrete) adaptation and decouple the rules from the actual implementation of the adaptation. This approach also supports the specification of application aware adaptation [17] and application transparent adaptation [21, 3] by respectively giving the control and implementation of the (A)ction of ECA rule to the application or to the environment.

Policy Manager (PM). The Reference Model for Open Distributed Processing (RM-ODP) Enterprise Language [13] comprises concepts, rules and structures for the specification of a community, where a community comprises objects (human, software, or combinations thereof) formed to meet an objective. The Enterprise Language focuses on the purpose, scope and policies of the community, where an enterprise policy is a set of rules with a particular purpose related to the community's purpose. We see such an approach as providing useful concepts for high-level modelling of a distributed system in general and pervasive systems in particular. The goals of roles can change due to a lack of resources required to achieve a task, for example. This implies that policies can be altered and changed dynamically depending on the context. The policy manager ensures that policy specifications described as *Obligation, Prohibition and Permission* associated with enterprise roles are respected in pervasive environment. The policy manager enables consistent addition, deletion and modification of policies. The Policy Manager is also responsible for maintaining consistency and resolving conflicts between role's objectives.

4.3. Service layer

A dynamic and open environment is characterised by the frequent appearance of new services and communication protocols. A unified mechanism is required to access services and communication protocols. This layer wraps services and protocols to fit into the m3 modelling requirements. The wrapping allows upper layers to interact with the service layer using the event-based paradigm. This layer provides: *(i)* at least the notification and discovery services. All the services fulfill a role, accessed as components using event notification service. The discovery service communicates via the notification service to the rest of the m3-RTE environment. *(ii)* Universal interface to the upper layers that enables the use of communication protocols such as SMTP, HTTP, TCP/IP or security protocol transparently. The current protocol independent interface is similar to the Linda tuple space model [12] and evolves towards the SOAP protocol [22] to achieve greater openness.

5. ARCHITECTURE PROTOTYPE

Several of the described concepts have been already tested in the prototype m3-RTE environment. The goal of the m3-RTE prototype is to create a test bed run-time environment for the current and future concepts in pervasive computing. This section discusses the event notification service used in the prototype coordination manager, prototypes of main architecture components (context, adaptability and policy managers) and examples of application adaptations.

5.1. m3 managers

Coordination Manager. Event notification is the building block of m3-RTE. Messages are sent to an intermediate system to be forwarded to a set of recipients. The benefits are reduced dependencies between components and as a result greater flexibility. We use the DSTC Elvin [6] notification system. Elvin messages are routed to one or more locations, based entirely on the content of each message. Elvin uses a client-server architecture for delivering notifications. Clients establish sessions with an Elvin server process and are then able to send notifications for delivery, or to register to receive notifications sent by other components. Clients can act, anonymously, as both producers and consumers of information within the same session. The Elvin subscription language allows to express complex regular expressions

In m3-RTE, the coordination manager executes MEADL specifications by transforming them into XML which in turn is parsed and transformed into Elvin subscriptions using Python [18]. Elvin's data is encoded in SOAP 1.1 [22] to provide for the use of different communication paradigms in the future.

Context Manager. Currently, the context manager is able to manage device descriptions in an RDF (Resource Description Framework) graph. In addition, our previous work on both application context (application requirements and its current state) and user context are currently being incorporated into the m3 context manager [9]. Context information also includes location information for users and devices.

Adaptation Manager. Several adaptability methods have been prototyped including insertion of variety of filters, migration of objects from resource poor sites to the static network and sending the result of the operation back to the object's client, restriction of an object interface (e.g. allowing access to subset of operations only) [10], adaptation of Web content [11].

Policy Manager. The Policy Manager extends context information by adding descriptions of roles and policies associated with roles. Our Policy Manager prototype is in an early stage of development and is currently able to manage simple policies such as Permission and Prohibition. We use concepts from MEADL to specify policy rules.

5.2. Application example

One of the applications adapted by m3-RTE is the Tickertape application. This application was used to test the architecture support for component coordination, management of a variety of context descriptions and a variety of adaptations methods.

Tickertape is an application that gives visual scrolling display of Elvin (event) traffic. It displays notifications to which the user subscribed. In the prototype we use it for chat-style messages.

We use m3-RTE to adapt the tickertape user interface rendering and the communication protocol according to the device capabilities and user preferences provided by the CM. The CM has an abstract description of the class of devices such as Palm, Solaris Ultra10, Nokia7110 that contains their capabilities (e.g. WAP 1.0, WAP 1.2 [25], touch-screen, Netscape ...). The AM has the adaptation rules that select a required component to exchange Elvin messages with the appropriate device (e.g selection of proxies, gateways). The MEADL script executed by the Coordination Manager forwards a tickertape connection request to the AM. The list of subscribed channels for roles is known by the CM from the user profile. The content of Elvin messages to be forwarded and the communication protocols to be used are chosen by the AM. As a result Tickertape was adapted to several different device types.

Another application built to operate in m3-RTE is an adaptive email client/server application [9]. The application is built as a set of cooperating components each implementing a particular functionality of the e-mail service. The application can be dynamically adapted to context changes in three different ways: *(i)* a variety of filters (attachment compression, reduction of image attachments, format conversion) can be inserted between the email client and the email server, *(ii)* interfaces available to the client can be restricted (e.g. only short messages can be read), *(iii)* some components of the email client (e.g. search the user's mailbox for a specific pattern) can be migrated from the client device if there is not enough processing power in the device.

The openness of the m3 architecture is demonstrated by the fact that we only added less than ten lines of code into the MEADL and AM to plug a new component that enables tickertape viewing on different devices. m3-RTE also demonstrates (i) a universal approach to adaptation which can support a large set of adaptation mechanisms, (ii) dynamic definition of event coordination between the context manager and the adaptability manager, and (iii) component based applications.

6. CONCLUSION

This paper describes an open architecture used as a testbed to build adaptable enterprise applications for pervasive environments. It leverages heterogeneous devices, existing mobility related standards and protocols. We have identified context, adaptation and policy management as fundamental elements of pervasive computing applications, and shown how our architecture integrates these three notions. The use of a role-based component model and MEADL coordination gives the m3 architecture the ability to provide dynamic plug and play, and yet effectively coordinate enterprise components. The use of notification service as the main communication paradigm within the m3 architecture enables a loose form of integration of components (or roles), permitting architectural reconfigurability as reactions to the ever-changing contexts of applications or occurrences of (a)synchronous events in a pervasive environment. Work is being carried out on both an extension to the prototype and on further adaptive applications in order to fully test the concepts introduced by the m3 architecture.

References

[1] Acharya, A. Ranganathan, M., Saltz,J. "A language for Resource-Aware Mobile Programs" *Mobile Object Systems: Towards the Programmable Internet, pages 111-130. Springer-Verlag, April 1997. Lecture Notes in Computer Science No. 1222.*

[2] Banavar, G., Beck, J., Gluzberg,E., E., Munson, J., Sussman, J. and Zkowski, D. "Challenges: An application Model for Pervasive Computing" *6th Proc annual Intl. Conference on Mobile Computing and Networking MOBICOM 2000, Boston August 2000*

[3] Bianchi,G., Campbell, A.T, Liao, R. " On Utility-Fair Adaptive Services in Wireless Networks" *Proc of the 6th Intl Workshop on QoS IEEE/IFIP IWQOS'98 Napa Valley CA, May 1998*

[4] Blair,G,. Blair,L.,Issarny, V,. Tuma, P,. Zarras, A,. The Role of Software Architecture in Constraining Adaptation in Component-Based Middleware Platforms. *Middleware 2000 Proc LNCS 1795 - IFIP/ACM NY, USA, April 2000*

[5] Composite Capabilities/Preference Profiles CC/PP - W3C - `http://www.w3.org/Mobile/CCPP/`

[6] Arnold. D., Segall, B., Boot,J., Bond,A., Lloyd,M. and Kaplan,S Discourse with Disposable Computers: How and why you will talk to your tomatoes, Usenix Workshop on Embedded Systems (ES99), Cambridge Massachusetts, March 1999 also `http://elvin.dstc.edu.au/`

[7] Davies, N. , Friday, A.Wade, S. and Blair, G. "A Distributed Systems Platform for Mobile Computing" *ACM Mobile Networks and Applications (MONET), Special Issue on Protocols and Software Paradigms of Mobile Networks, Volume 3, Number 2, August 1998, pp143-156*

[8] Demers,A., Petersen, K.,Spreitzer, M., Terry,D., Theimer, M., Welch,B. "The Bayou Architecture: Support for Data Sharing among Mobile Users" *Proceedings of the Workshop on Mobile Computing Systems and Applications, Santa Cruz, California, December 1994, pages 2-7.*

[9] Indulska J., Bond A., Gallagher M., "Support for Mobile Computing in Open Distributed Systems", *Proc. of the IEEE Region Ten Conference, Delhi, India, December 1998.*

[10] Gallagher, M "A nomadic Computing Architecture for Open Distributed Computing", Ph.D Thesis - University of Queensland , Submitted September 2000.

[11] Henricksen, K. and Indulska. J., "Adapting the Web Interface: An Adaptive Web Browser", Proceedings Australasian User Interface Conference 2001, *Australian Computer Science Communications, Volume 23, Number 5, 2001.*

[12] Wyckoff, P., McLaughry,S. W., Lehman, T. J. and Ford,D. A. "TSpaces", *IBM Systems Journal, August 1998* also `http://www.almaden.ibm.com/cs/TSpaces/`

[13] Information Technology - Open Distributed Processing - Reference Model - Enterprise Language (ISO/IEC 15414 | ITU-T Recommendation X.911) July 1999

[14] Joseph A., Kaashoek F. "Building reliable mobile-aware applications using the Rover toolkit" *MOBICOM '96. Proceedings of the second annual international conference on Mobile computing and networking, pages 117-129'*

[15] Kon, F. et al Monitoring, Security, and Dynamic Configuration with dynamicTAO Reflective ORB *Middleware 2000 Proc LNCS 1795 - IFIP/ACM NY, USA, April 2000*

[16] Medvidovic N, Taylor "A Framework for Classifying and Comparing Architecture Description Language " *Proc Software engineering Notes, ESEC/FSE'96 - LNCS Vol 22 numer 6 November 1997*

[17] Noble, B., Satyanarayanan, M., Narayanan, D. Filton J.E, Flinn J.,Walker K. , "Agile Application Aware Adaptation for Mobility" *16th ACM Symposium on Operating System Principles 1997*

[18] Python programming Language `http://www.python.org`

[19] Renesse,v-R. Birman, K., Hayden,M,., Vaysburd, A,., Karr, D. "Building Adaptive systems using Ensemble" *Cornell University Technical Report, TR97-1638, July 1997.*

[20] Rakotonirainy A., Bond A., Indulska,J,. Leonard.D. SCAF: A simple Component Architecture Framework. *Technology of Object-Oriented Languages and systems TOOLS 33 - June 2000 - IEEE Computer Society - Mont St Michel France*

[21] Satyanarayanan, M. The Coda Distributed File System *Braam, P. J. Linux Journal, 50 June 1998*

[22] Simple Object Access Protocol (SOAP) 1.1 `http://www.w3.org/TR/SOAP/`

[23] Extensible Markup Language (XML) 1.0 `http://www.w3.org/XML/`

[24] Want, Z. and Garlan D., "Task-Driven Computing". *Technical Report, CMU-CS-00-154, School of Computer Science CMU May 2000*

[25] Wireless Application Protocol - WAP Forum Specifications `http://www.wapforum.com/what/technical.htm`

DESIGN AND EVALUATION OF A QOS PROVISIONING SERVICE

A.T. van Halteren, G. Fábián, E. Groeneveld
KPN Research, PO Box 96, 7500 AB Enschede, The Netherlands.
{a.t.vanhalteren,g.fabian}@kpn.com
SERC, P.O. Box 424, 3500 AK Utrecht, The Netherlands
erik@serc.n

Abstract Middleware provides distributed objects with a software infrastructure that offers a set of well-known distribution transparencies. These transparencies enable the rapid introduction of applications for heterogeneous, distributed systems. However, to support guaranteed Quality of Service (QoS) system-specific QoS mechanisms need to be controlled. Accessing the low-level mechanisms directly by applications crosscuts the transparency offered by the middleware and limits portability and interoperability. The challenge for next-generation middleware is to support application-level QoS requirements, while maintaining the advantages of the distribution transparencies. This paper presents three contributions: (1) An architecture for a QoS-aware software infrastructure for distributed objects (2) A framework for a QoS provisioning service (QPS) and (3) An evaluation of the QPS framework by means of a prototype that supports performance

Keywords: QoS control, adaptive middleware, framework, prototyperequirements.

1. INTRODUCTION

Middleware is gaining wide acceptance as a generic software infrastructure for distributed applications. A growing number of applications are designed and implemented as a set of collaborating objects using object middleware, such as CORBA, EJB and (D)COM(+), as a software infrastructure that facilitates distribution transparent interactions. However, quality aspects of these interactions cannot be specified nor enforced by current object middleware, resulting in a best-effort QoS.

In order to support QoS sensitive applications, system-specific QoS mechanisms such as OS scheduling mechanisms and network reservation mechanisms need to be controlled. Allowing applications to directly access and control these mechanisms would crosscut the distribution transparencies offered by the middleware layer and would reduce the portability and interoperability of distributed object applications.

To avoid this, next generation object middleware should offer abstractions for management and control of the system level QoS mechanisms. These abstractions should take into account that new interfaces to OS resources and new network protocols are expected to appear as the result of ongoing research efforts. In addition, a changing run-time environment must be handled, such as system and network load that influences the QoS capabilities.

In summary, the architecture of next generation middleware has to meet the challenge of (1) evolutionary changes of the system level QoS mechanisms and (2) run-time dynamic changes of the environment.

1.1. Paper structure

This paper is organised as follows. Section 2 describes an architecture for positioning QoS support in open distributed systems. Section 3 gives an overview of the requirements on a middleware-based software infrastructure that offers QoS support to distributed objects. Section 4 presents our solution in the form of an infrastructure service for QoS provisioning, which is an extensible service for making middleware QoS-aware. Section 5 evaluates this framework and gives an overview of our implementation. Section 6 relates our work to other QoS-aware middleware solutions. Finally, this paper is completed in Section 7 with our conclusions.

2. QOS PROVISIONING IN OPEN DISTRIBUTED SYSTEMS

We use a layered architecture to structure the problem space and position the functions that provide QoS support in an open distributed system.

In this architecture, three functional layers are distinguished, each with distinct responsibilities, offering services to adjacent layers on top and using services of adjacent layers below. Orthogonal to the layers, three planes are identified: data transfer, control and management. The architecture is depicted in Figure 1.

At the middleware layer, the responsibilities of the planes are as follows. The *data transfer plane* consists of the functions that provide the 'traditional', i.e. non-QoS related, distribution transparencies. In case of CORBA, examples of these functions are the Portable Object Adapter (POA), the GIOP protocol engine or a CDR encoder.

The *control plane* is responsible for controlling the QoS mechanisms and monitoring the achieved QoS level to ensure adequate end-to-end quality of service levels. The scope of the control plane is limited to a single association between objects.

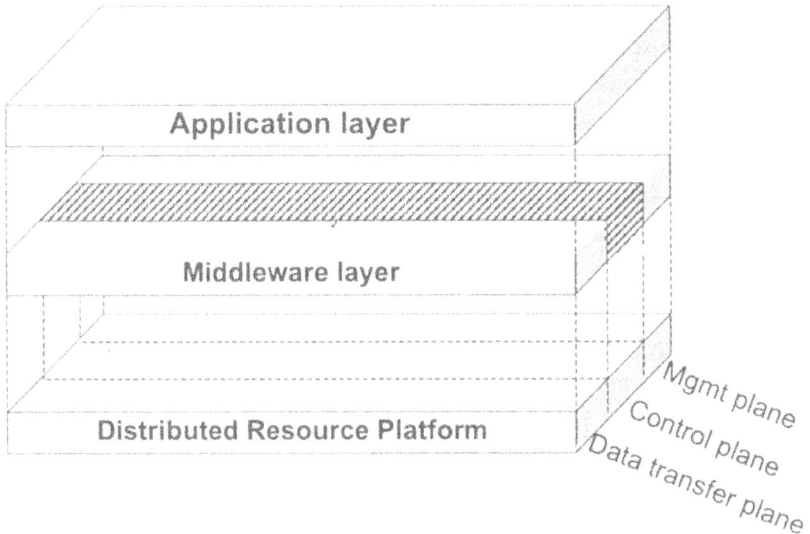

Figure 1. Layers and planes of open distributed systems

The *management plane* contains functions for long term monitoring, such as the gathering of statistics, and the instantiation and configuration of control plane functions. The scope of the management plane is beyond a single association since management actions have an effect on multiple associations.

The focus of this paper is on the control plane; therefore it is depicted as a hatched area in Figure 1.

3. REQUIREMENTS ON A QOS-AWARE MIDDLEWARE

The middleware layer is a natural place for brokering between QoS requirements of applications and the QoS capabilities of operating systems and networks. The aim of a QoS-aware middleware therefore is to provision QoS of applications in a heterogeneous distributed environment. Such a system has to deal with the diversity of low-level resource management mechanisms and the dynamic behaviour of the environment. In the literature, a number of requirements have already been identified on a QoS-aware middleware [11], [17]. The following requirements have been identified and are used as constraints on the design of our QoS provisioning service:

- Applications should be able to specify their QoS requirements using high-level QoS concepts. This frees application developers from having to know how to interact with the available system-level resource control mechanisms. Furthermore, applications become more portable since they are independent of the lower level mechanisms. Mapping the high level QoS specifications into parameters of resource control mechanisms should be done by the middleware.

- The software infrastructure should be modular and easily extensible with new interfaces to system level QoS mechanisms. This is essential to be able to deploy the software infrastructure on top of a wide variety of hardware, OS, and network infrastructures. Specifically, it should be possible to configure into the middleware components handling the control of different resource management mechanisms dynamically. Consequently, QoS control mechanisms are expected to offer standardised interfaces to the middleware, including reflective interfaces for run-time discovery.
- The software infrastructure should allow adaptive QoS support. In distributed environments the system behaviour is dynamic and only partially predictable. This requires adaptation that can be initiated both at the application and at the system level. At the application level this means that applications can change their QoS requirements dynamically, requesting higher (or lower) QoS. In such a case, the middleware should re-allocate system resources in order to meet the new requirements. Adaptation at system level on the other hand occurs when the availability of system resources drops, due to failure, system reconfiguration, increased user load or other non-predictable factors. Again, the middleware should re-allocate resources, and if possible, this should be completely transparent for applications. If the required QoS cannot be guaranteed, applications should be notified in order to see if they can adapt themselves to lower QoS levels.
- The software architecture should support policies for a) the QoS negotiation between client and server sides, and *b*) balancing and trading functions when resources are interchangeable. Many of the mechanisms used in a QoS-ware middleware are application area dependent. Policies offer a generic way to configure these mechanisms.

4. THE QOS PROVISIONING SERVICE

The QoS Provisioning Service (QPS) is a control plane service, because its actions are limited to a single association between a client and a server object. Such an association is also referred to as a client-server binding.

QPS acts as a broker between the application level QoS requirements and the available QoS mechanisms of the Distributed Resource Platform (DRP). In addition, QPS is responsible for maintaining a QoS agreement for the lifetime of a binding. Effectively, QPS is a broker and controller for QoS agreements.

The following sections give an overview of the lifecycle of QPS controlled bindings and present how each phase of the lifecycle is supported by QPS.

4.1. QPS lifecycle model

The lifecycle of bindings controlled by QPS revolves around the QoS level offered ($Q_{offered}$) by a server object, the QoS level required ($Q_{required}$) by a client object and the agreed QoS level (Q_{agreed}). The purpose of QPS is to control the resources of the DRP in such a way that some Q_{agreed} is negotiated and maintained for the lifetime of the binding. This agreed QoS is the result of a matchmaking process between the offered QoS of the server object and the required QoS of the client.

Figure 2 shows the five lifecycle phases of QPS for a single client-server binding. The lifecycle phases are inform, negotiate, establish, operate and release.

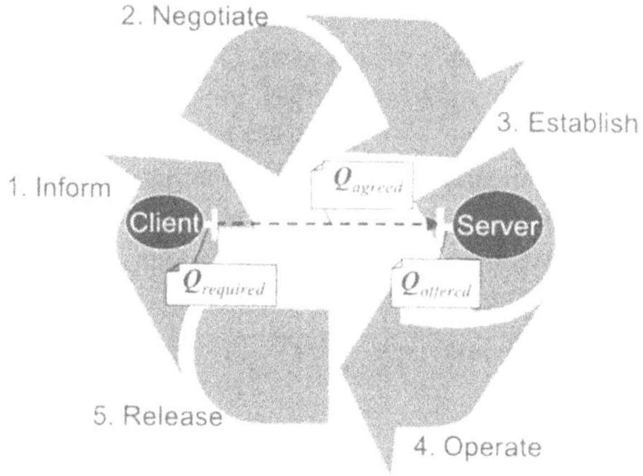

Figure 2. QoS support lifecycle in QPS

In the inform phase the client specifies its $Q_{required}$and the server specifies its $Q_{offered}$. The offered QoS is defined as the intended QoS that a server can offer if sufficient resources are available at the time a client binds to the server. QPS will generally accept a $Q_{offered,}$unless a single server object by itself intends to consume more resources than the computing system where it is deployed can offer.

During the negotiate phase, QPS initiates a negotiation procedure between the client, the server and the DRP to see if an agreement can be reached. A successful negotiation results in a Q_{agreed}that is then associated with the binding, and resources are reserved for the binding. During the establish phase, QPS assigns the resources that have been reserved during the previous phase, so other bindings cannot claim these resources. These can be communication, storage and processing resources.

Once sufficient resources have been assigned to the binding, Q_{agreed} must be maintained. This means correcting drifting quality levels, for example, by re-allocating system resources or, in case it is not possible, by informing applications to take appropriate actions. Applications can subsequently decide to lower their $Q_{required}$ and request a re-negotiation, or end their binding. This is the operate phase. Finally, when the client does not further need the binding (this is indicated explicitly by the client) system resources are released.

In this paper we focus on the first three phases. Details of the operate phase design can be found in [1]. We don't describe the release phase, since this phase is only concerned with releasing the resources claimed during the negotiate and establish phase. The next sections describe the QPS components and how QPS supports the inform, negotiate and establish phases.

4.2. QPS implementation

The QPS framework is implemented as a CORBA service and is designed to use standard CORBA extension hooks. QPS uses the Portable Object Adapter [16], the Portable Interceptor [10] and the Open Communications Interface [6]. Since QPS uses standardized ORB extension hooks, it can work with any standard ORB implementation that implements these extension hooks.

Figure 3 shows the standard ORB components and the QPS specific extension components. On the server side, the POA is extended with a dedicated Servant-Locator and a Negotiator object for managing servants with an offered QoS. On the client side QPS provides a QoSRepository (QR) interface for managing QoS requirements of clients.

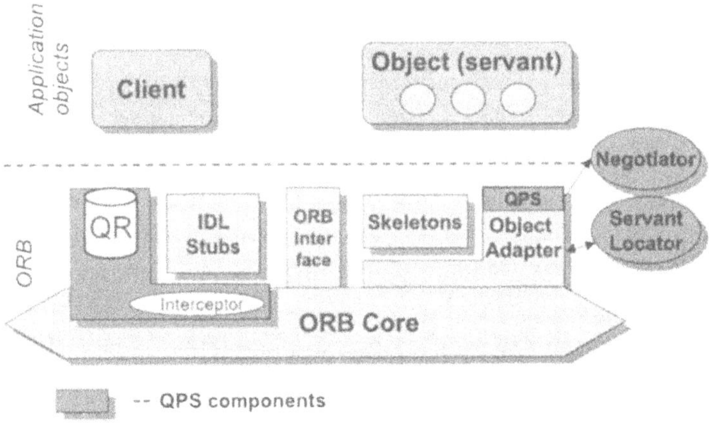

Figure 3. QPS components

4.3. Inform phase

Server application objects with offered QoS are registered at a dedicated POA, the QPS Object Adapter (QOA). These objects also register their $Q_{offered}$ with the QOA. QoS offers are expressed as XML documents. The structure of a QoS specification in XML format is inspired by the QML specification [5]. Use of XML technology has the advantage that standard parsers are available and that additional QoS dimensions can easily be incorporated into the QoS specification format. Clients can use the same XML document structure for specifying $Q_{required}$and register their requirements with the QoSRepository.

The QR and the QOA provide the same generic interfaces to client and server objects for informing QPS about their required and offered QoS.

4.4. Negotiate phase

The purpose of the negotiation phase is to reach an agreement between the client and the server about a sustainable and acceptable QoS level Q_{agreed}.The QoS negotiation is initiated by a client application that instructs QPS to start the negotiation. As a result, QPS sends $Q_{required}$ to the server-side, using a DII request directed at the target object. $Q_{required}$ is received by the QOA and forwarded to the negotiator together with an identifier for the target object. The negotiator uses this identifier to obtain the $Q_{offered}$and then calculates a Q_{agreed}. Calculation of Q_{agreed}can exploit different strategies. The default strategy in QPS results in a Q_{agreed} that is equal to $Q_{offered}$, whenever $Q_{required}$ is smaller than $Q_{offered}$ if sufficient resource are available such that$Q_{offered}$ can indeed be guaranteed. Negotiation fails when $Q_{required}$ is bigger than $Q_{offered}$. The default negotiation strategy can be overridden by a more sophisticated way to reach an agreement.

At any time in the lifetime of a binding, a client can register a new $Q_{required}$ and can initiate a negotiation.

4.5. Establish phase

When the negotiation is successful we enter the establish phase. At this stage the client and server have a common understanding of $Q_{agreed}$and resources at the middleware and DRP layers have been reserved. During the establish phase the resources are assigned to the binding and administered so that they can be released when the binding is released. In addition, a monitoring and control loop is instantiated to ensure that Q_{agreed}can be maintained for the operate phase.

5. QPS EVALUATION

The QPS components have been implemented in order to validate the feasibility of the QPS architecture[12]. In addition to the framework, a QPS plugin has been implemented that is able to reserve network resources. The design of this plugin, called QIOP, and its use for reserving network resources for CORBA method invocations are presented in the next sections.

5.1. QIOP

QIOP is an inter-ORB protocol that conveys standard inter-ORB messages via dedicated channels offering guaranteed QoS for messages sent through these channels. QIOP offers an ORB all the facilities needed to convey General Inter-ORB Protocol (GIOP) messages, in a similar way as IIOP does. The IIOP protocol specifies how GIOP messages are transported over TCP/IP connections. However, the IIOP protocol cannot provide guarantees on throughput and/or delay for message delivery. With QIOP such guarantees can be provided. In QIOP, RSVP control messages are used to investigate the availability of network resources.

QIOP builds on the acceptor/connector pattern [15]. It uses the Open Communication Interface (OCI) [3] to register and interact with the ORB. Figure 4 shows how a QIOP transport connection is established.

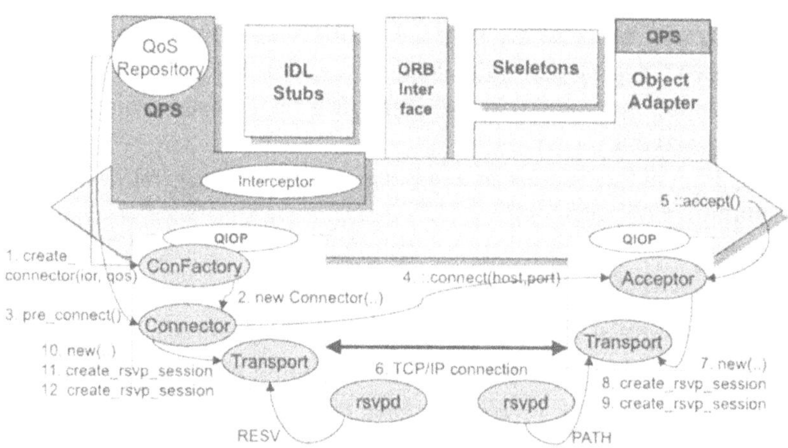

Figure 4. QIOP interactions

The QoSRepository uses the QIOP ConFactory to create a Connector. The Connector establishes a TCP/IP connection with the server side and creates QIOP transport objects. These transport objects create two RSVP sessions, one for network traffic from the client side to the server side and one for network traffic in the opposite direction. This is necessary because RSVP can only reserve network resources for a unidirectional flow.

The Transport objects create RSVP reservations for both RSVP sessions according to Q_{agreed}.

5.2. Results of QPS & QIOP

To demonstrate the benefits of QIOP over IIOP, we've conducted some experiments. The demonstration system consists of three PCs running Linux. One PC serves as a host for client objects, another PC serves as a host for a server object. The third PC is configured as a router with two Ethernet interfaces that connect to the client and server hosts. All PCs run the KOM-RSVP implementation [7]; furthermore, the client and the server hosts run ORBs with QPS and QIOP extensions.

In the experiment, two client objects are running on the client host; one with a QoS requirement $Q_{required}$ and one without a QoS requirement. Both clients connect to a single server object (i.e. they use the same object reference). As a result, the client without QoS requirements will communicate using IIOP whereas the other client will communicate using QIOP. To show the behaviour of QIOP in a saturated network, a heavy data stream, with occasional bursts was injected into the network. Figure 5 shows the response times of the two clients.

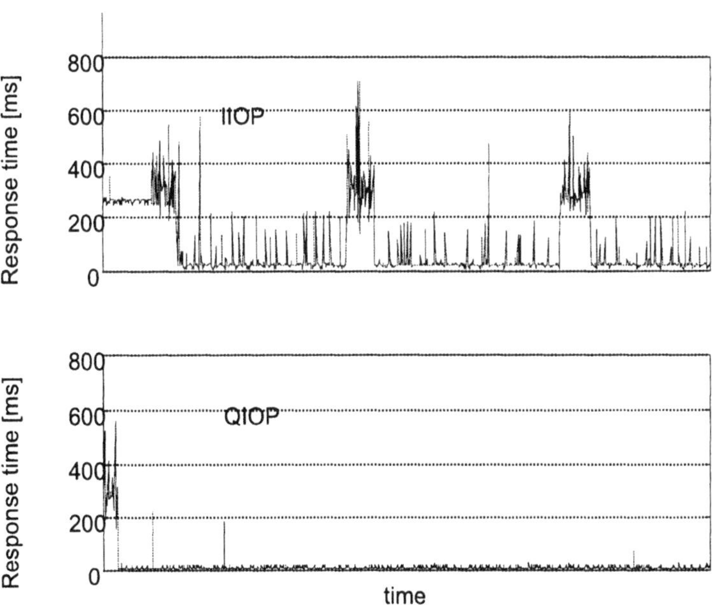

Figure 5. Response times in saturated network

The figure shows that the response times for messages carried over QIOP are not sensitive to heavy traffic bursts on the network (they all stay below 100 ms), whereas messages carried over IIOP can really suffer from large delays. This demonstrates that applications with more stringent requirements on the response time of remote object invocations can benefit from QPS with a QIOP plugin.

6. RELATED WORK

QoS-aware middleware is being developed in several projects, with different focuses. To limit the scope of this overview, we describe here only those systems that *a*) enable applications to specify their QoS requirements using high-level language concepts and *b*)realise resource adaptation. Per focus, three main QoS-aware middleware groups can be identified: general purpose middleware, real-time middleware and multimedia middleware.

The general purpose architectures differ mainly in their approach to resource reservation and adaptation mechanisms. QuO [18] is a CORBA based framework for configuring distributed applications with QoS requirements. It comes with a suite of description languages that allow applications to specify the interdependencies between QoS properties and system objects, thereby configuring the adaptive behaviour of the underlying system. QuO however uses code-weaving. This means that at compile time the code for QoS control is entangled with code for data-transfer. As a result, QuO only allows QoS mechanisms to be added at design time. Quartz [17] is another QoS-aware middleware. In Quartz, QoS concepts are introduced at system and application levels, with configurable mappings between the two. In Quartz, however, there is no reconciliation mechanism between required and realisable QoS. System agents that configure and monitor resources and balance their use carry out adaptation. MULTE-ORB [8][11] is another QoS-aware middleware that supports configurable multiple bindings. A QoS requirement is specified per binding, together with policies for negotiating QoS and for performing connection management. The QoS configuration and management system is however ChorusOS and SunOS specific. Similarly to QPS, in MULTE-ORB, QoS is controlled by feedback control loops.

OMG's Real-Time CORBA (RT-CORBA) specification [9] is targeted at real-time distributed systems. Applications specify policies that guide selection and configuration of protocols. RT-CORBA supports explicit binding in order to validate the QoS properties of bindings. After binding time, however, protocols may not be reconfigured. TAO [14] is a real-time CORBA ORB implementation targeted at hard real-time systems.

QoS aware multimedia middleware concentrates on QoS provisioning for multimedia streams. The requirements for such a platform are specified in the reTINA project [13]. Multimedia platforms are developed in the DIMMA project [2] at APM in Cambridge, and in the Adapt [4] project that extends the COOL ORB. From the previously mentioned platforms, TAO implements the CORBA A/V streaming. Furthermore, Quartz and MULTE-ORB support streaming too.

7. CONCLUSIONS

Next generation middleware must meet the challenge of evolutionary changes and run-time changes in a heterogeneous distributed computing environment, in order to provide distributed objects with support for QoS. This paper presents an architecture for QoS-aware middleware that separates the QoS support functions from 'traditional' data transfer functions. The QoS support functions at the middleware layer are further separated into control and management plane functions.

The QoS Provisioning Service (QPS) is our framework that enables control plane functions to be added to off-the-shelf object middleware, for controlling the QoS of individual client-server associations. QPS follows a 5 phase lifecycle model to establish and control a QoS agreement between a client and a server.

The QPS framework implementation presented here uses standard CORBA extension hooks, which makes QPS a portable CORBA service. We have presented QIOP, a communication module that uses RSVP for reserving network resources and demonstrated its performance benefits compared to communication over IIOP.

Future work includes the application of the QPS lifecycle to manage the QoS of multimedia streams, and implementing a more advanced interface between QPS and system level QoS control mechanisms.

Acknowledgments

The contributions of this paper are the result of our participation in the AMIDST project (`http://amidst.ctit.utwente.nl`). We thank the project members and in particular Lodewijk Bergmans, Marten van Sinderen, Luís Ferreira Pires and Ing Widya for their valuable discussions and input.

References

[1] L. Bergmans, A. van Halteren, L. Ferreira Pires, M. van Sinderen and M. Aksit, *A QoS-Control Architecture for Object Middleware*, Proceedings of the 7th IDMS Workshop, October 17-20, 2000, Enschede, The Netherlands.

[2] DIMMA Team, *DIMMA Design and Implementation*, ANSA Phase III, Technical Report APM.2063.01, Sept. 1997.

[3] N. Fischbeck, E. Holz, O. Kath and V. Vogel, *Flexible support of ORB interoperability*, 1999.

[4] F. Fitzpatrick, G.S. Blair, G. Coulson, N. Davies and P. Robin, *Supporting Adaptive Multimedia Applications through Open Bindings*, 4th International Conference on Configurable Distributed Systems (ICCDS'98), Annapolis, Maryland, USA, May 1998.

[5] S. Frolund and J. Koistinen, *Quality of Service Specification in Distributed Object Systems Design*, Proceedings of the 4th USENIX Conference on Object-Oriented Technologies and Systems (COOTS), Santa Fe, New Mexico, April 27-30, 1998.

[6] A.T. van Halteren, A. Noutash , L.J.M. Nieuwenhuis and M. Wegdam, *Extending CORBA with specialized protocols for QoS provisioning*. Proceedings of International Symposium on Distributed Objects and Applications (DOA'99), September 1999.

[7] M. Karsten, J. Schmitt and R. Steinmetz, *Implementation and Evaluation of the KOM RSVP Engine*, IEEE InfoCom 2001.

[8] T. Kristensen and T. Plagemann, *Enabling Flexible QoS Support in the Object* Request *Broker COOL*, 20th International Conference on Distributed Computing Systems (ICDCS'00), Taipei, Taiwan, April 2000.

[9] Object Management Group, *The Common Object Request Broker: Architecture and Specification* OMG document formal/00-10-33. October 2000.

[10] Object Management Group, *Portable Interceptors*, OMG Document orbos/99-12-02 ed., December 1999.

[11] T. Plagemann, F. Eliassen, B. Hafskjold, T. Kristensen, R.H. Macdonald and H.O. Rafaelsen *Flexible and Extensible QoS Management for Adaptive Middleware*. International Workshop on Protocols for Multimedia Systems (PROMS 2000), Cracow, Poland, October 2000.

[12] http://quamj.sourceforge.net/

[13] Chorus Systems, *Requirements for a Real-Time ORB*, ReTINA, Tech. Report RT/TR-96-8, May 1996.

[14] D.C. Schmidt, A.S. Gokhale, T.H. Harrison and G. Parulka,. *A High-Performance End System Architecture for Real-Time CORBA*. IEEE Communications Magazine, Vol. 35, No. 2, February 1997, pp. 72-77.

[15] D.C. Schmidt, *Acceptor and Connector: Design Patterns for Initializing Communication Services",* in Pattern Languages of Program Design (R. Martin, F. Buschmann, and D. Riehle, eds.), Reading, MA, Addison-Wesley, 1997.

[16] D.C. Schmidt and S. Vinoski, *C++ Servant Managers for the Portable Object Adapter*, SIGS C++ Report, Vol. 10. No. 8, September 1998.

[17] F. Siqueira and V. Cahill, *Quartz: A QoS Architecture for Open Systems*, 20th International Conference on Distributed Computing Systems (ICDCS'00), Taipei, Taiwan, April 2000.

[18] J. Zinky, R. Schantz, J. Loyall, K. Anderson and J. Megquier *The Quality Objects (QuO) Middleware Framework*. Workshop on Reflective Middleware (RM 2000), New York, USA, April 2000.

VII

MOBILE AGENTS

INTEGRATING MOBILE AGENTS AND NEURAL NETWORKS FOR PROACTIVE MANAGEMENT

Klaus Herrmann, Kurt Geihs
Johann Wolfgang Goethe-University
Department of Computer Science
Robert-Mayer-Str. 1
60325 Frankfurt / Main, Germany
{klaus,geihs}@vsb.cs.uni-frankfurt.de

Abstract The management of modern computer networks and distributed systems comprises big challenges due to the complexity of nowadays network environments. It requires a decentralized approach in order to be efficient, effective, scalable, and flexible. Moreover, it has to be proactive since identifying and preventing problems *before* they affect users becomes increasingly important. Several research projects have identified mobile agents as a possible solution for decentralized management, while others have used neural networks to make predictions and achieve proactiveness. We propose a management system which integrates both technologies to achieve proactiveness in a decentralized fashion. The result is a distributed management system that employs intelligent mobile components. This paper discusses our approach and presents the design and implementation of a prototype application that puts the proposed ideas to practice.

Keywords: Mobile Agents, Network Management, Proactive Management, Neural Networks, Prediction

1. INTRODUCTION

With the rapid growth of modern computer networks the management of these networks and their distributed applications has gained strategic importance. Moreover, new trends like the integration of fixed corporate networks and wireless terminal devices like laptops and palmtops introduce new levels of complexity for network management. These tendencies towards larger networks and more complexity and heterogeneity have triggered two development strands in distributed system management which are still only partially connected:

- **Decentralization:** By distributing the management intelligence within the managed network the system gains flexibility, scalability, and robustness.

- **Intelligent data analysis tools:** Manual analysis of management data from large, heterogeneous networks has become impractical or even impossible. By employing intelligent techniques, relevant information can be extracted from large sets of seemingly unstructured data.

While there are many research projects that either concentrate on decentralizing network management or on using intelligent analysis methods, the integration of both aspects has been rarely studied yet. This is mainly due to several conflicting properties of large scale intelligent systems and flexible decentralization mechanisms.

In this paper we will discuss how *mobile agents* (MAs) can employ *artificial neural networks* (NNs) to achieve intelligent data analysis in a decentralized fashion. In section 2 we describe the requirements and examine MAs and NNs with respect to network management. Section 3 will motivate the integration of MAs and NNs and discuss general technical challenges of this approach. We give a concrete design and analyze its properties. Section 4 introduces the IntraManager system which is an implementation of the proposed design for the management of IP networks. Finally, sections 5 and 6 will present related work and conclusions.

2. REQUIREMENTS AND TECHNOLOGIES

2.1. Decentralized and Proactive Management

When IAB and ISO developed their original network management (NM) standards more than a decade ago they assumed that a centralized approach would be appropriate to solve most NM problems. In these frameworks one or more central *manager* applications communicate with a set of *NM agents* that are installed on the managed nodes and serve as a data base for NM information. Putting intelligence on the managed nodes was not an option at that time because a small footprint approach was needed. Thus, these management frameworks did not include facilities to dynamically decentralize NM intelligence within the managed network.

The NM community quickly realized that NM had to be decentralized to handle the growing demands. The basic idea behind this decentralization is to express a NM task as a piece of *mobile code* [Baldi et al., 1997] which is sent to a managed device to monitor and control it locally. Decentralization can lead to some considerable improvements [Goldszmidt, 1993]. *Micro management* can be avoided, i.e. sequentially issued management commands can be encapsulated into one mobile code entity and need not be transmitted separately. Instead of collecting raw NM data to analyze it at the central location, mobile NM code can be sent to the devices to process the data where it originates. This leads to much more scalable applications because the processing load and network load are distributed over the whole network. A notable increase in robustness is achieved by avoiding *central points of failure* and *bottlenecks*. Moreover, an NM application based on mobile code is adaptable to dynamic changes within the managed network by adding or removing NM functions at managed nodes on the fly during runtime.

Today, the necessity for decentralization in NM standards seems to be generally agreed upon. Projects like the RMON MIB [Waldbusser, 2000] and DISMAN [Levi and Schoenwaelder, 1999] within the IETF (*Internet Engineering Task Force*), and the research initiated by Goldszmidt and Yemini with their *Management by Delegation* approach (MbD) [Goldszmidt, 1993] prove this fact. MbD was the first project that made use of *mobile code* to delegate NM tasks to managed nodes. Other researchers (e.g. [Kooijman, 1995], [Zapf et al., 1999], [El-Darieby and Bieszczad, 1999]) followed the same principle using different technologies.

Besides decentralization, another NM topic has gained considerable attention as managed networks continue to grow in size, complexity and importance. Such networks produce vast amounts of NM data which makes intelligent data analysis technologies a necessity. Furthermore, administrators seek for *proactive* NM tools that help to detect and prevent problems beforehand in order to avoid down times and financial losses.

A logical consequence of these observations is the integration of both decentralization and proactiveness into one framework. Such a framework should allow proactive, mobile NM tasks to manage the nodes of a network autonomously, i.e. without constant interventions from a central manager. To achieve the decentralization we chose mobile agents (MAs), while the aspect of proactiveness can only be realized by applying some intelligent prediction method that enables a NM tool to plan *one step ahead.* In our case we needed a very flexible mechanism in order to avoid frequent manual calibration which would interfere with the idea of autonomous decentralized NM tasks. Automatic adaptation to new and changing patterns in the measured data was important. Therefore, we chose artificial neural networks (NNs) as a prediction mechanism.

The next two sections will discuss MAs and NNs in more detail and motivate our decision for these technologies.

2.2. Intelligent Mobile Agents

Software agents are *self-contained, autonomous* software entities that can *perceive their environment, react to it in a timely fashion* and possibly change it according to their *goals.* They exhibit *goal-directed behavior* and thus are *proactive*. Agents can *interact with each other* through some kind of common *agent communication language*. They *act on behalf* of some human being or another software entity. In addition agents are called *mobile* if they are able to *migrate* to other hosts. Depending on the mechanisms that determine their bevahior, they may also be called *intelligent* (according to [Wooldridge and Jennings, 1995]).

Mobile intelligent agents appear to be a very attractive paradigm for complex, dynamic and distributed software. Agents are self-contained and generally use a message-based communication scheme. This leads to a highly flexible and modular approach. In addition, the concept of autonomy facilitates modular software systems whose modules (agents) are mobile and only loosely coupled. Therefore, a high degree of robustness can be introduced when designing agent-based software. Autonomy is mainly achieved through giving agents their own flow of control which enables them to actively take decisions.

All of the described abilities make mobile intelligent agents a good choice for decentralized NM (compare section 2.1). NM tasks can be represented as agents. When such an agent is mobile it becomes a *mobile manager* acting on behalf of an entity situated on a higher hierarchical level.

In the design of our own agent-based NM framework [Zapf et al., 1999] we use the notion of *health agents*. Such an agent monitors and controls a certain aspect of the *health* [Goldszmidt, 1993] of one or more managed nodes. Health agents are mobile but possess only a limited mobility scope. They can be viewed as intelligent agents that exploit their mobility for initial distribution and dynamically changing the degree of NM decentralization. After their migration to a primary target host they may autonomously react to changes in the network (or the NM policy) by moving away from or closer to their target host(s). As a reaction to the observed state they can spawn other MAs which may use their mobility to fix problems.

As we show in [Zapf et al., 1999], the use of well-known management protocols, in particular SNMP, allows for a very flexible distribution of health agents within a given network of nodes. These protocols are used by health agents to collect data. An agent may be put directly on a managed node and use SNMP locally or, if the node does not allow the execution of agent software, it may manage the device from a nearby node by using SNMP remotely over *short distances*. This eliminates the need for an agent execution environment on every managed node and helps reduce the impact of management.

2.3. Artificial Neural Networks

An artificial neural network (NN) presents a simple computational model of a biological neural system. In a NN, a number of primitive computing units (the neurons) are arranged in interconnected layers. In a *feed-forward* NN each neuron of one layer is connected to every neuron of the next layer. Each connection has a weight attached to it, that is adjusted during a training process. Every neuron calculates the weighted sum over its inputs and filters this sum through a non-linear *activation function*[1]. The result is propagated through its output connections and may serve as input for other neurons. After training such a NN with examples from a data set, the *general structure* of the data manifests itself in the network's weights. When deployed to *new* data from the same source it can still isolate this structure, even in the presence of noise, i.e. the NN can *generalize*. It reproduces the mapping learned during the training phase. Their ability to learn many different concepts with just one computational model, their flexibility to adapt to changes in the input data, and the efficiency of trained NNs make them so attractive. NNs are often applied to data analysis problems of which we only have a somewhat blurred understanding and which are therefore hard to solve with *classical* mathematical models.

Gardner and Harle show in [Gardner and Harle, 1997] how *Kohonen self-organizing maps* – a special kind of NN – can be used to map sets of generated NM events to their root causes (*event correlation*). In [Jobmann et al., 1997] the authors make use of a simple 2-layer feed-forward NN to correlate alarms in cellular phone networks. A second very appealing application, which we will focus on in this paper, is *time series prediction*. As was shown in [Edwards et al., 1997] a 2-layer feed-forward NN can be successfully applied for predicting the traffic in a network. In [Biesterfeld et al., 1997] the authors use the same technique to predict the future location of a mobile device within a cellular network. The setup used in these cases is also adopted for our work: The NM parameter which is to be predicted is periodically measured at discrete time intervals and thus can be expressed as a time series $\{x_0, x_1, \ldots, x_k\}$ where x_i is the parameter's value at time index i and k is the time index of the most recent measurement. The goal is to predict x_{k+1} given the window of values $\{x_{k-n-1}, \ldots, x_k\}$. For example, a NN could take the last 12 hourly system load values ($n = 12$) and output the value for the next hour. The training and forecasting process we adopt is discussed in more detail in section 4.1. [Dorffner, 1996] presents a general discussions on NN architectures for time series prediction.

3. INTEGRATION

The basic idea of the integration of MAs and NNs – motivated in section 2.1 – is that MAs carry NNs with them to the managed nodes to generate predictions and use them to manage nodes proactively. This results in a distributed system that employs mobile and intelligent components. First, we will discuss the

[1] [Masters, 1993] presents NNs in a very exhausting, comprehensive, and practical manner.

potential conflicts that might occur in such a scenario. We will then derive a design which takes these conflicting properties into account.

3.1. Potential Conflicts

The heavy-weight character of NNs versus the need for light-weight MAs: The major preconception against NNs is that they are *heavy-weight*. However, it is important to distinguish several phases here: the design, the training and the application. As far as the first two phases are concerned, NNs can be called heavy-weight in a sense, since the construction and initial training of a NN generally is a time and data consuming task. But when this is done, they are actually a very compact representation of knowledge. A multi-layered feed-forward NN is characterized by the structural description (number of layers and number of neurons in every layer) and by the knowledge representation (the connection weights). The structural representation can be neglected because it consists of only a few bytes. The sample NN sketched in section 2.3 takes up less than 300 bytes. Thus, a MA with the typical size of a few KB[2] will not gain much *weight* by carrying it. Moreover, the resource consumption in the deployment phase is very low since calculating a forecast only takes a few simple mathematical operations.

The NN's inherent need for persistence versus the volatile nature of MAs: Training an NN, as we already stated, is a time and data consuming task. Therefore, the loss of the acquired knowledge has to be prevented by storing the trained NN persistently. How is this possible when NNs are used *and trained* by highly volatile MAs? Most existing persistence concepts for MA systems are specialized to achieve short-term error recovery, but not long term persistent storage.

The customization of NNs to local environments versus the roaming of MAs: The majority of NN applications involve a large degree of customization to a *local environment*[3] which is done during the training. For example, system load patterns vary among the hosts of a network because these hosts are used by different users with different habits. When a MA with an NN migrates to a specific node and trains the NN with the local system load values, the NN will learn the load patterns specific to this node. If the MA takes this trained NN to another node it will probably fail to generate correct predictions since this node exhibits different load patterns.

[2]This approximation is based on experience gained with our prototype implementation.

[3]In NM an environment may be defined as one host or a small portion of the network.

3.2. The Design

While the first potential conflict turned out to be no problem, the second and third conflict seem to be hard to handle when MAs carry NNs. But a general question has to be asked here: *Is it necessary and sensible for a MA to carry his one and only NN at all times?* It may be for some special applications[4]. But for the majority of cases, a less dynamic solution is not only sufficient but also necessary, especially when we look at the customization problem. The basic idea of our design is that NNs are bound to hosts rather than to MAs at runtime. At first, this might seem to be a contradiction to our goal. A description of the basic scenario will clarify the issues.

In this scenario we adopt the notion of health agents as described in section 2.2. A health agent is responsible for monitoring, predicting, and proactively controlling a certain aspect of the health of a single node or a set of nodes. At its start time a mobile health agent is given the NN, that it needs to perform its task. The node or network segment that the MA is assigned to defines its *environment.* Upon arrival, the MA delivers its NN to a local *NN-service* dedicated to maintaining numerous NNs belonging to different MAs (Figure 1a). Through this deposition of the NN, the MA is relieved from the burden of maintaining the NN. It measures the data and delivers it in regular intervals to the NN-service which in turn takes care of training the NN with the data, and generating predictions on demand (Figure 1b). If the MA migrates or terminates, the NN is swapped to persistent storage by the service for reuse later on (Figure 1c). If the MA returns at a later point in time, it does not need to remember that it already deposited its NN. When it tries to resubmit its original NN to the NN-service, the service notices that it already has the NN belonging to this MA in its repository and continues using it instead of registering a new one (Figure 1d). As the MA migrates to different hosts, it implicitly distributes its NN. After a while, several NN-services on different hosts hold separate copies of the NN which are customized for the respective host's environment. This rather simple design has the following properties:

The notion of NNs is implicitly split in two. The NN that is carried around by the MA can be viewed as an *NN-type*, whereas the NNs maintained by the NN-services are *NN-instances*. These instances share a common structure and ability to learn a specific problem but they possess individual identities and different internal states. This also defines a new binding scheme for the NNs: The NN-type is bound to the MA while the NN-instances are bound to the hosts. A MA that travels across several nodes does not use one NN, but it uses several

[4]Such applications involve the recognition of globally observable patterns, i.e. patterns that exhibit the same behaviour wherever the MA goes.

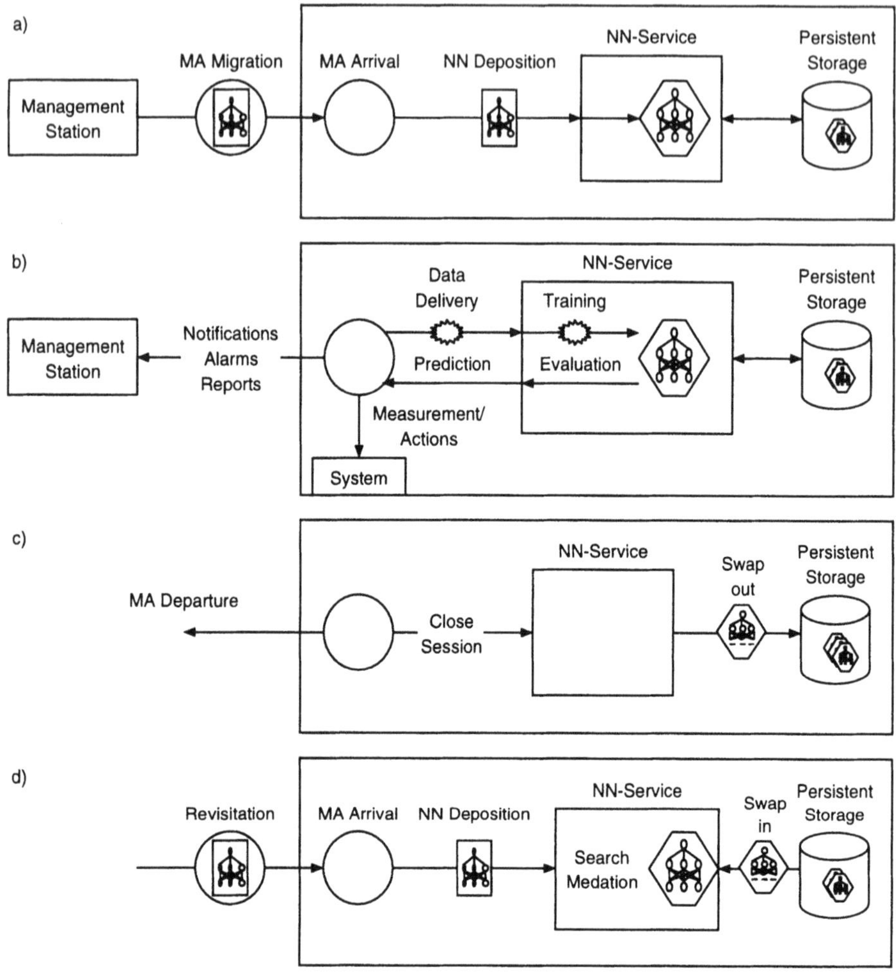

Figure 1. The basic scenario stages

customized instances of the same basic NN-type. This technique resolves the third conflict stated in section 3.1.

The MA does not have to take care of the NN's persistence and training. Therefore, the second conflict of section 3.1 is resolved.

The mechanism works transparently for the MA. On every visited host it executes the same operations: It registers its NN, requests predictions, and unregisters again before leaving. There is no need for the MA to hold a list of visited hosts in order to decide how to interact with a NN-service. Therefore, the deployment of the NNs is immune to the possible loss of an MA instance.

We achieve a decoupling of the *decision part* (the NN) and the *action-taking part* (the MA). The NN that decides what the future states of a system are, can be continuously trained and adapted to changing system characteristics. On the other hand, the MA whose code takes actions if the system state degrades, can easily be changed, removed or replaced without influencing the NN. This decoupling introduces a high degree of flexibility since the possible loss of a well-trained NN would make the replacement of a health agent very costly.

Summarizing these properties, we can conclude that the proposed design presents a good compromise between flexibility, persistence, and customization. It allows health agents to apply NNs in a decentralized way. At the same time highly mobile agents – let us call them *thin agents* – can be spawned by health agents and applied independently of the NN-usage to handle tasks autonomously that require such a high degree of mobility. All agents may communicate with each other to complete a common task cooperatively. Thus, we are able to fully exploit the advantages of MAs for NM. At the same time we can incorporate NNs as useful components in a decentralized NM system and achieve proactiveness through predictions. The issue of organizing NN training is discussed in the next section where we introduce a concrete prototype implementation of our design.

4. THE INTRAMANAGER SYSTEM

IntraManager is a scalable and flexible management system that decentralizes intelligence using MAs. It was designed to manage IP networks. However, we believe that the ideas proposed in our work can also be applied to other networks, like telephone or cellular phone networks since they rely on dedicated management platforms like TMN which could be enhanced. The IntraManager is build on the AMETAS agent system [Zapf et al., 1999]. IntraManager health agents can rely on several interfaces for measuring system parameters. These include e.g. SNMP agents and web server log files. A MA can use these data sources to calculate arbitrary health functions. Such a function may take several system parameters as input and evaluates to a single index characterizing the system state. This index is periodically calculated and compared with predefined thresholds to gauge the current state. If a threshold is exceeded for a certain amount of time, an action is invoked by the MA. The MA programmer can specify arbitrary actions for the different threshold events. The IntraManager system implements the design given in section 3.2. Thus, it is not only able to react to measured health indices but it can also predict them and derive proactive measures. The main motivation for the development of the IntraManager was the need for capacity planning within an enterprise network that has many low-bandwidth connections necessitating decentralized NM. Decisions have to be taken proactively concerning the extension of existing systems before the existing ones reach their limits. We are currently deploying the IntraManager prototype in such a testbed to investigate its applicability.

4.1. Automatic Training of Neural Networks

Our goal was to conduct proactive NM in a decentralized way to gain flexibility, scalability and robustness. Therefore, we gave a design that makes constant interventions by a central NM authority unnecessary and that is able to generate accurate predictions and take preventive actions. The framework requires the NN training to take place *automatically* at the managed nodes without central intervention. This poses a problem since the training process is generally the weak point of NNs. In practice, even a well-planned training process does not guarantee the success of a NN [Masters, 1993]. However, we assume a very specific application – the prediction of NM time series. Therefore, we can sooth this problem by introducing some constraints on the training process.

Helpful Constraints. The first constraint that is introduced by the nature of the problem is the fact that we do not have to deal with arbitrary functions. The time series observed in NM usually exhibit a superposition of several cyclic effects [Edwards et al., 1997]. Most NM parameters are directly or indirectly associated with human usage patterns which in turn obey to certain hourly, daily, weekly etc. cycles. Some of these cycles are known in advance which facilitates the construction of appropriate NNs. So these NNs can be constructed and tested centrally under human control and inserted into a central repository from which they are selected at the MA's start.

The second constraint is the choice of sample intervals in the magnitude of hours. That is, at the current stage we will not attempt to predict high-frequency data. Therefore, gaps in the measured data – which may appear when no measuring MA is present at the managed node – will only become critically large when the MA is absent for several hours. Gaps, i.e. missing values in the recorded time series, are a problem because this time series is to be used for the next training cycle of the NN. When the NN has already been trained it is possible to fill a gap in the time series by predicting the values in question. However, this can only be done when the gaps are not too large.

Another constraint can be applied concerning the NN *validation.* During the validation the trained NN is tested on a separate data set to ensure that it has good generalization capabilities. This task usually requires human supervision. However, the training and validation in the IntraManager context takes place *on-line*: A NN is trained with the collected data and validated during the deployment phase by comparing the predictions with the actually measured values. The difference of the two (*prediction error*) has a tendency to grow over time. When a certain error is exceeded, a new training run is initiated to accommodate the NN. Therefore, training and validation are ongoing processes [Edwards et al., 1997].

The Training and Prediction Process. For the actual training process the IntraManager uses the following scheme: In every *training epoch*, N random data samples – each consisting of an input window of length n and the $(n+1)$-th value as the target output – are presented to the NN. Subsequently the NN's weights are adjusted using the *conjugate gradient* method (see e.g. [Masters, 1993]). Several such *epochs* are conducted and the training run is stopped when the prediction error on the training data falls below some predefined threshold. We repeat this whole *training run* for a certain number of randomly initialized NNs and keep the NN which produces the lowest error. This NN is then deployed until the next training run is triggered (see section 4.1). Please note that the values of N and n are depending on the specific problem at hand and thus cannot be discussed here. Please refer to [Masters, 1993] and [Edwards et al., 1997] for a more general discussion on this topic.

The NNs used by the IntraManager have a single output neuron which enables them to predict *one* future value. To predict a longer window of values a *closed-loop forecast* can be conducted during which the predicted values are fed back into the NN as part of the input for the next forecast. The result is a small forecast time series enabling us to take proactive actions.

It should be noted that having a single output neuron does not really limit the power of the system. Having multiple output neurons for different time offsets usually renders the training much more difficult since it becomes harder for the training algorithm to minimize the prediction error. On the input side, one may actually use arbitrary data besides the pure time window (see section 2.3). Any kind of information that can be measured and that might be helpful for the training process can be used. One NN is dedicated to predict a specific system parameter or a compound index calculated from a number of parameters. To predict k different parameters one would use k NNs which can be operated by the same MA.

5. RELATED WORK

Several researchers have studied the application of NNs in NM. Kohonen self-organizing maps (SOM) are applied for event correlation in [Gardner and Harle, 1997]. A SOM is trained with alarms and learns to associate them with specific information on the root cause of the alarm. [Leray et al., 1996], [Biesterfeld et al., 1997], [Edwards et al., 1997], [Frank et al., 1999], and [Jobmann et al., 1997] present applications of feed-forward NNs similar to the one explained in section 2.3 for predictive and correlative purposes. The first major commercial application of NNs in proactive NM was recently introduced by Computer Associates. Their so-called *Neugents* are immobile agents using *functional link neural networks* to identify systems states and detect critical changes in their environment.

The application of NNs in combination with MAs to solve NM problems has not been addressed yet. An attempt to integrate MAs with an AI technique is made in [El-Darieby and Bieszczad, 1999] where the expert system JESS is used to correlate events within a MA system. However, they do not elaborate on the technical problems involved with this approach.

6. CONCLUSIONS

Our research integrates mobile agents and neural networks, two major technologies in contemporary distributed system management research. The goal of this integration is to enable MAs to use NNs for the prediction of future system behavior and to achieve decentralized proactiveness. We have designed and implemented an extension to our MA-based IntraManager system, that combines both technologies and shows that distributed system management can benefit substantially from this integration. Our future research will concentrate on the training process in specific application scenarios and its implications.

References

[Baldi et al., 1997] Baldi, M., Gai, S., and Picco, G. (1997). Exploiting Code Mobility in Decentralized and Flexible Network Management. In *Proceedings of the First International Workshop on Mobile Agents, MA'97, Lecture Notes in Computer Science Nr. 1219, Springer Verlag, 1997, ISBN: 3-540-62803-7*, Berlin, Germany.

[Biesterfeld et al., 1997] Biesterfeld, J., Ennigrou, E., and Jobmann, K. (1997). Neural Networks for Location Prediction in Mobile Networks. In *Proceedings of the International Workshop on Applications of Neural Networks to Telecommunications 1997 (IWANNT'97), Lawrence Erlbaum Associates*, Melbourne, Australia.

[Dorffner, 1996] Dorffner, G. (1996). Neural Networks for Time Series Processing. *Neural Network World*, 6(4):447–468.

[Edwards et al., 1997] Edwards, T., D.S.W.Tansley, Frank, R., and Davey, N. (1997). Traffic Trends Analysis Using Neural Networks. In *Proceedings of the International Workshop on Applications of Neural Networks to Telecommunications 1997 (IWANNT'97), Lawrence Erlbaum Associates*, pages 157–164, Melbourne, Australia.

[El-Darieby and Bieszczad, 1999] El-Darieby, M. and Bieszczad, A. (1999). Intelligent Mobile Agents: Towards Network Fault Management Automation. In *In Proceedings of the Sixth IFIP/IEEE International Symposium on Integrated Network Management*, pages 611–622, Boston/USA.

[Frank et al., 1999] Frank, R., Davey, N., and Hunt, S. (1999). Applications of Neural Networks to Telecommunications Systems. In *Proceedings of the European Congress on Intelligent Techniques and Soft Computing, EUFIT'99*, Aachen, Germany.

[Gardner and Harle, 1997] Gardner, R. D. and Harle, D. A. (1997). Alarm Correlation and Network Fault Resolution using Kohonen Self-Organising Map. In *Proceedings of IEEE Globecom'97, Vol.3*, pages 1398–1402, Phoenix, Arizona.

[Goldszmidt, 1993] Goldszmidt, G. (1993). On Distributed System Management. In *Proceedings of the Third IBM/CAS Conference*, Toronto, Canada.

[Jobmann et al., 1997] Jobmann, K., Tuchs, K.-D., Wietgrefe, H., Fröhlich, P., Nejdl, W., and Steinfeld, S. (1997). Using Neural Networks for Alarm Correlation in Cellular Phone Networks. In *Proceedings of the International Workshop on Applications of Neural Networks to Telecommunications 1997 (IWANNT'97), Lawrence Erlbaum Associates*, Melbourne, Australia.

[Kooijman, 1995] Kooijman, R. (1995). Divide and Conquer in Network Management using Event-Driven Network Area Agents. http://netman.cit.buffalo.edu/doc/papers/koo9505.ps, Technical Univerity of Delft, The Netherlands.

[Leray et al., 1996] Leray, P., Gallinari, P., and Didelet, E. (1996). A Neural Network Modular Architecture for Network Traffic Management. In *Proceedings of IEEE-CESA'96 IMACS multiconference, Symposium on Control, Optimization and Supervision, vol.1 of 2*, pages 1091–1094.

[Levi and Schoenwaelder, 1999] Levi, D. and Schoenwaelder, J. (1999). Definitions of Managed Objects for the Delegation of Management Scripts (RFC 2592).

[Masters, 1993] Masters, T. (1993). *Practical Neural Network Recipes in C++*. Academic Press, ISBN 0-12-479040-2.

[Waldbusser, 2000] Waldbusser, S. (2000). Remote Network Monitoring Management Information Base (RFC 2819).

[Wooldridge and Jennings, 1995] Wooldridge, M. and Jennings, N. (1995). Intelligent Agents: Theory and Practice. *The Knowledge Engineering Review*, 10(2):115–152.

[Zapf et al., 1999] Zapf, M., Herrmann, K., and Geihs, K. (1999). Decentralized SNMP Management with Mobile Agents. In *Proceedings of the International Symposium on Integrated Network Management (IM'99)*, pages 623–635, Boston/USA.

SECOND PRICE AUCTIONS

A Case Study of Secure Distributed Computing

Bart De Decker[1], Gregory Neven[2], Frank Piessens[3], Erik Van Hoeymissen[1]

[1] *K.U.Leuven, Dept. Computer Science, Celestijnenlaan 200A, B-3001 Leuven, Belgium*

{Bart.DeDecker,Erik.VanHoeymissen}@cs.kuleuven.ac.be

[2] *Research Assistant of the Fund for Scientific Research, Flanders, Belgium (F.W.O)*

Gregory.Neven@cs.kuleuven.ac.be

[3] *Postdoctoral Fellow of the Belgian National Fund for Scientific Research (F.W.O.)*

Frank.Piessens@cs.kuleuven.ac.be

Abstract Secure distributed computing addresses the problem of performing a computation with a number of mutually distrustful participants, in such a way that each of the participants has only limited access to the information needed for doing the computation. Over the past two decades, a number of solutions *requiring no trusted third party* have been developed using cryptographic techniques. The disadvantage of these cryptographic solutions is the excessive communication overhead they incur.

In this paper, we use one of the SDC protocols for one particular application: second price auctions, in which the highest bidder acquires the item for sale at the price of the second highest bidder. The protocol assures that only the name of the highest bidder and the amount of the second highest bid are revealed. All other information is kept secret (the amount of the highest bid, the name of the second highest bidder, ...). Although second price auctions may not seem very important, small variations on this theme are used by many public institutions: e.g., a call for tenders, where contract is given to the lowest offer (or the second lowest).

The case study serves two purposes: we show that SDC protocols can be used for these kind of applications, and secondly, we assess the network overhead and how well these applications scale. To overcome the communication overhead, we use mobile agents and semi-trusted hosts.

Keywords: Secure distributed computing, SDC, mobile agents, second price auction, agents, semi-trusted execution platform

1. INTRODUCTION

Secure distributed computing (SDC) addresses the problem of distributed computing where some of the algorithms and data that are used in the computation must remain private. Usually, the problem is stated as follows, emphasizing privacy of data. Let f be a publicly known function taking n inputs, and suppose there are n parties (named $P_i, i = 1 \ldots n$), each holding one private input x_i. The n parties want to compute the value $f(x_1, \ldots, x_n)$ without leaking any information about their private inputs (except of course the information about x_i that is implicitly present in the function result) to the other parties. An example is voting: the function f is addition, and the private inputs represent yes ($x_i = 1$) or no ($x_i = 0$) votes. In case an algorithm is to be kept private, instead of just data, one can make f an interpreter for some (simple) programming language, and let one of the x_i be an encoding of a program.

In descriptions of solutions to the secure distributed computing problem, the function f is usually encoded as a boolean circuit, and therefore secure distributed computing is also often referred to as *secure circuit evaluation.*

It is easy to see that an efficient solution to the secure distributed computing problem would be an enabling technology for a large number of interesting distributed applications across the Internet. Some example applications are: auctions ([8]), charging for the use of algorithms on the basis of a usage count ([9, 10]), querying a secret database ([6]), various kinds of weighted voting, protecting mobile code integrity and privacy ([10, 5]), ...

Secure distributed computing is trivial in the presence of a globally trusted third party(TTP): all participants send their data and code to the TTP (over a secure channel), the TTP performs the computation and broadcasts the results. The main drawback of this approach is the large amount of trust needed in the TTP.

Solutions without a TTP are also possible. Over the past two decades, a fairly large variety of solutions to the problem has been proposed. An overview is given by Franklin [3] and more recently by Cramer [2] and Neven [7]. These solutions differ from each other in the cryptographic primitives that are used, and in the class of computations that can be performed (some of the solutions only allow for specific kinds of functions to be computed). The main drawback, however, of these solutions is the heavy communication overhead that they incur.

In this paper, we investigate a case study: *second price auctions.* Here, the highest bidder wins but has to pay the second highest bid. The final outcome will only reveal the name of the winner and the amount of the second highest bid. All other bids and even the name of the second highest bidder remain secret. We have chosen this application, because it illustrates the merits of SDC, and is somewhat exemplary for many other useful applications. For instance, the authority and many public institutions request for quotations before awarding the job/purchase to the lowest or second lowest offer. The reader can easily verify that determining the lowest (or second lowest) offer, without revealing the other quotations, is only a small variation on our case study.

In this case study, we try to be as specific as possible. We will show how SDC can be used in this application. Moreover, we will look at the performance. In particular, we examine the communication overhead and the scalability of the application in terms of number of participants. Although the communication overhead seems prohibitively high, a reasonable remedy is proposed, using mobile agents and semi-trusted sites. Indeed, mobile agents employing SDC protocols can provide for a trade-off between communication overhead and trust. The communication overhead is alleviated if the communicating parties are brought close enough together. In our approach, every participant sends its representative agent to a trusted execution site. The agent contains a copy of the private data x_i and is capable of running an SDC-protocol. Different participants may send their agents to different sites, as long as these sites are located closely to each other. Of course, a mobile agent needs to trust his execution platform, but we will show that the trust requirements in this case are much lower than for a classical TTP. Also, in contrast with protocols that use unconditionally TTPs, the trusted site is not involved directly. It simply offers a secure execution platform: i.e. it executes the mobile code correctly, does not spy on it and does not leak information to other mobile agents. Moreover, the trusted host does not have to know the protocol used between the agents. In other words, the combination of mobile agent technology and secure distributed computing protocols makes it possible to use a *generic* TTP that, by offering a secure execution platform, can act as TTP for a wide variety of protocols in a uniform way. A detailed discussion of the use of mobile agent technology for advanced cryptographic protocols is given in [7].

The sequel of the paper is organized as follows: in section 2, we review one of the SDC protocols that will be used by the application; a design of the the application, second price auctions, is given in section 3; in this section, we also examine the communication overhead and tackle the scalability issue. In section 4, we introduce a modus operandi for the application. Finally, in section 5, we summarize the main outcomes of this paper.

2. SECURE DISTRIBUTED COMPUTING USING GROUP-ORIENTED CRYPTOGRAPHY

In [4], Franklin and Haber propose a protocol that evaluates **a boolean circuit** on data encrypted with a homomorphic probabilistic encryption scheme for any number of participants. It resembles the protocol for two parties, proposed by Abadi and Feigenbaum ([1]).

To extend the idea of [1] to the multi-party case, an encryption scheme is needed that allows anyone to encrypt, but needs the cooperation of all participants to perform a decryption. In a joint encryption scheme, all participants know the public key K_{pub} while each participant $P_1, \ldots, P_n$ has his own private key $K_1, \ldots, K_n$. Using the public key, anyone can create an encryption $E_S(m)$ of some message m, where $S \subseteq \{P_1, \ldots, P_n\}$, such that the private key of each participant in S is needed to decrypt. More formally, if D_i denotes the decryption with P_i's private key, the relation between encryption and decryption is given by

$$D_i(E_S(m)) = E_{S \setminus \{P_i\}}(m)$$

The plaintext m should be easily recoverable from $E_\emptyset(m)$.

In the joint encryption scheme used by Franklin and Haber, a bit b is encrypted as

$$E_S(b) = \left[g^r \mod N,\ (-1)^b \left(\prod_{j \in S} g^{K_j} \right)^r \mod N \right]$$

where $N = pq$, p and q are two primes such that $p \equiv q \mod 4$, and $r \in_R Z_N$. The public key is given by $[N, g, g^{K_1} \mod N, \ldots, g^{K_n} \mod N]$ where each K_i represents the private (secret) key of participant P_i.

This scheme has some additional properties that are used in the protocol:

- *XOR-Homomorphic.* Anyone can compute a joint encryption of the XOR of two jointly encrypted bits. Indeed, if $E_S(b) = [\alpha, \beta]$ and $E_S(b') = [\alpha', \beta']$, then $E_S(b \oplus b') = [\alpha\alpha' \mod N, \beta\beta' \mod N]$.

- *Blindable.* Given an encrypted bit, anyone can create a random ciphertext that decrypts to the same bit. Indeed, if $E_S(b) = [\alpha, \beta]$ and $r \in_R Z_N$, then

  $$\left[\alpha g^r \mod N,\ \beta \left(\prod_{j \in S} g^{K_j} \right)^r \mod N \right]$$

  is a joint encryption of the same bit.

- *Witnessable.* Any participant can withdraw from a joint encryption by providing the other participants with a single value. Indeed, if $E_S(b) = [\alpha, \beta]$, it is easy to compute $D_i(E_S(b))$ from

  $$W_i([\alpha,\ \beta]) = \alpha^{-K_i} \mod N$$

First of all, the participants must agree on a value for N and g, choose a secret key K_i and broadcast $g^{K_i} \mod N$ to form the public key. To start the actual protocol, each participant broadcasts a joint encryption of his input bits. For an XOR-gate, everyone simply applies the XOR-homomorphism. The encrypted output of a NOT-gate can be found by applying the XOR-homomorphism with a default encryption of a one, e.g. $[1, -1]$.

However, it is the AND-gate that causes some trouble. Suppose the encrypted input bits for the AND-gate are $\hat{u} = E(u)$ and $\hat{v} = E(v)$. To compute a joint encryption $\hat{w} = E(w) = E(u \wedge v)$, they proceed as follows:

1 Each participant P_i chooses random bits b_i and c_i and broadcasts $\hat{b}_i = E(b_i)$ and $\hat{c}_i = E(c_i)$.

2 Each participant repeatedly applies the XOR-homomorphism to calculate $\hat{u}' = E(u') = E(u \oplus b_1 \oplus \ldots \oplus b_n)$ and $\hat{v}' = E(v') = E(v \oplus c_1 \oplus \ldots \oplus c_n)$. Each participant broadcasts decryption witnesses $W_i(\hat{u}')$ and $W_i(\hat{v}')$.

3 Everyone can now decrypt $\hat{u}'$ and $\hat{v}'$. We have the following relation between $w' = u' \wedge v'$ and $w = u \wedge v$:

$$
\begin{array}{rcl}
w' & = & u' \wedge v' \\
 & = & (u \oplus b_1 \oplus \cdots \oplus b_n) \wedge (v \oplus c_1 \oplus \cdots \oplus c_n) \\
 & = & (u \wedge v) \;\oplus\; (u \wedge c_1) \;\oplus \cdots \oplus\; (u \wedge c_n) \\
 & & \qquad\quad \oplus\; (b_1 \wedge c_1) \;\oplus \cdots \oplus\; (b_n \wedge c_1) \\
 & & \qquad\quad \vdots \qquad \vdots \qquad\qquad\qquad \vdots \\
 & & \qquad\quad \oplus\; (b_1 \wedge c_n) \;\oplus \cdots \oplus\; (b_n \wedge c_n) \\
 & & \qquad\quad \oplus\; \underbrace{(b_1 \wedge v)}_{w_1} \;\oplus \cdots \oplus\; \underbrace{(b_n \wedge v)}_{w_n} \\
 & = & (u \wedge v) \oplus w_1 \oplus \cdots \oplus w_n
\end{array}
$$

Each participant is able to compute a joint encryption of w_i: he knows b_i and c_i (he chose them himself) and he received encryptions $\hat{c}_j$ from the other participants, so he can compute $E(b_i \wedge c_j)$ as follows:

- If $b_i = 0$, then $b_i \wedge c_j = 0$, so any default encryption for a zero will do, e.g. $[1, 1]$.
- If $b_i = 1$, then $b_i \wedge c_j = c_j$, so $\hat{c}_j$ is a valid substitution for $E(b_i \wedge c_j)$.

$E(u \wedge c_i)$ and $E(v \wedge b_i)$ can be computed in an analogous way. He uses the XOR-homomorphism to combine all these terms, blinds the result and broadcasts this as $\hat{w}_i$.

4 Each participant combines $\hat{w}'$ and $\hat{w}_j$ ($j = 1 \ldots n$), again using the XOR-homomorphism, to form $\hat{w} = E(w)$.

When all gates in the circuit have been evaluated, every participant has a joint encryption of the output bits. Finally, all participants broadcast decryption witnesses to reveal the output.

3. SECOND PRICE AUCTIONS

In this section we consider second price auctions, where there is one item for sale and there are n bidders. The item will only be sold if the bid of one participant is strictly higher than the other bids. In all other cases there is no winner. The clearing price is the second highest bid. The requirements for this type of auction are the following:

- if there is no winner, nothing is revealed;
- if there is a winner:
  - the identity of the highest bidder is revealed, but the highest bid remains secret;
  - the 2nd highest bid is revealed, but the identity of the 2nd highest bidder is kept secret;
  - no other information (other bids) are to be revealed.

For three participants X, Y and Z, the boolean circuit is shown in Figure 1. The inputs to the circuit are 32-bit bids[1]. The output is the identity of the winner, represented by the bits $R1$ and $R0$ ($R1R0 = 00$ no winner, 01 winner is X, 10 winner is Y, 11 winner is Z), and the clearing price. If there is no winner, the clearing price is set to zero. To determine the winner, the circuit uses three comparators and a number of AND and OR gates. To determine the clearing price, four multiplexers are used. Consider the situation where X makes the highest bid. In this case $G1 \wedge G2 = 1$, $L1 \wedge G3 = 0$, $L2 \wedge L3 = 0$ and $R1R0 = 10$, so the second input to the final multiplexer will be chosen. The input on this line is determined by the bids made by Y and Z. If $Y > Z$ then $G3 = 1$ and Y will be selected as the clearing price. In the other cases ($Y < Z$ or $Y = Z$) Z will be the clearing price.

Our goal is to estimate the communication overhead of an implementation of secure distributed second price auctions with the protocol proposed by Franklin and Haber. The auction is designed as a boolean circuit and the communication overhead for secure circuit evaluation is estimated. The communication overhead is determined by the following steps in the protocol:

- broadcast of the encrypted input bits of each participant;
- evaluation of an AND gate:
  - broadcast of the encrypted bits $E(b_i)$, $E(c_i)$;
  - broadcast of the decryption witnesses $W_i(\hat{u}')$, $W_i(\hat{v}')$;
  - broadcast of the blinded $\hat{w}_i$;
- broadcast of the output decryption witnesses.

The associated communication overhead is:

[1] In reality, fewer bits (e.g. 8 or 16) would suffice.

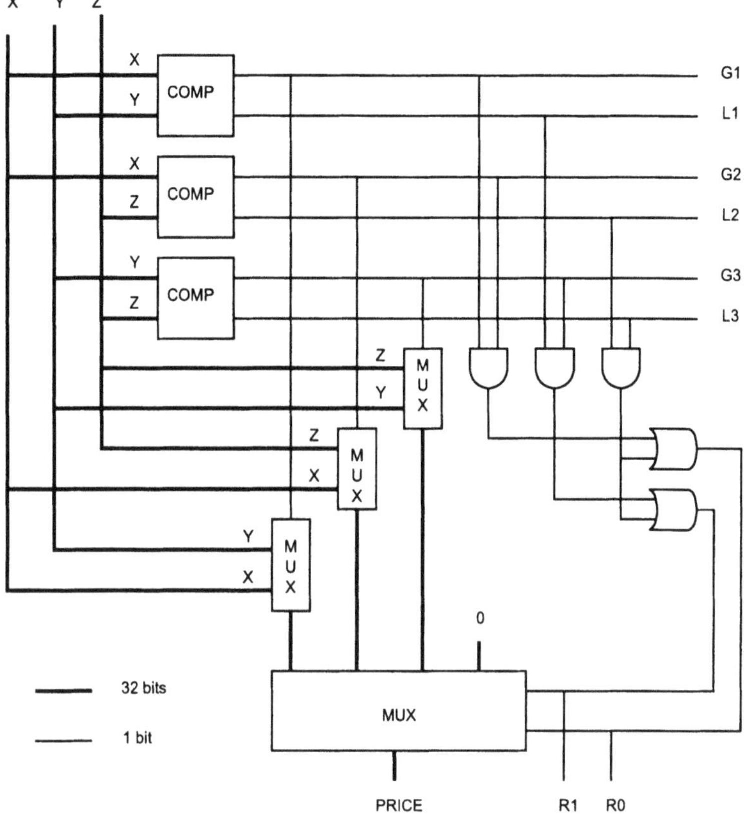

Figure 1. Boolean circuit implementation of second price auctions.

- $2 \cdot |N| \cdot in_i \cdot n$ for the broadcast of the input bits;
- $8 \cdot |N| \cdot n$ for the evaluation of an AND gate;
- $|N| \cdot out \cdot n$ for the decryption broadcast.

where $|N|$ is the length of N in bits, which is the same as the number of bits needed to represent an element of Z_N^*, in_i is the number of input bits of participant i, n is the number of participants and *out* is the number of output bits of the circuit. In order to estimate the communication overhead, we need to be able to determine the number of AND gates in the boolean circuit (note that each OR gate can be implemented with AND and NOT gates). Each comparator can be built with 374 AND-gates[2]

[2]The boolean function $A > B$, can be expressed as $A_0.\overline{B_0} + (A_0.B_0 + \overline{A_0}.\overline{B_0}).(A_1.\overline{B_1} + (A_1.B_1 + \overline{A_1}.\overline{B_1}).(A_2.\overline{B_2}...))$. Hence if A and B are k-bit numbers, $1 + 6(k-1)$ AND gates are needed. Both functions, $A > B$ and $B > A$, are needed for each comparator.

For $n > 3$ participants, the circuit changes as follows. The number of comparators needed is now $\binom{n}{2} = n \cdot (n-1)/2$. The final multiplexer will need to distinguish between $n+1$ different cases, i.e. n possible winners or no winner at all. The other n multiplexers are there to select the clearing price out of $n-1$ bids when there is a winner. The number of AND gates needed for each multiplexer as a function of the number of inputs m is shown in Figure 2. Besides the comparators and the multiplexers, some additional AND and OR gates are needed. However, the number of these gates is negligible compared to the number of gates needed for the comparators and multiplexers. In summary, the circuit has a total gate complexity of $O(n^2)$.

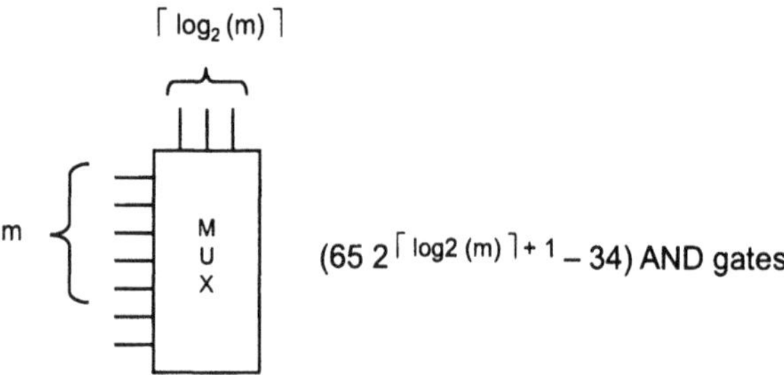

Figure 2. Number of AND gates needed in a mulitplexer

The results of estimating the communication overhead for this circuit as a function of the number of participants n are summarized in Table 1[3]. Franklin and Haber's protocol is linear in the number of broadcasts, so the total message complexity is $O(n^3)$. However, it must be noted that this only holds on a network with broadcast or multicast functionality, such that the communication overhead of sending a message to all participants is the same as that of sending a message to a single participant. In absence of such infrastructure, the total message complexity is $O(n^4)$.

Table 1. Network overhead of secure second price auctions

n	4	16	32
Overhead (MB)	15	1000	8000

[3]We choose $|N|$ to be 1024 bits.

4. MODUS OPERANDI

From the previous section, it should be clear that the design of the application has pros and cons:

- A major advantage is that our solution does not require a globally trusted third party that plays the role of the arbiter.
- The worst drawback is the immense communication overhead and the fact that the solution does not scale very well.

There exists a trade-off between 'trust' and 'communication overhead' in both options, the first one using a TTP and the solution that uses SDC. In this section, we investigate this trade-off and present a nice remedy for the communication overhead.

If a globally trusted third party is used, every participant, P_i, has to send its private bid x_i to that TTP who will select the highest bidder, determine the second highest bid, and disseminate its decision to the participants $P_i, i = 1..n$ (see Figure 3). Of course, before sending its private data to the TTP, every P_i

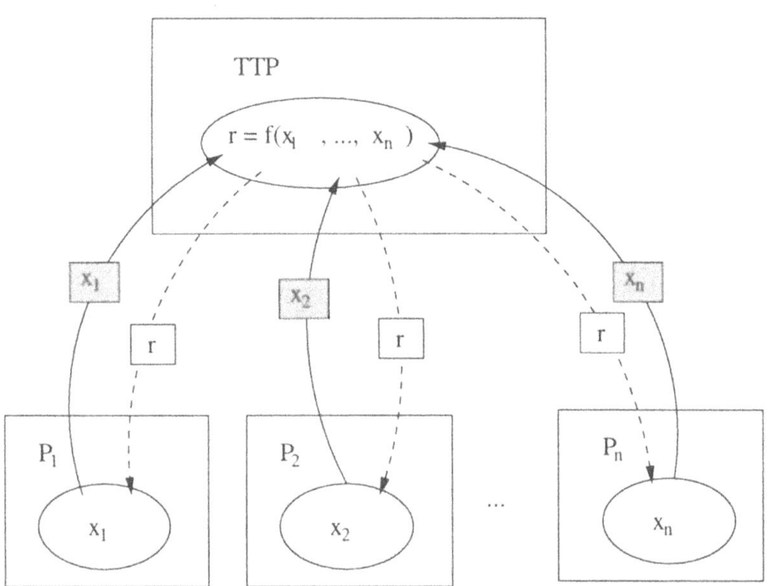

Figure 3. 2nd Price Auction Using a TTP.

must first authenticate the TTP, and then send x_i through a safe channel. This can be accomplished via conventional cryptographic techniques. It is clear that this approach has a very low communication overhead: the data is only sent once to the TTP; later, every participant receives the result of the computation. However, every participant should uncondionally trust the TTP. It is not clear whether n distrustful participants will easily agree on one single trustworthy site. If this site is compromised, all secrets, x_i may be compromised! Also, the site needs the appropriate software for this particular application. Hence, for every new 'application' new software needs to be installed. Therefore, the participants not only need to trust the (security of) the site, but also the software for this application.

In our approach (see Figure 4), the trust requirements are really minimal: every participant P_i trusts its own execution site E_i, and expects that the other participants provide correct values for their own inputs. (Note that in this protocol, a participant cannot cheat, because of the use of witnesses.) Although our approach is very attractive, it suffers extensive communication overhead and does not scale well.

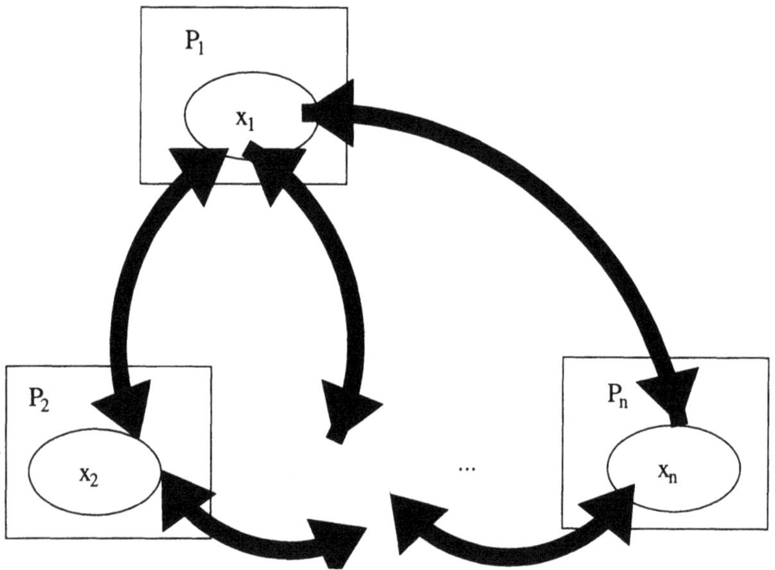

Figure 4. 2nd Price Auction Using SDC.

The communication overhead of SDC-techniques can be remedied by introducing semi-trusted execution sites and mobile agents (see Figure 5). Every participant P_i sends its representative, agent A_i, to a trusted execution site E_j. The agent contains a copy of the private data x_i and is capable of running a SDC-protocol. It is allowed that different participants send their agents to different sites. The only restriction being that the sites should be located closely to each other, i.e. should have high bandwidth communication between them. Of course, every execution site needs a mechanism to safely download an agent. However, that can be easily accomplished through convential cryptographic techniques. The amount of large distance communication is moderate: every participant sends its agent to a remote site, and receives the result from its

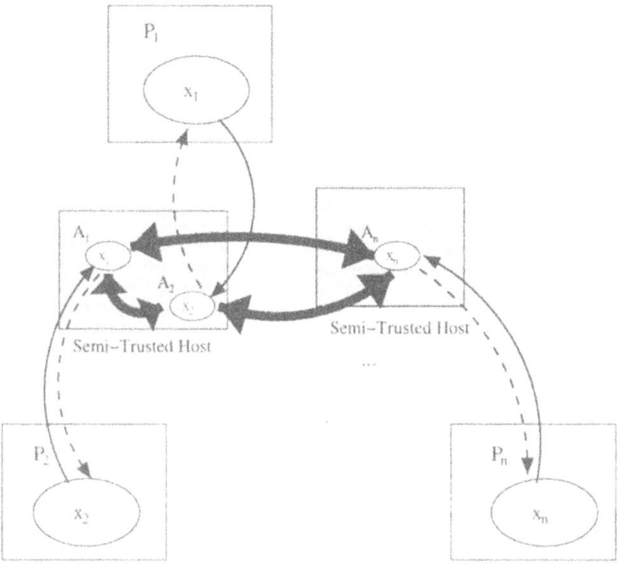

Figure 5. 2nd Price Auctions Using Agents (SDC) and Semi-Trusted Sites.

agent. The agents use a SDC-protocol, which unfortunately involves a high communication overhead. However, since the agents are executing on sites that are near each other, the overhead of the SDC-protocol is acceptable. No high bandwidth communication between the participants is necessary, and there is no longer a need for one single trusted execution site. The agents that participate in the secure computation are protected against malicious behaviour of other (non-trusted) execution sites by the SDC-protocols. That is sufficient to make this approach work. Moreover, in contrast with the approach where one uses an unconditionally trusted third party, the trusted sites are not involved directly. They simply offer a *secure execution platform*: the trusted hosts do *not* have to know the protocol used between the agents. In other words, the combination of mobile agent technology and secure distributed computing protocols makes it possible to use *generic* trusted third parties that, by offering a secure execution platform, can act as trusted third party for a wide variety of protocols in a uniform way. Finally, the question remains whether it is realistic to assume that participants can find execution sites that are close enough to each other. Given the fact however that these execution sites can be *generic*, we believe that providing such execution sites could be a commercial occupation. Various deployment strategies are possible. Several service providers, each administering a set of geographically dispersed "secure hosts", can propose their subscribers an appropriate site for the secure computation. The site is chosen to be in the neighborhood of a secure site of the other service providers involved. Another approach is to have execution parks, offering high bandwidth communication facilities, were companies can install their proprietary "secure site". The park itself could be managed by a commercial or government agency.

5. CONCLUSIONS

This paper demonstrates that second price auctions, and many other relevant applications, can be implemented by using SDC protocols. That way, the participants can make sure that all confidential information is kept secret. The major disadvantage, the overwhelming communication overhead, can be remedied through the use of mobile agents and semi-trusted sites. There is no need for one generally trusted site, nor does the program code have to be endorsed by all participants. The trusted execution sites are generic and can be small (which might allow to draft a formal security for these sites). The communication overhead of secure distributed computing protocols is no longer prohibitive for their use since the execution sites are located closely to each other.

References

[1] M. Abadi and J. Feigenbaum, "Secure circuit evaluation, a protocol based on hiding information from an oracle," Journal of Cryptology, 2(1), p. 1–12, 1990

[2] R. Cramer. "An introduction to secure computation", in LNCS 1561, pp 16–62, 1999.

[3] M. Franklin, "Complexity and security of distributed protocols," Ph. D. thesis, Computer Science Department of Columbia University, New York, 1993

[4] M. Franklin and S. Haber, "Joint encryption and message-efficient secure computation," Journal of Cryptology, 9(4), p. 217–232, Autumn 1996

[5] S. Loureiro and R. Molva, "Privacy for Mobile Code", Proceedings of the workshop on *Distributed Object Security*, OOPSLA '99, p. 37–42.

[6] G. Neven, F. Piessens, B. De Decker, "On the Practical Feasibility of Secure Distributed Computing: a Case Study", Information Security for Global Information Infrastructures (S. Qing, J. Eloff, ed.), Kluwer Academic Publishers, 2000, pp. 361-370.

[7] G. Neven, E. Van Hoeymissen, B. De Decker, F. Piessens, "Enabling Secure Distributed Computations : Semi-trusted Hosts and Mobile Agents", to appear in Networking and Information Systems Journal 3 (2001).

[8] N. Nisan, "Algorithms for selfish agents", *Proceedings of the 16th Annual Symposium on Theoretical Aspects of Computer Science*, Trier, Germany, March 1999, p. 1–15.

[9] T. Sander and C. Tschudin, "On software protection via function hiding", *Proceedings of the second workshop on Information Hiding*, Portland, Oregon, USA, April 1998.

[10] T. Sander and C. Tschudin, "Towards mobile cryptography", *Proceedings of the 1998 IEEE Symposium on Security and Privacy*, Oakland, California, May 1998.

[11] T. Sander, A. Young, M. Yung, "Non-Interactive CryptoComputing for NC^1", preprint.

SPECIFICATION AND VERIFICATION OF A DYNAMIC RECONFIGURATION PROTOCOL FOR AGENT-BASED APPLICATIONS

Manuel Aguilar Cornejo*, Hubert Garavel,
Radu Mateescu, and Noël de Palma
INRIA Rhône-Alpes, 655, avenue de l'Europe, F-38330 Montbonnot St. Martin, France
Manuel.Aguilar@imag.fr, {Hubert.Garavel, Radu.Mateescu, Noel.De-Palma}@inria.fr

Abstract Dynamic reconfiguration increases the availability of distributed applications by allowing them to evolve at run-time. This paper deals with the formal specification and model-checking verification of a dynamic reconfiguration protocol used in industrial agent-based applications. Starting from a reference implementation in JAVA, we produced a specification of the protocol using the Formal Description Technique LOTOS. We also specified a set of temporal logic formulas characterizing the correct behaviour of each protocol primitive. Finally, we studied various finite state configurations of the protocol, on which we verified these requirements using the CADP protocol engineering tool set.

Keywords: compositional verification, distributed application, dynamic reconfiguration, LOTOS, mobile agent, model-checking, specification

1. INTRODUCTION

As computing resources become decentralized, the development of distributed applications receives increasing attention from the software engineering community. These applications are often complex and must satisfy strong reliability and availability constraints. To avoid stopping an entire distributed application for maintenance operations (e.g., repair, upgrade, etc.), it is essential to provide mechanisms allowing distributed applications to be reconfigured at run-time. Such mechanisms should ensure a proper functioning of the application regardless of run-time changes (e.g., creation or deletion of agents, replacement of agents, migration of agents across execution sites, modification of communication routes, etc). Moreover, these mechanisms should not induce heavy penalties on applications during maintenance operations.

*This author was partially supported by CONACYT-SFERE and UAM Iztapalapa, Mexico.

Dynamic reconfiguration has been studied and implemented in various middlewares, such as CONIC [13], ARGUS [2], and POLYLITH [23]. In some approaches, e.g., POLYLITH, dynamic reconfiguration is part of the applications developed on top of the middleware, thus transferring to application developers the responsibility to ensure consistency after reconfiguration. In other approaches, e.g., CONIC and ARGUS, the middleware is extended with (application-independent) dynamic reconfiguration features.

This paper studies the protocol for dynamic reconfiguration of agent-based applications defined in [20], which follows the latter approach. This protocol has been implemented in the middleware platform AAA (*Agents Anytime Anywhere*) [1, 21], which allows a flexible, scalable, and reliable development of distributed applications. The protocol has been experimented on several industrial applications developed in cooperation with BULL, and especially on an application for managing a set of network firewalls [21]. In this application (included in BULL's NETWALL security product), each firewall produces a log file of audit information; agents are used to manage logged information, to provide filtering functionalities that can be added and customized lately according to customer requirements, to correlate and coordinate multiple firewalls, and to deploy a set of log management applications over the firewalls.

As this dynamic reconfiguration protocol is non-trivial, it was suitable to ensure its correctness using formal methods, and especially to establish that reconfiguration preserves the consistency of the application. Starting from the informal description of the protocol given in [20] and a JAVA implementation that was already in use, we produced a formal specification of the protocol using the ISO Formal Description Technique LOTOS [12]. We then identified a set of safety and liveness properties characterizing the desired behaviour of each reconfiguration primitive of the protocol. To verify whether these correctness properties hold for the LOTOS specification, we used the *model-checking* approach [3]; verification was carried out using CADP [6], a protocol engineering tool set providing state-of-the-art compilation, simulation, and verification functionalities.

This article is organized as follows. Section 2 presents the AAA agent-based middleware and its dynamic reconfiguration protocol. Section 3 describes the LOTOS specification of the protocol. Section 4 reports about the verification process performed using CADP. Finally, Section 5 discusses the results and gives directions for future work.

2. THE DYNAMIC RECONFIGURATION PROTOCOL

In this section, we first introduce the AAA distributed agent model. Then, we state the dynamic reconfiguration problem and present the principles of the reconfiguration protocol under study.

2.1. The AAA distributed agent model

In the AAA model [1], the basic software elements are *agents* executing concurrently on several *sites*. Each agent has only one execution flow (single-thread). Agents are connected by *communication channels*, i.e., unidirectional point-to-point links. Agents can synchronize and communicate only by sending or receiving messages on communication channels, which play the role of references to other agents.

Agents behave according to an *event-reaction* scheme: when receiving an event on a communication channel, an agent executes the appropriate reaction, i.e., a piece of code that may update the agent state and/or send messages to other agents (including the agent itself).

The AAA infrastructure ensures that agents and communications satisfy certain properties [1] listed in the table below. The dynamic reconfiguration protocol relies upon some of these properties, and especially the *causality* property (also called *causal ordering*) [24, 16].

AGENT PROPERTIES	
Persistency	Agent lifetime is not bounded to the duration of execution (however, this does not ensure consistent state retrieval after failures).
Atomicity	Upon receipt of an event, the reaction of an agent is either fully executed or not executed at all.
Configurability	Agent attributes and references to other agents can be changed at run-time by a third party (e.g., an administrator).
COMMUNICATION PROPERTIES	
Asynchrony	No assumption is made on transmission speed, allowing applications to be designed and implemented in a time-independent manner.
Reliability	Message delivery is guaranteed in spite of network failures or system crashes and without any involvement from the application.
Causality	Messages are delivered in the same order as they are sent.

2.2. Dynamic reconfiguration

Dynamic reconfiguration of an agent-based application encompasses (at least) four possible changes in the structure of the application at run-time: *architectural changes* (creation or deletion of agents, modification of communication routes), *migration changes* (modification of the placement of agents on execution sites), *agent implementation changes*, and *agent interface changes*. The dynamic reconfiguration protocol under study takes into account only the first two aspects.

Figure 1 shows an example of application reconfiguration involving the migration of an agent across two sites. This example will be used throughout this section.

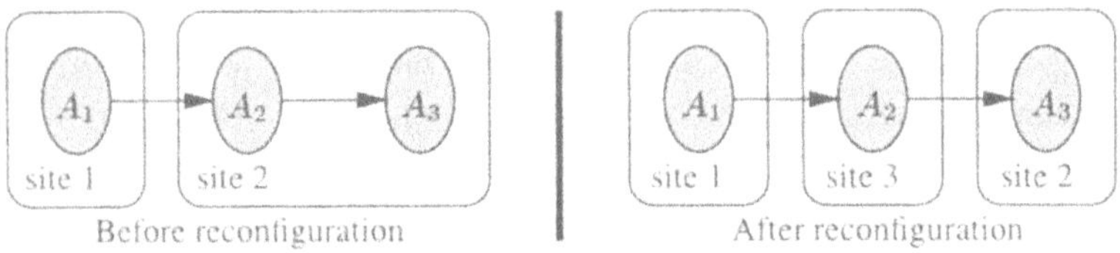

Figure 1. Migration of agent A_2 from site 2 to site 3

Dynamic reconfiguration must preserve *consistency* [14]: after reconfiguration, the application should be able to resume its execution from its global state prior to reconfiguration. Figure 2 shows an inconsistency that may occur during the reconfiguration depicted on Figure 1: message m_3 is lost because while it was in transit, its destination (agent A_2) has migrated from site 2 to site 3.

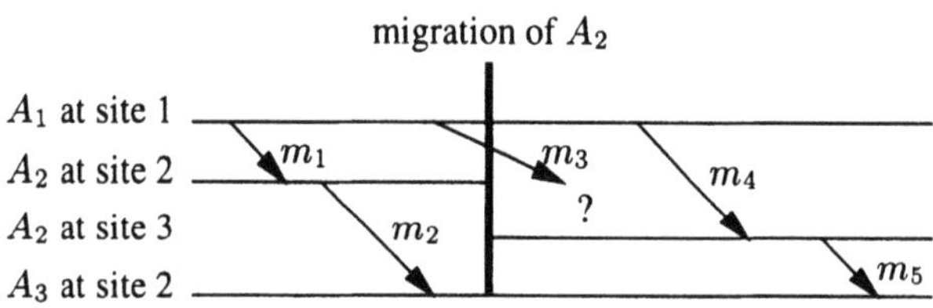

Figure 2. Inconsistency arising from migration of A_2 from site 2 to site 3

To avoid inconsistencies, three issues must be taken into account:

- *Agent naming:* references to migrating agents must be properly updated (e.g., assuming that agent names include site information, the reference to agent A_2 used by agent A_1 when sending message m_3 may become outdated after A_2 has moved from site 2 to site 3).

- *Agent states:* after an agent has been reconfigured, it must be able to resume its actual computation from its former state (e.g., agent A_2 must resume its computation on site 3 from its state on site 2 prior to migration).

- *Communication channels:* messages in transit during a reconfiguration must be preserved and properly redirected to their destination agents after reconfiguration (e.g., message m_3 should reach A_2 after A_2 has migrated to site 3).

2.3. Principles of the protocol

To ensure consistency in presence of agent migration, different approaches have been proposed, such as checkpointing [17] (which performs a rollback of the application to its last consistent state, on which reconfiguration is performed), forwarding techniques [22] (which temporarily replace a migrating agent by a *forwarder* responsible for redirecting incoming messages to the new location of the agent), and transparent protocols for location-independent communication [25] (which avoid reference updates between agents by preserving agent names).

Checkpointing techniques require the additional cost of maintaining consistent distributed snapshots of the application (i.e., the agent states and the messages in transit) and of rollbacking. Forwarding techniques induce residual dependencies that may affect application reliability (e.g., in case of a forwarder failure). The AAA agent-based middleware does not provide location-independent communications, but rather reliable communication and agent management primitives.

For these reasons, the dynamic reconfiguration protocol described in [20] does not rely on these techniques. It is derived from the protocol used in CONIC, but improved to take advantage of the properties (event-reaction model, asynchrony, persistency) guaranteed by the AAA middleware. The protocol associates to each application a particular agent, named *configurator*, which is responsible for handling all reconfiguration commands. The configurator maintains a view of the application configuration (placement of agents on sites and communication routes between agents), determines if a reconfiguration command can be performed, executes the corresponding actions, and updates the configuration view accordingly. Unlike a forwarder, the configurator can handle more complex reconfiguration primitives, such as code replacement and agent deletion.

The communication infrastructure provided by the AAA model can be seen as a logical bus that carries all messages between application agents and/or the configurator. Each agent is referenced by an address $\langle a, s \rangle$, where s is the identifier of the current site of the agent and a is the local identifier of the agent on site s. When an agent moves across different sites, its address must be updated appropriately (note that the local identifier may also change when the agent migrates to another site).

The following reconfiguration primitives are supported by the protocol: `ADD` (addition of a new agent to the application), `DELETE` (removal of an agent from the application), `MOVE` (migration of an agent to another site), `BIND` and `REBIND` (creation and modification of a communication channel between two agents). The implementation of the `REBIND`, `MOVE`, and `DELETE` primitives must avoid inconsistencies. Intuitively, when an agent is under reconfiguration, its execution must be suspended; in the event-reaction model, this can be obtained by ensuring that the agent receives no more events during its reconfiguration. The preconditions for a safe execution of the reconfiguration primitives can be summarized as follows: *all communication channels involved must be empty (i.e., must not contain any message in transit) before reconfiguration can occur.*

The dynamic reconfiguration protocol implementing these primitives can be defined using a notion of *abstract state* for application agents. At any time, an agent can be in one of the three abstract states listed in the table below.

STATE	MEANING
Active	The agent can execute normally and communicate with other agents according to the event-reaction model.
Passive	The agent can react to events but cannot send any event to other agents; all events that it must send are delayed until its reactivation.
Frozen	The agent does not receive any event anymore; all agents having a reference towards it are passive and the corresponding channels are empty.

During the execution of reconfiguration commands, the configurator forces certain agents into appropriate abstract states in order to preserve consistency. Roughly speaking, to reconfigure an agent A or one of its outgoing channels, the configurator implements the following protocol:

1. Compute the *Change Passive Set*, noted $cps(A)$, which contains all the agents having a communication channel directed to A: these agents must be made passive in order to freeze A. For the `REBIND` primitive, $cps(A)$ is empty, but A itself must be made passive.

2. Passivate all agents in $cps(A)$. So doing, all agents with references to A are becoming passive and all communication channels directed to A are progressively flushed. When this is complete, agent A is frozen (except in the case of `REBIND`, where A is made passive, but not frozen).

3. Send the reconfiguration command to A. The causal ordering property ensures that this command will only be received when A is frozen (although the configurator never knows exactly when A is frozen).

4. Activate all agents in $cps(A)$. Agents in $cps(A)$ that have received messages while they were passive must react to these messages as soon as they are reactivated. In the case of `REBIND`, agent A is reactivated when it receives the `REBIND` command.

3. FORMAL SPECIFICATION

In this section we give a brief overview of LOTOS and then we detail the specification of the dynamic reconfiguration protocol.

3.1. Overview of LOTOS

LOTOS (*Language Of Temporal Ordering Specification*) [12] is a Formal Description Technique standardized by ISO for specifying communication protocols and distributed systems. Its design was motivated by the need for a language with a high abstraction level and strong mathematical basis, which could be used for the description and analysis of complex systems. LOTOS consists of two "orthogonal" sub-languages:

The data part is based on the well-known theory of algebraic abstract data types, more specifically on the ACTONE specification language [4]. A data type is described by its sorts and operations, which are specified using algebraic equations.

The behaviour part is based on process algebras, combining the best features of CCS [19] and CSP [11]. A concurrent system is usually described as a collection of parallel processes interacting by rendezvous. Each process behaviour is specified using an algebra of operators (see the table below). Processes can manipulate data values and exchange them at interaction points called *gates*.

BEHAVIOUR OPERATOR	INTUITIVE MEANING
`stop`	Do nothing.
G !V ?X:S ; B	Interact on gate G, sending value V and receiving in variable X a value of sort S, then execute B.
B_1 [] B_2	Execute either B_1 or B_2.
[E] -> B	If E is true then execute B, else do nothing.
B_1 |[$G_1, ..., G_n$]| B_2	Execute B_1 and B_2 in parallel with synchronization on gates $G_1, ..., G_n$ (||| means no synchronization).
`exit`	Terminate successfully.
B_1 >> B_2	Execute B_1 followed by B_2 when B_1 terminates.
P [$G_1, ..., G_n$] ($V_1, ..., V_n$)	Call process P with gate parameters $G_1, ..., G_n$ and value parameters $V_1, ..., V_n$.

3.2. Architecture of the protocol

The architecture of the LOTOS specification (see Figure 3) consists of a configurator agent and n application agents. All agents are modelled as LOTOS processes, which execute concurrently and communicate through a software bus (an abstraction of the AAA infrastructure), which is also modeled by a LOTOS process. Agents can send and receive messages (events) via the gates `SEND` and `RECV`, respectively. The `Bus` process acts as an unbounded buffer (initially empty) accepting messages on gate `SEND` and delivering them on gate `RECV`.

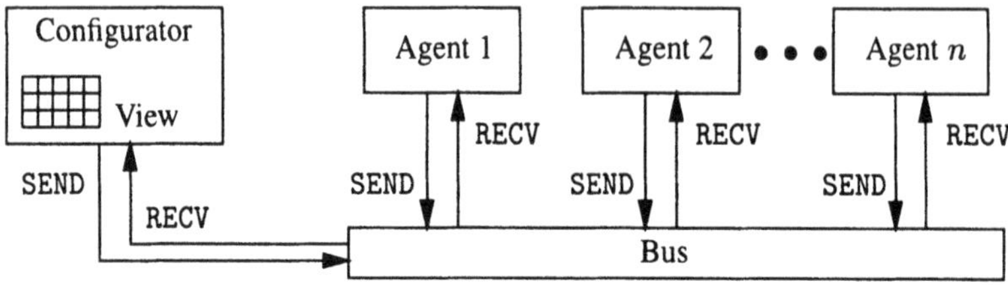

Figure 3. Architecture of the dynamic reconfiguration protocol

Dynamic agent creation is modelled in a finite manner by considering a fixed set of `Agent` processes that initially are all "dead" (an auxiliary abstract state, noted DEAD, meaning that the agent is not part of the application) and will be progressively added to the application.

3.3. Configurator agent

The configurator agent is responsible for keeping track of the application configuration and for executing the reconfiguration commands coming from some external user. Since we seek to study a general behaviour of the protocol, we do not specify a particular user, letting the configurator behave as if it would receive an infinite sequence of arbitrary reconfiguration commands.

The `Configurator` process has two parameters: the application configuration C (initially empty) and the address set R of agents currently in the DEAD state. The configuration C is modelled as a list of tuples $\langle\langle a, s\rangle, A\rangle$, where $\langle a, s\rangle$ is the address of an agent present in the application and A is the set of agent addresses towards which the agent has a reference (output channels). The `Configurator` process has a cyclic behaviour: it chooses a reconfiguration command non-deterministically, executes the appropriate operations, and calls itself recursively with an updated configuration. In the following example, we only detail the MOVE primitive, the other reconfiguration primitives being specified similarly.

```
process Configurator [SEND, RECV] (C:Config, R:AddrSet) : noexit :=
   (* ... other reconfiguration primitives *)
   (choice A:Addr, S:SiteId []
      [(A isin C) and (getsite (A) ne S)] ->
      (let A2:Addr = newaddr (S, C) in
         Passivate [SEND, RECV] (cps (A, C)) >>
         SEND !A !confaddr !MOVE !A2 !dummy;
            RECV !confaddr !A2 !ACK !dummy !dummy;
               Activate [SEND, RECV] (A, A2, cps (A, C)) >>
               Configurator [SEND, RECV]
                  (setaddr (A, A2, setchan (cps (A, C), A, A2, C)), R)
      )
```

```
  )
endproc
```

The address A of the agent to be moved and its destination site identifier S are chosen non-deterministically. The agents in the set *cps*(A) are made passive by calling the auxiliary process Passivate. Then, a MOVE command is sent to agent A, which must respond with an acknowledgement upon completion of its migration to site S. The agents in *cps*(A) are then reactivated by calling the auxiliary process Activate, which also notifies them with the new address A2 of agent A. Finally, the Configurator calls itself recursively with a modified configuration obtained from C by updating the address of agent A and the output channels of the agents in *cps*(A).

3.4. Application agents

Application agents execute the code of the application according to the event-reaction model and must also react to the reconfiguration commands sent by the configurator agent. Since we focus on the reconfiguration protocol itself rather than on the agent-based applications built upon it, we consider only one application-level message (called SERVICE) sent between agents.

The Agent process has four parameters: its current abstract state S, its current address A, the set R of agent addresses (output channels) towards which it has a reference and a boolean B indicating whether a message was received while it was passive (this may occur during the migration of another agent towards which the current agent has an output channel). The Agent process has a cyclic behaviour: it receives an event, executes the corresponding reaction according to its current abstract state S, and calls itself recursively with the parameters updated appropriately. In the following example, we only detail the reaction of an agent to the MOVE command, the other reconfiguration commands being specified similarly.

```
process Agent [SEND, RECV] (S:State, A:Addr, R:AddrSet, B:Bool):noexit:=
  (* ... other reconfiguration commands *)
  [S eq ACTIVE] ->
     RECV !A !confaddr !MOVE ?A2:Addr !dummy;
        SEND !confaddr !A2 !ACK !dummy !dummy;
           Agent [SEND, RECV] (S, A2, R, B)
  []
  [S eq PASSIVE] ->
     RECV !A !confaddr !MOVE ?A2:Addr !dummy;
     ([B] ->
       (choice A3:Addr [] [A3 isin replace (A, A2, R)] ->
        SEND !A3 !A !SERVICE !dummy !dummy;
           SEND !confaddr !A2 !ACK !dummy !dummy;
              Agent [SEND, RECV] (ACTIVE, A2, replace (A, A2, R), false)
       )
```

```
    []
    [not (B)] -> SEND !confaddr !A2 !ACK !dummy !dummy;
       Agent [SEND, RECV] (ACTIVE, A2, replace (A, A2, R), false)
    )
endproc
```

The migration is specified simply by changing the agent address. If the agent is active, it simply sends an acknowledgement with its new address A2 back to the configurator, and then calls itself recursively with an updated address. If the agent is passive (this can happen only if it has an output channel directed to itself), it first reacts to the events received from other agents while it was passive, then sends an acknowledgement to the configurator, and finally becomes active, updating its address and its output channels.

4. MODEL-CHECKING VERIFICATION

To analyze the behaviour of the dynamic reconfiguration protocol, we used the CADP tool set, which we briefly present. We then express the correctness properties of the protocol and give experimental results regarding model-checking verification.

4.1. Overview of the CADP tool set

CADP (CÆSAR/ALDÉBARAN Development Package) [6] is a state-of-the-art tool set dedicated to the verification of communication protocols and distributed systems. CADP offers an integrated set of functionalities ranging from interactive simulation to exhaustive, model-based verification. In this case-study, we used the following tools of CADP:

CAESAR.ADT [8] and **CAESAR** [10] are compilers for the data part and the control part of LOTOS specifications, respectively. They can be used to translate a LOTOS specification into a Labelled Transition System (LTS), i.e., a state-transition graph modelling exhaustively the behaviour of the specification. Each LTS transition is labelled with an action resulting from synchronization on a gate, possibly with communication of data values.

EVALUATOR 3.0 [18] is an on-the-fly model-checker for temporal logic formulas over LTSs. The logic considered is an extension of the alternation-free μ-calculus [5] with action predicates and regular expressions. The tool also provides diagnostics (examples and counterexamples) explaining the truth value of the formulas.

BCG_MIN is a tool for minimizing LTSs according to various equivalence relations, such as strong bisimulation, observational or branching equivalence, etc.

SVL 2.0 [9] is a tool for compositional and on-the-fly verification based on the approach proposed in [15]. Compositional verification is a mean to avoid state explosion in model-checking by dividing a concurrent system into its parallel components (e.g., the configurator agent, application agents, and the bus), generating (modulo some abstractions) the LTS corresponding to each component, minimizing each LTS and recombining the minimized LTSs to obtain the whole system.

4.2. Correctness properties

To express the correct behaviour of the dynamic reconfiguration protocol, we expressed a set of relevant properties about its behaviour. Two main classes of properties are usually considered for distributed systems: *safety properties*, stating that "something bad never happens", and *liveness properties*, stating that "something good eventually happens" during the execution of the system. For the dynamic reconfiguration protocol under study, we identified, together with the developers of the AAA middleware, 10 safety and liveness properties characterizing either the global behaviour of the protocol or the particular behaviour of each reconfiguration primitive. These properties are shown in the table below (the S and L superscripts indicate safety and liveness, respectively).

No.	Correctness Property
P_1^L	There is no deadlock in the specification.
P_2^L	Every reconfiguration command is eventually followed by an acknowledgement.
P_3^S	There is a strict alternation between commands and acknowledgements.
P_4^L	Every command sent to the bus is eventually delivered to its receiver.
P_5^S	Initially, no event can be sent before at least one agent has been created.
P_6^S	Initially, no application event can be sent before the underlying channel has been created.
P_7^L	Every event sent to a migrating agent will be delivered properly.
P_8^S	After a move command has been sent, the target agent cannot receive any event until it completes its migration.
P_9^S	Every event sent to a channel being rebound will be delivered before the rebind completes.
P_{10}^S	An agent that has been removed from the application cannot execute anymore.

Then, we expressed these properties in regular alternation-free μ-calculus, the temporal logic accepted by the EVALUATOR 3.0 model-checker. This logic allows to succinctly encode safety properties by using regular modalities of the form $[\mathsf{R}]\,\mathsf{F}$, which state the absence of "bad" execution sequences characterized by a regular expression R. For instance, property P_3 is encoded by the formula $[\mathsf{T}^*.\texttt{SEND\_CMD1}.(\neg\texttt{SEND\_ACK})^*.\texttt{SEND\_CMD2}]\,\mathsf{F}$, where the action predicates SEND_CMD1, SEND_CMD2, and SEND_ACK denote the emission of two reconfiguration commands and of an acknowledgement, respectively.

4.3. Verification results

As model-checking verification is only applicable to finite-state models (of tractable size), we considered several instances of the protocol involving a finite number of agents, sites, and reconfiguration commands. The experimental results regarding LTS generation are shown in the table below. For each instance, the table gives the LTS size (number of states and transitions) and the time required for its generation using CADP. All experiments have been performed on a 500 MHz Pentium II machine with 768 Mbytes of memory.

AGENTS	SITES	COMMANDS	STATES	TRANS.	TIME
2	2	ADD, BIND, REBIND	77	84	9"
2	2	ADD, DELETE, BIND, REBIND	4 424	5 832	43"
2	2	ADD, BIND, REBIND, MOVE	599 474	832 864	4'25"
3	1	ADD, DELETE	493	639	15"
3	1	ADD, BIND	3 391	5 031	32"
3	1	ADD, BIND, REBIND	590 119	935 397	5'13"
3	1	ADD, BIND, MOVE	646 592	917 796	5'46"

As expected, the LTS size increases rapidly with the number of agents present in the instance, because the number of possible application configurations is exponential in the number of agents. Using the EVALUATOR 3.0 model-checker, we verified that all temporal properties given in Section 4.2 are valid on each instance considered. The average verification time of a property over an LTS was about one minute.

5. CONCLUSION AND FUTURE WORK

In this paper, we used the ISO language LOTOS [12] and the CADP verification tool set [6] to analyse a protocol for dynamic reconfiguration proposed in [20] and used in the AAA platform [1].

The LOTOS specification developed (about 900 lines) provides a non-ambiguous description of the protocol and a basis for future development and experimentation of new reconfiguration primitives. Using model-checking and temporal logic, we were able to verify the correct functioning of the protocol on various configurations involving several agents, sites, and reconfiguration primitives. This experiment increased the confidence in the correctness of the protocol and demonstrated the usefulness of formal methods for agent-based applications.

Three future research directions are of interest. Firstly, to improve scalability, the protocol could be extended to use a distributed configurator instead of the current centralized solution. Secondly, the validation activity could be continued on larger configurations of the protocol and more detailed specification of the AAA communication infrastructure. Thirdly, one could investigate the generation of test suites for the JAVA implementation of the protocol, by using the TGV tool [7] recently integrated in CADP, which allows to automatically derive test suites from user-defined test purposes.

Acknowledgments

We are grateful to Frédéric Lang for his careful reading and valuable comments on this paper, and for his assistance in using the SVL tool.

References

[1] L. Bellissard, N. De Palma, A. Freyssinet, M. Herrmann, and S. Lacourte. An Agent Platform for Reliable Asynchronous Distributed Programming. In *Proceedings of SRDS'99 (Lausanne, Suisse)*, 1999.

[2] T. Bloom and M. Day. Reconfiguration and Module Replacement in Argus: Theory and Practice. *Soft. Eng. Journal*, 8:102–108, 1993.

[3] E. M. Clarke, O. Grumberg, and D. Peled. *Model Checking*. MIT Press, 2000.

[4] J. de Meer, R. Roth, and S. Vuong. Introduction to Algebraic Specifications Based on the Language ACT ONE. *Computer Networks and ISDN Systems*, 23(5):363–392, 1992.

[5] E. A. Emerson and C-L. Lei. Efficient Model Checking in Fragments of the Propositional Mu-Calculus. In *Proc. of LICS'86*, pp. 267–278.

[6] J-C. Fernandez, H. Garavel, A. Kerbrat, R. Mateescu, L. Mounier, and M. Sighireanu. CADP (CÆSAR/ALDÉBARAN Development Package): A Protocol Validation and Verification Toolbox. In R. Alur and T. A. Henzinger, editors, *Proc. of CAV'96 (New Brunswick, NJ, USA)*, LNCS vol. 1102, pp. 437–440.

[7] J-C. Fernandez, C. Jard, T. Jéron, L. Nedelka, and C. Viho. Using On-the-Fly Verification Techniques for the Generation of Test Suites. In R. Alur and T. A. Henzinger, editors, *Proc. of CAV'96 (New Brunswick, NJ, USA)*, LNCS vol. 1102, pp. 348–359.

[8] H. Garavel. Compilation of LOTOS Abstract Data Types. In S. Vuong, editor, *Proc. of FORTE'89 (Vancouver, Canada)*, pp. 147–162. North-Holland, 1989.

[9] H. Garavel and F. Lang. SVL: a Scripting Language for Compositional Verification. In *Proc. of FORTE'01 (Cheju Island, Korea)*, Kluwer Academic, 2001.

[10] H. Garavel and J. Sifakis. Compilation and Verification of LOTOS Specifications. In L. Logrippo, R. L. Probert, and H. Ural, editors, *Proc. of PSTV'90 (Ottawa, Canada)*, Kluwer Academic, pp. 379–394.

[11] C. A. R. Hoare. *Communicating Sequential Processes*. Prentice-Hall, 1985.

[12] ISO/IEC. LOTOS–A Formal Description Technique Based on the Temporal Ordering of Observational Behaviour. Int. Std. 8807, ISO, Genève, 1988.

[13] J. Kramer and J. Magee. Constructing Distributed Systems in CONIC. *IEEE Trans. on Soft. Eng.*, 15(6):663–675, 1989.

[14] J. Kramer and J. Magee. The Evolving Philosophers Problem: Dynamic Change Management. *IEEE Trans. on Soft. Eng.*, pp. 1293–1306, 1990.

[15] J.-P. Krimm and L. Mounier. Compositional State Space Generation from LOTOS Programs. In Ed Brinksma, editor, *Proc. of TACAS'97 (Enschede, The Netherlands)*, LNCS vol. 1217.

[16] P. Laumay, E. Bruneton, L. Bellissard, and S. Krakowiak. Preserving Causality in a Scalable Message-Oriented Middleware. C3DS 3rd Year Report Deliverable, ESPRIT Long Term Research Project no. 24962 (http://www.newcastle.research.ec.org/c3ds), 2001.

[17] M. Litzkow and M. Solomon. Supporting Checkpointing and Process Migration Outside the UNIX Kernel. In *Proc. of the USENIX Winter Conference (San Francisco, USA)*, pp. 283–290, 1992.

[18] R. Mateescu and M. Sighireanu. Efficient On-the-Fly Model-Checking for Regular Alternation-Free Mu-Calculus. In S. Gnesi, I. Schieferdecker, and A. Rennoch, editors, *Proc. of FMICS'2000 (Berlin, Germany)*, GMD Report 91, pp. 65–86. Full version available as INRIA Research Report RR-3899.

[19] R. Milner. *Communication and Concurrency*. Prentice-Hall, 1989.

[20] N. De Palma, L. Bellissard, and M. Riveill. Dynamic Reconfiguration of Agent-Based Applications. In *Proc. of ERSADS'99 (Madeira Island, Portugal)*, 1999.

[21] N. De Palma, L. Bellissard, D. Féliot, A. Freyssinet, M. Herrmann, and S. Lacourte. The AAA Agent-based Message Oriented Middleware. Tech. Report 30, C3DS Public Tech. Report Series, ESPRIT Project no. 24962, 2000.

[22] M. L. Powell and B. P. Miller. Process Migration in DEMOS/MP. In *Proc. of the 6th ACM Symp. on on Operating System Principles*, pp. 110–119, 1983.

[23] J. M. Purtilo. The POLYLITH Software Bus. ACM TOPLAS, 16(1):151–174, 1994.

[24] M. Raynal, A. Schiper, and S. Toueg. The Causal Ordering Abstraction and a Simple Way to Implement It. *Inf. Proc. Letters*, 39(6):343–350, 1991.

[25] P. Sewell, P. T. Wojciechowski, and B. C. Pierce. Location-Independent Communication for Mobile Agents: A Two-Level Architecture. In *Proc. of ICCL'98 (Chicago, USA)*, LNCS vol. 1686, pp. 1–31.

VIII

MANAGEMENT & MONITORING

WIDENING TRADITIONAL MANAGEMENT PLATFORMS FOR MANAGING CORBA APPLICATIONS

Markus Debusmann, Reinhold Kroeger
Fachhochschule Wiesbaden - University of Applied Sciences
Department of Computer Science, Distributed Systems Laboratory
Kurt-Schumacher-Ring 18
D-65197 Wiesbaden, Germany
{debusman|kroeger}@informatik.fh-wiesbaden.de
http://wwwvs.informatik.fh-wiesbaden.de

Abstract During the past years, enterprises became more and more dependent on the business processes that are often implemented using CORBA middleware. Todays management platforms ignore the dependency between applications and their middleware, and thus give up valuable information sources that are required for proactive management.

In this paper an Integration System is presented by which traditional management platforms are widened for managing CORBA applications. Thus, the investments for an existing management platform are protected. The Integration System consist of a flexible and highly available Integration Agent and the Generic Management Interface for querying management-relevant information from CORBA applications.

Keywords: CORBA, application management, management platforms

1. INTRODUCTION

Today, IT-supported business processes are the vital spots of all enterprises. To cover heterogeneity in hardware and software and to support adaptability, these business processes are frequently implemented on the basis of multi-tier architectures using a middleware layer as glue for integrating the various application components. Due to its rich functionality, CORBA [OMG, 1998b] has received broad acceptance within industry and is thus used for implementing business-critical applications more and more.

In addition, novel applications in the area of Web-based electronic business, require high availability (24x7), short response times and other service-oriented criteria in order to achieve customer satisfaction and their long-term binding. These requirements can only be met by establishing an application management strategy that permanently monitors the status of the running application environment. Furthermore, so-called proactive management is necessary which, based on extracted information from all layers of the system, detects creeping problems and leads to corrective actions before real failures occur.

Traditional management platforms, like HP IT/Operations [HP, 1997] or Tivoli Management Environment (TME) [Tivoli, 1998] were more oriented towards element management and often only provide a very limited type of application management. Usually, existence of application processes is checked at the operating system level, and application log files may be parsed locally, checking for relevant events actively notified by the application.

In many companies large data processing centers operate the business-critical applications in three shifts. The operation requires an administration center ("Leitstand") that reflects a considerable investment also regarding the specific skills of the administrators. An individual administrator may be responsible for managing a series of different applications or infrastructure components. For him, the view upon a managed system must be as simple as possible and the frequency of events appearing on his console must be kept low in order to ensure their correct and timely processing. Especially when running a distributed CORBA application, the multiplicity of components involved and their static and dynamic relationships are hardly to supervise without any computer-based assistance. To protect the investment, operating concepts for new types of applications, like modern multi-tier CORBA-based flight information systems, have to be invented which ensure a seamless integration into the existing management environment.

As described in [Hegering et al., 1999] CORBA gains increasing significance as a management architecture and thus will serve as a basis for building management platforms in the future. Approaches like JIDM [OG, 1997] provide a simple mapping of SNMP and OSI management information models onto CORBA and vice versa and thus provide interoperability. But for short-term to mid-term solutions an integration of CORBA applications into existing management plarforms beyond simple interoperability is required.

This paper presents a solution to this dilemma. The focus of the paper is on a solution, the Integration System and its central component the Integration Agent, for integrating CORBA-based applications into a traditional management environment. The approach presented here was developed in a joint research and development project between the Distributed Systems Laboratory of Fachhochschule Wiesbaden - University of Applied Sciences, and Lufthansa Systems GmbH, Kelsterbach, Germany. The project focussed on integrating CORBA-based flight information applications into traditional management platforms, HP IT/Operations in this case. To achieve this, a so-called

Integration System has been developed which is placed between the management platform and the CORBA application. The integration system hides the complexity of the managed distributed application from the administrator and allows a seamless integration into the management platform. The integration system is itself also based on CORBA.

The paper is organised as follows. Section 2 identifies the requirements for managing CORBA applications from the perspective of a data processing center in more detail. The overall architecture of the proposed solution is outlined in section 3. It mainly identifies General Management Interfaces and the Integration Agent as constituent components of the integration system. The Generic Management Interface is presented in section 4 while the concept of the Integration Agent is described in section 5 with special emphasis on its modularity and reliability. In section 6 the cascaded configuration of Integration Agents is described which solves the distributed case in general. The paper closes with a summary in section 7.

2. REQUIREMENTS FOR MANAGING CORBA APPLICATIONS

In large scale data processing centers any viable solution for managing CORBA applications has to be integratable into the existing management platform. Typical simple interfacing procedures are based on processing various application and system logs, on checking the existence of processes and on executing commands/scripts in order to launch some actions in the managed system. To achieve this, the management station of an administrator communicates with its management agents running locally on the managed nodes. Furthermore, any acceptable solution has to be as generic as possible, i.e. it should be easily adaptable to other upcoming CORBA applications, and should be highly independent of the ORB used, taking into account that no OMG management interfaces have been standardised so far.

Managing highly available applications (99,98%) as stated for modern e-business applications requires a management system that is also highly available. Generally it is expected that the management system itself is even more reliable and robust than the managed system.

In contrast to classical centralised mainframe applications, for CORBA applications the management system has to control a possibly large number of nodes and components involved. Furthermore, a CORBA application is essentially dependent upon the CORBA middleware components and the used CORBA services. Thus, all the underlying components and services have to be taken into account as well. But even modern management platforms generally have no specific build-in model which reflects the structure and the capabilities of a CORBA-based environment. While this simplifies and unifies the view of all the managed systems, it also gives up a number of valuable information sources especially needed for proactive management which aims at early detection and removal of latent faults. In this case knowledge of the internal state of the application is generally required. This is especially true when a dynamic reconfiguration of the application during runtime has to be supported in order to meet the availability requirements.

As a result, in order to advice corrective actions the management system has to determine a global picture of the managed CORBA application by aggregating and correlating status information from the individual application components and all the underlying middleware, system and network components the application is relying on.

3. GENERAL ARCHITECTURE

Figure 1 depicts the high-level architecture of the proposed Integration System (IS) for managing CORBA applications using existing management platforms. The IS consists of the Integration Agent (IA) and the Generic Managing Interface (GMI). The IA collects management-relevant information from all layers of the managed environment: from the application layer, the CORBA layer, the system layer, and the network layer.

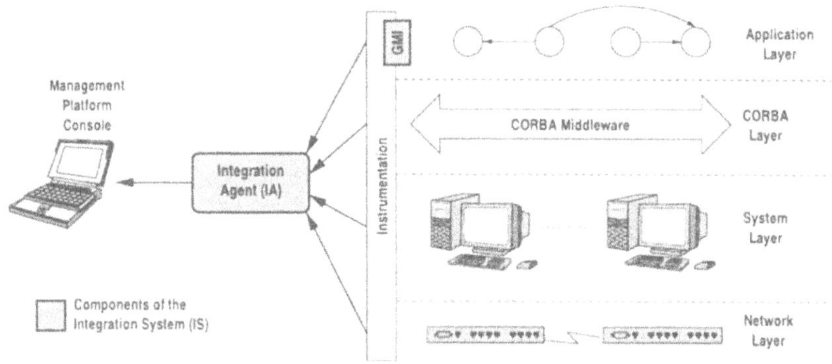

Figure 1. Overall architecture of a solution for managing CORBA applications

From each layer the information is extracted via a layer-specific instrumentation, respectively. In the application layer generic Portable Interceptors [OMG, 1999] in combination with an Application Response Measurement (ARM) instrumentation [TOG, 1998] have been successfully evaluated for performance management [Kloos, 2000] and will be the method of choice in the future. Currently hand-coded instrumentation is often used. Due to missing standardisation, the extraction of information from the CORBA layer depends on the facilities provided by the middleware platform used. If management support is provided, the CORBA layer typically appears as an SNMP private MIB extension, e.g. for IONA OrbixManager [IONA, 1998] or BEA Manager [BEA, 1998]. For the system layer and the network layer a number of information sources exist, like UNIX syslog and utilities, NT event log and system monitor, or SNMP MIBs [Stallings, 1999].

The main focus of the Integration Agent is the monitoring of the upper two layers. To provide high-quality metrics, information collected from the application layer and the CORBA layer is validated against information collected from the two lower layers.

In order to check the correct functioning of the application logic, to ensure progress and to compute service-oriented performance metrics the IA issues probing test transactions against all critical application objects and middleware services. In analogy to the network 'ping' utility for checking reachability these probing transactions have been called 'application pings'. The corresponding functions have been realised as part of the GMI which is a CORBA interface attached to all relevant CORBA application components. The GMI is covered in detail in section 4. As described above, the CORBA services which cannot be enhanced by a GMI have to be monitored as well in an appropriate manner. For them, service requests are issued which are used for error detection and measuring response times thus excluding stuck-at problems or overload situations. As an example, the CORBA Naming Service [OMG, 1998a] is queried to assure that all necessary CORBA application objects are registered. Subsequently, these can be checked via test transactions supplied through their management interfaces.

All the described checking and validating logic is encapsulated in the IA which constitutes the second type of components of the Integration System. An Integration Agent collects information from different sources, processes incoming notifications, executes validating logical functions, computes metrics and communicates with the traditional management platform, if so desired. The needed high level of adaptability of an IA and its basic fault-tolerance are its main non-functional properties. As will be seen, an IA can exhibit CORBA client and CORBA server functionality. Thus, IAs may be cascaded for covering distributed environments and for supporting aggregation and abstraction (see section 6).

The computed metrics and events generated by the IA are offered to traditional management platforms. The mechanism for providing these types of information is an implementation issue. A possible solution is using the API provided by the management platform directly from the Integration Agent.

4. A GENERIC MANAGEMENT INTERFACE FOR CORBA APPLICATIONS

The Generic Management Interface extends the CORBA application via a static CORBA IDL interface and enables management applications to access management-relevant information from the application objects. The GMI supports the following functions defined in CORBA IDL: *list* (query the information model offered by the application object), *get* (read a variable), *set* (write to a variable), *action* (invoke an operation through the GMI), and *ping* (execute a test transaction, a so-called *application ping*).

The information exchanged via the methods of the GMI is encoded using the Extensible Markup Language (XML) [W3C, 2000]. An XML Document Type Definition (DTD) defines the formats of the exchanged XML documents. This solution has the advantage that the methods of the management interface are always the same, i.e. all application objects that support the GMI can be managed by the same manager. The concrete management information and functionality is individually defined for each managed object type by its associated information model.

Compared to the CORBA `any` type, the use of XML has several advantages. XML supports the definition of grammars that determine the format of the interchanged information which provides great flexibility. In addition, XML is in a human readable format and is supported by numerous tools which enormously support the development and test phase. From a performance perspective, the integration of an XML parser is not a lightweight solution. But on the other hand, the use of CORBA `any` and their dynamic decomposition using the CORBA `DynAny` is also a very expensive approach.

Figure 2 depicts the integration of the GMI into an application object. Of course, the taken approach requires application-specific code for defining and supporting the offered information model. Requests to the GMI are passed to an XML parser that analyses the XML documents given as parameters to the requests. After parsing the XML documents, an access controller handles the interaction with the application logic, e.g. the value of some application variables may be read or a reconfiguration action may be executed. The result is transformed back into an XML document and returned to the caller of the GMI.

Using the application ping the business logic of the application object can be checked. During an application ping all relevant parts of the application object should be involved. To the outside world the result generally is a simple boolean value representing the status of the application object (red/green decision). But it is also possible to have a more fine-grained result represented as a numerical value or an enumeration. Furthermore, the caller of the application ping may take a timestamp immediately before the call and when it returns.

From measuring this response time of the probing transaction the caller may also deduce some load information.

The GMI enables a flexible monitoring and customizing of application objects during runtime as needed by the IA. Furthermore, not discussed here in detail, a CORBA client for the GMI with a graphical user interface has been developed which allows for visualising internal variables and metrics of the running application according to the exposed information model.

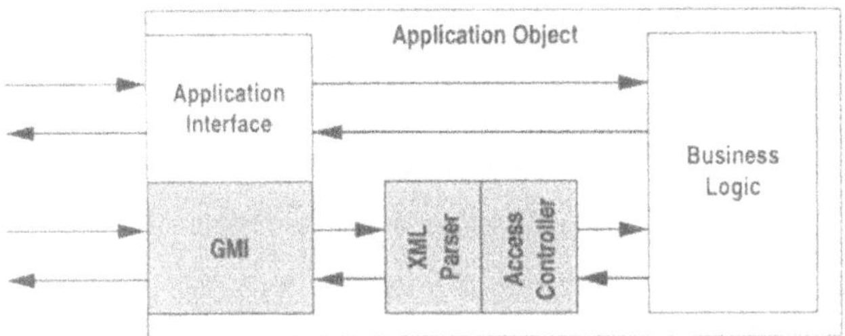

Figure 2. Integration of the Generic Management Interface into an application object

5. CONCEPT OF THE INTEGRATION AGENT

This section describes the Integration Agent with special emphasis on how its main design goals, namely modularity and high availability, have been achieved. Due to these features, it is well-suited to extend existing management platforms for the ability to manage CORBA applications.

Modularity is required in order to integrate a large number of different information sources and to adapt the management logic to the specific project needs. The IA provides a framework for dynamically loading modules at runtime that provide the actual functionality of the IA. This framework is also the basis for defining a hierarchy of operating modes to cope with failure situations.

The principal structure of the IA is depicted in Figure 3. The central component is the Module Manager. It provides a generic mechanism for dynamically loading modules into the IA and activating them during runtime. Loaded modules are under control of the Module Manager.

Furthermore, the Module Manager provides a framework for concurrent communication between modules. Communication is based on asynchronous messaging, and thus enables concurrency within the IA. To achieve this, the Module Manager has an internal pool of threads that handle incoming messages. The number of threads in the thread pool is limited and all threads are created during initialisation. This prevents performance losses because of thread creation and deletion. In addition, an inflation of the process is prevented.

Modules are divided in so-called action modules, event modules, and logic modules respectively. Action modules are used for carrying out desired actions

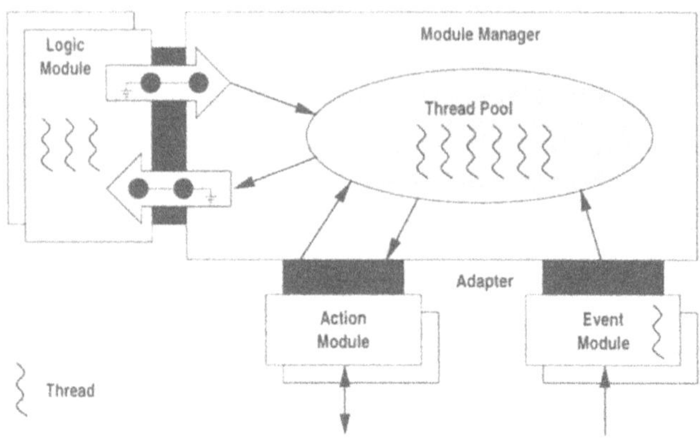

Figure 3. Internal architecture of the Integration Agent

in the managed system, e.g. querying an information source or starting/stopping a process. An action module has to implement a simple generic interface that is used by the Module Manager to communicate with the module. All functionality required to communicate with the outside world is encapsulated by an action module and thus transparent for the Module Manager. In principle, action modules are of relatively small complexity. Compared to the Module Manager, action modules are passive. They are activated if a thread of the Module Manager executes methods of an action module.

Event modules are used for integrating event sources into the IA. In contrast to action modules, event modules are active and wait for the monitored system to submit an event, e.g. sending an SNMP trap or writing a log entry. In case an external event is detected, the event module generates an internal event that is handled by the logic modules.

The logic modules are the driving components of the IA and implement the intrinsic management algorithms. Logic modules are started by the Module Manager. Subsequently, they run concurrently to the Module Manager, i.e. they normally create their own internal threads that handle the necessary tasks. Logic modules are able to send commands to action modules and process their results. Furthermore, logic modules can handle events that were sent from event modules. In addition, logic modules can also sent their own events, e.g. if one logic module detects a critical situation it may advertise this by sending events to other logic modules.

The adapter implements a common interface between the Module Manager and the modules. It abstracts from the various module types and is responsible for the dynamic loading and unloading of a module.

So far, a number of concrete modules are available. Action modules exist for sending SNMP requests, for executing shell scripts and programs, and for performing CORBA method invocations (CORBA client). An event module is implemented that analyses a proprietary log format. Furthermore, logic modules exist for checking system configurations, for writing a logfile to the IT/O management platform, and for offering a Generic Management Interface (CORBA server) as described in section 4. The latter module enables the distribution of Integration Agents as described in the following section.

High availability is an essential characteristic of a management system when managing business-critical applications. To assure high availability the IA applies a self-checking process pair, continuous self-diagnosis, and hierarchical operating modes.

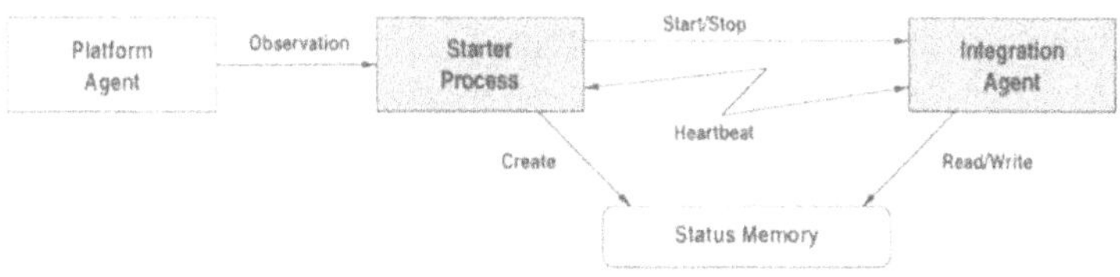

Figure 4. Relationship between the Starter Process and the Integration Agent

The operating system´s view upon the IA is illustrated in Figure 4. The IA is a process under the control of a so-called starter process which starts and stops the IA. The complexity of the starter is relatively small thus ensuring a high level of correctness. The IA and the starter process regularly exchange heartbeat signals to indicate each other that they are working correctly. If the starter does not receive a signal it assumes that the IA is no longer running or hangs and restarts it again. In case the IA does not receive a heartbeat signal from the starter it shuts down itself. To complete a supervising chain, the existence of the starter is ensured by the traditional management platform.

The status memory, a shared memory segment that is created by the starter during initialisation and loaded from a file, is used for storing relevant status information of the IA which is intended to survive crashes of the IA. After a restart the IA reads from the status memory and thus can immediately resume from its saved state. Each module has its own section within the shared memory segment and is responsible to assure the consistency of its part of the shared memory segment by setting a consistency flag after all write operations to its section have been processed successfully. The last consistent state of the module is kept in the shared memory segmentt itself and is used after a crash.

By self-diagnosis of the loaded modules and the Module Manager error detection takes place. If loaded modules are considered faulty or if their operating preconditions are no longer valid they are swapped out of the IA. To provide an orderly service, so-called operating modes have been introduced. Each mode is characterised by a set of successfully running modules. The modes depend successively on each other, i.e. the higher the operating mode the more functionality is integrated into the IA by the loaded modules. The Module Manager will always try to be in the highest possible operating mode thus automatically adapting to the current problem situation.

Within the cooperation with Lufthansa Systems the following three modes were identified and realised. *Mode 0 (Hardcore)* comprises the basic functionality. Within this mode the IA only depends on services provided by the operating system, i.e checking the existence of processes through a system module, log processing and SNMP. In *Mode 1 (CORBA Client)* the IA has the ability to invoke methods of CORBA server objects. Within *Mode 2 (CORBA Server)* the IA exports its internal information through a logic module with Generic Management Interface (see section 4), i.e. the information may be queried by other IAs that are at least running in Mode 1.

6. CASCADING INTEGRATION AGENTS

In general, the CORBA client functionality of the Integration Agent enables the supervision of a distributed CORBA application by a single IA. If the information collected through the CORBA client module has to be validated against node-specific constraints, local views of other IAs are required. For example, the overall application may be in a correct state if a certain number of application objects run on the available server machines. This requires a two-level checking: first, the application objects have to be reached via an application ping, and second, the number of object instances on the different nodes have to be checked. This problem can be solved by cascading IAs.

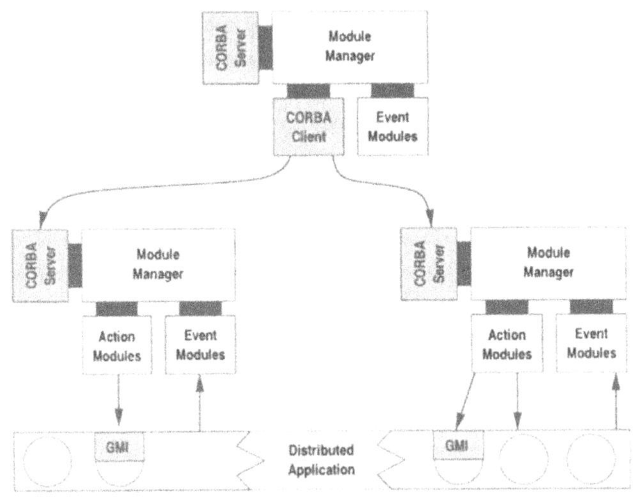

Figure 5. Hierarchical arrangement of Integration Agents

By establishing a hierarchical configuration of IAs as illustrated in Figure 5 several views of individual IAs can be aggregated into a more complex view. The local IAs export their information model through their CORBA server module (logic module). A superior IA uses its CORBA client module (action module) to query the CORBA server modules of the secondary IAs. The information queried by the superior IA through its CORBA client module can be reexported through its CORBA server module so that a hierarchy of any depth can be configured.

The aggregation of several local IA views by one superior IA simplifies the view upon the managed system. For management tools querying information from the superior IA the distribution of the managed components is transparent. This simplifies the integration of the IA into an existing management platform.

7. SUMMARY

Traditional management platforms have deficiencies in managing CORBA applications. Application-internal information that is a prerequisite for proactive management can often not be extracted because processes are regarded as black boxes. This paper presents an Integration System consisting of the Integration Agents and the Generic Management Interface for managing CORBA applications using existing management platforms. The central component is the Integration Agent that collects and aggregates metrics from the managed system and interacts with traditional management platforms.

The Generic Management Interface was developed for extracting management-relevant information from CORBA applications. The interface consists of a static CORBA IDL interface that is integrated into the application. The exchanged messages are flexibly defined using XML.

The Integration Agent is characterised by two main concepts: modularity and high availability. Flexibility is achieved by modules that can be dynamically loaded into and swapped out of the Integration Agent. High availability is achieved by implementing the Integration Agent as a self-checking process pair. In addition, the Integration Agent runs in various operation modes whereas the current mode is determined by continous self-diagnosis. Several Integration Agents may be configured in a cascading manner. This hides the distribution of the managed application to the administrator and thus simplifies management.

The Integration System is implemented and was easily integrated into an HP IT/Operations management environment. The Generic Management Interface was well accepted by application developers and administrators. Currently, the Integration System is in its test phase.

Acknowledgments

The authors like to thank Christoph Weyer from Fachhochschule Wiesbaden for his ideas and implementation work concerning the module manager framework. We also thank Dirk Lindner, Arno Schaefer, Thomas Kullmann, Pascal Mougnon, and Thomas Piwek from Lufthansa Systems for their support and numerous valuable discussions.

References

[BEA, 1998] BEA (1998). *BEA Manager Reference Manual 2.0.* BEA Systems.

[Hegering et al., 1999] Hegering, H.-G., Abeck, S., and Neumair, B. (1999). *Integrated Management of Networked Systems: Goals, Architectures, and their Operational Application.* Morgan Kaufmann Publishers.

[HP, 1997] HP (1997). *HP OpenView IT/Operations Concepts Guide.* Hewlett Packard. B4249-90011, Version A.04.00.

[IONA, 1998] IONA (1998). *OrbixManager User's Guide.* IONA.

[Kloos, 2000] Kloos, D. (2000). Performance Management of CORBA Applications Using a Generic Instrumentation. Diploma thesis, Distributed Systems Laboratory, Fachhochschule Wiesbaden - University of Applied Sciences, Germany. (in German).

[OG, 1997] OG (1997). *Inter-Domain Management: Specification Translation.* The Open Group. Document No. 509.

[OMG, 1998a] OMG (1998a). *CORBAServices: Common Object Services Specification.* Object Management Group.

[OMG, 1998b] OMG (1998b). *The Common Object Request Broker: Architecture and Specification.* Object Management Group. Revision 2.3.

[OMG, 1999] OMG (1999). *Portable Interceptors.* Object Management Group. Document no.: orbos/99-12-02.

[Stallings, 1999] Stallings, W. (1999). *SNMP, SNMPv2, SNMPv3, and RMON 1 and 2.* Addison-Wesley, 3rd edition.

[Tivoli, 1998] Tivoli (1998). *TME 10 Framework User's Guide.* Tivoli Systems. Version 3.6.

[TOG, 1998] TOG (1998). *Systems Management: Application Response Measurement (ARM) API.* The Open Group. Document no.: C807.

[W3C, 2000] W3C (2000). *Extensible Markup Language (XML) 1.0.* World Wide Web Consortium. Second Edition, W3C Recommendation.

LIVE UPGRADE TECHNIQUES FOR CORBA APPLICATIONS*

L. A. Tewksbury, L. E. Moser, P. M. Melliar-Smith
Department of Electrical and Computer Engineering
University of California, Santa Barbara, CA 93106
tewks@alpha.ece.ucsb.edu, moser@ece.ucsb.edu, pmms@ece.ucsb.edu

Abstract The ability to perform *live software upgrades* is essential for long-running applications that provide critical services. Program modifications are necessary as programmer errors and new user requirements are uncovered. If software is to remain relevant, it must be upgradable. The Eternal Evolution Manager allows distributed CORBA applications to be upgraded while they continue to provide service. In addition to avoiding planned downtime, the Evolution Manager accomplishes the difficult tasks inherent to software evolution with minimal help from the application programmer. With our live upgrade techniques, and the underlying fault tolerance of the Eternal System, we can allow applications to run forever.

1. INTRODUCTION

Halting an executing application to modify its source code has traditionally involved difficult tradeoffs. The importance of the intended code improvement must be weighed against the revenue loss that is inevitable when an application incurs planned downtime. It might never be feasible to bring down critical computer systems, such as those that control the life support systems in spacecraft or hospitals. Oftentimes, software modifications to fix programming errors or to improve functionality are forsaken because an application must provide continuous service.

---

*The research in this paper has been supported by DARPA/ONR Contract N00174-95-K-0083, DARPA/AFOSR Contract F3602-97-1-0248 and MURI/AFOSR Contract F49620-00-1-0330.

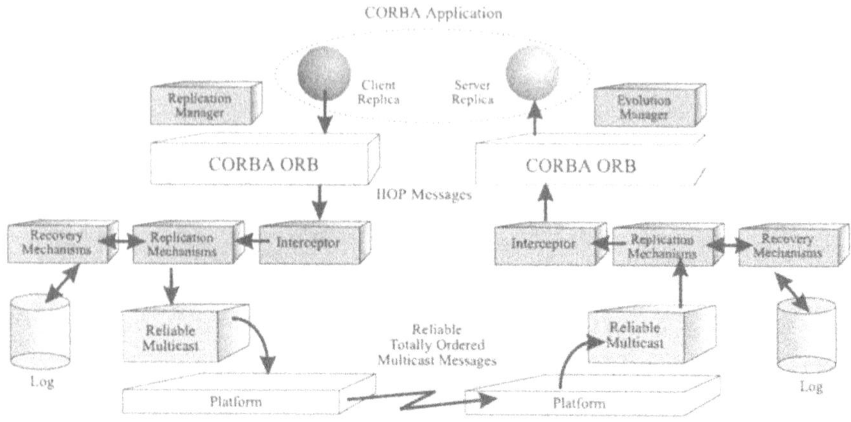

Figure 1. The Eternal System.

1.1. Fault Tolerant CORBA

The Common Object Request Broker Architecture [12] (CORBA) allows distributed client/server objects to interoperate, regardless of the operating system, platform or programming language being used. Clients invoke the methods defined in the server's Interface Definition Language (IDL) interface, through an Interoperable Object Reference (IOR) without knowing where the server resides in the network. The Object Request Broker (ORB) routes invocations and responses between distributed client and server objects.

The Eternal system, shown in Figure 1, provides CORBA applications with transparent fault tolerance. The Interceptor diverts the CORBA invocations and responses to the underlying Totem [10] protocol, which reliably multicasts the messages to all of the members of the recipient object group. The Logging-Recovery Mechanisms allows objects to recover from faults by initializing a new replica's state with the state of its object group. The Evolution Manager uses the object replication necessary for achieving fault tolerance to achieve live upgrades of CORBA application objects. [1]

The Replication Mechanisms place replicas into object groups. Assuming an active replication scheme, any invocation to the object group is received and responded to by all of the object replicas in the same order. Duplicate invocations and responses are suppressed so that replicas remain consistent.

[1] If evolution is required but fault tolerance is not, the objects are replicated only during the upgrade. Because the Replication Manager already provides replication to achieve fault tolerance, and because an application that requires no downtime from an upgrade will most likely require no downtime due to faults, replication for evolution effectively incurs no additional overhead beyond that required for fault tolerance.

Replicas can be added to (and removed from) object groups and the Replication Mechanisms ensure that the new replicas receive the proper messages. Thus, we kill and start individual replicas during an upgrade without interrupting the behavior of the object group as a whole.

2. THE ETERNAL EVOLUTION MANAGER

The Eternal Evolution Manager (composed of the Preparer and the Upgrader) upgrades CORBA applications without interrupting their execution. The Preparer, with application programmer assistance, performs static analysis of the original and new versions of an application. The Upgrader uses the results of this static analysis to perform a fully-automatic live upgrade. An application's performance is minimally impacted while an upgrade is underway, and entirely unaffected otherwise. The steps that must take effect during an upgrade are complicated, and would be tedious and error-prone for a human to perform. We automate most of these steps. The programmer is not required to maintain aspects of the old code (such as the old IDL interfaces) when writing the new version of the code. But objects must inherit from and implement the `Checkpointable` interface if they are intended to be upgradable, and, indeed, if they are to be recoverable by the fault tolerance part of the Eternal system. The `Checkpointable` interface contains a method *get_state()* that retrieves the state of an object and a method *set_state()* that initializes the state of an object. We aim to handle all *reasonable* code modifications, including those to an object's interface, method implementations, and renaming, removing or adding an instance variable, etc. Replacing an old version of an application with a completely unrelated new version is unreasonable as there is no way to transition between such "versions".

The Eternal Preparer compares the old version of the code *P_old* and the new version of the code *P_new* in preparation for the live upgrade. This offline analysis automatically generates *state transfer* code and, with application programmer assistance, generates *state conversion* code [15]. Whenever a replica is added to an object group, state is transferred from the object group to the new replica. The Preparer automatically generates the intermediate code *P_inter*, a superset of *P_old* and *P_new*, which executes during the transition between *P_old* and *P_new*. State conversion is needed during this transition if the structure of *P_old*'s state differs from the structure of *P_new*'s state. Additionally, the Preparer supplies the Upgrader with the necessary upgrade steps.

2.1. The Eternal Upgrader

The Upgrader performs a series of individual replacements which "nudge" the application towards an upgraded state but which neither affect its behavior nor interrupt the executing application. The replicas being upgraded are replaced, one at a time [2], by their intermediate versions, which continue to execute the old methods. While one replica is down during this replacement, the other member(s) of the object group continue to provide service, masking the replacement from the application. Once all of the intermediate versions are executing, and once the object group is quiescent, we effect an *atomic switchover* after which only the new methods are executed. Because of the underlying reliable totally-ordered multicasts within the Eternal system, all of the replicas receive the switchover messages at the same logical time and, thus, the state of the upgraded replicas remains consistent. Then, to clean up the application, the intermediate object replicas are replaced, one at a time, with final versions containing only the new version of the code.

2.2. An Example Upgrade

The upgrade process is simplest when the new version of an object has an interface that is syntactically and semantically identical to the interface of the old version. *An interface-preserving upgrade* can be isolated from the other application objects. When an object's interface changes during an upgrade, the situation becomes more complex. Consider a *coordinated upgrade* in which the original server contains a method *B.m(void)* that is upgraded to *B.m(int)*. Upgrading the *B* servers before upgrading the *A* clients can result in invalid client invocations of *B.m(void)* on the new server.

We use *coordinated upgrade sets* to upgrade multiple objects concurrently. The clients that invoke a method undergoing an interface change must be upgraded at the same time as the modified server to provide the correct parameters for the invocation. The mechanics of a coordinated upgrade strongly resemble those of an interface-preserving upgrade. We therefore only describe the more complicated scenario, shown in Figure 2. The figure shows the sequence of invisible replacements performed during the coordinated upgrade of a simple application.

2.3. Quiescence

An object cannot be upgraded unless it is *quiescent* (not executing any of its methods). For example, consider a method *A.m()* that invokes a method *B.n()*. If *B.n()* has been invoked but has not completed, then *B* is not quiescent, because it is executing, and *A* is not quiescent because it is stalled waiting for a response from *B*. Note that the invocations discussed here are synchronous. We cannot

[2]The replicas are replaced individually because we aim to preserve the fault tolerance of the application during the upgrade.

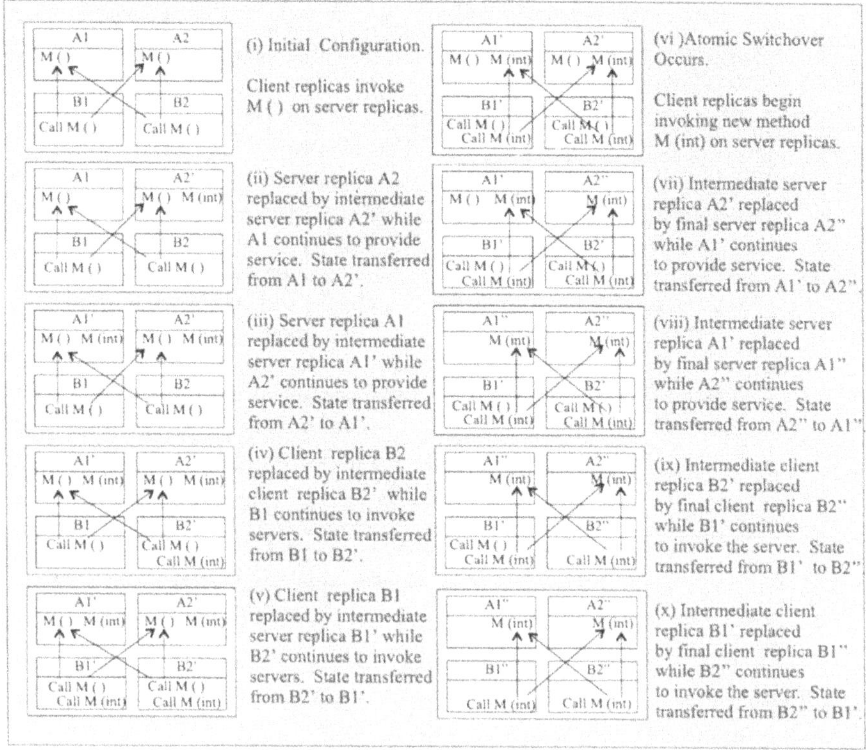

Figure 2. The invisible replacements performed during a coordinated upgrade.

Replica A1	Replica A2	Replica A3

aMethod() {
a++; ⇐ *state transfer*
b = a + b;
c = a*2+b;
}
	aMethod() {
	a++;
	b = a + b; ⇐ *state*
	c = a*2+b; *transfer*
	}
		aMethod() {
		a++;
		b = a + b;
		c = a*2+b; ⇐ *state*
		} *transfer*

Figure 3. Upgrading without waiting for quiesence yields indeterminate results.

ensure the quiescence of an object with asynchronous operations unless the completion of those operations is signaled to the Upgrader.

An object must be quiescent when it undergoes an invisible replacement and during the atomic switchover, both of which involve a transfer of state. To see why this condition is necessary, consider transferring the state of three replicas *A1*, *A2* and *A3* of the same object when they are executing *aMethod()*. The replicas have finished executing the lines of code indicated by the arrows in Figure 3, and hence have different states. Eternal suppresses duplicate messages

<table>
<tr><th>original Count class</th><th>new Count class</th></tr>
<tr><td><pre>
interface Count {
    void updateCount();
}
class Count {
    int countVal;
    int countDir;
    void updateCount() {
        if (countDir == 1)
            countVal++;
        else if (countDir == -1)
            countVal–;
    }
    void changeDirection(int dir) {
        countDir = dir;
    }
}
</pre></td><td><pre>
interface Count_new {
    void updateCount(in long inc);
}
class Count_new {
    int countVal;
    int countDir;
    void updateCount(int inc) {
        if (countDir == 1)
            countVal += inc;
        else if (countDir == -1)
            countVal -= inc;
    }
    void changeDirection(int dir) {
        countDir = dir;
    }
}
</pre></td></tr>
</table>

Figure 4. The old and new versions of the Count class.

so we cannot predict which of the replicas' *get_state()* operations will return, and a deterministic state cannot be returned. Similarly, receiving the state at a non-quiescent point would result in an inconsistent result.

3. UPGRADE CODE GENERATION

Our live upgrade methodology utilizes an intermediate period, during which the old code coexists with the new code within the automatically generated intermediate code. Before the *switchover*, the intermediate code behaves like the old version of the code and after the *switchover*, the intermediate code behaves like the new version of the code. By encapsulating the old and new functionality within a single object, switching between the executing code versions is expedited.

Consider a class `Count` whose *updateCount()* method increments or decrements `countVar`. The new version of the method increases or decreases `countVar` by `inc`. Both classes are shown in Figure 4.

The Preparer parses the two classes and automatically generates the intermediate class `Count_inter` shown in Figure 5. It contains a member variable `switchFlag`, indicating whether the switchover has occurred, and which determines whether incoming messages are "handled" by the old code or the new code. The methods defined in the intermediate object are a superset of those defined in both the old and the new code versions. The old state variables are kept distinct from the new state variables by appending the variables with either the *_old* or the *_new* suffix. The state of the old variables is transferred (and

```
interface Count_inter {
    void updateCount();
    void updateCount(in long inc);
}
class Count_inter {
    unsigned short switchFlag;
    int countVal_old, countDir_old;
    int countVal_new, countDir_new;
    void UpdateCount() {
        if (switchFlag == 0) {
            if (countDir_old == 1) countVal_old++;
            else if (countDir_old == -1) countVal_old–;
        }
    }
    void UpdateCount(int inc) {
        if (switchFlag == 1) {
            if (countDir_new == 1) countVal_new += inc;
            else if (countDir_new == -1) countVal_new -= inc;
        }
    }
    void ChangeDirection(int dir) {
        if (switchFlag == 0) countDir_old = dir;
        else countDir_new = dir;
    }
    void set_state() {
        countVal_new = countVal_old;
        countDir_new = countDir_old;
    }
}
```

Figure 5. Automatically generated intermediate code for the `Count` object.

original IDL	intermediate IDL 1	intermediate IDL 2	new IDL
UpdateCount()	UpdateCount() UpdateCount_(int)	UpdateCount_(int) UpdateCount(int)	UpdateCount(int)

Figure 6. The old, intermediate and new versions of the `Count` class.

converted, if necessary) to the new variables entirely within the intermediate object, avoiding an unnecessarily time-consuming encoding and decoding of state. By breaking the method implementation encapsulation of `Count` and `Count_new` within `Count_inter`, the *set_state()* method can assign the (most likely) private state variables directly, without using their (possibly lacking) accessor functions.

Methods cannot be overloaded in IDL interfaces, so the `Count_inter` IDL code shown in Figure 5 (which contains both *UpdateCount()* and *Update-*

Count(int)) will not compile. We have presented the sample intermediate code this way for the sake of simplicity. The Preparer actually generates two different intermediate objects (see Figure 6), temporarily renaming the *UpdateCount* method. The atomic switchover occurs when *intermediate IDL1* is executing.

4. WRAPPER FUNCTIONS

Table 1. Wrapper function feasibility.

Original Method	New Method	Feasibility
aMethod(int i, int r)	aMethod(int i)	trivial
aMethod(float i)	aMethod(int i)	trivial
aMethod()	aMethod(int i)	questionable

Wrapper functions translate between syntactic and semantic differences in methods and their synthesis requires significant programmer assistance. Some method signature upgrades cannot be masked with wrapper functions. The examples shown in Table 1 illustrate the feasibility of using wrapper functions for different types of method upgrades.

The first method upgrade in Table 1 eliminates a parameter from the new method. After receiving user verification that the i variables are equivalent, translation between the two methods is accomplished by not passing the second parameter to the new method. The wrapper function that is automatically generated is

```
aMethod(int i, int r) {
  wrappedObj → aMethod(i);
}
```

The second method upgrade in Table 1 changes the type of a method parameter. It is simple to convert from a float to an integer, and, with input from the application programmer, translation between less obvious types changes is tractable.

It is much more difficult to write a wrapper function for an upgrade that adds information to a method. The Preparer cannot automatically generate wrapper code that initializes i for the third upgrade in Table 1, although the application programmer might be able to provide an initialization routine.

4.1. Wrapper Functions to Handle Pure CORBA Clients

In Figure 7, `ClientObj` invokes *InvokeMiddleTier (int iDelay, int rDelay)* on `MiddleObj`. After waiting *iDelay* seconds, `MiddleObj` invokes *UpdateCount()*

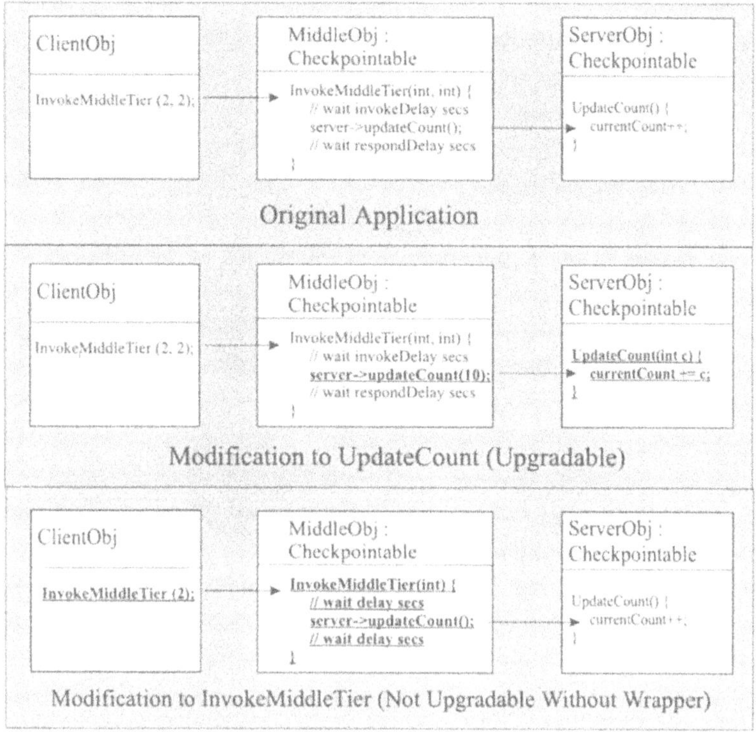

Figure 7. Example illustrating the use of wrapper functions during an upgrade.

on `ServerObj`, incrementing *currentCount*. `MiddleObj` then waits *rDelay* seconds before returning. One possible upgrade, the middle component in Figure 7, is for `MiddleObj` to pass an integer *c* to `ServerObj`, instructing `ServerObj` to increase *currentCount* by *c*. The coordinated upgrade set for this upgrade consists of the `ServerObj` replicas and the `MiddleObj` replicas, both of which are upgradable.

But how can the application programmer upgrade *InvokeMiddleTier (int, int)* to the method *InvokeMiddleTier (int)* (the lower component of Figure 7)? Because `ClientObj` invokes *InvokeMiddleTier*, it too must be upgraded. But `ClientObj` is a pure client; it does not implement the *Checkpointable* interface (it does not implement any interface), so it cannot undergo a live upgrade.
`MiddleObj` can undergo an coordinated upgrade without disturbing `ClientObj` by using a wrapper function. A wrapper function is easy to generate for the *InvokeMiddleTier* upgrade, however, not all method upgrades can be masked by a wrapper function. The presence of pure clients in an application can make it impossible for otherwise upgradable objects to undergo certain upgrades, and the pure clients themselves cannot be upgraded. Even if the interfaces used by

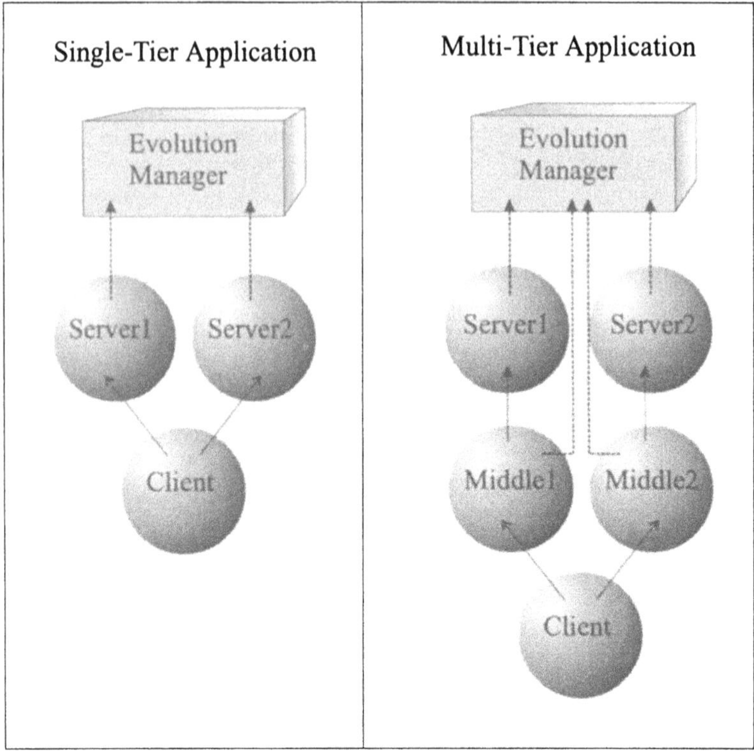

Figure 8. The single-tier and two-tiered applications undergoing upgrades.

pure clients can be modified, wrapper functions will permanently reside in the application.

Therefore, it is desirable to minimize the number of pure clients in an application. If the clients are made to implement the *Checkpointable* interface, the formerly pure client objects are effectively transformed into client/server objects. However, the server functionality is invoked only by the Eternal infrastructure. As far as the application is concerned, the object remains a client.

5. PERFORMANCE MEASUREMENTS

The Evolution Manager is implemented using Vertel's e*ORB2.1 and runs over a network of 360 MHz UltraSparc 5's running Solaris 8. Measurements were taken to ascertain the performance degradation experienced by an application during an upgrade.

We took measurements on an interface-preserving upgrade of a single-tier application, and an interface-changing upgrade of a two-tier application, both of which are shown in Figure 8. In the single-tier application, the client sends a constant stream of invocations to a doubly replicated server. In the two-tier application, the client sends a constant stream of invocations to a doubly replicated middle object, which then invokes a doubly replicated server. Both upgrades change one of the server's methods, but the second upgrade changes a server's interface.

Five experiments were performed on each application. The first two experiments measure the throuhput of the application in an isolated configuration (not connected to the Evolution Manager). The third and fourth experiments measure the throuhput of the application in a non-isolated configuration without starting the upgrade. The non-isolated configuration includes all of the objects and connections shown in Figure 8. The isolated and non-isolated case were tested separately to determine how connection establishment alters application performance. We also wanted to determine how much killing and restarting replicas degrades performance. For the second and fourth measurements, we manually killed and restarted the application objects, mimicking the object group membership changes that occur during an upgrade's invisible replacements. The final throuhput measurements were performed while the live upgrade was underway.

Table 2. Application performance during an upgrade.

Configuration being Measured	Roundtrip	Penalty
Interface-Preserving Isolated:		
(1) Client invokes two server replicas (baseline)	152	–
(2) Both server replicas killed/restarted 2xs	132	13%
Interface-Preserving Non-Isolated:		
(3) Client invokes two server replicas	135	11%
(4) Both server replicas killed/restarted 2xs	115	24%
(5) Both servers upgraded (duration 8.9 s)	98	35%
Interface-Changing Isolated:		
(1) Client invokes two tiers (baseline)	57	–
(2) All server replicas killed/restarted 2xs	52	9%
Interface-Changing Non-Isolated:		
(3) Client invokes two tiers	48	16%
(4) All server replicas killed/restarted 2xs	43	25%
(5) All servers upgraded (duration 19.5 s)	38	33%

The experimental results are shown in Table 2. The single-tier (two-tier) application experienced four (eight) kill/restarts, and hence four (eight) transfers of state. To maintain replica consistency, replicas queue messages while state is transferred. Also, the underlying Totem relable multicast protocol [10] is slowed down during membership changes. These two effects decrease the throuhput by 13% (9%).

Both applications experience performance degradation while running in the non-isolated configuration. The extra Evolution Manager objects run on additional hosts, and because Totem is based on a logical token passing ring, extra hosts increase the round-trip time of the token. The extra hosts and the extra connections combine to decrease the throuhput of the single-tier (two-tier) application by 11% (16%).

The combined effects of killing and restarting replicas, and running the application in a non-isolated configuration result in a 24% (25%) decrease in throuhput. The performance penalty for performing a live upgrade is not substantially larger. The single-tier (two-tier) upgrade takes 8.9 (19.5) seconds and decreases throuhput by 35% (33%). The Evolution Manager competes with the application for computing resources, and the upgraded objects are briefly stalled during the switchover.

These are preliminary results. Neither the Evolution Manager, nor the underlying protocols has been performance tuned. In particular, the underlying protocols are not optimized for the frequent object group membership changes that live upgrades require. However, it is our assessment that these are extremely reasonable results, especially because these experiments represent a worst-case scenario in several ways. It is unlikely that the applications being upgraded will undergo the message invocation bombardment experienced by these example applications. Also, the upgrades were performed very rapidly for these experiments. The Evolution Manager performed one invisible replacement after the other, as quickly as possible. The upgrade's impact would be dampened by spreading the upgrade out over a larger timescale. Future experiments will investigate more reasonable upgrade durations and the impact of state size and achieving quiescence on the performance of an application undergoing an upgrade.[3]

6. RELATED WORK

Kramer and Magee's classic evolving philosophers paper [8] concerns itself with the structural issues involved in dynamic reconfiguration. All of the objects being upgraded are passivated, as are all of the objects that can invoke these objects. This *passive set* includes all of the objects that can initiate a nested operation that eventually invokes an object being upgraded. In a highly connected system, this technique can significantly hinder the application's availability during an upgrade. Goudarzi and Kramer [6] quiesce a group of objects being upgraded, the *BSet*, by only blocking the *non-BSet* objects that invoke the *BSet* during the quiescence algorithm. Bidan *et al* [1] have developed a

[3]The state in both of these examples was small, and the nature of these applications ensured that quiescence would be reached quickly.

Dynamic Reconfiguration Manager (DRM) for CORBA that passivates a group of objects undergoing reconfiguration. Only the links between the group being made passive and the objects external to that group are blocked, not the external objects themselves.

The Simplex architecture [5] executes multiple versions of a program simultaneously and shields the old code from the new version until its correctness is established. However, the types of upgrades allowed by Simplex are limited. Feiler [3] has developed an offline analysis tool that determines when the upgrade of one component will require the upgrade of additional components in the system. Syntactic, type and semantic incompatibilities in the component connections are considered.

Senivongse [16] has developed a mediator that makes the evolution of server objects transparent to their clients. A mapping operator (similar to Eternal's wrapper functions) transforms and forwards the client's old requests to the new server, and then transforms and forwards the new server's responses to the old client. The generation of these mapping operators is semi-automatic. One problem with this technique is that multiple upgrades to a server yield multiple mapping operators performing multiple forwards, degrading performance. The application programmer ensures that an upgrade can be masked by mapping operators.

Bloom [2] used the Argus system [9] to replace modules while preserving their state. The lack of subtyping in Argus limits the types of upgrades that can be performed. Adding a method to an object changes the object's type, and if an invocation returns an object of this changed type, type correctness is violated and the upgrade cannot be performed.

Hauptmann and Wasel [7] accomplish live upgrades by including the upgrade code within a separate application thread. This code must exist in any upgradable application object even when no upgrade is underway. Additionally, significant programmer assistance is required to generate the upgrade-specific code, although the authors state that a tool could be written to automate much of this work. The authors assume that as long as the interfaces remain the same, the upgrade of multiple components can be broken up into a sequence of independent upgrades, but do not explain how correct program semantics is maintained. Felber [4] includes a brief conceptual discussion a replication-based solution to on-line upgrades using the Object Group Service (OGS) in his dissertation, but does not provide much discussion of on-line upgrade issues.

Podus [14] is an example of a system that loads new code into memory and changes the binding of procedures to perform live upgrades. Methods are upgraded when they are not executing, and the method upgrades are ordered such that a new version of a method cannot invoke an old version of another method. The drawback of this approach is that the mechanisms used to achieve the dynamic upgrade are complicated and require specialized compilers and linkers.

7. CONCLUSIONS AND FUTURE WORK

The Eternal Evolution Manager enables live upgrades of distributed CORBA applications by exploiting a reliable totally-ordered multicast protocol and object replication. The aim is to automate as much of the upgrade process as possible both to reduce programmer errors and to encourage previously infeasible application upgrades.

We have successfully performed interface-preserving and interface-changing live upgrades on simple applications and are convinced that our live upgrade mechanisms work properly. The next step is to perform an upgrade with alarge coordinated upgrade set. We plan to investigate ways to circumvent the anticipated coordinated quiescence bottleneck, including using wrapper functions to reduce the size of the coordinated upgrade set, and using semantic program knowledge (obtained from the application programmer) to break an application version change into multiple upgrades with smaller coordinated upgrade sets. We also plan to investigate programming styles and techniques that minimize the amount of time that the Upgrader must wait for a coordinated upgrade set to become quiescent.

References

[1] C. Bidan, V. Issarny, T. Saridakisand, and A. Zarras, "A dynamic reconfiguration service for CORBA," *Proc. of the 4th Intl. Conf. on Configurable Distributed Systems*, Annapolis, MD (May 1998), pp. 35-42.

[2] T. Bloom and M. Day, "Reconfiguration and module replacement in Argus: Theory and practice," *Software Engineering Journal* (March 1993), pp. 102-108.

[3] P. Feiler and J. Li, "Consistency in dynamic reconfiguration," *Proc. of the 4th Intl. Conf. on Configurable Distributed Systems*, Annapolis, MD (May 1998), pp. 189-196.

[4] P. Felber, "The CORBA Object Group Service: A Service Approach to Object Groups in CORBA," Ph.D. Thesis, École Polytechnique Fédérale de Lausanne, (1998).

[5] M. Gagliardi, R. Rajkumar and L. Sha, "Designing for evolvability: Building blocks for evolvable real-time systems," *Proc. of the IEEE 1996 Real-Time Technology and Applications Symposium*, Brookline, MA (June 1996), pp 100-109.

[6] K. M. Goudarzi and J. Kramer, "Maintaining node consistency in the face of dynamic change," *Proc. of the 3rd Intl. Conf. on Configurable Distributed Systems*, Annapolis, MD (May 1996), pp. 62-69.

[7] S. Hauptmann and J. Wasel, "On-line maintenance with on-the-fly software replacement," *Proc. of the 3rd Intl. Conf. on Configurable Distributed Systems*, Annapolis, MD (May 1998), pp. 70-80.

[8] J. Kramer and J. Magee, "The evolving philosophers problem: Dynamic change management," *IEEE Transactions On Software Engineering*, vol. 16, no. 11 (November 1990), pp. 1293-1306.

[9] B. Liskov, "Distributed programming in Argus," *Communications of the ACM* (March 1988), pp. 300-313.

[10] L. E. Moser, P. M. Melliar-Smith, D. A. Agarwal, R. K. Budhia and C. A. Lingley-Papadopoulos , "Totem: A fault-tolerant multicast group communication system" *Communications of the ACM*, vol. 39 , no. 4 (April 1996), pp. 54-63.

[11] L. E. Moser, P. M. Melliar-Smith and P. Narasimhan, "Consistent object replication in the Eternal system," *Theory and Practice of Object Systems* vol. 4, no. 2, (1998), pp. 81-92.

[12] Object Management Group, "The Common Object Request Broker: Architecture and Specification," Revision 2.4.2, OMG Technical Document Formal/2001-02-01, Object Management Group (February 2001).

[13] Object Management Group, "Online Upgrades Request for Information," OMG Technical Document realtime/2000-08-01 (August 2000).

[14] M. Segal and O. Frieder, "On-the-fly program modification: Systems for dynamic updating," *IEEE Software* (March 1993), pp. 53-65.

[15] L. A. Tewksbury, L. E. Moser and P. M. Melliar-Smith, "Automatically generated state transfer and conversion code to facilitate software upgrades," *Maintenance and Reliability Conf. Proc.*, Gatlinsburg, TN (May 2001).

[16] T. Senivongse, "Enabling flexible cross-version interoperability for distributed services," *Proc. of the Intl. Symposium on Distributed Objects and Applications*, Edinburgh, Scotland (September 1999), pp. 201-210.

RACCOON — AN INFRASTRUCTURE FOR MANAGING ACCESS CONTROL IN CORBA

Gerald Brose
Institut für Informatik, Freie Universität Berlin, Germany
gerald.brose@acm.org

Abstract Object-level security management of CORBA applications is not sufficiently supported by current management architectures. This paper presents a language-based approach and an infrastructure for managing fine-grained access control policies for CORBA objects at an abstract level.

Keywords: CORBA, Access Control, Security Policies, Management

1. INTRODUCTION

The complexity inherent in distributed systems constitutes a major problem for overall security because of the significant potential for human error. This applies especially in the area of security management. A basic premise of this work is that the correct design, specification, and management of security policies is a central problem in distributed systems because these tasks are both error–prone and by their very nature security–critical. We argue that the potential damage caused by inadequate handling of policies is significant, and that current methods or management tools do not provide adequate support to security administrators.

This paper focuses on one particular aspect of security policy management in CORBA environments, viz. access control. Access control is concerned with preventing unauthorized accesses to shared resources and is used to enforce a given set of security requirements. "Commercial" security policies [Clark and Wilson, 1987] usually concentrate on integrity requirements, but access control can also be used to enforce confidentiality, general resource usage restrictions (availability), or even coordination policies in CSCW systems [Edwards, 1996]. These requirements are addressed in access control policies, which describe which accesses in a system are authorized and which are not. In our use of the term, policies are represented in terms of a formal access model and can be evaluated by an access control mechanism.

To support the management of access policies for CORBA objects, it is necessary to define appropriate management abstractions. These abstractions serve two purposes. First, they allow managers to deal with large–scale systems by abstracting from individual entities such as objects, users, and access rights, i.e., they hide details that are too numerous to handle individually. Examples of abstractions of this kind include domains of objects, user groups, and views. Second, they can be used to hide implementation details that are too involved to be intelligible to security managers, such as an individual operation invocation in a complex object–oriented application protocol. Roles and views are examples of abstractions of this second kind.

An important aspect of access control in object–oriented systems is that it is not sufficient to consider run–time management in isolation. Because of the potentially large number of objects and complex interaction patterns in object–oriented applications, a security administrator cannot be expected to completely understand the internal logic of all applications running under his supervision. The security implications of, e.g., introducing a new right or object type into a running system might be unclear, so managers need security documentation at an adequate level of abstraction. This information can only be provided by application designers, however, so some form of cooperation and communication between developers, deployers and managers is required.

We propose a separate design document that must be delivered with an application in the form of a descriptor file, which can be read by deployment and management tools. It is the responsibility of application developers to prepare this document as an input to the subsequent deployment and management stages in the application life cycle. To do so, policy designers use a specific design language, the *View Policy Language* (VPL).

The remainder of this paper is structured as follows. Section 2 presents a language–based approach to this problem. In section 3, we describe the security architecture required for managing access control in CORBA based on VPL. Section 4 discusses related work. The paper concludes with a summary and an outlook on future work in section 5.

2. VIEW–BASED ACCESS CONTROL POLICIES

The central concept of the access control model proposed in [Brose, 1999, Brose, 2000] and presented in this section is the higher–level modelling concept of a *view* for authorizations. Using views, policies can be written and understood in terms of sets of related authorizations. A view is a named set of access rights, which are both permissions or denials for operations on objects. While access decisions are based on individual rights, views are the units of description and authorization assignment. They are defined statically as part of a policy specification. Figure 1 shows an example of a view definition in VPL.

```
view Reading
    controls Document
    restricted_to Staff
{
    allow
        read;
        find;
};
```

Figure 1. A view definition.

Views are defined as authorizations for objects of a single IDL interface, which is referenced in the `controls`–clause of the view definition. In the example, the view `Reading` controls the IDL type Document, which means that this view can only be assigned on objects of this type or one of its subtypes. Permissions are listed after the keyword `allow`, denials would be introduced by `deny`. In the example, only operations to read the document and to find words within the document are allowed. A view can be restricted to the roles listed in a `restricted_to` clause so that it is not possible to assign the view to other roles. The `Reading` view can only be assigned to the role `Staff`.

The introduction of this concept is motivated by the observation that generic rights such as "read", "write", and "execute" are not adequate for describing authorizations in large–scale systems comprised of typed objects. Generic or uninterpreted rights are ill–suited for application–level access policies in these systems because they provide no means to impose external structure by defining relationships or constraints. Moreover, it is difficult to capture the rich semantics of operations in object–oriented systems with just a small set of generic rights. Generic rights thus lead to modelling problems in the design of access policies and are hard to manage.

To solve the problems outlined above, we propose a new access model that is based on the classical access matrix model by Lampson [Lampson, 1974]. Unlike Lampson's matrix or the standard CORBA access model [OMG, 1998], matrix entries do not contain simple generic rights but named and typed sets of rights, i.e., views. Matrix rows in the model correspond to roles, so a matrix entry represents the authorizations assigned to a role for the particular object denoted by the matrix column. Table 1 illustrates such a matrix.

The notion of roles used here is that of the $RBAC_3$ model [Sandhu et al., 1996]. In $RBAC_3$, roles can be organized into role hierarchies, and role constraints such as mutual exclusion can be expressed. Figure 2 shows role definitions in VPL.

Table 1. Access matrix with view entries.

Role \ Object	f: Folder	chapter: Document	contract: Document
Secretary	Lookup	Reading	Reading
Author	Lookup Appending	Reading Updating	Reading
Editor	Listing Appending Removing	Reading	Reading
Manager	Lookup	Reading	Updating

```
roles
   Staff;
   Author;
   Secretary:  Staff; // Secretary is senior to Staff
   Editor:  Staff {
      maxcard  4 // no more than 4 editors
   };
   Manager:  Staff {
      excludes Author // managers may not be authors
   };
```

Figure 2. Role definitions.

VPL can be used to express implicit authorizations and exceptions, and allows designers to specify priorities that determine how conflicts between permissions and denials are resolved. Moreover, it is possible to statically specify dynamic rights changes using the `schema` language construct. Figure 3 illustrates how views are assigned and removed in response to the IDL operation create, which acts as a trigger. The schema in the example is defined to react to operations on objects whose type has the same name as the schema, i.e., on DocumentFactory objects. The modifier `with assign option` in the `assigns` clause is equivalent to SQL's grant option and means that the receiving principal may delegate the view `Managing` to other principals at his discretion. The identifiers `result`, `caller`, and `this` are dynamically bound to the result of the create operation, the DocumentFactory object itself, and the caller, respectively. A second effect of the create operation is that the `Creating` view is removed from the caller's matrix entry for the DocumentFactory object, assuming that this view was required to call create in the first place.

By fixing the target data model to IDL, it is possible to define a number of static type checks that help to catch policy specification errors early. For example, it can be checked that views are well–formed with respect to the IDL

```
schema DocumentFactory {
   create
      assigns
         Managing with assign option on result to caller
      removes
         Creating on this from caller
}
```

Figure 3. A VPL schema for document creation.

type they control. Additionally, it can be verified that schema clauses comply with role restrictions defined in views, and that conflicts between permissions and denials are resolvable at runtime.

3. AN INFRASTRUCTURE FOR ACCESS CONTROL MANAGEMENT

A number of infrastructure components and tools are required to allow application developers and managers to work with the model abstractions presented in the previous section. The first tool that is required in the life cycle of an access policy is a VPL compiler, which is needed to type–check policy descriptions and compile them into a descriptor file format. Similar to EJB descriptors [Sun Microsystems, 2000], the VPL compiler produces an XML file. The contents of this file is deployed to a role and view repository, respectively, which make role and view constructs accessible at runtime. XML was chosen as an intermediate format so that deployment tools can rely on standard XML parsing libraries and a document type description (DTD) rather than having to implement a full VPL compiler. Deploying new roles potentially involves role renaming, either to prevent name clashes with existing roles, or in order to identify new roles with already existing roles that have the same function but different names. Figure 4 depicts the development and deployment process.

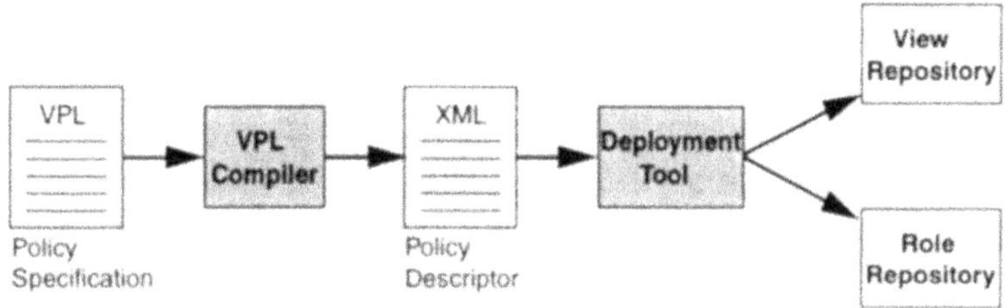

Figure 4. Policy compilation and deployment.

3.1. Operation and Management

Any mechanism for controlling access to CORBA objects must be able to intercept and check all possible accesses, i.e., the mechanism must be interposed between the object and its callers and not be bypassable. This property is known as *complete mediation* in [Department of Defense, 1985], where the entire mechanism is termed *reference monitor*. The most straightforward allocation of this functionality is to perform access checks in the address space of the process hosting the object implementation. CORBA interceptors are a convenient way to implement this mechanism, and the CORBA Security Service specifies an access control interceptor for this purpose. Our own implementation also uses interceptors.

The UML diagram in Figure 5 illustrates how accesses are transparently intercepted and checked in CORBA. The interceptor calls an AccessDecision object which requires an access policy to determine whether the interceptor can allow the access and let the request pass, or whether it must deny the access by signaling the CORBA system exception NO_PERMISSION to the caller. This exception is not shown in the diagram.

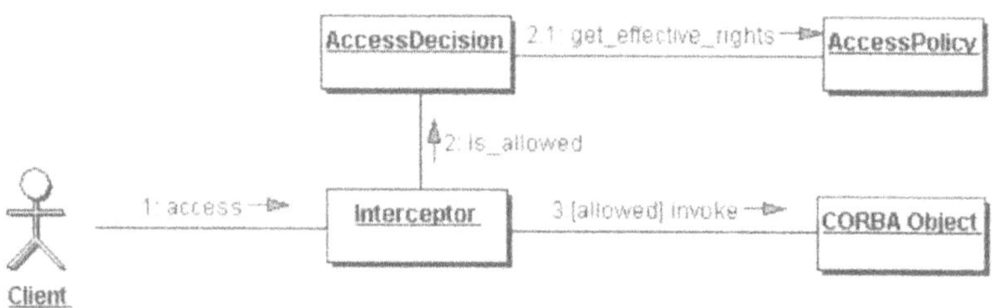

Figure 5. Access Control with Interceptors.

While interceptors are the standard implementation of reference monitor functionality, they are not the only option. It is just as possible to define reference monitors on a per–node or even per–subnet basis rather than only per–process. Moving the reference monitor further away from the protected object has implications for the extent of the object's trusted computing base (TCB), however. In the case of a per–process interceptor implementation, the TCB comprises the target platform's hardware, operating system, middleware, and security service implementation. Delegating this functionality to a component outside the target node, e.g., to an application–level firewall, means placing trust not only in the firewall, but also in any machine within the interior network because operation invocations from these machines do not pass through the firewall and thus remain unchecked.

An interceptor needs access control information to be able to make access decisions, viz. information about the caller and its roles, about the target, and the requested access operation. In addition, it needs access to the access policy for the target object. Figure 6 gives an overview of the components that are involved in an access decision and need to be adapted to the specific access control model used here. The interceptor and the AccessDecision object reside within the server hosting the target object and have been omitted from the diagram. In the remainder of this section, we discuss these infrastructure components, their relationships, and their management interfaces in more detail.

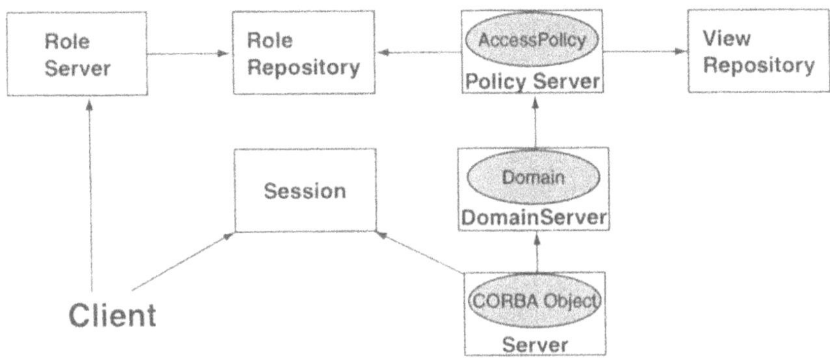

Figure 6. Raccoon architecture.

3.2. Sessions and Role Server

In the CORBA security framework, information about callers is represented as security attributes and stored in *Credentials* objects. Credentials objects are created on the client side as the result of authentication and stored in the client–side context. Before an operation is invoked, the client runtime system needs to establish a security association or *Session* with the server and transmit its credentials. In our approach, the credentials associated with sessions contain information about the caller's roles. This section describes the necessary role management components, which are not defined by the CORBA Security Service.

Role information is provided in the form of X.509v3 certificates that contain the principal's public key and a single role name in an extension field of the certificate. Upon request, these certificates are created, signed, and returned by a role server component. A *role certificate* is a binding between a principal identifier (a public key) and a role name, and this binding can be verified by checking the role server's signature.

The role server does not need to establish the identity of clients requesting role certificates because a role certificate itself does not convey any authorizations to its holders, and because callers must authenticate separately with the individual servers anyway. However, the role server may still choose to authenticate clients and restrict access to role information if this information is considered sensitive. Because role information about a principal is used to derive authorization information, access control interceptors must verify the authenticity and freshness of the information using the role server's public key. They must also verify that the caller is indeed the subject of the role certificates it presents. Caller authentication is achieved by relying on SSL transport connections.

The process of requesting certificates and storing them locally as credentials is performed by the security service on the client side, which is also responsible for sending these certificates to the server. The basic model of interaction with the role server is thus "client–pull" and allows security–aware clients to select a subset of roles for subsequent accesses rather than presenting the full set of certificates. This can be desirable for two reasons. First, a client might wish to use only the minimal set of roles required to carry out a certain task in order to restrict the potential damage of Trojan horses, or of its own mistakes in using the application. Second, our access model supports assigning explicit denials to certain roles so that a client might in fact be more restricted in his actions when using the union of all his roles than when using only a specific subset of roles. The client can perform this role selection using standard CORBA security API calls for credentials management.

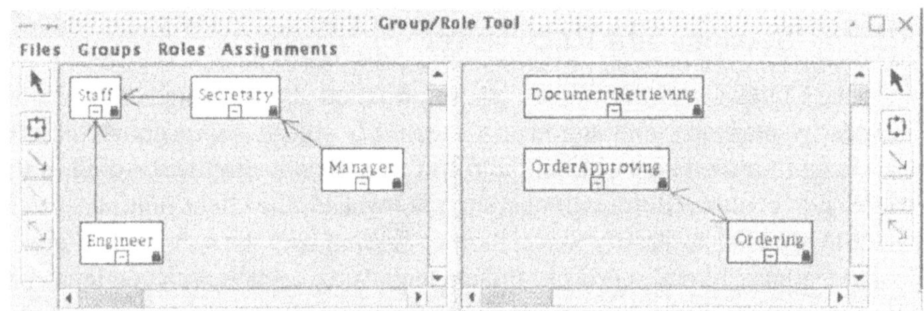

Figure 7. Role Management GUI.

The role server provides administrators with the GUI shown in Figure 7, which supports managing groups, roles, and role constraints. The left half of the window displays information about principals in the form of a group hierarchy. In the right panel, the example shows three roles and a mutual exclusion constraint between the two roles `OrderApproving` and `Ordering`, which is shown as a double–headed arrow. This role information itself is not kept in the role server but stored separately in the role repository. The assignment of groups of principals to roles is performed by drawing an arrow from a group in the left panel to a role in the right panel.

3.3. Domain Server

In large distributed systems, objects are typically not managed individually but grouped into management domains. For this reason, the individual CORBA object in Figure 6 is not directly associated with a policy. This allows managers to structure large systems into manageable subsystems and to model the diverse spheres of management authority and responsibility that are frequently found in large organizations. This section presents a model for and an implementation of a service for CORBA that supports grouping objects into domains, the construction of domain hierarchies, and the assignment of policies to domains. The service itself is policy–neutral. It can also be used as a generic mechanism to attach arbitrary dynamic properties to CORBA objects and is more flexible than the OMG–specified Property Service [OMG, 1997] because it does not require managed objects to implement service–specific interfaces. More information on the domain service can be found in [Brose et al., 2001].

The CORBA specification [OMG, 1999a] defines interfaces for policies and domains but no service API for managing the life cycle of domain objects, the construction of domain hierarchies, or the membership of objects in domains. An object may be a member of multiple domains, but CORBA requires that every object must be a member of at least one domain. Domains may only be associated with one policy of a given type. Individual domains are thus free of conflicts between policies of the same type, such as one access control policy allowing an access and another policy rejecting the same access.

As in [Sloman and Twidle, 1994] and [ISO/IEC, 1996], a policy domain is basically a relation between a set of member objects and a set of policies. Hierarchical relationships between domains are an important means of expressing delegation of responsibility between authorities and can also model refinement between policies. We model domain hierarchies as acyclic directed graphs, with edges representing subdomain relationships. A domain's policies also apply to the members of its subdomain, and changes in parent domain policies may affect objects in subdomains. Policy changes in subdomains, however, only affect the members of that domain and its subdomains.

Assuming that policies of different types are entirely orthogonal, there can be no direct policy conflicts within a single domain. Policy conflicts are possible between policies of different domains, however, because objects can be members of more than one domain, and because a domain's policies also apply in its subdomains in a hierarchy. The domain management service therefore supports the allocation of conflict resolution strategies in the form of *meta policies* [Hosmer, 1993]. A meta policy may, e.g., define a general precedence rule for policies in domains, such as "policies closer to the root of the domain graph take precedence".

A meta policy is basically another policy that is associated with a domain and must be interpreted by an enforcement mechanism. We do not attach any more semantics to a meta policy than that it applies to policies of a given type that in turn apply to the objects in the domain. As with other policies, the actual meaning is determined by the mechanism. Meta policies need not be restricted to conflict resolution as in [Kühnhauser, 1999] and [Lupu and Sloman, 1999], but can be regarded as general policy operators that are implemented by the individual policy enforcement mechanisms.

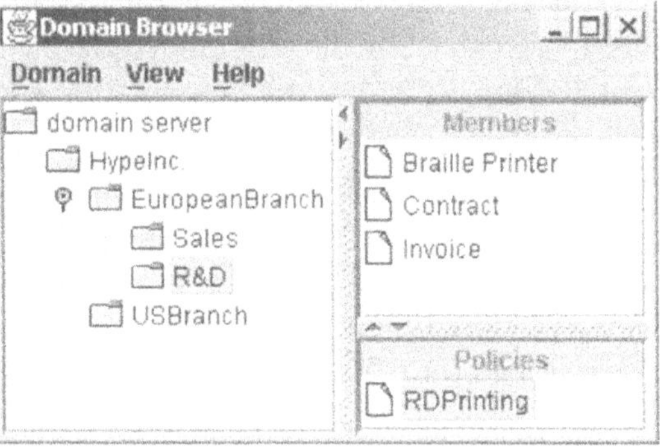

Figure 8. The Domain Browser.

The implementation provides a GUI management tool with which domain services can be used centrally by an administrator. This Domain Browser is shown in Figure 8. It includes an editor for generic policies that can be written as simple lists of name–value pairs and can be conveniently configured to provide different graphical policy editors for different policy types. VPL, e.g., requires a different editor, which is shown in Figure 9.

3.4. Policy Server

The editor tool shown in Figure 9 combines information from different sources. The upper left panel shows information about the objects in the policy domain, which is part of the domain server. The upper right panel shows the access policy itself, i.e., assignments of views to roles on the objects selected in the left panel. In this case, the `Staff` role holds a `Faxing` view on the printer object in the domain. The complete access policy is represented by a separate CORBA object of type AccessPolicy, which implements the view–based access matrix model.

The policy editor supports adding new views on the objects and types in the domain. In the lower half of the window, the policy editor displays the definition

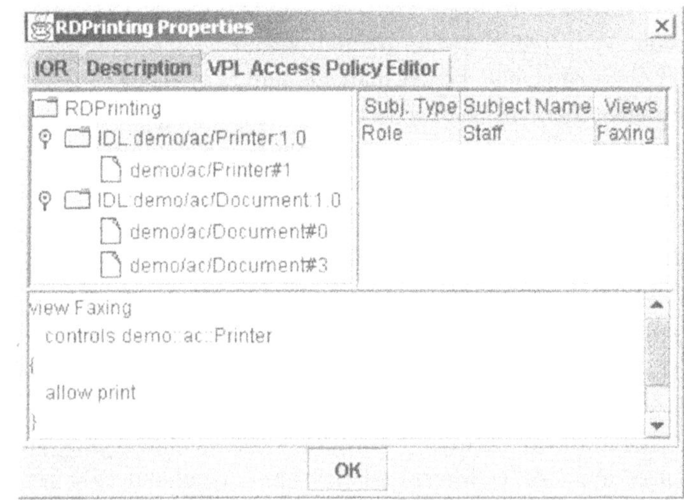

Figure 9. The VPL Policy Editor.

of the view `Faxing` that it retrieved from the View Repository in response to the selection of this view in the upper right panel. Finally, the editor can also display IDL type information in the lower panel if an IDL type name is selected. For this purpose, it requires access to a CORBA Interface Repository.

4. RELATED WORK

An existing management product that supports security management in CORBA environments is [Tivoli, 2001], which comprises a comprehensive suite of tools. Tivoli does not specifically address access control management at the level of application objects, and provides no separate specification language. The CORBA security service product by [Adiron, 2001] does provide an access control language, but this language is not object–oriented and limited to the restricted standard model of access control in CORBA.

Our basic approach of relying on a separate, abstract language for the specification of non–functional aspects of applications can be compared to *Aspect–Oriented Programming* (AOP) [Kiczales et al., 1997]. AOP also relies on separate *aspect languages* that are processed by a tool called *aspect weaver*. This tool generates code for aspects such as concurrency and distribution, and performs the integration of functional code with aspect code. There is currently no aspect language in AOP that addresses access control. The use of descriptor files that are processed by deployment tools is common in environments such as EJB [Sun Microsystems, 2000] or the CORBA Component Model (CCM) [OMG, 1999b], both of which also support the expression of simple access policies in descriptors. Both descriptor languages do not provide adequate management abstractions, however, and only support access control decisions at the granularity of types, not individual objects.

In the context of policy–based management, a number of general–purpose policy languages have been proposed, e.g. [Sloman and Twidle, 1994, Koch et al., 1996, Tu et al., 1997]. The information models underlying these languages are more general than the CORBA object model, and they do not offer higher–level authorization concepts like views. These languages are thus not suitable for collaborative use by CORBA application developers, who have to provide an initial policy design, and security managers, who subsequently deploy, refine and manage the policy. We argue that for such an approach, it is necessary to sacrifice some generality for better integration with design abstractions, i.e., IDL interfaces.

A general framework for defining arbitrary access control policies is proposed in [Jajodia et al., 1997], where policies are formulated as a set of rules in a logic–based language. This model leaves open all design decisions about how implicit authorizations are derived, how rights propagate in groups, which conflict resolution strategies are used, and how priorities are employed. Rules embodying these design decisions have to be defined first as part of a policy library. The data model for protected objects is also left open and has to be described separately.

5. SUMMARY AND FUTURE WORK

This paper presented a language–based approach to the problem of managing application–level access control policies in CORBA. We discussed a view and role–based access model and presented the runtime infrastructure required to manage policies according to our access model. A prototypical Java implementation of the Raccoon architecture was done using the CORBA implementation [JacORB, 2001]. The prototype implements the subset of the CORBA Security Service that is relevant for access control and replaces its standard access model. Moreover, it extends the security service with role and domain management components.

To demonstrate the feasibility of the approach, we plan to evaluate the performance implications of the proposed architecture, and to conduct a more complex application case study. The prototypical implementation has not been specifically designed to withstand denial of service attacks, which would require appropriate replication of services. Another direction for future work is to use VPL for managing application–level firewalls for CORBA.

Acknowledgments

This work is funded by the German Research Council (DFG). The author would like to thank Peter Löhr and Nicolas Noffke for fruitful discussions.

References

[Adiron, 2001] Adiron (2001). http://www.adiron.com/.

[Brose, 1999] Brose, G. (1999). A view–based access model for CORBA. In Vitek, J. and Jensen, C., editors, *Secure Internet Programming: Security Issues for Mobile and Distributed Objects*, LNCS 1603, pages 237–252. Springer.

[Brose, 2000] Brose, G. (2000). A typed access control model for CORBA. In Cuppens, F., Deswarte, Y., Gollmann, D., and Weidner, M., editors, *Proc. ESORICS 2000*, LNCS 1895, pages 88–105. Springer.

[Brose et al., 2001] Brose, G., Kiefer, H., and Noffke, N. (2001). A CORBA domain management service. In *Proc. KiVS 2001*.

[Clark and Wilson, 1987] Clark, D. D. and Wilson, D. R. (1987). A comparison of commercial and military computer security policies. In *Procs. IEEE Symposium on Security and Privacy*, pages 184–194.

[Department of Defense, 1985] Department of Defense (1985). Department of Defense Trusted Computer System Evaluation Criteria. DoD 5200.28-STD.

[Edwards, 1996] Edwards, W. K. (1996). Policies and roles in collaborative applications. In *Proc. Computer Supported Cooperative Work (CSCW)*, pages 11–20.

[Hosmer, 1993] Hosmer, H. H. (1993). The multipolicy paradigm for trusted systems. In *Procs. ACM New Security Paradigms Workshop*, pages 19–32.

[ISO/IEC, 1996] ISO/IEC (1996). *Information Technology — Open Systems Interconnection — Security Frameworks for Open Systems: Overview*. International Standard, ISO/IEC 10181-1:1996(E).

[JacORB, 2001] JacORB (2001). http://www.jacorb.org.

[Jajodia et al., 1997] Jajodia, S., Samarati, P., Subrahmanian, V. S., and Bertino, E. (1997). A unified framework for enforcing multiple access control policies. In *Proc. International Conference on Management of Data*, pages 474–485.

[Kiczales et al., 1997] Kiczales, G., Lamping, J., Mendhekar, A., Maeda, C., Lopes, C., Loingiter, J.-M., and Irwin, J. (1997). Aspect–oriented programming. In *Proc. ECOOP*, LNCS. Springer.

[Koch et al., 1996] Koch, T., Krell, C., and Krämer, B. (1996). Policy definition language for automated management of distributed systems. 2nd International Workshop on Systems Management, IEEE Computer Society.

[Kühnhauser, 1999] Kühnhauser, W. (1999). *Metapolitiken*. GMD Research Series. GMD.

[Lampson, 1974] Lampson, B. W. (1974). Protection. *ACM Operating Systems Reviews*, 8(1):18–24.

[Lupu and Sloman, 1999] Lupu, E. C. and Sloman, M. (1999). Conflicts in policy–based distributed systems management. *IEEE Transactions on Software Engineering*, 25(6):852–896.

[OMG, 1997] OMG (1997). *CORBAservices: Common Object Services Specification*.

[OMG, 1998] OMG (1998). *Security Service, Revision 1.5*.

[OMG, 1999a] OMG (1999a). *The Common Object Request Broker: Architecture and Specification, Revision 2.3*.

[OMG, 1999b] OMG (1999b). *CORBA 3.0 New Components Chapters*. OMG, TC Document ptc/99-10-04 edition.

[Sandhu et al., 1996] Sandhu, R. S., Coyne, E. J., Feinstein, H. L., and Youman, C. E. (1996). Role–based access control models. *IEEE Computer*, 29(2):38–47.

[Sloman and Twidle, 1994] Sloman, M. and Twidle, K. (1994). Domains: A framework for structuring management policy. In Sloman, M., editor, *Network and Distributed Systems Management*, chapter 16. Addison–Wesley.

[Sun Microsystems, 2000] Sun Microsystems (2000). *Enterprise JavaBeans Specification, Version 2.0, Final Draft.*

[Tivoli, 2001] Tivoli (2001). http://www.tivoli.com.

[Tu et al., 1997] Tu, M., Griffel, F., Merz, M., and Lamersdorf, W. (1997). Generic policy management for open service markets. In *Proc. International Conference on Distributed Applications and Interoperable Systems (DAIS'97)*, pages 212–222, Cottbus, Germany. Chapman & Hall.

IX

SHORT PAPERS II

TOOL-ASSISTED SECURITY ASSESSMENT OF DISTRIBUTED APPLICATIONS

Peter Herrmann, Lars Wiebusch, and Heiko Krumm
Universität Dortmund, FB Informatik, LS IV
D - 44221 Dortmund, Germany

Abstract The CORBA security services support the flexible provision of security features. Their employment, however, has to be tailored to the assets and threats of a system. We relate the corresponding analysis and design of CORBA systems with traditional security analysis, risk assessment, and countermeasure planning as it is in the scope of information system security standards. Since security analysis tends to be difficult and error-prone, we combine that proposal with our object-oriented security analysis and modeling approach. It employs object-oriented modeling techniques and tool-assistance in order to facilitate the analysis and assure its quality even in case of extensive systems.

Keywords: Security analysis, risk assessment, Common Criteria, CORBA security services, object-oriented security analysis

1. INTRODUCTION

The growing importance of the CORBA platform ([OMG, 1997]) and the existing needs for application security analysis and design plead for the provision of an approach which is devoted to the efficient security analysis of CORBA-based applications. In particular the objectives expressed in the appendix E of the CORBA security services specification ([OMG, 2000]) aim to the assurance of trustworthiness of information systems. They should be linked with the general international security certification standard conceptions, in particular with the notions and procedures of the Common Criteria ([ISO/IEC, 1998]). Analysis and design of secure systems, however, is usually expensive and laborious since well-educated specialists have to analyze the systems in detail under consideration of recommendations and standards (e.g., baseline protection cf. [BSI, 1999] or certified levels cf. [SOGIS, 1991, ISO/IEC, 1998]). Moreover they have continuously to consult the rapidly growing security information bases (e.g., [CERT, 2001]).

Meanwhile many procedures for the corresponding analysis and design of secure systems were proposed (cf. overview in [Baskerville, 1993]). They comprise series of phases devoted to system identification, asset valuation and security objective definition, weakness and threat identification, assessment of risks, and finally planning, design, and evaluation of suitable countermeasures. In [Herrmann and Krumm, 2001] we proposed the new approach of object-oriented security analysis. While existing approaches are based on classical data base and information system techniques like dictionaries, data repositories, and decision trees, we apply explicit object-oriented modeling and enhanced object-oriented techniques. Our tool adopts the conceptions of object-oriented design tools of computer-aided software engineering and supports the comfortable interactive design of graphical model definitions. In fact, our tool re-uses open-source modules of the Argo project ([TIGRIS, 2000]). We represent system and security objectives by means of an object instance diagram. Special support results from libraries of predefined object classes which model system component types and define basic methods for automated class-specific analysis and evaluation.

The automated threat analysis and countermeasure introduction of the tool is mainly based on the conception of graph rewrite systems (cf. [Bardohl et al., 1999]). A rewrite system consists of a set of rewrite rules where a rule is a pair of graph patterns, a pre-pattern and a post-pattern. Moreover an application condition and effect functions can belong to a rule. A rule can be applied to a graph if an instance of its pre-pattern can be found in the graph. The application replaces the instance of the pre-pattern by a corresponding instance of the post-pattern. The patterns are object configuration patterns. So, pre-patterns can correspond to scenarios which come along with vulnerabilities and post-patterns can augment those scenarios with representations of threats.

In the sequel we report on the adaption of class libraries and rewrite rules to the security analysis of CORBA based distributed applications.

2. OBJECT-ORIENTED ANALYSIS

ISO/IEC published a set of common criteria (CC) to standardize security evaluations of IT systems ([ISO/IEC, 1998]). Moreover it provides a methodology for detecting vulnerabilities and for developing countermeasures in order to reduce the risks. Figure 1 delineates the main notions of the CC. Computer systems and system components are assets for their owners. The assets are exposed to various security risks since they contain vulnerabilities which can be utilized by malicious threat agents. To minimize the risks, asset owners impose countermeasures reducing vulnerabilities. The countermeasures, however, may contain vulnerabilities themselves which have to be reduced by other countermeasures.

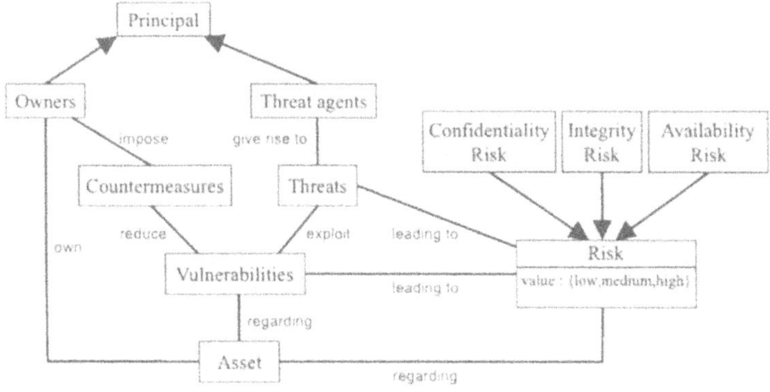

Figure 1. Security classes and associations

Our approach supports the CC compliant system identification by a library of asset classes like networks, stations, applications, and data as well as associations between the classes. The tool supports the creation of asset and association instances resulting in a UML object diagram of the system. Thereafter the assets have to be evaluated in order to define the requirements for protection. According to the potential damage each asset is assigned with either one of the four security levels of baseline protection *maximum*, *high*, *moderate*, and *low* or with one of seven evaluation assurance levels introduced in the CC. One can assign different security levels for an asset with respect to each of the three security objectives confidentiality, integrity, and availability.

The next phase identifies firstly vulnerabilities and thereafter threats on the assets. It is supported by libraries of vulnerability classes and threat classes. Moreover two rewrite rule libraries exist. One detects and documents vulnerabilities, the other adds corresponding threats. The interactive valuation of the seriousness of threats concludes the phase.

Then risks are modeled by objects augmenting pairs of assets and vulnerabilities. Moreover, the value of a risk is calculated from the security level of the asset and the seriousness of the vulnerability (cf. [Courtney, 1977]). That risk assessment is again supported by a class and a rewrite rule library. An interactive classification of risks follows and decides if a risk is not acceptable and must be reduced by countermeasures.

A countermeasure class library and a countermeasure introduction rewrite rule set support the last phase. Attributes of countermeasure objects describe protection levels and prizes which influence the automated selection of measures and the computation of achieved security levels. Since countermeasures may have vulnerabilities themselves, the analysis has to iterate the phases in order to check the extended system.

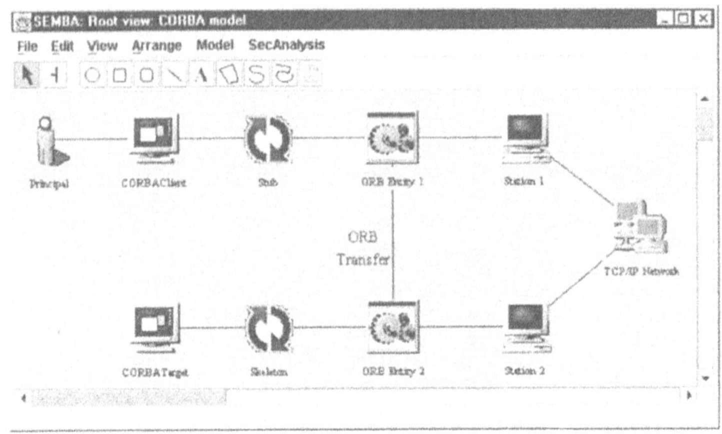

Figure 2. Object model of the CORBA architecture

3. ANALYSIS OF CORBA APPLICATIONS

In order to enable security analysis according to the CORBA security services specification ([OMG, 2000]), we extended the set of system asset classes by CORBA-specific components like client and target objects, stubs, skeletons, and ORB components. Moreover classes were added specifying countermeasures like principal-authenticator objects or credential objects. Figure 2 depicts an UML object diagram of a CORBA-based system. Here, the CORBA client and target objects and the principal accessing the client are described by the objects *Client*, *Target*, and *Principal* while the objects *Stub* and *Skeleton* model the access points of the IDL-based interface. The ORB specification consists of the underlying hardware platform (*Station 1*, *Station 2*, *Network*) and of the ORB software components (*ORB Entity 1*, *ORB Entity 2*).

Next, we will sketch the security analysis of a small part of the system. In a first step, we evaluate the client object and assume that a damage of the client object caused by a malicious attack may lead to a considerable disruption of the institution. Therefore, according to [BSI, 1999], we evaluate it with the security level *High*.

Thereafter the tool identifies vulnerabilities of the client object which may cause threats. With respect to user access, objects may be vulnerable in two manners: At first, an object is not able to recognize the true identity of a principal which may be exploited by masquerade based attacks. At second, an object has to enable access to system resources in order to fulfill given privileges. That may be utilized for an extension of the granted privileges. The tool therefore assigns the two vulnerability objects *Inability to recognize true identity* and *Utilization of not granted privileges* to *Client*. Likewise threat objects are added describing threats based on wrong identities or exceeded privileges. The seriousness of the vulnerabilities is rated to *Maximum* since *Client* is not protected by countermeasures yet.

In the next step the tool assesses the risks for *Client*. The confidentiality, integrity, and availability risks are calculated based on the security level *High* of the object *Client* and the seriousness values *Maximum* of the vulnerabilities. By using a special risk matrix (cf. [Herrmann and Krumm, 2001]), the tool calculates the value *High* for all three risks of the client. Since these risks are unbearable, suitable countermeasures have to be imposed. Therefore the security analysis is continued.

The CORBA security specification ([OMG, 2000]) intends the use of a principal-authenticator object and credential objects to provide authentication and access control. The principal-authenticator object authenticates principals requesting access to a CORBA system resource by authentication methods like passwords, smart cards, or biometric systems. Moreover, it maintains an access control list describing the privileges of the particular principal. The principal-authenticator object creates credential objects which can be forwarded to objects the principal wants to access. A credential object testifies that the principal was authenticated by the principal-authenticator object and contains information enabling the accessed object to check the principal's privileges for compliance with its own security policy. If an object does not contain security related functions, the checks are performed by the ORB. In our example, the tool introduces a principal-authenticator object and credential objects to reduce the two vulnerabilities of the client object. Moreover, it has to decide which authentication method to impose. Since password-based authentication systems offer too weak protection for an asset facing a high risk, the tool selects a smart card system which is the least expensive of the remaining alternatives. Finally, the tool assigns the security level *High* to the principal-authenticator object and to the credential objects since these objects guard an asset also rated with *High*.

Since the principal-authenticator and credential objects carry vulnerabilities themselves which intruders may use to reduce their protection, a second iteration of the security analysis is performed for the extended system consisting of the original CORBA example and the added safeguards. This iteration leads to the introduction of unique signatures and timestamps for credentials in order to protect them against attacks during network transfer.

4. CONCLUDING REMARKS

We considered the needs for standard compliant security assessment of distributed CORBA-based applications and reported on the principles of a new approach for that purpose. It combines object-oriented modeling of CORBA security issues and Common Criteria. Moreover it focuses on tool-assistance and automation. Current work is devoted to the enhancement of the libraries and to practical experiments. Future work aims to the integration of support for the second major task in the provision of secure systems, namely proper operation and management of the security components. It will utilize results from current work on general model-based security management (cf. [Lück et al., 2001]).

References

[Bardohl et al., 1999] Bardohl, R., Taentzer, G., Minas, M., and Schürr, A. (1999). Application of graph transformation to visual languages. In *Handbook on Graph Grammars, Volume 2*, Chapter 1. World Scientific.

[Baskerville, 1993] Baskerville, R. (1993). Information Systems Design Methods: Implications for Information Systems Development. *ACM Computing Surveys*, 25(4):375–414.

[Booch et al., 1999] Booch, G., Rumbaugh, J., and Jacobson, I. (1999). *The Unified Modeling Language User Guide*. Addison-Wesley Longman.

[BSI, 1999] BSI (1999). *IT Baseline Protection Manual*. Bundesamt für Sicherheit in der Informationstechnik, www.bsi.de.

[CERT, 2001] CERT (2001). Current information bases and advisories. www.cert.org.

[Courtney, 1977] Courtney, R. (1977). Security Risk Assessment in Electronic Data Processing. In *AFIPS Conf. Proc. of the National Computer Conference 46*, pages 97–104, Arlington. AFIPS.

[Herrmann and Krumm, 2001] Herrmann, P. and Krumm, H. (2001). Object-oriented security analysis and modeling. In *Proc. 9th International Conference on Telecommunication Systems*, pages 21–32, Dallas. ATSMA, IFIP.

[ISO/IEC, 1998] ISO/IEC (1998). *Common Criteria for Information Technology Security Evaluation*. ISO/IEC. International Standard ISO/IEC 15408.

[Lück et al., 2001] Lück, I., Schäfer, C., and Krumm, H. (2001). Model-based Tool-Assistance for Packet-Filter Design. In *Policies for Distributed Systems and Networks*, LNCS 1995, pages 120–136, Bristol. IEEE, Springer-Verlag.

[OMG, 1997] OMG (1997). *A Discussion of the Object Management Architecture*. Object Management Group (OMG).

[OMG, 2000] OMG (2000). *Security Services Specification, Version 1.5*. Object Management Group (OMG), CORBA.

[SOGIS, 1991] SOGIS (1991). *Information Technology Security Evaluation Criteria (ITSEC)*. EC advisory group SOGIS.

[TIGRIS, 2000] TIGRIS (2000). *ArgoUML Vision*. Tigris. argouml.tigris.org/vision.html.

SERVICE ORIENTED APPLICATION MANAGEMENT – DO CURRENT TECHNIQUES MEET THE REQUIREMENTS?

Rainer Hauck, Igor Radisic

Munich Network Management (MNM) Team, University of Munich, Dept. of CS

Oettingenstr. 67, D-80538 Munich, Germany. Phone: +49-89-2178-2155|2167, Fax: -2262

{hauck|radisic}@informatik.uni-muenchen.de

Abstract Besides the conclusion of agreements about quality of service (QoS), one of the major prerequisites for a global service market are means to monitor the fulfillment of those agreements. From a user's perspective, the time needed to complete a service transaction represents one of the most critical QoS parameters. As most electronic services are usually based on distributed applications, obviously the same techniques can be used to measure the performance of electronic services as well as the underlying applications. In recent years several techniques evolved to monitor the application performance. However, the new aspect of service orientation adds relevant new requirements that are to be posed on such solutions. This paper evaluates the various techniques from a service oriented point of view and presents open research questions.

Keywords: Distributed Applications, Application Performance Monitoring, Service Performance, Electronic Service, Quality of Service

1. INTRODUCTION

As the analysis of agreements between providers of so called *electronic services* (e-services) and their customers shows, one of the most important prerequisites for a successful business relationship is the fulfillment of the agreed quality of service. Usually several problems arise from not fulfilling the agreement that lead to consequences ranging from penalties to be paid by the provider to breaking up the agreement. The discipline of *service management* provides and develops tools, techniques and methodologies to support the provider in fulfilling his agreements.

As current e-services are usually based on distributed applications (*application services*), it is actually possible to use the same techniques to manage both the e-services and the underlying applications. As a consequence there are several new requirements emerging from service orientation in application management: the main focus changes from application deployment and configuration to monitoring and controlling proper fulfillment of the agreed QoS. From a customer's point of view the most interesting QoS parameter in this context is the time needed to successfully complete a transaction. Taking too much time resolves into user's discontent which is to avoid. As providers are strongly interested in fulfilling the agreed QoS parameters, the ability to react in time is most relevant to the provider in case application performance degradation is noticed and thus the violation of an SLA is possible. On the other hand customers want to verify the fulfillment of their SLAs. Thus, for both sides means to monitor the duration of transactions are necessary.

In recent years several techniques evolved to monitor the performance of distributed applications. This paper presents a classification and a criteria-based rating of existing approaches in the area of application performance monitoring from a service oriented point of view. Furthermore, the analysis is used to identify and structure open research questions.

The requirements to be posed on the different approaches have been derived from a generic service model [8]. As already mentioned, one of the most important requirements is to monitor **service-oriented parameters** (e.g., transaction duration, service availablity). Of similar importance is the monitoring of **actual user experience** (as opposed to drawing samples) and the availability of **in-depth information** to allow providers to easily identify root causes of problems. Further requirements are **minimal effort** for all participants, **minimal performance impact** on the application service to be monitored, the possibility to do **real-time monitoring** as well as **general applicability** of the solution (concerning e.g., operating systems, programming languages).

2. CLASSIFICATION OF APPROACHES

In recent years a number of approaches to application performance monitoring have evolved. To alleviate evaluation of specific techniques, the following section introduces a classification gained from a survey of currently existing solutions by applying the requirements mentioned above. Eventually, the most

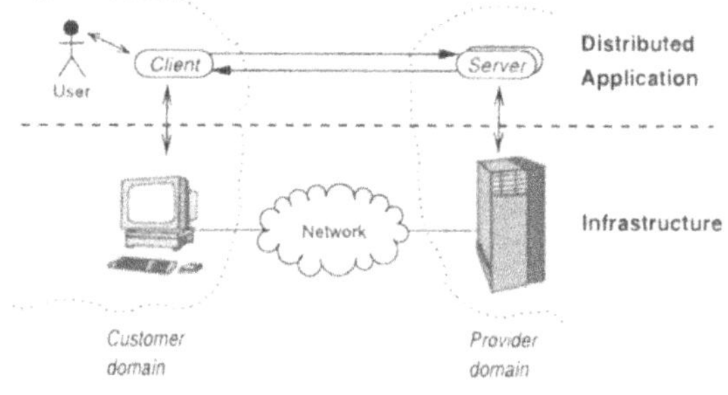

Figure 1. Distributed application scenario

prominent representatives of the different classes – both current products and existing standards – are briefly introduced. Figure 1 shows a simple model of a distributed application as well as its underlying infrastructure. The measurement of performance parameters can either take place at the application itself or in the infrastructure (both at the network and the systems). When measuring the application itself, approaches that solely focus on the client-side of the application can be distinguished from those taking into account the application as a whole (client- *and* server-side). This leads to the following four classes of techniques: *Monitoring of network traffic, system-level monitoring, client-side application monitoring* and *application-wide monitoring*. The following paragraphs explain these four techniques along with a number of subordinate techniques in greater detail.

2.1. Monitoring of network traffic

A wide spread technique to identify QoS problems of applications in networks is scanning the network traffic in order to detect transaction-like behavior. Looking at IP-based networks, traffic occurring successively between the same pair of source and destination address is called a *flow* that, in combination with the application's port number, helps to find out start and end point of a client request and its response. In case of high-speed networks an evaluation of the measured data mostly cannot be done on-the-fly and therefore flows are recorded in real-time but analyzed at a later date. If network nodes (e.g., routers) do not support recording of flows, especially suited devices (so called *probes*) are installed in the network that provide the needed functionality. Advantages of this method are that no source code access is needed and every application that communicates over the network can be monitored.

Nevertheless, there are several disadvantages. As usually only transactions of standard applications can be detected automatically the system administrator must have in-depth knowledge about protocols of custom-designed applications to configure probes in that way that they distill individual transactions. Even worse, many protocols are used for different purposes than originally designed (e.g., SOAP uses *HTTP* for its RPC mechanism), which further increases complexity. In case of encrypted communication monitoring of network traffic is not suitable at all. As mentioned above, due to massive data volumes in high-speed networks the data analysis cannot be done in real-time and therefore cannot be used to react in time when a problem occurs. Additionally, it is impossible to determine the reason of a QoS degradation as long as it is not a network failure. Furthermore, time stamps are not taken from a user's point of view but at the network meter point.

Overall, solely monitoring network traffic is not suited well for application service performance monitoring as this technique was originally developed and used to detect network failures, for capacity planning and for reporting. There are several working groups within the IETF that develop standards in the field of network based (application) performance monitoring: e.g., *IP Performance Metrics (IPPM)* [13] and *Realtime Traffic Flow Measurement (RTFM)* [3]. Several companies offer probes and analyzing software using this technique: e.g., *CompuWare's EcoSCOPE* [6], and *Apptitude's MeterFlow* [2].

2.2. System-level Monitoring

A second approach to application performance management is to measure system-level parameters like CPU usage, memory utilization, number of open files or run state of a process or a thread. By mapping processes and threads to applications, status information about the application is gained. The main advantage of this approach is the great experience gathered over the last years which allows easy collection of the data. It is relatively easy to read this kind of information from the system and provide it to management systems via well-defined interfaces.

However, there are major drawbacks of this technique as well: The basic problem of this solution is that it cannot provide the QoS parameters agreed with customers. Information about the state of the underlying systems is of minor importance to technically not versed customers. Mapping of system-level information to user-oriented parameters is often impossible. Even if a process is running perfectly from a systems view, the transactions a user is interested in might still be failing. Therefore, the monitoring of system-level parameters can be invaluable for a provider to monitor overall system performance but cannot be used for measuring actual application performance and verifying SLAs.

The IETF makes heavy use of this approach by providing a number of MIBs (e.g., SysAppl MIB [12]) concerning the area of application management. A lot of management tools, like HP Perfview [10] also follow this approach.

2.3. Client-side application monitoring

Monitoring solely from client's side is the third class of techniques we discovered. In contrast to the methods mentioned so far it is possible to measure the actual time an application needs to complete a transaction, i.e. it is metered from a user's perspective. Nevertheless, this class of techniques still suffers from one general problem: it is possible to detect an application's malfunction in the moment it happens but it still does not help in finding the root cause of the problem. Therefore in general this class of techniques is only useful to verify fulfillment of SLAs from a customer's point of view, but additional techniques have to be used for further analysis in order to detect the reason of a QoS problem. Our studies revealed two basic methods that are applied to monitor from a client's perspective: *synthetic transactions* and *GUI based solutions*. The following paragraphs describe these two approaches in more detail.

Synthetic Transactions: This method uses simulated transactions in order to measure the response time of an application server and to verify the received responses by comparing them to previously recorded reference transactions. Several simulator agents, acting as clients in a network, send requests to the application server of interest and measure the time needed to complete a transaction. In case response time exceeds a configurable threshold or the received server response is incorrect in some way, the agents usually inform the manager by generating events.

As solely synthetic transactions are monitored and not real transactions initiated by actual users, this technique is only useful to take a snapshot of a server's availability, but not to verify the fulfillment of service level agreements. To get measurement data close to actual user experience, the interval between simulated transactions has to be reduced to a minimum. As a consequence the application service could experience serious performance degradation. Further problems arise from agent deployment in large networks.

Currently there are several companies providing either product solutions for performance monitoring using synthetic transactions, like *Geyer & Weinig's GW-TEL INFRA-XS* [15], or offering a service for testing the availability of application services, like *Jyra In-Site* for Web-/E-Commerce Server [11], using this technique.

GUI based solutions: To be able to meter the actual user transactions but to avoid the need for accessing the client application's source code, a new approach was recently developed: As every user request both starts and ends with using/changing a GUI element at the client side (e.g. clicking a web link and displaying the appropriate web page afterwards), simply observing GUI events delivers the needed information about start and end points of user transactions. A software agent installed at client site devices gathers the transaction data of interest from a user's point of view.

The advantages of this technique are that the actually occurring transaction duration is measured and that it can be applied to every application service client. Furthermore, only very little performance impact is caused on the monitored application.

However, we discovered two major problems. First of all, mapping GUI events to user transactions is a difficult task regarding non-standard applications and therefore requires additional effort by the administrator. Secondly, the only agents using these technique known by the authors, are agents by *Candle ETEWatch* [9] that are currently available only for MS Windows platforms.

2.4. Application-wide monitoring

As mentioned before, client-based monitoring cannot identify the reason for performance degradation or malfunction of an application. Therefore solutions that monitor both from the client- and from the server-side are necessary. As details about the application and problems within the application cannot be gathered externally, these approaches rely on information supplied by the application itself. Our studies have shown two basic classes that allow application-wide monitoring. These are *application instrumentation* and *application description*. These two classes are described in the following paragraphs in greater detail.

Application instrumentation: Application instrumentation means insertion of specialized management code directly into the application's code. The required information is sent to management systems by using some kind of well-defined interface. This approach can deliver all the service-oriented information needed by an administrator. The actual status of the application and the actual duration of transactions is measured and any level of detail can be achieved. Subtransactions within the user transactions can be identified and measured.

However, application instrumentation is not very commonly used today. This is mainly due to the complexity and thus the additional effort posed on the application developer. The developer has to insert management code manually when building the application. Subtransactions have to be correlated manually to higher-level transactions. As the source code is needed for performing instrumentation, it definitely has to take place during development.

Examples for approaches using application instrumentation are the *Application Response Measurement API (ARM)* [4] jointly developed by HP and Tivoli and the *Application Instrumentation and Control API (AIC)* [5] developed by *Computer Associates*. Both approaches have recently been standardized by the Open Group. ARM defines a library that is to be called whenever a transaction starts or stops. Subtransactions can be correlated using so called correlators. Thus the duration of the transaction and all subordinate transactions can be measured. AIC in contrast was not explicitely developed for performance measurement but might be used in this area as well. It defines an application library to provide management objects that can transparently be queried using a client library. Additionally, a generic management function can be called through the library and thresholds of certain managed objects can be monitored regularly. Both ARM and AIC suffer from all the problems mentioned above and thus are not in wide-spread use today.

Application description: As most of the applications in use today somehow deliver status information but are not explicitely instrumented for management, application description techniques can be used. As opposed to the instrumentation approach, no well-defined interface for the provisioning of management

Table 1. Summary

Techniques \ Requirements		Service–oriented parameters	Actual user experience	In–depth information	Minimal effort	Minimal impact	Real–time measurement	General applicability
Monitoring of network traffic		o/–	o	–	–	o/+	–	++
Monitoring of system parameters		––	o	o/+	o	++	++	++
Client–based monitoring	Synthetic Transactions	+	––	––	++/+	––	++	++
	GUI–based Monitoring	++	++	––	–	++	++	–
Application–wide monitoring	Application instrumentation	++	++	++	––	+	++	o
	Application description	o	o	o	–	++	+	++

information exists. The description therefore comprises where to find the relevant information and how to interpret it. Examples might be scanning of log files or capturing status events generated by the application.

The major advantage of application description techniques is that it can be applied to legacy applications without requiring access to the source code. It can be done by a third party after application development, while the reasonable approach again is to provide the description by the developer.

Application description faces two major problems: The information available typically is not easy to map to the information needed by the administrator. Especially in the area of performance management typically only little information is available. Moreover monitors are needed to extract the information from the application. Only very little information can be gathered by standard monitors and thus specialized monitors must be developed for every application.

The most prominent representative of application description suited for performance monitoring is the *Application Management Specification (AMS)* [1]. Most other approaches, like the *CIM Application Schema* [7] mainly focus on configuration management. An example for a tool making use of application description is *Tivoli Business System Manager* [14], which reads in AMS based *Application Description Files (ADF)* to learn about the application or business system to be managed.

3. OPEN RESEARCH QUESTIONS

Table 1 summarizes the results of our analysis. As can easily be seen, none of the currently existing techniques completely meets the requirements of service oriented application management. Either they simply cannot deliver the data needed or they suffer from high complexity.

In our opinion application instrumentation is the only reasonable way to overcome the problems of today's application performance management. However, due to the enormous efforts posed on the developer nowadays it is hardly ever used. This immediately leads to a number of research questions that have to be tackled in the future. The following enumeration provides an overview of the most important open research questions concerning application instrumentation:

Instrumentation methodology: A methodology for the developer must be provided in order to alleviate the task of identifying relevant measurement points. Current application techniques simply offer APIs to be called from an application but give no hint about where to actually place the calls in the code. The instrumentation definitely has to take place during application development and thus the instrumentation methodology must be integrated into the software development process.

Automation and tool support: To further alleviate a developer's task a great amount of automation and tool support must be achieved. Therefore, means to facilitate or even automate the instrumentation process must be developed. E.g., in the area of component based application development the code required to measure response time of an individual component might entirely be generated by a development tool.

Correlation of subtransactions: Means to avoid the cumbersome correlation of subtransactions to their parent transactions are desperately needed. The idea of transporting unique transaction identifiers through the application as parameters is awkward to say the least. In some cases (e.g., component bases development, third party instrumentation) this approach even makes an instrumentation nearly impossible. By correlating transactions, e.g., using the identifiers of the underlying control flows, this could be simplified by far.

Integration with remaining existing techniques: Finally, a tighter integration of application instrumentation with the existing techniques is required in order to deliver an exhaustive overview of the status of the application to be monitored.

4. CONCLUSION

The paper focused on evaluating the different approaches currently used for performance monitoring of distributed applications. Therefore a classification and analysis of available approaches has been done. Overall result was, that current techniques are not sufficient to solve today's service management problems. The paper concludes with open research questions in the area of application performance management that – in our opinion – are most important to be tackled in the forthcoming years.

Our current work focuses on the research questions raised above. Especially in the area of component based application development some promising prototypes are under development that might lead to a high degree of instrumentation automation. In the area of automated transaction correlation we already have achieved some first substantial progress which is about to be published soon.

Acknowledgments

The authors wish to thank the members of the Munich Network Management (MNM) Team for helpful discussions. The webserver of the MNM Team is located at `http://wwwmnmteam.informatik.uni-muenchen.de`.

References

[1] Application Management Specification. Version 2.0, Tivoli Systems, 1997.

[2] Apptitude. MeterFlow Network Decision Data Engine. Technical White Paper, January 2000.

[3] N. Brownlee, C. Mills, and G. Ruth. RFC 2063: Traffic flow measurement: Architecture. RFC, IETF, January 1997.

[4] Application Response Measurement (ARM) API . Technical Standard C807, The Open Group, July 1998.

[5] Application Instrumentation and Control (AIC) API, Version 1.0. Technical Standard C910, The Open Group, November 1999.

[6] Compuware. Ecoscope — analyzing networked application performance, 2001, `http://www.compuware.com/products/ecosystems/ecoscope/`.

[7] DMTF Application Working Group. Application MOF Specification 2.5. CIM Schema, Distributed Management Task Force, December 2000.

[8] M. Garschhammer, R. Hauck, H.-G. Hegering, B. Kempter, M. Langer, M. Nerb, I. Radisic, H. Roelle, and H. Schmidt. Towards generic Service Management Concepts – A Service Model Based Approach. In *Proc. of the 7th Int. IFIP/IEEE Symposium on Integrated Management*, May 2001.

[9] Hurwitz Group. Candle captures the "user experience". Technical White Paper, September 1998.

[10] Hewlett–Packard Company. HP Management Software Products, 2001, `http://www.managementsoftware.hp.com/`.

[11] Jyra. Jyra In–Site@PSINet, 2000, `http://in-site.jyra.com/`.

[12] C. Krupczak and J. Saperia. RFC 2287: Definitions of system-level managed objects for applications. RFC, IETF, February 1998.

[13] V. Paxson, G. Almes, J. Mahdavi, and M. Mathis. RFC 2330: Framework for ip performance metrics. RFC, IETF, May 1998.

[14] Tivoli Systems, Inc. Tivoli Business System Manager, 2001, `www.tivoli.com/products/index/business_system_mgr`.

[15] Geyer & Weinig. Portofolio – INFRA-XS, 2000, `http://www.gwtel.de/`.

JAVA CLASS LOADING TECHNIQUES IN THE HARNESS METACOMPUTING FRAMEWORK

Dawid Kurzyniec and Vaidy Sunderam
Emory University, Dept. of Math and Computer Science
1784 N. Decatur Rd, Atlanta, GA, 30322, USA
{dawidk,vss}@mathcs.emory.edu

Abstract Harness is an Java-centric metacomputing system based on a principle of dynamic reconfigurability not only in terms of participating computing resources, but also the capabilities of the virtual machine itself. The central feature of the system is a "plug-in" mechanism built upon Java dynamic class loading services enabling integration of new functionality in the run time. In this paper we describe new flexible, framework based Java class loading techniques and their application in the Harness system.

1. INTRODUCTION

Harness [4, 8] is a metacomputing framework based upon such experimental concepts as dynamic reconfigurability and extensible distributed virtual machine. The underlying motivation behind Harness is to develop a metacomputing platform for the next generation, incorporating the inherent capability to integrate new technologies as they evolve. The first motivation is an outcome of the perceived need in metacomputing systems to provide more functionality, flexibility, and performance, while the second is based upon a desire to allow the framework to respond rapidly to advances in hardware, networks, system software, and applications.

Harness attempts to overcome the limited flexibility of traditional software systems by defining a simple though powerful architectural model of a software backplane which is configured dynamically by attaching "plug-in" modules providing various services. Those "plug-in" modules are simply packages of cooperating Java classes and possibly related resources, and the dynamic "plug-in" loading is based upon underlying Java class loader capabilities to locate and load classes and resources from the dynamically changing set of software repositories.

Current implementation of Harness class loader fails to satisfy two desired features: to support loading classes from Java archive (JAR) files [5], as they improve code integrity and reliability with *package sealing* [5] and digital signatures, and to supply uniform and reliable caching mechanism reducing potentially expensive network access. This paper overviews the flexible class loader framework, intended to support a wide range of possible dynamic class loading models, and describes its application in the Harness system.

2. CLASS LOADERS IN JAVA

The concept of a class loader evolved together with the Java technology. Primarily it was designed to allow users to load to the Java VM classes coming from various non-standard sources such as downloaded from the network, fetched from a database, or even generated on-the-fly. Beginning from the JDK 1.1, class loaders support finding not only classes but also other resources such as images, icons, or sound files. Also, the class signers has been introduced to improve the security model.

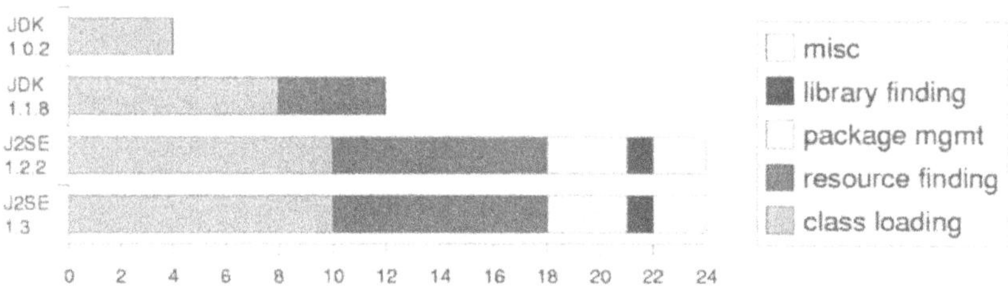

Figure 1. Class Loader API evolution

Java 2 platform brought substantial changes to the class loader capabilities. Its semantics were refined [7] and it has been tightly integrated with the newly established Java Security API [9]. A few new classes were introduced: the `java.security.SecureClassLoader`, intended as a basis for user-defined class loaders incorporating Java security model, and the `java.net.URLClassLoader`, which enables loading data from Java archive (JAR) files [5] and includes support for downloadable extensions [2]. Moreover, in addition to finding and loading classes and resources class loader became responsible to define and keep track of packages and control native library linking. Additionally, the notion of parenthood and request delegation has been introduced improving the run-time model. The evolution of a class loader API (that is, the set of `public` and `protected` methods of class `java.lang.Classloader`) is illustrated in Figure 1.

3. FLEXIBLE CLASS LOADER FRAMEWORK

Although class loaders are used when there is a need for some application-specific way to find classes, resources, or libraries, they often have much in common. For example, many of them might want to read data from JAR files or download it from the network; similarly, many class loaders treats classes and resources uniformly rather than having separate routines for dealing with them. These similarities, however, do not comprise a common denominator. For that reason, full advantage of a generic class loader can be taken only when its structure is *modular*, so the users can choose and configure the modules they are willing to use in their implementations. Unfortunately, none of the class loaders provided as a part of Java platform is flexible enough to be appropriate for this purpose.

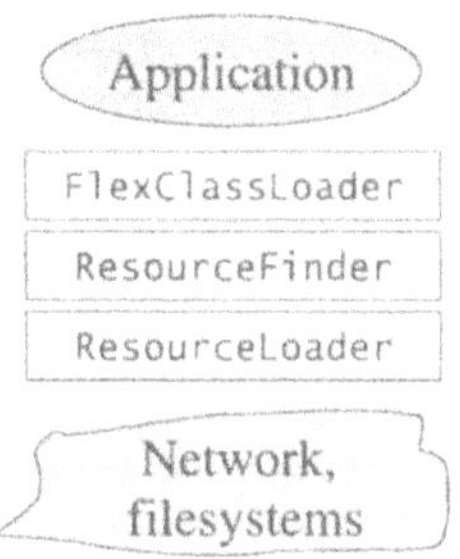

Figure 2. Structure of Flexible Class Loader Framework

The flexible class loader framework presented here is an example of such modular structure, as illustrated in Figure 2. It is based on the observation that the typical class loader, apart from doing its low level duty, must perform independent activities like searching for requested data, being able to download it from the network and manage JAR files. Taking this into account, it becomes reasonable to split the whole functionality into three layers:

- the class loader itself, serving as an interface to an application,
- the resource finder, encapsulating the searching algorithm but unaware of differences between classes, libraries, and other resources,
- the resource loader, responsible for managing JAR files and downloading data from the network.

The full description of the framework is out of scope of this paper. Note, however, that as the most specific part of each class loader is its resource searching algorithm, many sophisticated ones can be derived from this scheme just by customization of the resource finder layer. Also, because many class loaders require the capabilities to cache code downloaded from the network, we introduced the `CachingResourceFinder` providing those as a part of the framework.

4. CLASS LOADING IN HARNESS

Harness uses specific class loading scheme: classes can be retrieved from various software repositories, possibly maintained by independent organizations.

Each time the class is to be loaded, the system searches for it subsequently on the repository search path. As long as all classes are kept in repositories as separate files and there is a direct mapping between directory paths and package names, the lookup can be performed easily just by specifying proper URLs. Thus, the only activity required to make given class visible to Harness system is to put it on appropriate directory path in the software repository.

4.1. Hierarchical Resource Lookup

The simple class lookup model described above gets complicated if we wish to include JAR files as an option to store classes and resources. It is not obvious how JAR files should be stored in repositories to retain simplicity of making the classes and resources available to Harness system. It is important to note that they must be stored in some designated places known by the class loader, because many Internet protocols (including HTTP as an important special case) do not provide reliable mechanisms to query for directory contents.

As a solution, we provide notion of hierarchical resource lookup based on the package-oriented organization of the Java language. The Java deployment strategies encourage to store in JAR files only single packages, consisting of related classes and resources and providing some concrete functionality. Making such JAR file layout a requirement, it becomes possible to establish a naming contract as follows: the name of the JAR file should be the same as the last part of appropriate package name, and the JAR file itself should be stored where directory of that name would be normally expected. For example, JAR file wrapping package `edu.emory.mathcs.harness` should be named `harness.jar` and be placed on the `edu/emory/mathcs` path.

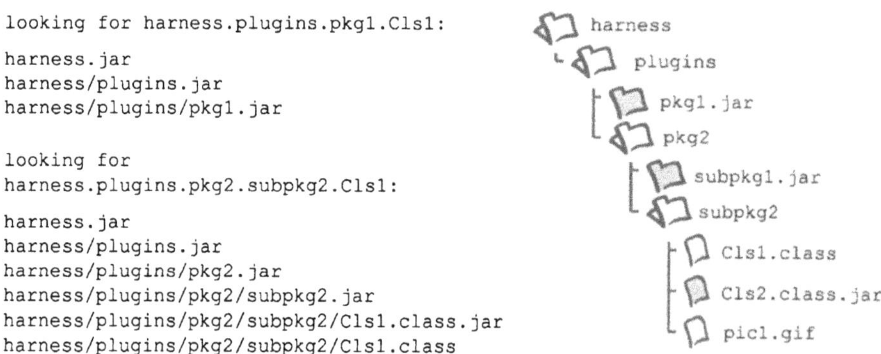

Figure 3. Examples of Hierarchical Resource Lookup

The Figure 3 shows two examples of the hierarchical resource lookup based on such naming contract. When looking for a class or resource, the algorithm goes downward directory structure trying to search JAR files starting from the outermost one possible. If it fails, the traditional lookup method is eventually adopted making the whole approach backward compatible.

The algorithm was implemented in the class derived from the framework's `CachingResourceFinder` and inheriting its caching capabilities. The new class loader is therefore automatically equipped with uniform and flexible caching mechanism, replicating remote structures of software repositories as the classes and resources are loaded.

4.2. Benefits for Harness

In the Harness system, the class loader plays important role as it is responsible to provide background layer for linking "plug-in" services. The new class loading approach will be beneficial here as it allows to take advantage of JAR file features and as it provides uniform caching mechanism:

- JAR files can be digitally signed and can contain certified code. This will enable security improvement in a Harness system, allowing system administrators to include certificates in security policies.
- JAR files are compressed, so data will be faster downloaded from the network.
- JAR files may contain meta-information related to JAR file as a whole or to its separate entries. Using this meta-information, Harness will be able to avoid performing complex byte-code analysis of the classes being downloaded (the system performs such analysis in order to decide if it can run the "plug-in" in its own Java VM or if it should spawn another one).
- Complex plug-ins, which contain a bunch of classes and resources, will be maintained more easily by storing them in single JAR file. Also, the package consistency and versioning will be improved by taking advantage of JAR package attributing and sealing.

5. CONCLUSIONS AND FUTURE WORK

This paper overviews the flexible class loader framework, which simplifies development of application-specific class loaders and consists of the set of customizable classes providing commonly needed functionality. The ongoing work on the application of the framework in the Harness system is described, including the hierarchical resource lookup algorithm which supports loading resources stored in software repositories.

The future work plans include enabling Harness to take advantage of "plug-in" modules containing native code [1, 6]. To retain high portability, these modules are intended to carry out native source files rather than precompiled libraries; the compilation process would occur "just in time" on the target platform. This technique would benefit from described class loader framework in several ways: first, the Java classes and native source files comprising the "plug-in" could be bundled together in the elegant JAR file. Next, the code certification and digital signatures could be used to assure reliability, which is essential when native code is considered. And finally, the general-purpose caching services provided by the new class loader would support management and caching of native libraries once they were compiled on a target platform.

References

[1] M. Bubak, D. Kurzyniec, and P. Łuszczek. Creating Java to native code interfaces with Janet extension. In M. Bubak, J. Mościnski, and M. Noga, editors, *Proceedings of the First Worldwide SGI Users' Conference*, pages 283–294, Cracow, Poland, October 11-14 2000. ACC-CYFRONET.

[2] The Java extension mechanism. `http://java.sun.com/j2se/1.3/docs/guide/extensions/index.html`.

[3] P. Gray, V. Sunderam, and V. Getov. Aspects of portability and distributed execution of JNI-wrapped code. Available at `http://www.mathcs.emory.edu/icet/sp.ps`.

[4] Harness project home page. `http://www.mathcs.emory.edu/harness`.

[5] Java archive (JAR) features. `http://java.sun.com/j2se/1.3/docs/guide/jar/index.html`.

[6] Java Native Interface. `http://java.sun.com/j2se/1.3/docs/guide/jni/index.html`.

[7] S. Liang and G. Bracha. Dymanic class loading in the Java Virtual Machine. Available at `http://www.java.sun.com/people/gbracha/classloaders.ps`.

[8] M. Migliardi and V. Sunderam. The Harness metacomputing framework. In *Proceedings of the Ninth SIAM Conference on Parallel Processing for Scientific Computing*, San Antonio, Texas, USA, March 22-24 1999. Available at `http://www.mathcs.emory.edu/harness/PAPERS/pp99.ps.gz`.

[9] Java security home page. `http://java.sun.com/j2se/1.3/docs/guide/security/index.html`.

DESIGNING AND IMPLEMENTING AN OBJECT-RELATIONAL DATA WAREHOUSING SYSTEM

Bodgan Czejdo[1], Johann Eder[2], Tadeusz Morzy[3], Robert Wrembel[3]

[1] *Department of Mathematics and Computer Science, Loyola University*
St. Charles Ave., New Orleans, LA 70118
czejdo@loyno.edu

[2] *Institut für Informatik-Systeme, Universität Klagenfurt*
Universitätsstr. 65, A-9020 Klagenfurt, Austria
eder@ifi.uni-klu.ac.at

[3] *Institute of Computing Science, Poznań University of Technology*
Piotrowo 3A, 60-965 Poznan, Poland
morzy@put.poznan.pl, Robert.Wrembel@cs.put.poznan.pl

Abstract In this paper we present some of the results achieved while realising an international research project aiming at the design and development of an Object-Relational Data Warehousing System ORDAWA. Important goals of the project are to develop techniques for the integration and consolidation of different external data sources in an object-relational data warehouse, the construction and maintenance of materialised relational as well as object-oriented views, index structures, query transformations and optimisations, and techniques of data mining. The achievements discussed in this paper concern the application of materialised object-oriented views in the process of building an object-relational data warehouse.

Keywords: object-relational data warehouse, operational data store, object-oriented view.

1. INTRODUCTION

Organisational decision support systems require a comprehensive view of all aspects of an enterprise. Information collected in an enterprise are often of different data format and complexity (e.g. relational, object-relational, and object-oriented databases, on-line multimedia data stores, Web pages, spreadsheets, flat files etc.). Therefore, one of the important issues is to provide an integrated access to all these heterogeneous data sources.

There are two basic approaches to data integration: the *mediated* approach and the *data warehousing* approach [1]. In the first one, a global query is decomposed and transformed into queries for each of the data sources. The results of each of the queries are then translated, filtered, and merged to form a global result.

Whereas in the *data warehousing* approach, data of interests coming from heterogeneous sources are extracted, filtered, merged, and stored in an integrating database, called *data warehouse*. The data are also enriched by historical and summary information. Then, queries are issued for this data warehouse.

The advantages of the data warehousing approach to data integration are as follows: (1) queries operate on a local centralised data repository, that reduces access time to data, (2) queries need not be decomposed into different formats and their results need not be integrated, (3) a data warehouse is independent of other data sources, that may be temporary unavailable. However, a data warehouse has to be kept up to date with respect to source data, by periodically refreshing it. A data warehouse is often implemented as the set of materialised views.

This paper describes some of the results achieved while realising an international research project aiming at the design and development of an Object-Relational Data Warehousing System – *ORDAWA* [2]. The project is conducted in co-operation of the Institute for Informatics-Systems at Klagenfurt University, the Institute of Computing Science at Poznañ University of Technology, and the Department of Mathematics and Computer Science at Loyola University. Important goals of the project are to develop techniques for the integration and consolidation of different external data sources in an object/relational data warehouse, the construction and maintenance of materialised relational as well as object-oriented views, index structures, query transformations and optimisations, and techniques of data mining. The achievements discussed in this paper concern the application of materialized object-oriented views in the process of building an object-relational data warehouse.

2. OBJECT-RELATIONAL DATA WAREHOUSE

The more and more frequent need to create, store, and manage data of a complex structure and behaviour leads to the make use of object-relational (e.g. *Oracle8*, *Extended Parallel Server*, *IBM DB2 UDB*) or object-oriented databases (e.g. *Objectivity/DB*, *ObjectStore*, *Versant*). These complex data, similarly as relational, will be the subject of the integration and analysis in a central repository – a data warehouse. To this end, the data model of such a data warehouse should support complex types in order to reflect the complexity of source information. Moreover, object data use the methods and these methods should also be available in the integrated system, in order to retain the functionality and information as well as to be able to process the information. Therefore, many research papers suggest to use an object-relational or object-oriented data model (cf. [3, 4]) as a common model for integrating heterogeneous data sources.

Our object-relational data warehousing architecture is presented in Figure 1. An intermediate layer, called an *operational data store* (ODS) is built between data sources and a data warehouse [5, 6]. An operational data store is a subject-oriented set of data coming from one or more data sources. While loading an ODS, data are extracted from data sources, transformed to a common data model of an ODS, and preintegrated. Then, the content of various operational data stores is again integrated and loaded into a central data warehouse.

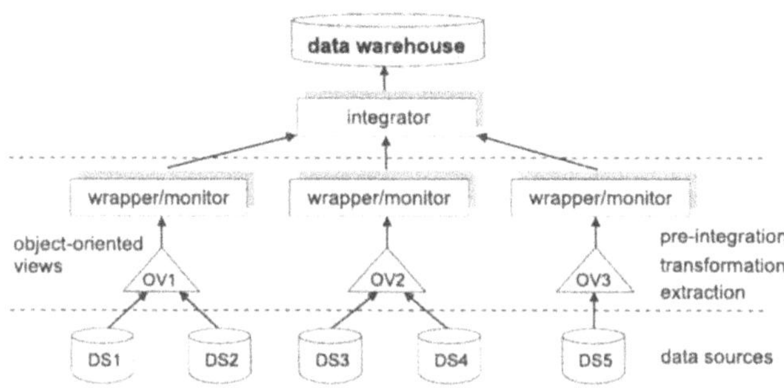

Figure 1. The application of object-oriented views in a data warehouse architecture

The main differences between a data warehouse and an operational data store are as follows. Firstly, the content of an ODS changes more frequently than the content of a data warehouse. Secondly, data in an ODS are near current with respect to the corresponding data in data sources. Next, data in an ODS can be updated but the updates do not propagate down to data sources. And finally, the aggregation level of data in an ODS is very low.

The purpose to build an ODS is to separate long lasting, time consuming processing, e.g. On-Line Analytical Processing queries, from data sources. Since OLAP queries operate on data in an ODS, they do not interfere with the processing in data sources. Furthermore, an ODS may be designed and tuned especially for a particular pattern of processing, whereas the underlying data sources may be designed and tuned for other kind of processing, e.g. OLTP. For the reason of tuning one may need to change the structure of source data in an ODS, e.g. merge some source information, project some attributes, introduce data redundancies.

From the implementation point of view, an ODS is seen as the set of materialised object-oriented views.

While materialising an object-oriented view one has to consider the materialisation of structure as well as the materialisation of methods. The materialisation of methods is important firstly because this technique allows to increase performance of methods whose computation take long time. Secondly, by materialising methods one is able to transform behaviour of objects to relational model. In this case materialised methods are just seen as attributes having persistent values. However, not all methods are good candidates for the materialisation. For example, method comparing or looking for similarities between two pieces of information can not be easily materialised. For these reasons, a data warehousing system has to provide means for the materialisation of methods as well as for invoking and computing methods when needed, i.e. should be able to maintain the behaviour that is not easy to materialise.

To sum up, by using object-oriented views for modelling and implementing operational data stores we achieved the following goals: (1) we are able to extend data warehousing into object-oriented data sources; (2) due to the expressiveness of an object-oriented data model we are able to transform one data model to another and this transformation may be supported by methods defined in a view; moreover, the restructuring of source data in an operational data store can be easier.

3. THE CONCEPT OF AN OBJECT-ORIENTED VIEW

In our approach, called *View Schema Approach* (*VSA*), we draw on the model of an object-oriented database, presented in [7], which we extended by the following concepts supporting object-oriented views, their materialization and maintenance: (1) view class, (2) view object, (3) view schema, (4) mappings between database schema and views, and (5) mappings between objects in a database and those in views.

An *object-oriented view* is defined as a *view schema* of an arbitrary complex structure and behavior [8]. A view schema is composed of view classes. Each *view class* is derived from one or more *base classes*, i.e. classes in a database schema. A view class is derived by an OQL-like command. View classes in a view schema are connected by inheritance and aggregation relationships. Several view schemas can be created from the same base schema.

A given view schema can be explicitly materialised. The materialisation of a view schema results in the materialisation of its view classes. When materialising the instances of a given view class it is possible to materialised the structure of objects and results of some methods applicable to view objects.

After objects have been materialised in a view, the maintenance of consistency between base objects and those materialised in a view becomes an important issue. In our approach we have developed three following techniques for propagating modifications from source objects to their materialised counterparts in a view schema: (1) deferred on commit incremental refreshing, (2) deferred on demand incremental refreshing, and (3) deferred on demand complete refreshing. Only certain view classes are allowed to be refreshed incrementally.

In order to incrementally propagate the modifications from base to view objects we have developed additional data structures, called *Class Mapping Structure*, *Object Mapping Structure*, and *Log*. The first two structures represent mappings between base and view classes as well as between their instances, cf. [8, 9]. Whereas *Log* stores records describing operations performed on base objects, cf. [9].

4. SUMMARY

The application of object-oriented views in the process of building an object-relational data warehouse system is very promising. Object-oriented views are important mechanisms providing an integrated access to data of various structures. It is due to the following facts:
object-oriented features, especially methods, may facilitate data transformation, integration, and analysis in an object-relational data warehouse;
the high expressiveness of an object-oriented data model makes object-oriented views suitable for the transformation and integration of many different data sources that use various data models.

Several approaches to object-oriented views were proposed in scientific publications (see [9, 10] for an overview). But they provide a limited functionality for the application in the process of data warehousing. Our *View Schema Approach* is more general and it encompasses other approaches. Moreover *VSA* allows to materialize a view schema and maintain its consistency by using one of the three maintenance techniques. *VSA* has been implemented as a prototype and evaluated in a series in experiments. The results are presented in [9].

Further research within the *ORDAWA* project will focus on: query transformation and optimisation techniques in data warehousing environment, techniques and algorithms for data mining in data warehousing environment, the maintenance of summary data for periodically changing dimension data as well as the maintenance of a data warehouse schema and data in the presence of changes made to the schemas of source databases [11].

References

[1] Widom J.: Research Problems in Data Warehousing, Proc. of the 4th Int. Conference on Information and Knowledge Management (CIKM), 1995, pp. 25-30

[2] J.Eder, H.Frank, T.Morzy, R.Wrembel, M.Zakrzewicz, Designing an Object-Relational Database System: Project ORDAWA. Proc. of challenges of the ADBIS-DASFAA 2000 Conference, Prague, Czech Republic, 2000, pp.223-227

[3] Bukhres O. A., Elmagarmid A. (eds.): Object-Oriented Multidatabase Systems: A Solution for Advanced Applications, Prentice Hall, 1996

[4] Fankhauser P., Gardarin G., Lopez M., Munoz J., Tomasic A.: Experiences in Federated Databases: From IRO-DB to MIRO-Web. Porc. of the VLDB Conference, USA, 1998, pp. 655-658

[5] Inmon W. H.: Building the Data Warehouse, 2nd edition. John Wiley & Sons, 1996

[6] Jarke M., Lenzerini M., Vassiliou Y., Vassiliadis P.: Fundamentals of Data Warehouses. Springer-Verlag, 2000, ISBN 3-540-65365-1

[7] Abiteboul S., Hull R., Vianu V.: Foundation of Databases. Addison-Wesley Publishing Company, 1995

[8] Wrembel R.: On Materialising Object-Oriented Views. In Barzdins J., Caplinskas A. (eds.): Databases and Information Systems. Kluwer Academic Publishers, March 2001, ISBN 0-7923-6823-1, pp. 15-28

[9] Wrembel R.: The Construction and Maintenance of Materialised Object-Oriented Views in Data Warehousing Systems. PhD thesis, Poznañ University of Technology, Institute of Computing Science, March 2001

[10] Motschnig-Pitrik R.: Requirements And Comparison of View Mechanisms for Object-Oriented Databases. Information Systems, Vol. 21, No. 3, 1996, pp. 229-252

[11] Czejdo B., Messa K., Morzy T., Putonti C.: Design of Data Warehouses with Dynamically Changing Data Sources. In Proc. of the Southern Conference on Computing. The University of Southern Mississippi, October, 2000

DISTRIBUTED TRANSACTIONS FOR ODMG FEDERATED DATABASES

Damir Becarevic and Mark Roantree
Interoperable Systems Group
Dublin City University, Ireland
damirb@compapp.dcu.ie

Abstract Global transactions are still an issue for federated database systems. In the IOMPAR project, one of the goals is to develop a transaction protocol for ODMG databases which act as wrappers to information systems in a federation. In this short paper we describe an architecture for transporting secure data in a federated database system. Our on-going work involves providing the transaction service which can guarantee global transactions within our architecture.

1. INTRODUCTION

Federated database systems are comprised of heterogeneous information systems and use an integrated schema to provide a global interface for users and applications. Global transactions submitted at the federated layer are divided into set of subtransactions to be executed at local databases. This research is focused on the development of a secure transaction architecture for object databases operating in a federated database architecture. Research is conducted under the IOMPAR (Internet Object Management: Privacy ARchitecture) project in Dublin City University [8]. The IOMPAR project is focused on the provision of an architecture and services for the execution of complex transactions in a secure environment. The strategy is to reuse existing (standard) technologies where possible and only supply those layers that are required: security, a flexible transaction manager, and multimedia handling.

IOMPAR uses the OASIS federated architecture described in [7], which uses the ODMG model [4] as its common model. OASIS provided an architecture and services to construct federated schemas for heterogeneous systems [5]. This architecture did not provide security, support for behaviour in views, or multimedia support. Since the majority of database systems are not ODMG databases, a wrapper language for mapping local schemas to ODMG schemas was developed and implemented. Please refer to [9] for a description of federated architectures and issues, and to [2] for a description of research work using object-based federated systems.

The motivation for this research is as follows: a global transaction service needs to extract data from local databases, compare sub-results and compute the final result for each global transaction. This means that data is moved from one database to another in the form of objects. Transaction consistency for all modifying operations must be guaranteed at both the local and global levels. There are many problems and issues which arise with global transactions across multiple heterogeneous systems. This research attempts to solve some of these problems as we construct a new global transaction manager for a federation of databases which uses an ODMG canonical model.

2. RESEARCH DETAILS

In this Section we introduce the concept of the Secure Communication Architecture (SCA) for ODMG databases. The architecture provides an object transport infrastructure and distributed transaction control system for object transfer.

2.1. Secure Communication Architecture Overview

The Secure Communication Architecture (SCA) extends the Object Transport Architecture presented in [1] for the OASIS project. The SCA provides transaction control and common protocol for transfer of data between systems which employ an ODMG wrapper. Each database and its corresponding interconnecting layers form one node in the federated system. At a high level, the SCA consists of three modules: The Transport Service, Local Transaction Service and Global Transaction Service as illustrated in Figure 1.

The Transport Service manages the transport of objects and commands between nodes in the distributed system. The protocol used for the encapsulation of metadata and commands is XML. XML is convenient as a data interchange format for incompatible data sources, because data encoded using XML can be easily interpreted by different types of systems. The object data is not encoded in XML, but using a protocol that support binary data encoding. Protocol encoded data is transported over a CORBA transport channel, as CORBA [6] provides the low level transport infrastructure needed for the physical transfer of data. The separation of data and metadata transport protocols is to improve performance since XML has a large overhead caused by markup information.

The Local Transaction Service manipulates a local database and ensures local transaction consistency. It performs read and write operations on both data and metadata stored in the database. The execution of a series of modifying

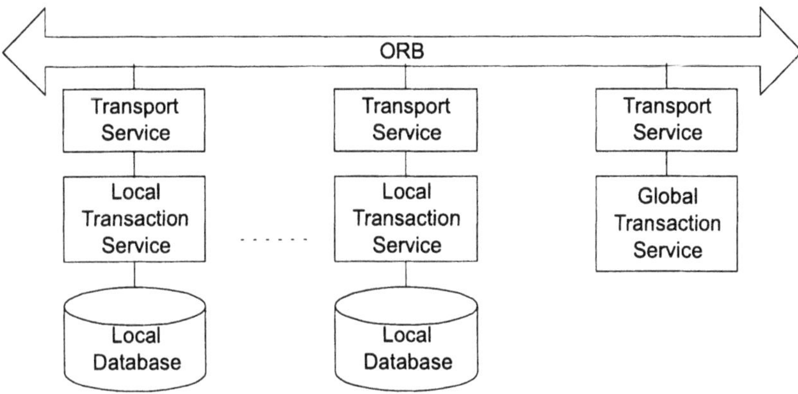

Figure 1. The Secure Communication Architecture

operations in a single global transaction is guaranteed by the local transaction manager.

The Global Transaction Service is positioned at the federated layer and controls execution of distributed transactions. It initiates global transactions and ensures transaction consistency and global serialization using a new protocol suitable for global transactions. This protocol forms the main part of this research task within the IOMPAR project. The GTS generates a set of commands and submits them to local databases for execution.

2.1.1 The Transport Service. The Transport Service performs protocol coding/decoding and transport for objects and commands. The Protocol Coder module transforms metadata and transaction commands into an XML representation. The format for XML encoding of ODMG objects is OIFML introduced in [3]. Data types, attribute names and relations in OIFML are defined by XML tags. Metadata values are placed between attribute start tag and the attribute end tag, while complex data structures are represented by tag hierarchies. This XML transport protocol is capable of encoding ODMG metadata, OQL commands, and messages. Object data is transported in some protocol that supports binary data encoding. Encoding format of transport protocol is called protocol metadata and is defined in XML.

At the target node the metadata transfer is decoded and verified against the local database schema using the Local Transaction Service. Protocol metadata is used for decoding of data protocol, so the receiving side does not need to have previous knowledge of object data encoding format. Constructed memory structures representing transported objects are delivered to the Local Transaction Service. The Transfer Agent is a CORBA object that can function both as

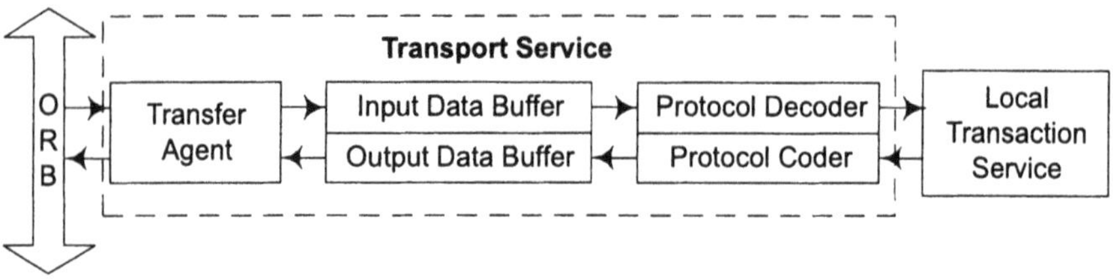

Figure 2. The Transport Service

a sender and as a receiver for data transport. The transport packages are transferred between nodes as binary data streams. Received packages are placed in the Input Data Buffer for processing by the data decoder.

2.1.2 The Local Transaction Service. The Local Transaction Service is the operational centre for each local database node. It consists of six modules as illustrated in Figure 3.

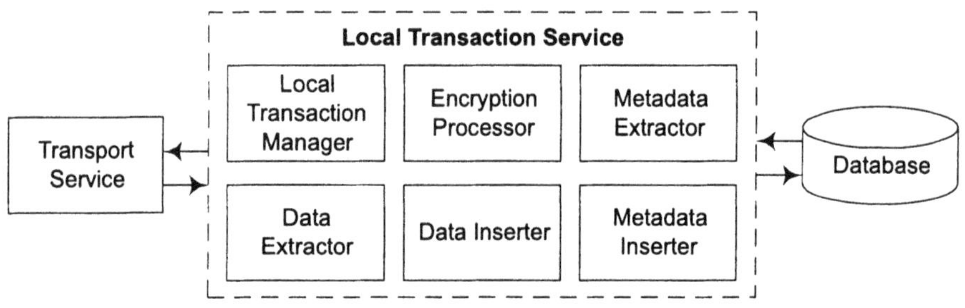

Figure 3. The Local Transaction Service

The Local Transaction Manager receives decoded commands and data from the Transport Service. It analyzes commands and activates other Local Transaction Service modules. Commands can be classified as: transaction commands such as `begin transaction`, `commit`, `rollback`; metadata manipulation commands such as create class definition and edit class definition; and data manipulation commands such as create modify objects.

The Encryption Processor performs encryption and decryption of data. Not all data or commands need be encrypted, so the Encryption Processor can selectively encrypt only specified property values.

The Metadata Extractor reads metadata information from the schema repository of the local database. Extracted metadata is passed to the Transport Service for XML encoding and transported to the target system.

The Data Extractor reads data values from the database. It can extract specified property values if required. Prior to transfer, the Encryption Processor is called.

The Metadata Inserter creates new class definitions and delete existing ones. For deleted class definition, all objects belonging to this class are also deleted.

The Data Inserter module is responsible for all data manipulations on physical data. All operations are performed within a transaction session started by the Local Transaction Manager.

2.1.3 The Global Transaction Service. The Global Transaction Service (GTS) is positioned at the federated level of the architecture. The GTS analyses global transactions and divides them into a set of subtransactions that are submitted to local database nodes for execution. The priority level[1] is specified for each subtransaction by the client who submitted the global transaction. If a high priority is required, then the atomicity of the corresponding subtransaction must be guaranteed by the two-phase-commit protocol. Otherwise, the subtransaction is considered a low priority, and it is submitted to the LTS but does not require completion (for the global transaction to succeed). For the global transaction to succeed, all high priority subtransactions must successfully commit. The Local Transaction Service determines if a global subtransaction is executable based on information of transaction capabilities of the local database system. If the LTS cannot support the required transactional protocol, the global transaction is aborted.

3. CURRENT RESEARCH

In this short paper we provided an overview of the framework in which our proposed global transaction service will operate.

Our current focus is on examining current research in the field of distributed transaction management for heterogeneous database systems. This information will provide input into the development of our own ODMG-based transaction manager. We are also focused on providing a detailed specification for transport of data (as binary streams) and metadata and decoding information (as XML data). Binary protocols should support binary data encoding and efficient transport of large volumes of multimedia.

[1]Priority levels are part of our work on a transaction taxonomy and are not covered here.

Work is already underway on a prototype developed in C++ using the Versant 6.0 ODMG databases and Oracle 8i object-relational databases operating on both Windows and Linux platforms. The middleware system is Iona Orbix 2000, a CORBA development environment for Windows and Linux.

References

[1] Byrne R, Roantree M., *An Object Architecture for ODMG Databases*, Proceedings of the 34th Hawaii International Conference on System Sciences.

[2] Bukhres O. and Elmagarmid A. (eds.), *Object-Oriented Multidatabase Systems*, Prentice Hall, 1996.

[3] G. M. Bierman, *Using XML as an Object Interchange Format*, ODMG web url: www.odmg.org, May 2000.

[4] Cattel R. et. al. (eds.) (2000). *The Object Data Standard: ODMG 3.0*, Morgan Kaufmann.

[5] Oasis Project. *www.compapp.dcu.ie/~oasis*, 2000.

[6] Orfali R. and Harkey D. (1998) *Client/Server Programming with Java and CORBA*, Wiley.

[7] Roantree M., Murphy J. and Hasselbring W. *The OASIS Multidatabase Prototype*. ACM Sigmod Record 28:1, March 1999

[8] Roantree M., *The Iompar Project: Secure Transport of Complex Objects*, Technical Report IOM-001, November 2000

[9] Sheth A., Larson J. *Federated Database systems for Managing Distributed Heterogeneous and Autonomous Databases*, ACM Computing Surveys, 22:3, pp 183-236, ACM Press, 1990

Author Index

Sponsors

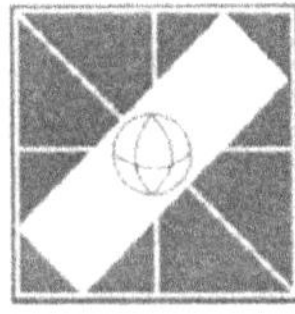

IFIP WG6.1

European Commision - Human Potential Programme

UMM, Kraków, Poland

Polish State Committee for Scientific Research

IONA

SOLIDEX®

COMARCH

Microsoft
Research

PTI

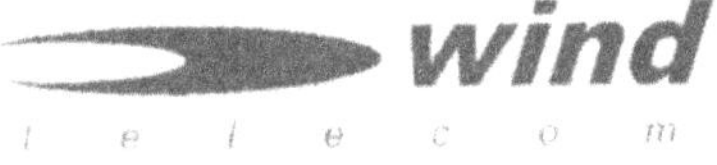
wind
t e l e c o m

www.ingramcontent.com/pod-product-compliance
Ingram Content Group UK Ltd.
Pitfield, Milton Keynes, MK11 3LW, UK
UKHW020429200726
13857UKWH00002B/352

* 9 7 8 1 4 7 5 7 8 3 2 6 1 *